T0301928

The Rise of the New Economic Powers and the Changing Global Landscape

THE RISE OF THE NEW ECONOMIC POWERS AND THE CHANGING GLOBAL LANDSCAPE

HAICO EBBERS

Nyenrode Business University, The Netherlands

World Scientific

NEW JERSEY • LONDON • SINGAPORE • BEIJING • SHANGHAI • HONG KONG • TAIPEI • CHENNAI • TOKYO

Published by

World Scientific Publishing Co. Pte. Ltd.

5 Toh Tuck Link, Singapore 596224

USA office: 27 Warren Street, Suite 401-402, Hackensack, NJ 07601

UK office: 57 Shelton Street, Covent Garden, London WC2H 9HE

Library of Congress Cataloging-in-Publication Data

Names: Ebbers, H. A. (Hendrikus Andreas), 1961–   author.
Title: The rise of the new economic powers and the changing global landscape /
    Haico Ebbers, Nyenrode Business University, The Netherlands.
Description: New Jersey : World Scientific, [2023] | Includes bibliographical references and index.
Identifiers: LCCN 2022032898 | ISBN 9789811263118 (hardcover) |
    ISBN 9789811263125 (ebook) | ISBN 9789811263132 (ebook other)
Subjects: LCSH: Economic history--21st century. | International trade. | Globalization.
Classification: LCC HC59.3 .E234 2023 | DDC 330.9--dc23/eng/20220906
LC record available at https://lccn.loc.gov/2022032898

British Library Cataloguing-in-Publication Data

A catalogue record for this book is available from the British Library.

For any available supplementary material, please visit
https://www.worldscientific.com/worldscibooks/10.1142/13048#t=suppl

Desk Editors: Aanand Jayaraman/Lai Ann

Typeset by Stallion Press
Email: enquiries@stallionpress.com

Printed in Singapore

Preface

For several years now, the full-time MSc program at Nyenrode Business University includes a course on the New Economic Powers. Why? I firmly believe that our students will soon live and work in a world no longer dominated by the West.

Granted, in the decades to come, western countries will remain the most prosperous with (much) higher incomes than those in the major emerging countries. They will also hold on to their position in technology, and soft power and democratic institutions that have created prosperity ensure that the West retains its immense influence on global rules. The western middle class will continue to be an important market, and western companies will stay key players on the world stage.

The end of western domination

However, the West can no longer dominate the global community as it has done in the past. Today's world is pluralistic, and the larger emerging markets are becoming increasingly influential. Todays graduates, the future managers, will face new competitors, new competitive strategies, new markets, and a middle class with different consumption patterns and ideas. Students who choose a government career, either centrally or locally, will also face a new world where the West immediately feels the repercussions of choices made in China, India, or Indonesia. We have seen many examples in recent years: stock market volatility, inflation due to higher commodity prices, takeovers of iconic companies, and rising tourist numbers, which are about to pick up after a dramatic decline due to COVID-19.

New Economic Powers

At Nyenrode Business University, we think it is imperative for our students, entrepreneurs and policy makers to know what is happening in emerging markets. I choose to focus on the nine most important emerging markets of today and, indeed, of the future: the New Economic Powers or the NEP-9. The NEP-9 are China, Brazil, Indonesia, India, Mexico, South Africa, South Korea, Russia, and Turkey. These countries can, individually or in different partnerships, change the global landscape. Taking a large and heterogeneous group as a starting point is complex. Still, there are many fundamental similarities between these countries. In many cases, their differences are caused only by the difference in their development process.

A common characteristic among the NEP-9 countries is the need to rebalance the economy and society

---

For example, each NEP-9 is going through a development process called *rebalancing*. This means these countries are developing growth strategies that ensure their economies transition from easy growth based on more labor and machinery to growth based on technological advances and increased productivity. This process aims to avoid the *middle-income trap*. NEP-9 countries also show strong similarities in the role of government; a government that is much more active to complement the market compared to the West. Additionally, they all believe in the benefits of international trade, direct investments, and globalization in general, provided they are in service of domestic priorities and considerations. The NEP-9 take the cautious view regarding global integration and feel the autonomy of the nation state must be guaranteed, which tends to bring them into conflict with the principles of the World Trade Organization and the International Monetary Fund. Conflict certainly does not mean the NEP-9 want to do away with these multilateral institutions. However, they ask these organizations to recognize and adapt to the new global situation. The NEP-9 are staking their claim in the discussions about the rules and future of globalization and international organizations.

Choices Made in This Book

Writing a book about nine emerging economies and their effects on the principal aspects of the globalization process requires choices. Choosing which countries to include in the NEP-9 is inherently arbitrary. I had to defend the inclusion of South Korea several times, emphasizing the country's technological status and its specific role in the Asian region as an investor and political bridge builder, which you will also read about in this book. South Korea is also included because it is a unique illustration of the importance of government policy. At the end of the Second World War, the living standards in North and South Korea were very similar, whereas 40 years later, in the early 1990s, there were already huge differences. By 2022, South Korea's level of prosperity is comparable to the United Kingdom and New Zealand. In contrast, North Korea's level of wealth is estimated to be lower than in countries like Chad and Sierra Leone. This vast gap emerged within three generations. Cultural aspects, geographical differences, and not knowing the required policies for wealth creation cannot explain this difference. It is mainly attributable to the differences in specific government policies.

The focus on longer term trends and developments

A second choice is to focus on long-term trends, abstracting from short-term actions, crises, and conflicts, to avoid getting swept up by current events and issues. When the Chinese government rolled out a massive stimulus package to counter the economic effects of the 2008–2009 financial crisis, western media claimed these policies were the start of a reduced role of the market in favor of the government. In retrospect, this conclusion was arguably incorrect. The Chinese government has held on to its policy of retreat in the economic sphere. Still, western media were bent on interpreting the stimulus package and did so incorrectly, as evidenced by China's current stimulus package implemented to counter the COVID-19 crisis. This package was significantly smaller than those rolled out by governments in the West (and Japan). Between 2008 and 2022, the Chinese government has stuck to the long-term process of achieving sustainable economic development focused on rebalancing, even if specific periods of crisis require extraordinary (government) measures.

So, I will look primarily at long-term developments and search for the fundamental pillars that support the choices and policies of the NEP-9. This is a complex process. Predictions are difficult to make, even in the short term. Often, short- and long-term developments happen in parallel and interweave. Sudden policy changes, political choices, pandemics, military tensions, or new governments can throw off the most meticulously researched forecasts. In a sense, I had a personal experience on this. COVID-19 forced the closure of all schools in the Netherlands on March 15, 2020, just being in the mid of a lecture cycle for the part-time MSc program at Nyenrode. I remember sending my students an email on March 18, 2020, to inform them about the first online lecture. I also confidently expressed my hope that we could meet up again physically for the final classes in early May. Needless to say, this prediction of the near future did not pan out.

The changing world: see what happened after the Russian invasion in the Ukraine

---

I wrote this preface in late January 2022. Who could have imagined how different the world would look a month later? After the first proof readings, I asked my editor if it was OK to write some words on the Russian invasion in Ukraine at the end of February 2022 and fortunately, he was able to incorporate some additional words in this preface. Obviously, some of the analyses on Russian economy, international trade and foreign direct investments in this book are caught up by the latest reality. The short-term effects of the Russian invasion were seen immediately on the financial markets and the development of local currencies such as the ruble. This kind of situation usually produces a lot of short-term speculative behavior and the volatility that comes with that. Clearly, we can scrap Russian economic growth forecasts for this year and the next. And this also relates to other NEP-9 countries, western advanced nations and developing countries. They now witness tough economic circumstances with rising energy-and commodity prices, supply shortages and political instability. In the short term, the announced sanctions will turn weak economic growth into a severe recession. Since February 2022, Russia has been disconnected from global institutions. Russia had to withdraw from the WTO and had to reduce its international diplomatic network substantially. It is also clear that it lost credibility in many parts of the world, which harms its soft power and reduces its geo-political influence. All these effects will have longer-term implications for Russia's integration and connection to the rest of the world.

Cynically, the Ukraine invasion shows why Russia was selected in the NEP-9. It has enormous natural resources and is a large military power. Although, geo-political power is under attack, there are several countries that backed the Russian decisions.

I found it not surprising that the scheduled BRICS summit on June 23, 2022 continued with the theme of "Foster High-quality BRICS Partnership, Usher in a New Era for Global Development". Searching for alliances, especially in challenging times, is essential for the NEP-9 countries. It is the only way large emerging markets may change the global governance design and shape the new global landscape: cooperative in specific issues and pragmatic in dealing with differences. We see this with respect to Indonesia and Turkey. They are both quite silent on the brutal Russian invasion in Ukraine. For Brazil and Mexico, the war in Ukraine is about the fight of the expanding NATO and the Russian narrative of protecting national sovereignty.

However, over time, the Russian invasion of Ukraine may also put pressure on relationships within the BRICS and NEP-9. In recent years, China and Russia have grown closer politically, as reflected in bilateral trade and investment. At the same time, China is dependent on the global economy and open borders. China is deeply integrated into the world economy, much more so than Russia. Additionally, China has massively invested in the One Belt One Road initiative, with the idea of connecting the East and the West, but whether that is possible without Russia is questionable. China also has considerable interests in Africa. Many African countries consider the Russian incursion into sovereign Ukraine as a form of colonialism and expect China to express clear disapproval. Not doing so will create significant problems for China, as these countries will wonder: How does China regard *our* national sovereignty? Other long-term effects rising from the War may fit the analyses in different chapters. For example, the current trend of regionalism will be accelerated, hard power becomes increasingly important, the enormous migration flow in Europe may solve labor shortages and perhaps out of control oil and gas prices give a boost to working on the green GDP.

If short-term forecasts are uncertain, long-term projections are inherently more challenging. For example, in the early 1960s, experts thought world population growth would peak in 2026. We now know population growth reached its peak in the late 1960s and has been declining ever since. Another example that shows the complexity of long-term assessment is the vision of Francis Fukuyama. In 1989, he concluded: *What we may be witnessing is not just the end of the Cold War or the passing of a particular period of post-war history, but the end of history as such: that is, the end-point of mankind's ideological evolution and the universalization of western liberal democracy as the final form of human government* (*The End of History*, 1989, p. 3). The chapters of this book will show you this conclusion was premature. The past few years have proven that the liberal democracies of the West cannot deliver on their promises. The NEP-9 countries show that there are alternative systems available and that an universal liberal democracy is not the only system that creates prosperity, well-being, stability, and equality. The recent developments in Ukraine tell us declaring the Cold War over was also premature. Despite these complexities, this book regularly discusses long-term predictions, backed by remarks and clarifications on how to read the numbers.

We cannot ignore that the NEP-9 are becoming significant players in all aspects of the globalization process. That is the new reality, which at times caused discomfort and uncertainty in the West. Domestic employment comes under pressure, companies go abroad, and companies from countries "different" from us take over iconic enterprises. However, the new reality also creates opportunities. The middle class in NEP-9 countries is growing, NEP-9 companies launch new innovative products, and the realization that the western liberal economic system is not a panacea and that (thankfully) there are alternative economic systems and choices is slowly taking hold. Looking at other countries with different systems, understanding each other, and learning from each other are essential. To do so, it is necessary to put developments in the correct, long-term context. In this respect, we are still far removed from the day when discussions and negotiations are no longer needed because western liberal democracy has "won," as Fukuyama concluded. Now, more than ever, it is necessary to understand why governments, voters, consumers, and producers in the NEP-9 countries do what they do. After all, we will increasingly feel the consequences and effects of these choices.

Providing insight into long-term developments, whether back or forward-looking, can be done through qualitative terms such as *in recent times, in the past, better than before, an increase in prosperity in the far future*, and *the coming years*. At the same time, some clarification through quantitative overviews is helpful. Here, it is essential to indicate how the data were obtained, which assumptions were made and that the data reflect a (moderate) consensus view. We must also remember that even moderate forecasts can show substantial differences in various areas, as the overviews concerning the global middle class and investment flows show. We must focus on what matters rather than quarrel about what the numbers are actually showing. Consider, for example, how the BBC reported the number of daily COVID-19 casualties at the beginning of the pandemic. Each day, they showed viewers how many people had died during the previous 24 hours and within 28 days of a positive COVID test. After a while, we were only talking about the numbers. Much attention was given to their (in)accuracy and presentation. For example, some people died in hospital from other conditions but tested positive for COVID-19. Should these be included in the data? Instead of putting so much energy into debating the correctness of the data, it would be much better to explain the data and how they guided the choices. This book has a lot of numbers to support the narrative, to facilitate the analysis. Nothing more and nothing less.

An economic approach within the context of political realities

---

A third choice made in this book is its economic approach within a political context. In the lectures for the Global Immersion Programs in China (Renmin university) and Singapore and Dubai at SPJain, it makes sense to complement the economic approach with political realities. After all, economics and political choices are so deeply intertwined in these countries that it is impossible to discuss one without the other. The same goes for all NEP-9 countries, and as a result, political aspects are included but placed within the economic analysis. I will look at democracy, corruption, and economic systems and their (possible) effects on the level of prosperity. We will analyze how the middle class is linked to the political elite and connect this to the role the middle class plays in the development process. A look at increased urbanization in NEP-9 countries focuses on its economic effects and analyzes the various urbanization plans rolled out by governments.

Again, we must take politics into account. After all, the enormous growth in countries like China and India did not result from better advice from economists or a sudden change in national cultural aspects. It is the political choices. Politics is inherent to economic analyses of the NEP-9. These political aspects are woven into the fabric of this book through the role governments play in economic processes.

Many questions and often no black and white answers

This brings me to the fourth choice I made in this book: a broad, integrative approach that does not always allow for unambiguous answers to essential questions. The analysis of urbanization in the NEP-9 mentioned earlier clearly reflects this integrative approach. It goes hand in hand with technological developments, special economic zones, income inequality, and even how urbanization affects overall happiness. Economics may be the hook on which the analysis is hung, but the broad view is an essential guiding principle.

The world has dramatically changed since I started writing this book in March 2020. The question is whether the underlying foundations of the globalization process have also changed. I have tried to provide answers or, at least, to discuss which factors we must consider in the search for answers. A book is inevitably selective, but each chapter is an essential element in understanding the process of globalization and the role the NEP-9 play in it.

The Chapters and Topics

Chapter 1 sheds light on why our NEP-9 cluster includes these specific countries. Some require no further explanation, such as China and India, but we will elaborate on others. Considerations include economic size in the coming decades, but also regional (Turkey), geopolitical (South Africa), demographic (Mexico), and sectoral aspects (South Korea).

In Chapters 2 and 3, I analyze how these countries have been able to generate wealth and address how we should measure wealth. Looking at a wide range of human indicators, we see they are clearly catching-up with the traditional economic powers. A key learning point about this catching-up is that the NEP-9 have been able to combine the benefits of the market with the stability that government intervention can bring. For them, one cannot exist without the other. Except for South Korea, the NEP-9 countries all have middle-income status. Their policies aim to enable the transition to high-income status. In doing so, they must look beyond GDP or income, including also human indicators, while staying within environmental boundaries set by nature.

Chapter 4 analyzes the most important differences and fundamental similarities between the nine NEPs. We highlight the differences from an economic perspective (export-driven versus a large domestic market), a political perspective (democracy versus autocracy), and a geopolitical perspective (hard versus soft power). There are many similarities in how these countries view the current global landscape and how they shape their economic policies.

Chapters 5 and 7 discuss the NEP-9's mixed feelings about globalization and the functioning of multilateral institutions such as the WTO and the IMF. Globalization and global institutions are valuable and necessary, but national governments must have the freedom to intervene when necessary. We will discuss in detail the discomfort felt about the way the globalization process is currently developing.

Between the analyses of the globalization process (Chapter 5) and the role of global organizations (Chapter 7) is a chapter on international trade. Here too, we see that the NEP-9 countries acknowledge the benefits of international trade and the functioning of markets in general but demand strategic domestic autonomy. They do not see protectionism and the roll-out of various non-tariff barriers as a step backward from multilateral free trade. They are molding international trade to positively impact their national economy precisely because they are going through so many different transitions at once, all of which can be disruptive.

Finally, Chapter 8 looks at foreign direct investments (FDIs). Here, again, we see restraint. In principle, the NEP-9 welcome foreign investors and companies; after all, they bring with them technological and managerial knowledge, and new products become available to the growing middle class. At the same time, they realize that not all investments are good. Think, for example, of highly polluting production processes that make little use of local workers and where there are no links to domestic companies. In that case, we can question the benefits of this type of investment. Therefore, the NEP-9 governments play a vital role in creating a suitable investment climate for specific investments.

NEP-9 countries: various formal and informal alliances

The NEP-9 are particularly important (and increasingly so) because they find each other in various formal and informal alliances. Examples are the BRICS, G20, and WTO and bilateral partnerships between the NEP-9 countries, often focusing on only economic cooperation because of sensitive political issues. For example, China is one of the largest investors in Turkey and, together with Germany and Russia, its largest trading partner. At the same time, there are significant political sensitivities between the two countries. China refuses to label the PKK as a terrorist organization, and Turkey is issuing Turkish passports to Uyghur asylum seekers. We see this among most NEP-9 countries: deeper economic ties and joint action on geopolitical issues, for which bilateral political sensitivities are temporarily shelved. Turkey and Russia enjoy intensive economic relations despite conflicting interests in the Caucasus and the Middle East. There is far-reaching trade integration between China and Indonesia, with bilateral trade increasingly happening in local currencies despite tensions in the South China Sea. China and India collaborate economically within the BRICS and Asian Infrastructure Investment Bank while at the same time hashing out longstanding border conflicts in the Himalayas.

Despite the conflicts and sensitivities, these largest emerging markets, individually and in different partnerships, will significantly influence the new global landscape because of four interrelated factors:

1. Economic catching-up in the NEP-9 is pushing forward and will irrevocably lead to greater geopolitical influence.
2. The role played by the government will remain prominent despite the upward development.
3. The government will remain an important factor in future trade and investment relations with other countries.
4. There is growing discomfort in the NEP-9 about how multilateral institutions manage the globalization process.

To a large extent, these four factors, explored in-depth in the following eight chapters, will determine the shape of the new global landscape. Helped by its broad, integrative approach and deliberately non-technical language, this book is accessible for both economists and non-economists who want to understand the changing global landscape better.

I hope you enjoy reading *The Rise of the New Economic Powers and The Changing Global Landscape*.

About the Author

Haico Ebbers is Professor of International Economics at Nyenrode Business University in the Netherlands. Professor Ebbers studied International Economics and macro-economics at the University of Groningen. In 1991, he joined Nyenrode and completed his PhD in 1996. Professor Ebbers is guest professor at various national and international universities, including some top universities in China. He was visiting professor at China Europe International Business School (CEIBS) in Shanghai between 1996 and 2006 and is still active as visiting professor at Renmin University in Beijing. Furthermore, he is visiting professor at SP Jain School of Global Management in Singapore, Dubai and Sydney. He is recognized as one of the leading thinkers in the field of EU–China economic relations. In the previous years, he developed Global Immersion programs for MBA and MSc students in emerging markets with a strong focus on the pros and cons of globalization.

Acknowledgments

The book could not be written without support. My thanks go to Christa Jongeling for her translation and editing work and to the editorial team of World Scientific, in particular to Aanand Jayaraman for all the help, suggestions, and patience. Special thanks to Jeroen van den Brandhof for developing the figures and tables. Jeroen, it was a great pleasure that we continued our cooperation after the work you did on my previous book *Unravelling Modern China* (2019).

Contents

Chapter 1

Why a Book on New Economic Powers?

1.1 From Some General Remarks Toward One Chapter and a Whole Book

In 2004, I co-authored a Dutch textbook on globalization, trade, and foreign direct investments (Jagersma and Ebbers, 2004). The emphasis of that book is firmly on the West: the western middle class, the western attitude toward multilateral institutions, western companies, and the western model of economic development in which the market plays a large role. This focus was the logical choice at the time, as at the start of the new millennium, western multinationals were the drivers of globalization. The western middle class was the largest consumption market, and western countries dominated organizations such as the World Trade Organization (WTO) and IMF. Technological innovations emerged from the United States, Japan, and a few European countries. Despite the dot. com crash of 2000 and the economic crises that followed, the prevailing economic paradigm was "more market, less government" — the system implemented in western countries. Asian, Latin American, Eastern European, and African countries were seen primarily as pools of cheap labor, not yet as interesting markets. Consequently, foreign direct investments flowed primarily from developed, industrialized countries to developing, cheap labor countries.

Our 2004 book discussed the development of emerging markets in terms of GDP and human development indicators such as life expectancy and education. We emphasized common characteristics, such as

1

the route to a diversified economy, growing welfare, and a relatively large role of government in economics. Although there were early signs that because of their successful development process and opening up to the rest of the world, certain emerging markets could be attractive from a market perspective, in 2003, we decided not to dedicate a separate chapter to them. We discussed the emerging markets from a bird's eye view; the emerging Asian market or the emerging Latin American market, for example. Again, this choice made sense at the time. Remember, in 2003, the size of the Indian economy, measured in nominal gross domestic product (GDP), was only 30% of that of the United Kingdom. In the same year, even Texas, with its 21 million inhabitants, had a larger GDP than India, with its 1.1 billion citizens. The Chinese economy was smaller than both the Italian economy and the economy of California, and in 2003, the combined share of Brazil, India, Indonesia, and Turkey in world exports was lower than that of individual countries, such as Italy and Canada (UN, 2003). The global economic and political impact of the emerging markets, even larger ones, was still marginal.

The size of the Indian economy was only 30% of that of the
United Kingdom in 2003

We did spend a few words on the commonly named Asian Miracle, the Asian success in economic catch-up, by mentioning the development process of the newly industrializing countries of Southeast Asia (the commonly named Asian Tigers), but that was it. For example, we did not mention the BRIC: Brazil, Russia, India, and China. I remember vivid discussions on whether we should refer to the 2001 Goldman Sachs report on the BRIC countries: *Building Better Global Economic BRICs*. Ultimately, we decided not to, as we questioned the soundness of the assumptions and methodology of the report. Don't forget that in 2003, we were in the middle of the American boom period, with high economic growth. Add to this the collapse of the Union of Soviet Socialist Republics (USSR) and Francis Fukuyama's 1989 essay *The End of History*, in which he stated that western liberal democracy would become the only system of government to enjoy widespread normative support. In this era of "triumph of capitalism," the BRIC report was interesting but only as a possible scenario in the longer-term future.

Furthermore, in 2003, we decided not to touch upon the rising middle class of emerging markets. Neither did we mention companies from emerging markets in our overviews of the largest and most successful companies and brands. By and large, in the early 2000s, the middle class was based in the West. Differences in definition aside, the consensus was that only a tiny fraction of the global middle class was located in (the larger cities in) specific emerging markets. In 2003, Asia, Latin America, Eastern Europe, and Africa constituted less than 10% of the global middle class. China and India had a negligible share of around 1% of global middle-class consumption (OECD, 2010). The emerging-market middle class was also considerably poorer than the middle class in the West. International travel was far out of reach for them: we hardly found any middle-class visitors from outside Europe during the 2004 Olympic Games in Athens.

In the early 2000s, the global middle class was based in the West

---

Companies from emerging markets were barely visible on the international stage. In the early 2000s, a handful of companies from India (M&M), China (Huawei technologies and Lenovo), Brazil (Ambev), Mexico (Cemex), and South Africa (SAB Millar) were successful, but these were exceptions. And despite their international expansion, at the time, they were driven primarily by domestic operations. One could argue that in the early 2000s, the West still dominated the global landscape in almost all aspects.

1.1.1 *The catching-up*

In 2016, I published a new textbook on globalization (Ebbers, 2016). A little over a decade is a mere blip in historical context, but it is a long time indeed in a discussion on the importance and role of emerging markets in the global landscape. Within this decade, we saw dramatic changes in the role of (large) emerging markets in trade, investments, politics, and finance. Companies and brands from emerging markets entered the western markets, such as China-based Alibaba and Xiaomi; the latter was founded only in 2010. Other successful examples are Etihad Airlines from the United Arab Emirates, America Movil (Mexico), JBS (Brazil), Turkish Airlines, and Indian-based Infosys and Wipro. Moreover, in 2015, the global middle class (defined as people earning between 11 and 110 dollars in purchasing power a day) rose from 1.5 billion people in 2006 to almost three billion people, with half of them situated in emerging markets (Kharas, 2017). In the same year, China's nominal GDP was 65% of that of the US, but measured in purchasing power, China's GDP was already larger than that of the US. The top 15 largest economies worldwide contained new players, such as China, India, Russia, Brazil, Indonesia, and Mexico, both in nominal GDP as well as GDP in purchasing power parity.

Clustering of emerging markets is possible and needed

Emerging markets had a prominent role in the new book. It discussed the role of emerging markets in the globalization process in relation to international trade and foreign investments and clusters of emerging markets and their perspectives on the role of the WTO. I emphasized that organizing emerging markets in clusters, like the BRICs, EAGLES, Next-11, and Nest Eagles (more on them later), is a way to measure the combined power of these countries: A power that would change the face of globalization with new rules, new competitors, a new role of the government, and a new middle class. I strongly felt that despite their differences, for the sake of analysis and research, it is indeed possible to discuss clusters of emerging markets as one group. Although I am well aware that it is dangerous to focus on common denominators, I intentionally concentrated on the general picture and the commonalities of these countries, leaving aside the differences and some country-specific issues. Simplification and deduction are required to come to general conclusions.

Despite this prominent role, the focus of the 2016 book was still on the advanced economies of the western world. Although they experienced massive economic growth, in 2015, the economies of both India and Brazil were still considerably smaller than the economy of California, and the gap in income per capita between fast-growing emerging markets and the western, industrialized countries remained enormous.

1.1.2 *A new book is needed*

Today, the most important emerging markets require a book devoted solely to them. I will explore their common characteristics, as well as their differences, and look at the role they play in globalization. This book aims to help you understand shifts in the political, economical, and societal landscape of these countries and recognize the choices these countries are making, as they *will* affect you as a consumer, worker, policymaker, marketeer, strategist, (global) citizen, or voter. Their growing impact on the world stage is visible everywhere. Just look at some of the anecdotal evidence of a growing middle class in emerging markets. Of the almost 700,000 tickets sold abroad for the 2018 World Cup in Russia, soccer fans from emerging economies, such as Colombia, Brazil, Mexico, Argentina, Peru, and China, were all in the top 10 of foreign attendees traveling from abroad to enjoy matches. Quite a difference from the 2004 Olympic Games in Athens. The World Bank and the Brookings Institute now consider 36% of the Chinese population (lower) middle class (2020). For Mexico, that percentage is 70% (2020): a dramatic increase compared to the early 1990s (World Bank, 2021).

We are also witnessing the growing visibility of companies from emerging markets. I was surprised to see Alipay, TikTok, Hisense, Gazprom, and Qatar Airways among the biggest official sponsors of UEFA Euro 2020. The growing impact also holds for political issues. The political, social, and constitutional changes in Turkey, the new role of China (under President Xi Jinping) and India (under Prime Minister Narendra Modi) in world economics and politics, the polarization in politics in Brazil and Indonesia, and the aggressive stance of Russia in international relations may all affect globalization and the globalization process. Whether economic or political in nature, choices made by the largest emerging markets will be felt globally.

The catching-up: a continuing process

Another reason we need to understand the new role of the largest emerging markets is that their rise and development will continue throughout the coming decades. Unfortunately, we will likely see short-term economic crises, such as those experienced in Brazil and South Africa, in early 2021. We may also expect more political and social unrest, such as was seen in Turkey and India in 2020 and 2021, but the consensus view is that a different world will have emerged by 2050. We are moving toward an emerging market century. Before the COVID-19 pandemic, the consensus was that China would overtake the US as the world's largest economy in terms of nominal exchange rate around 2028. In 2016, China was already the largest economy in purchasing power parity (IMF, 2020; PWC, 2017). The latest growth forecasts include the impact of COVID-19 on the US and the Chinese economies in 2020 and 2021. These show that because of the strong recovery of the Chinese economy in 2020, compared to the contraction of the US economy, China could become the world's largest economy in terms of nominal exchange rate (or market exchange rate) even some years earlier (IMF, 2021).

We will continue to see the shift of global economic power away from established advanced economies, especially those in Europe, toward the emerging economies of Asia and elsewhere. Figure 1.1 shows that in 2050, six countries in the top 10 largest economies will be emerging markets, whether we refer to GDP in market exchange rate or in purchasing power parity (Chapter 2 will explain the difference). Figure 1.1 also shows the relative size of the economies. For example, in terms of purchasing power parity, in 2021, the Chinese share in the global economy (18.7%) was substantially larger than the importance of the US in the global economy (15.9%).

GDP nominal	2021 US$ billion		2050 US$ billion		GDP PPP	2021 US$ billion		2050 US$ billion
1 US	22.939	1 China	49.853	1 China	27.071	1 China	58.499
2 China	16.862	2 US	34.102	2 US	22.939	2 India	44.128
3 Japan	5.103	3 India	28.021	3 India	10.181	3 US	34.102
4 Germany	4.230	4 Indonesia	7.275	4 Japan	5.633	4 Indonesia	10.502
5 UK	3.108	5 Japan	6.779	5 Germany	4.843	5 Brazil	7.540
6 India	2.946	6 Brazil	6.532	6 Russia	4.447	6 Russia	7.131
7 France	2.940	7 Germany	6.138	7 Indonesia	3.530	7 Mexico	6.863
8 Italy	2.120	8 Mexico	5.563	8 Brazil	3.437	8 Japan	6.779
9 Canada	2.015	9 UK	5.369	9 France	3.322	9 Germany	6.138
10 South Korea	1.823	10 Russia	5.127	10 UK	3.276	10 UK	5.369
11 Russia	1.647	12 Turkey	4.078	11 Turkey	2.873	11 Turkey	5.184
13 Brazil	1.645	13 South Korea	3.539	13 Mexico	2.685	18 South Korea	3.539
15 Mexico	1.285	30 South Africa	1.939	14 South Korea	2.503	27 South Africa	2.570
16 Indonesia	1.150			32 South Africa	861		
21 Turkey	795						
33 South Africa	335						

Share in world nominal GDP, 2021									
US	China	Japan	Ger.	UK	India	France	Italy	Canada	SK
24.2	17.8	5.4	4.5	3.3	3.1	3.1	2.2	2.2	1.9

Share in world PPP GDP, 2021									
China	US	India	Japan	Ger.	Russia	Indo.	Brazil	France	UK
18.7	15.9	7.0	3.9	3.4	3.1	2.4	2.4	2.3	2.3

Share in world nominal GDP, 2050									
China	US	India	Indo.	Japan	Brazil	Ger.	Mexico	UK	Russia
18.5	13.1	10.7	2.7	2.6	2.5	2.3	2.1	2.0	1.9

Share in world PPP GDP, 2050									
China	India	US	Indo.	Brazil	Russia	Mexico	Japan	Ger.	UK
20.0	15.1	12.1	3.4	2.6	2.4	2.3	2.2	2.0	1.8

Figure 1.1:   GDP development between 2021 and 2050, specific countries.

Source: IMF (2021) and PWC (2017).

With several large emerging markets in the shared driver seat, the world is changing fast. This will profoundly impact countries, companies, consumers, and workers in these emerging markets, and those in western, developed economies. Interestingly, people in these western economies are losing faith in globalization. Changes, particularly rapid ones, create discomfort and a perceived lack of control. Imagine hearing you will get new neighbors. You do not know them and cannot predict how they will behave. You must build a relationship and find a new balance, living next door to each other. Whether it is new neighbors or an emerging market, often we see a defensive reaction. Feeling uncertainty and discomfort about rapid changes is nothing new. Consider this quote from French journalist and politician J.J. Servan-Schreiber, from his book *The American Challenge* (1968): "Europe is an unprepared victim to the US capitalist predator with its far superior management, technology, and capital. Including its soft power in the field of culture and movies; the US would take over the French economy and society."

Discomfort about the new neighbors

Today, we see the same reaction to the rise of China or the takeover of iconic national companies by firms from emerging markets. It was also clearly visible in the slogans used during the Brexit campaign (*Taking Back Control*) and the 2016 American elections (*America First*). When I was teaching in an international MBA program in Sydney in 2019, I asked the opinion of my students about the development by several EU countries of setting up a screening mechanism for investments aimed to block takeovers by Chinese, Brazilian, Mexican, or Indian companies. One student had recently read an article about the Asian giant hornet spotted for the first time in the United States and made this comparison: "They can wipe out entire bee colonies within hours, and the same will happen with western companies."

1.2 Growing Importance

The growing importance of the largest emerging markets is striking in many respects: demographically, economically, geopolitically, culturally, technologically, and environmentally.

1.2.1   *Demographics and economics*

Demographics have shifted and will continue to move toward emerging markets. If the phrase "people are our greatest asset" is true, then emerging markets are rich indeed. In 2021, the population of emerging markets accounted for more than 87% of the world's population. In the top 10 countries with the highest population in 2021, nine are emerging markets. The only western country on that list is the United States. This development will continue in the coming decades (see Figure 1.2).

A large population is not always preferable. Dividing earned income over many people results in low(er) income per capita. A large population can also lead to a host of problems too numerous to dive into here. However, as we will see later on, a large population is beneficial for achieving longer-term development, especially if the population is relatively young and educated, as is the case in countries such as South Africa, India, Mexico, and Indonesia. A relatively young population means a country can achieve long-term development based on a growing labor force.

Demographics also relate to the explosion of the middle class. The OECD (2017) estimates that by 2030, Asia will represent 66% of the global middle class and 59% of middle-class consumption, compared to 28% and 23% in 2009. Western companies realize there is an opportunity for growth in emerging markets. The growth of the middle class is driving the development and implementation of emerging market strategies by companies, such as Unilever, Volkswagen, and Walmart. Today's emerging markets are becoming tomorrow's main markets.

Top 10 in 2021		Mln	%	Top 10 in 2050		Mln	%
1	China	1406	18.0	1	India	1639	16.8
2	India	1373	17.5	2	China	1402	14.4
3	United States	331	4.2	3	Nigeria	401	4.1
4	Indonesia	270	3.4	4	United States	379	3.9
5	Pakistan	225	2.9	5	Pakistan	338	3.5
6	Brazil	212	2.7	6	Indonesia	331	3.4
7	Nigeria	211	2.7	7	Brazil	229	2.3
8	Bangladesh	170	2.2	8	Ethiopia	205	2.1
9	Russia	146	1.9	9	Congo-DRC	194	2.0
10	Mexico	126	1.6	10	Bangladesh	193	2.0

Figure 1.2:   Population in millions and global share (%), 2021 and 2050.

Source: UN, Department of Economic and Social Affairs (2021).

As shown before, emerging markets will soon dominate the list of the world's largest economies, which translates into their growing significance in international trade and investment. From 2016 onwards, China and Russia have been mostly in the top 10 countries with respect to outward Foreign Direct Investments (UNCTAD, 2021). China is the biggest export country worldwide, and South Korea, Mexico, Russia, India, and Brazil are all in the top 25 of the largest exporters of 2020 (WTO, 2021). Also, the structure of international trade is changing fast. Traditionally, advanced economies dominated the export of services, such as management and consulting, computer and information service, but that is changing dramatically. In previous years, service export has been growing much faster in emerging markets than in western economies. In 2020, China overtook Spain, Italy, and Japan to become the 5th largest exporter of services in the world. India is in the top 10, and Thailand, Brazil, Indonesia, and Egypt are in the top 30 and moving up rapidly (WTO, 2021).

In many aspects, changes are going very fast

The same holds for emerging market companies. As we've already seen, companies from emerging markets are becoming common names for Western consumers and provide fierce competition for western multinationals in the global marketplace.

1.2.2 *Geopolitics*

The growing importance of emerging markets is also evident in geopolitics. Their international influence has increased substantially through the formation of the G-20 in 1999. The G-20 has superseded the G7 as the leading entity in global issues, and half of its members (19 countries and the EU) are large emerging markets, which are our New Economic Powers in the chapters to come. Growing political power is also evident in the increased voting share of the larger emerging markets in the International Monetary Fund. However, as we will find out later in the book, this voting share is still far below their *economic* power, which is why the larger emerging markets are demanding more voting power in the IMF. As we will see in Chapter 6, meeting this claim will automatically result in less voting power for western countries. Zero-sum games always produce winners and losers; quite different from the discussion on the effects of international trade in Chapter 6. There we will see that international trade may create a positive-sum game with only winners.

We are also witnessing the growth of soft power of China (the commonly named Beijing Consensus) and India (Mumbai Consensus), the topic of Chapters 5 and 7. Nye popularized the term in his 1990 book, *Bound to Lead: The Changing Nature of American Power*. In this book, he wrote: "when one country gets other countries to want what it wants might be called co-optive or soft power in contrast with the hard or command power of ordering others to do what it wants." Soft power influences by molding and shaping the preferences, views, and desires of others through culture, values, and policy.

Zero-sum game versus positive-sum game

One example is the popularity of the cultures of the emerging markets: not only movies from India (Bollywood) or Korean music (K-pop) but also food from Mexico and Indonesia, and the iconic companies from China and India. Today, several African countries are following the Chinese growth model instead of following IMF guidelines, not because they are forced to do so, but because of China's economic success and its growing soft power. The world is becoming more modernized and less westernized at the same time.

1.2.3 *Technology and the environment*

The global center of gravity for research and technology is rapidly shifting toward emerging markets. Look at the ranking of emerging markets in the annual Global Innovation Index (WIPO) and the Global Competitiveness Report (World Economic Forum): Countries such as China, India, Brazil, and Russia were in the top 10 in terms of expenditures on Research & Development in 2019. In 2003, I was working on the previously mentioned globalization book. Back then, the consensus view was that underdeveloped educational systems and a lack of regulations aimed at stimulating creative thinking and innovative behavior were seriously hampering innovation in emerging markets. However, over the last decade(s), several emerging markets have been striving to develop skills and talent through educational policies, often centered around free education for all, at least at the primary level. Their governments have supported these efforts with relevant increases in public spending on education and R&D. Countries like China and Turkey are highly advanced digitally. The same holds for South Korea. For example, smartphone penetration, the percentage of a population actively using a smartphone, is staggering in some larger emerging markets: Indonesia, Mexico, Turkey, China, and Russia were well above 55% in 2020 (Figure 1.3).

Finally, emerging markets share the responsibility of creating the climate crisis with the western world, but they can also play an essential part in solving it. To put it bluntly, the environmental situation in countries like China, India, and Russia is simply dramatic. You may remember the striking images of the skies in cities like Shanghai, Mumbai, or Moscow that emerged during the early days of the COVID-19 pandemic. The stark contrast between the clear blue skies during the global lockdowns and the smog-filled, pre-COVID days is a painfully vivid illustration of how bad things have gotten. In many emerging markets, coal is the leading cause of bad air quality, combined with low energy efficiency and, obviously, the enormous growth of car ownership. China was by far the largest market in terms of car sales in 2020, but India and Brazil are also in the top five. Mexico, Turkey, and Indonesia are all in the top 20 of the same list. Arguably, in many parts of these countries, water pollution may be an even bigger problem than air pollution. As we will see in Chapter 2, these countries are already overshooting the planetary boundaries in several respects.

Country	%		
United States	81.6	Iran	62.9
United Kingdom	78.9	Turkey	61.7
Germany	77.9	Indonesia	58.6
France	77.6	Mexico	54.4
South Korea	76.5	Thailand	54.3
Italy	75.9	Brazil	51.4
Russia	68.5	Philippines	37.7
China	63.8	South Africa	40.0
Japan	63.2	India	32.1
Vietnam	63.1	Pakistan	18.4

Figure 1.3: Smartphone penetration, 2020, selected countries.

Source: Statista (2021).

Despite this bleak picture, the larger emerging markets are also an essential part of the solution. Undoubtedly driven by the fact that they are the most vulnerable to rising temperatures, they have taken promising steps.

Emerging markets: taking responsibility and essential in finding solutions

---

Due to government subsidies, the share of plug-in electric vehicles in new passenger car sales in China was above 6% in 2020, compared to 2% in the United States. As we will see in the following chapters, China is one of the biggest adopters of clean energy. Indonesia is showing a strong commitment to significantly reducing its greenhouse gas emissions, driven by the demands of the growing urban middle class. Despite setbacks in the previous years, countries such as India have passed climate laws that should guarantee they succeed in reaching the climate objectives of the Paris Agreement of 2015, that were reaffirmed during the latest climate change conference in Glasgow in November 2021. Obviously, as we will witness throughout the book, good intention is one, but it is all about the execution of what has been put on paper by governments.

1.3 Emerging Markets: An Overview

The term emerging markets was introduced in 1981 when the World Bank promoted investing in specific developing countries. To attract investors, words such as "developing," "Third World," and "less developed" were replaced by more aspirational terms. Emerging markets were promoted as attractive, promising, and less risky than (other) developing economies. But, even back then, lumping together up-and-coming economies such as Thailand, Brazil, Argentina, Greece, Taiwan, India, and South Korea created discussions about the homogeneity of these countries or, rather, the lack thereof.

The rebalancing process

That discussion is ongoing: in the academic world, in the boardrooms of multinationals, amongst policymakers, and, consequently, on the pages of this book. Chapter 4 will delve into common characteristics and important differences. On the one hand, we see that emerging markets share some common characteristics. For example, most emerging markets are in the process of reorienting (or rebalancing) their economies toward activities with higher added value. They all are (selectively) opening up to the rest of the world and promoting more engagement with the global economy. As this transition process is ongoing, including high volatility and fast changes in the society, they all see the necessity for a relatively large and visible government.

On the other hand, lumping together different countries erases country-specific features and differences. On specific issues and in some areas, the differences between emerging countries are too large to be ignored. For instance, in 2020, private consumption made up only 40% of GDP in China but 70% in Turkey (Global Economy.com). Both China's and Russia's population is aging, while India's population is relatively young. There are also differences in trade openness. Think about closed economies, such as Nigeria, Egypt, and Iran, and open economies, such as Chili and the United Arab Emirates. Some emerging markets depend entirely on one or two commodities (Nigeria and Russia), while China and Mexico have diversified their export structure toward manufacturing.

1.3.1 *Clustering of emerging markets*

The biggest challenge facing this book is avoiding excessive simplicity or unmanageable complexity when going into detail. With this in mind, we will start by explaining the different clusters used by international organizations. The IMF divides the world into two major groups: advanced economies and emerging and developing economies. They do this by looking at GDP per capita, human indicators, such as healthcare and income distribution, export diversification, and the degree of openness regarding trade and investments. This division is debatable because some of these indicators may conflict. For example, is Qatar an advanced economy or an emerging and developing economy? Official IMF statistics consider Qatar an emerging market, even though it has the world's highest GDP per capita. However, the country also shows deep income inequality and scores poorly on several other human development indicators, putting it in the emerging market category. The same holds for many other oil-exporting countries.

Different aspects of categorization emerging markets

The World Bank established a categorization based exclusively on income level (gross national income per capita). Chapter 3 uses this categorization as the basis for discussing the middle-income trap. It has four levels:

1. Low-income countries
2. Lower-middle-income countries
3. Upper-middle-income countries
4. High-income countries

The WTO divides countries into three classes: developed countries, developing countries, and least developed countries. There are no criteria for these classifications, so countries may self-nominate their status. You might wonder why a country would classify itself as a developing or least-developed country, but as we will discuss in Chapter 7; the status of a developing or least-developed country comes with certain rights. For example, the WTO grants these countries longer transition periods for implementing the rules agreed upon in multilateral agreements.

Clustering of emerging markets is also done by banks, consultancy firms, and research institutes. The BRIC acronym first appeared in the aforementioned 2001 Goldman Sachs publication *Building Better Global Economic BRICs*. It identified four countries that, according to Goldman Sachs, would soon start to play an increasingly important role in the global economy: Brazil, Russia, India, and China. These countries were chosen based on two factors: the size of the population and the size of the economy. Goldman Sachs argued that, considering their rapid development, the combined economies of these countries will supersede the combined economies of the current richest countries by 2025. South Africa joined the BRIC cluster in 2010, which was duly renamed as BRICS. A surprising choice, considering the two deciding factors, but this decision was motivated by political considerations rather than economics and demographics. South Africa was seen as a gateway for investments from BRIC countries to the African continent and there was a feeling that the African continent should get a voice in the various international forums.

The wake-up call

The Goldman Sachs report of 2001 was a wake-up call of sorts, a warning that the world would be changing dramatically in the next decades. Before the 2001 report, some generalizations were made regarding fast-growing emerging markets. For example, the Asian Tigers was a term used to describe several booming economies in Southeast Asia, including Singapore, Hong Kong, South Korea, and Taiwan. In their report, *The East Asia Miracle,* the World Bank predicted in 1993 that the economies of the Asian Tigers would all grow dramatically in the decades to come. However, in the 1990s, these countries were relatively small, and their impact on the world economy and western countries remained modest. Opposite to the World Bank, the BRIC report made clear that the impact of the largest emerging markets on the world economy would soon be felt more strongly.

After 2001, many more acronyms were introduced into the discussion about emerging markets. Goldman Sachs launched the Next-11 in 2005. These are countries that all have the potential to become one of the 20 largest economies in the 21st century. They are Bangladesh, South Korea, Egypt, Indonesia, Iran, Mexico, Nigeria, Pakistan, the Philippines, Turkey, and Vietnam. Again, economic size and rate of development were important reasons to distinguish this group from other emerging markets. In 2006, Price Waterhouse Coopers presented the Emerging 7 (the E-7): the seven largest emerging markets whose combined GDP was expected to exceed the GDP of the G7 by 2020. It included Brazil, Russia, India, China, Mexico, Indonesia, and Turkey. In 2009, The Economist Intelligence Unit (EIU) clustered a group of emerging markets based on the size of their young populations and the level of diversification of the economy and export. Colombia, Indonesia, Vietnam, Egypt, Turkey, and South Africa are referred to with the acronym CIVETS. Individually, most of the CIVETS countries will remain regional players at most, overshadowed by their large neighbors China and India. However, according to the EIU, as a collective, they will surpass Europe, Japan, and Russia in terms of economic power by 2030.

Static versus dynamic clustering

In 2010, Banco Bilbao Vizcaya Argentaria (BBVA) Research launched the "EAGLEs" (Emerging And Growth Leading Economies), a diverse group of emerging markets, ranging from China and India to Mexico and Vietnam. The EAGLEs are emerging markets whose contribution to world economic growth in the medium and long term is expected to be larger than the combined average of the G6 economies (G7 excluding the US). This cluster is a dynamic concept where the EAGLEs' composition can change over time according to countries' forecasted performance. The latest adjustment (2016) saw the addition of countries such as Bangladesh, Egypt, and Vietnam. Besides the EAGLEs, BBVA has also created a cluster of 15 countries called "Nest-EAGLEs." In the latest update of 2016, the Nest-EAGLEs countries are also selected based on the (projected) increase of their GDP in the next 10 years (2014–2024). Countries that show an increase in their GDP over this decade that is larger than the average of the most industrialized countries (except the G7) are considered a Nest-EAGLE. Like the EAGLEs, the Nest-EAGLEs are a dynamic cluster that can change over time. Currently, the Nest-EAGLEs include, among others, countries such as Thailand, Argentina, Nigeria, Colombia, Poland, and South Africa.

1.3.2 *Emerging markets: Toward common features*

As you may have gathered by now, there is no one definition or categorization of an emerging market. However, we can determine some common features. First and foremost, "emerging" refers to the process of becoming more advanced. Their starting position (less advanced) tells us that emerging markets have a lower than average per capita income compared to advanced high-income countries. Most of the emerging markets have lower- or upper-middle-income status as indicated by the World Bank, meaning a Gross National Income per capita between 1,036 and 12,535 (2020) in US dollars.

Second, emerging markets are associated with relatively rapid growth that may continue for several decades. This fast economic development is usually driven by structural reforms toward industrialization, diversification of the economy, investment in education, and responsible reduction of trade and investment barriers. Responsible (smart) is a term used throughout this book to emphasize that reforms *must* be implemented in the correct sequence and with the correct speed. The third shared characteristic is that because of the multiple transitions happening simultaneously, emerging markets present a mix of both opportunity and risk. Falling fertility rates, improved healthcare, and continued urbanization are driving a demographic transition, often hand in hand with social, economic, technological, and political transformations. And all of this is happening in a relatively short timeframe. Uncertainty, change, volatility, risk, and opportunity are all key elements for defining and describing emerging markets.

Opportunity and risk

Transitions are often disruptive. Therefore, the fourth common feature is that in most emerging markets, the government plays a prominent role in guiding the transformation process. Examples are protecting domestic industries through trade barriers, implementation of industrial policies, helping local companies, involvement in the educational system, and building infrastructure. Although these interventions are essential, emerging markets also know that integration in the world economy (through trade and foreign direct investments) and market forces (which stimulate efficiency) are crucial preconditions for longer-term development. That is why they are looking for the optimum balance between the market and government. The balance these countries strike between market forces and government intervention will determine where their transformational processes will lead them. The outcome may be quite different from western markets.

1.4 New Economic Powers

The above introduction only uses the term emerging markets to refer to up-and-coming economies and does not distinguish between emerging markets and New Economic Powers (NEP). But, measured by economic power, some countries are clearly more important than others. In the first of a series of reports on rising economic powers, the US Congress introduced them as follows: "a small group of developing countries is transforming the global economic landscape. Led by China, India, and Brazil, these rising economic powers pose varied challenges and opportunities for the US" (Ahearn, 2011). This book substantially expands this leading group of China, India, and Brazil to nine countries: the NEP-9. First, let's clarify the concept New Economic Powers and discuss the nine countries of the NEP-9 and the reason for their inclusion in this new cluster.

What makes an emerging market a New Economic Power? For starters, NEPs are the largest emerging markets of today and, indeed, in the next two or three decades. They can influence not only their closest neighbors but also other regions and the rest of the world. Their influence stems

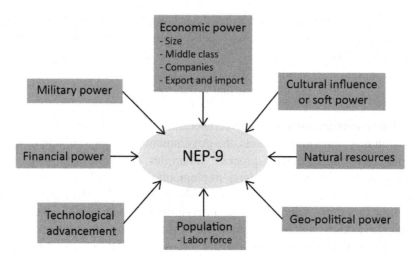

Figure 1.4:   Criteria that define a New Economic Power.

from, for example, their large population, a powerful military, the size of the economy, financial power, science, technology, and ideology, and this profoundly impacts other nations (see Figure 1.4).

Evidently, a high GDP or GDP per capita does not automatically make a country powerful. Luxembourg, Switzerland, Qatar, and Norway can boast some of the highest GDP per capita, but they are not driving the global economic engine; indeed, they are not even considered as a regional engine and they are not a force of influence in the globalization process.

For most New Economic Powers, globalization is a new phenomenon

Adding *New* emphasizes that these Economic Powers have joined the global community relatively recently. For example, the number of tourist arrivals in countries like India, Turkey, Brazil, and China has exploded in the last 20-odd years. Today, Turkey welcomes 53 million foreign tourists every year, compared to less than seven million in 1995 (World Bank, 2021). *New* also shows that they have only recently stepped onto the geo-political stage and into world economics. Finally, *New* tells us that human indicators in these countries have only recently started to improve, meaning that economic development and better healthcare and education are new phenomena for many of their citizens.

1.4.1 *Changing the global landscape*

Renaming these specific emerging markets *Economic Powers* acknowledges the economic, social, geopolitical, cultural, and technological impact of their development process on the region and worldwide. In this sense, we should see *economic* of this concept in a broader context. Economic power associates with other factors of power. For example, cultural power is related to economic success, and in most cases, economic power translates into (geo-)political and military power. This book argues (with some minor exceptions, such as the voting power discussion in the IMF) that power in itself is not a zero-sum game but a positive-sum game in which everyone wins. If India and Brazil take significant steps in fighting the climate crisis, the West also benefits. When we see economic progress and political stability in Turkey or South Africa, this is also good for the West.

In essence, the development of the NEP is creating a more multipolar world on four dimensions:

1. The balance of global economic power is shifting from the United States and the EU to non-western countries. The process of catching-up is ongoing, and Western economies may no longer be the largest, the fastest growing, the most competitive, the most dynamic, or the most dominant, neither economically nor militarily.
2. The monopoly of the West in technological advancement is disappearing. Technological progress originates more and more in the NEP and is spreading more easily to other countries due to better absorption capacity resulting from better education and integration through multinationals.
3. Attitudes and viewpoints of NEPs on multilateral institutions, building international alliances, and the role of the government in society tend to differ from western economies. These differences are reshaping the architecture of global governance.
4. The influence of the NEP on policy choices made by developing countries is increasing. Developing countries may follow the Chinese or Indian model instead of the US policy mix. Although the West may feel that the trade policies, domestic rules, and foreign policies of, for example, China, Russia, or Brazil are uncertain, unclear, and unfair, the attitude of many emerging markets is markedly different. They see credible and trustworthy international partners.

While the original BRIC cluster is often used interchangeably with the term "rising powers," our NEP-9 concept is broader. Figure 1.5 shows the nine New Economic Powers selected for this book, followed by the motivation for their selection.

A multipolar world

The NEP-9 includes regional powers, such as Indonesia, Mexico, Turkey, South Africa, and South Korea. This inclusion is in line with the EAGLEs' concept, which emphasizes the importance of second-tier NEPs. These second-tier NEPs are all growing toward economic heavyweights in the longer term. And although it is unlikely they will dominate the global landscape, their power can also be seen from a regional and sectoral perspective. For example, Brazil is a regional leader in Latin America. The country's influence, however, is not so much economic or military but exercised through its diplomatic power and intensive participation in multilateral and regional platforms. Turkey projects itself as a model for countries that from 2010 onwards went through the Arab Spring. Although its building-up of soft power stagnated in the last several years, Turkey's opening up and its continued efforts in balancing Islam and democracy still inspire certain Arab countries. The same holds for Indonesia as format for Asian countries. Finally, South Africa is seen as the leading voice of sub-Saharan Africa, and South Korea is a regional technological powerhouse. All these countries have a significant influence on regional affairs; they all

Figure 1.5:   NEP-9 on the world map.

are noteworthy players on the global stage, and they are all chipping away at the global dominance of the western countries (including Japan).

Regional and sectoral powerhouses

Economic power is perceived differently by different countries and peoples. Ask Australians and New Zealanders which country is the most powerful in the world, and they would probably say China. The same is heard in some Asian countries and maybe even Germany due to its trade emphasis on China. Ask the same question in Canada, Mexico, the Philippines, or South Korea, and you will get a very different answer. Citizens and policy-makers of these countries will say that the United States is the world's most powerful country. Yet another point of view: My students at SP Jain School of Global Management in Dubai always put Saudi Arabia in their top five of the most powerful nations. My Western MSc and MBA students in the Netherlands consistently say Germany and the United Kingdom are in the top five. European countries never feature in the answers my Uruguayan students in Montevideo give. They stress the importance of Brazil.

These wildly varying answers illustrate the subjectivity of economic or political power. Despite differences in perceptions, however, most respondents are thinking in absolutes, for example, the size of the economy, trade flows, foreign capital flows, and hard power through military expenditures.

1.4.2 *A short introduction to the NEP-9*

By many metrics, Brazil is a regional powerhouse. It is by far the largest economy in Latin America and has considerable resources to draw from. Its population is the 6th largest worldwide (2021). The country also has enormous natural resources and is one of the largest producers and export-ers of iron ore, sugar, soya beans, coffee, and meat. Brazil is also a front-runner in clean energy: Eighty percent of its electricity comes from hydropower. The PWC (2017) forecasts mentioned before predict that, in terms of GDP in purchasing power parity, Brazil will rank 5th in 2050. Brazil also has impressive diplomatic power. It is, together with India, the leading voice of developing nations in multilateral institutions and, due to its focus on multilateralism, able to act as a bridge in international negotiations.

The same holds for Turkey. The country proliferates itself as the bridge between Europe and Asia and between Christianity and Islam. Together with Indonesia, it is the world's most influential Muslim country and, in several aspects, an example to reformers after the Arab Spring that started in 2010. After discovering gas in the Black Sea, Turkey is on its way to becoming self-sufficient in its energy supply. In terms of demographics and economic size, Turkey is in the global top 20. According to Goldman Sachs, it could potentially move up to the top 10 by 2050, as Turkey's economic development after the mid-2000s has been particularly impressive. In international negotiations and geopolitical actions, Turkey may now be even more powerful in the Middle East than Germany, France, and the United Kingdom. The country has also increased its power in the Caucasus by actively intervening in the Nagorno-Karabakh conflict. Obviously, from time to time, Turkey does experience some economic and political crises. As was also the case in 2020 and 2021. Still, you should keep in mind that the book's focus is on longer-term development, and seen from that perspective, Turkey should be one of the NEP-9.

As the world's fourth most populous nation, Indonesia is now the world's 16th largest economy based on GDP in market exchange rates, and many predictions say it will become a top five country by 2050. Similar to Brazil, Turkey, and South Africa, its development process has been and will continue to be quite volatile, partly driven by cycles regarding commodities. But this volatility will not affect the longer-term rise toward global powerhouse status. Indonesia is relatively politically stable, and (local) democracy is quite resilient. From 2019 onwards, Indonesia has been part of the upper-middle-income countries, and almost 30% of its population falls into the (lower-)middle-class category. Note that in 1995, only 25 years ago, that percentage was around 3%. In 2050, it will have the third-largest middle-income population, trailing China and India. Indonesia also boasts a demographic bonus: Their 270 million citizens (2020) are relatively young.

Selecting the NEP-9: difficult choices

As a (relatively new) economic powerhouse, South Korea deserves its place amongst the NEP-9. It is the 10th largest economy in nominal GDP in 2020 (IMF, 2021). When I presented a paper on economic miracles in

Melbourne in the late 1990s, most Australians in the audience still thought of South Korea as a developing and agricultural country, including the high risks inherent to that status, a disrupting government interference, low wages, and cheap products. From a poor, rice-farming peasant economy in the 1950s, economic development in the 1970s accelerated. South Korea achieved the same welfare level per capita as Brazil already in the early 1980s. This upward trend continued, leading to the high-tech, developed nation it is today. Globally, South Korea is one of the most "wired nations," with almost all its households online. According to the Global Innovation Index, the country is in the top three of the most innovative nations worldwide between 2015 and 2021, driven by its hyper-competitive environment. Although a rich country in many aspects, it became more prominent as a regional powerhouse only recently. It is also more active in multilateral negotiations, driven by its increasing soft power through K-pop and Korean movies (e.g., Parasite in 2019). This Korean soft power also increased due to how the country dealt with the Coronavirus outbreak. Their handling of this health crisis was admired by their Asian neighbors and gained them appreciation on the global political stage. The unstable geopolitical situation in the region also makes South Korea a vital military force: Almost 3% of its GDP is spent on defense.

Needless to say, the NEP-9 also includes China. Whether the country will replace the US as the world's leading power soon or whether it will emerge as a superpower together with the US is not the issue. China is a superpower today and will continue to be in the decades to come. Its GDP in terms of purchasing power is expected to exceed that of the US by 40% in 2050 (IMF, 2020; PWC, 2017). China has the largest middle class by far, and in 2030, more than 25% of the global middle-class consumption will happen in China. China is the largest exporter and importer in the world. 35% of its export is statistically high-tech and we increasingly see Chinese brands appearing in the shopping streets of the West. Companies such as Alibaba, Baidu, and TenCent are shaping the digital transformation, with almost 70% smartphone penetration. China's soft power is growing, as several lesser developed countries look to China as a competitive economic and political model that could be an alternative to Western liberalism based on free-market economics. China is already a major military power and spends more on defense than India, South Korea, Russia, and Brazil combined. At the same time, China's military might is still much smaller than the US (World Bank, 2021).

Although Russia is not the Soviet Union 2.0, in many areas, it is indeed a superpower: A nuclear, energy, space, and military superpower.

Hard and soft power

Whenever the leaders of the US and Russia meet, it is reported on globally and without fail, framed as a meeting between two superpowers. Politically, Russia carries a lot of weight in the international arena. You may argue that it is boxing above its economic weight on the international scene. And even though it cannot rule like the USSR was able to do, Russia is directing much of what happens in several former Soviet countries. Furthermore, with the world's 11th largest GDP in market exchange rate (IMF, 2021), it's undoubtedly a significant economic power. It is forecasted (PWC, 2017) to be in the top 10 of the largest economies in 2050, driven by its natural resources. It is one of the largest suppliers of raw materials, including oil and gas, and the world leader in exporting wheat (2021). The country still has soft power in many parts of the world, driven mostly by its image as the main alternative to the US economic and political system. However, in the previous years, Russian geopolitical actions reduced its soft power substantially.

The status of India as a current and future global power is primarily motivated by its demographic dividend (a growing and young population) and its economic development after the turn of the century. India is considered a "demographic darling"; one-third of Indians are under 14, meaning the working-age population will grow during the next 20 years. India's economy has expanded dramatically in the previous two decades. In 1998, India was deeply poor, unable to reach even average global standards of human development. By 2050, India is projected to be the world's second-largest economy (overtaking the United States) and will account for 15% of the world's total GDP in purchasing power parity. Currently, the World Bank categorizes India as a lower-middle-income country. In addition to the size of its economy, India also has a space program and is one of the few nuclear powers. At the same time, India has several features of less developed nations. Income per capita is low, and there is enormous income inequality. Many economic and cultural barriers block the possibilities for and acceleration of social mobility. And it looks like COVID-19 is exceedingly hard on India and its poorest people. According to the IMF (2021), the Indian economy contracted by 9% in 2020. Culturally and politically, India is considered a powerful global influence and a positive example of liberal political, democratic, and economic development. Perhaps even more significantly, the cultural impact of Indian cuisine, literature, and movies on the world will get bigger. This soft power has been under pressure for a few years, however, due to increasing authoritarianism based on radical Hindu nationalism and regional social instability. In general, India's soft power remains strong, as the largest democracy in the world and the prevailing perception of India as a responsible international power and partner in multilateral institutions.

South Africa is not the largest economy on the African continent: after some statistical adjustments in previous years, the total economy of Nigeria is bigger (African Development Bank). However, I selected South Africa over Nigeria because the country holds a unique position not just in regional trade agreements but also in international platforms where it often represents Africa. Within the context of the African continent, South Africa is relatively stable politically and is considered the primary initiator of South–South cooperation in Africa. In the western perspective, South Africa is to the African continent as the US is to the rest of the world: the land of opportunity and a sort of ideological compass, driven by its remarkable transition to democracy in 1994. We saw political downturns, unrest, and pessimism in the previous decade, but the country still plays a leading role in promoting the revival of the African continent. But, crucially, this role is mainly bestowed upon the country by non-Africans. In the West, the country has considerable moral authority and diplomatic power in the same way Brazil has for Latin America. In terms of international trade, South Africa is the largest exporter of platinum in the world, with a share of 27%, and in 2020, it was the third largest exporter of iron ore.

Mexico is competing to become a top 10 country in terms of GDP based on purchasing power parity with countries such as France and the UK (2021). Projections say that Mexico will be the world's sixth largest economy by 2050. It is a manufacturing hub for global supply chains, which is quite a change from the 1980s. Within two decades, the nation transformed itself from a fuel exporter to a manufacturing export country. Today (2021), Mexico is the 10th largest exporting economy, mainly exporting to the United States. This economic picture is undoubtedly the opposite of the perception of Mexico held by many. A lot of Americans and other western people think of Mexico as a poor, agricultural, and underdeveloped country, dominated by drug cartels and impoverished people desperate to get into the United States. It is fascinating and saddening that my

Mexican students participating in international programs also have this negative image of their native country. They seem to have internalized the western perspective. Mexico has a large and young population, and like India and Indonesia, this will give them a demographic head start in the coming decades. There are clear barriers to capitalizing on this demographic dividend. Factors such as low-quality infrastructure and an enormous informal sector are big obstacles to overcome.

These are our nine New Economic Powers, the group of nations that forms the basis for the discussion of the changing global landscape in the following chapters.

1.5 NEP-9 Developments in Numbers: A First Look

The following chapters will dive into the growing importance (or the process of catching-up with developed countries) of the NEP-9 and the results of this progress. We will start with a first look at the changing economic landscape.

The catching-up process of developing countries began in Asia in the 1960s and 1970s, followed by others in the 1990s, and resulted from longer-term developments. This emphasis on the longer term is important to note. When considering long-term consequences, we use the average growth from year on year, despite knowing there were good and bad times. The same holds when we use forecasted growth rates. We focus on the average growth over a longer period, stepping away from short-term, cyclical patterns.

Exponential growth and the doubling time

By concentrating on longer-term developments, we can see that continuing differences in growth between countries dramatically impacts welfare. To measure long-term impact, we may use the commonly named *Rule of 70*. Essentially, divide 70 by the annual growth rate, and the answer will tell you how long it takes a value to double. Applying the *Rule of 70*, we can estimate how long it will take for a GDP or GDP per capita to double or the number of years it will take for a population to double. For example, at a GDP growth rate of 5%, it will take 14 years to double the economy (70 divided by 5). A population with a 2% annual growth would take 35 years to double (70/2). To illustrate the importance of the

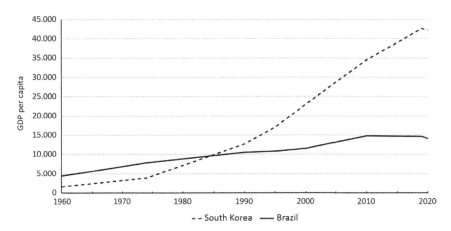

Figure 1.6: Economic development (GDP per capita in purchasing power parity in US$), Brazil and South Korea, 1960–2020.

Source: World Bank, World Development Indicators.

phenomenon of different long-term growth rates, we will look at the growth history of two of our NEP-9 countries: Brazil and South Korea.

Figure 1.6 shows the per capita GDP for Brazil and South Korea. The per capita GDP (or income) of these two countries snowballed during the 1960s and 1970s but then took sharply divergent paths. In 1960, Brazil's per capita GDP in purchasing power parity was $4,400, considerably higher than the $1,690 GDP per capita of South Korea. Both countries experienced rapid growth from 1960 to 1974, and by 1974, this resulted in much higher GDP per capita levels. By then, Brazil's GDP per capita was $7,880, while South Korean GDP per capita was $3,895. Both were able to double their per capita income within 11 (South Korea) and 15 (Brazil) years due to average annual growth of 6–7%.

Both countries were hit by the world recession and other external shocks in the 1970s and 1980s. While both countries were hit, South Korea recovered and even surpassed its prior growth rate, but Brazil stagnated. In 1990, Brazil's GDP per capita of $10,500 was now much lower than South Korea's ($12,700). By 2020, South Korea achieved the living standards of high-income Western Europe, with an income per capita of $43,100. By contrast, Brazil in 2020 had an income per capita of just $14,800 in purchasing power.

As you will see throughout this book, economic development does not automatically increase human development indicators, such as health, education, housing, and infant mortality. Still, you could say that economic growth is a precondition for the improvement of human indicators, as illustrated by the comparison of South Korea and Brazil.

Brazil versus South Korea: different development paths

The average number of years of schooling in South Korea is 12, versus seven in Brazil (UN, 2021). Brazil's infant mortality rate is nearly four times higher than South Korea's, 17.3 versus 4.5 per 1,000 live births (2020).

1.5.1 *Development between 1990 and 2020*

Figure 1.7 shows the development of GDP per capita in purchasing power parity of the NEP-9 between 1990 and 2020. It reveals several interesting

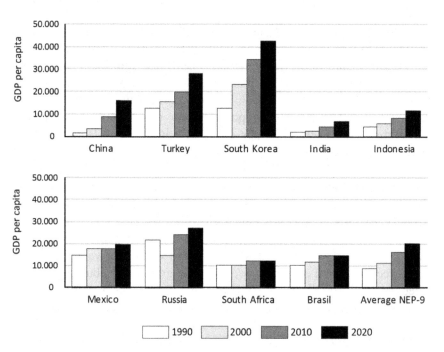

Figure 1.7:   GDP per capita in purchasing power parity, US$, 1990–2020.

Source: IMF (2021).

features. To begin with, although we cluster the NEP-9 countries, we can see significant differences in the various nations' development processes. China stands out with a staggering +1,000% growth of its GDP per capita in PPP between 1990 and 2020, a dramatic difference from South Africa and Brazil, which experienced much smaller increases in welfare in the same period. Despite their common characteristics, differences between the NEP-9 countries are consequential enough to merit discussion throughout the book.

Second, the economic development of the Asian countries is impressive, particularly when compared to both Latin American countries, which have witnessed only a moderate increase in GDP per capita. The third interesting feature is that the data clearly show the catching-up process. The average increase in GDP per capita of the NEP-9 between 1990 and 2020 is 132%. This percentage is considerably higher than welfare growth in western countries such as Italy (16%), Japan (30%), the UK (53%), and the US (55%) over the same period (IMF, 2021).

In all statistics, China stands out

A look at the development of the NEP-9's share in world exports reveals similar features (Figure 1.8). Again, China deserves mention, with its share rising from 1.2% (1990) to 10.8% (2020). India's, Mexico's, and Turkey's growing share in world exports are equally impressive. However, both Russia and South Africa have lost some of their share in global

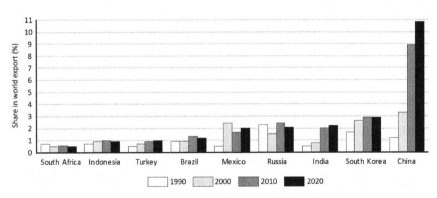

Figure 1.8:   NEP-9 percentage in world exports between 1990 and 2020.

Source: WTO (2021).

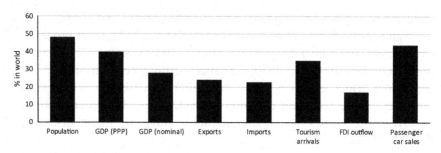

Figure 1.9:   Importance of NEP-9 today, 2020.

Source: UN, World Bank, IMF, UNCTAD, and WTO databases.

markets, as compared to 1990. The same holds for western countries, such as the US, the UK, Japan, and France. These all had a higher share in world exports in 1990 as compared to 2020.

These developments have resulted in the importance of the NEP-9 today. This book will discuss our changing world and the role of New Economic Powers in it. However, it is worth highlighting the distinct role played by China, given its size and impressive growth performance. In many aspects, the Chinese development process distorts the picture of the NEP-9 as presented, for example, in Figure 1.9. China's share in world export is 11%, representing almost half of the total share of the NEP-9 combined (WTO, 2021).

1.5.2 *Attention on China*

As you will see throughout the book, some statistics and discussions differentiate China from the other NEPs and pay this country special attention and justifiably so. China is the largest trading partner to over 130 countries, and the investment flow from China to other markets has accelerated exponentially in the previous decade. In 2019 and 2020, China was the largest investor in Bangladesh, Thailand, Malaysia, Ethiopia, the Middle East, and others (UNCTAD, 2021). Countries such as Australia, Thailand, and Brazil are deeply dependent on the Chinese economy for their growth, and the Chinese renminbi heavily influences the currencies of Vietnam and Turkey. What happens in China has a global impact. The rise of China, the competition it brings to the worldwide market, and the associated *China Price* (Harney, 2009) are felt in almost every corner of the globe. From the mid-2010s onwards, global financial markets have reacted strongly to choices made by the Chinese monetary authorities that could affect the value of the Chinese renminbi or the Chinese stock market. The Chinese–US trade war has affected numerous countries because, in one way or another, they are all connected to Chinese trade flows.

The global impact of China: "the China price"

In 2019, before COVID-19, China's share in the global demand for aluminum was almost 70%, and China's consumption as a percentage of world consumption of copper, nickel, and zinc was over 50% (World Bank, 2021). Undoubtedly, ongoing trends in China, such as accelerating urbanization, will impact (the volatility of) global prices. For example, in 2020, the price of zinc spiked by almost 50% between January and October, solely due to the Chinese economy expanding. China's domestic choices regarding sustainability issues will profoundly impact global warming. Sustainability is mentioned 35 times in the Chinese government's 13th five-year plan (2016–2020), and after the United States withdrew in 2017, China assumed a leading role in the Paris climate agreement. At the same time, China is the largest consumer of coal, and therefore, the biggest emitter of fossil fuel carbon dioxide (CO_2) emissions in 2020. China is responsible for almost 30% of the world's total CO_2 emissions (Rhodium Group, 2021), roughly twice the amount emitted by the United States. These figures relate to the whole economy; in China, emissions per person are still less than half of those of US citizens.

In 2021, we are acutely aware that choices made by Chinese policy-makers, their middle class, and companies will be felt worldwide. A marked change from just over a decade ago, when, in his State of the Union Address of January 2007 (White House Archives), President Bush referred to Iraq 35 times, Al Qaeda 25 times, and Iran five times, China popped up only once, in a non-economic context. Times have changed, and today, due to China's development after 2007, there are many reasons to single out China from other NEPs occasionally.

1.6 Is the World Truly Moving Toward the NEP-9? The Interpretation Issues

Interpretation is essential to writing this book. The same observations and data will have different people arriving at different conclusions. It depends on how information is merged and separated and the outcome depends on the focus, the expertise of the analyst, and the ethnocentric way of thinking.

For example, analyzing the Asian growth miracle has led to an unending debate (World Bank, 2016). Are these countries examples of successful state-directed industrialization, or do they prove opening up economies and market forces result in greater welfare levels? This framing requires a black or white answer: either one or the other. When adjusting the framing of the question, the Asian Miracle shows that a careful combination of market forces and government interference, rather than choosing a single strategy on principle, creates longer-term, inclusive welfare. Again, you could argue that, based on the Korean experience, both opening up and exporting, and aggressive trade intervention and government interference are required conditions for economic success. The most successful countries between 1990 and 2020 have intelligently combined the market and government.

Mostly, there is no black or white answer. For example, it is not the market OR the government but the market AND the government

---

We can follow this up by asking whether this Asian model can be a template for other developing or emerging markets. Is there an one size fits all strategy that works under all circumstances and for all countries? Unfortunately, the answer is negative. Advising developing countries to, for example, follow the Korean model is similar to advising an ambitious soccer player to follow the Lionel Messi model: imitate the best. Easy to say, easy to understand, but near impossible to execute.

The same interpretation issue holds for using statistics or the difficulty in separating short-term developments from longer-term changes. For example, India's 2020 negative economic growth caused by the COVID-19 pandemic must be separated from their 5% longer-term growth between 1990 and 2019. That is because, as we will see later in the book, longer-term and short-term growth drivers differ substantially. The 2008 financial crisis and the COVID-19 pandemic have negatively affected the NEP-9 in many ways. Think of the human and economic consequences in India, China, South Africa, and Brazil. The impact of COVID-19 on global oil and gas prices has negative implications for Russia. The fall in international trade hit countries like South Korea and

Indonesia hard. Unemployment in countries like Turkey and Mexico rose dramatically, resulting in a catastrophic reduction in income due to the absence of a mature social safety net. Despite all this, the global importance of these countries is still on the rise because of their relatively steep longer-term growth paths. As stated before, in longer-term forecasts and most scenarios, the impact of COVID-19 will result in an even faster catching-up process and a further acceleration of NEPs as essential engines driving the recovery of the world economy after 2020 (IMF, 2021).

1.6.1 *The analysis is relative in nature*

The aforementioned description focused on the rise of New Economic Powers and their growing role in world economics and politics. It is important to note that their development does not automatically mean that the US, Japan, and the EU are in irreversible economic decline. They are not. In the decades to come, these countries will remain the wealthiest countries in the world in terms of income per capita, highly ranked in competitiveness. Still, their economies may no longer be the largest, the fastest-growing, or the most dynamic, and they cannot dominate the world as they did before. Hence, be aware that we are talking about relative decline, not in absolute terms.

> *The western countries will remain the most prosperous, but they cannot dominate the world anymore*

Taking the COVID-19 crisis out of the equation, western countries are still forecasted to experience positive growth in the medium and longer term. The US is and will be leading in innovation and is home to the world's best universities. Demographic trends are also relatively favorable in the US compared to other advanced economies and some New Economic Powers. In addition, many European countries have the highest human welfare indices, relatively low-income inequality, and despite low growth, many EU countries still have the highest income per capita. In many ways, the balance of power in the international system looks broadly similar in 2020 as it did at the beginning of the millennium. The US is still the primary superpower in economic and military terms, and countries like France and the United Kingdom are ranked the highest in soft power. The OECD countries are overrepresented in multilateral institutions, such as the IMF and the World Bank, as they were 20 years ago. Countries such as the US, Japan, Sweden, and the Netherlands are still at the top of innovation indices, and the US dollar is still by far the most important international currency: today as well as in the medium- to longer-term future. A Chinese company selling smartphones to Brazil is likely to request payment in US dollars because it prefers to hold the reserve currency. Ironically, the financial crisis of 2008, and to a certain extent the COVID-19 pandemic, has reaffirmed and strengthened the role of the dollar and the US as a financial powerhouse (BIS, 2021).

I should emphasize that the global economy and the developments and forces shaping it are never straightforward. Clear-cut conclusions cannot always be drawn and will rarely point in one direction. A considerable part of the analysis in this book is interpreting numbers, developments, choices, and combining anecdotal evidence. Too great a focus on what is changing draws our attention away from what remains the same. But, we must not forget that what remains the same may be as important to the analysis as what is changing.

1.6.2 *Knowing the differences*

We must also be careful in defining essential concepts and choosing to use data and figures to substantiate our analyses. The first question I always ask my students at the start of my Immersion Program on globalization at SP Jain, Singapore, is "Which country is the largest foreign investor in Africa?" To ensure that all students focus on foreign direct investments (FDI), in advance, I define an FDI as a cross-border investment made by a company in one country aimed at obtaining a long-term interest in a foreign company in another country. I give my students four options: China, the United States, the United Kingdom, and France. Without fail, the vast majority of students select China, and indeed, if one looks at the inflow of FDI in a specific year, China was the largest investor between 2014 and 2017 (UNCTAD, 2020). But Chinese investments in Africa only started accelerating after the early 2000s (and began at a very low base point). Companies from the US, the UK, and France, however, have been investing in the African continent for many decades. Consequently, their ownership of assets had many years to build. And so, the total ownership of assets, or the commonly named stock of FDI, of China in the African continent is considerably less than the other three countries.

Interpretation of statistics is complex. For example, in China, consumption as a percentage of GDP is extremely low: below 40% in 2020.

There are no easy answers. Context is important

Compare this to 70% in Brazil and South Korea (IMF, 2021). At the same time, Chinese consumption growth is exceptionally dynamic, with growth figures of around 7% year-on-year between 2005 and 2019. The reason the Chinese consumption ratio is still low is that over the previous decades, GDP growth has also increased by 7%. Based on the consumption ratio, one would conclude that Chinese consumption is stagnant. A look at the bigger picture reveals that to be incorrect.

The same holds for commodity dependency as a characteristic of many emerging markets. Generally speaking, successful emerging economies can reduce their dependence on agriculture, energy, and raw materials and transform toward industrialization and manufacturing. The discussion of whether this transformation has been successful is in part based on the country's share of commodity exports in total exports. In Brazil, this share increased from 46% in 1998–2003 to 65% in 2014–2019 (WTO, 2021). This increase may cause some to argue that the transition toward manufacturing (and services) did not happen. However, the Brazilian manufacturing sector also increased substantially in absolute value. Manufacturing exports grew by 160% between 2003 and 2019, and agricultural commodity exports grew by an impressive 300%, driven mainly by strong increases in the price level of commodities. In this case, price spikes in commodities and agriculture blur the picture of Brazil's transformation process.

Although this book discusses the most recent data available, it builds analyses on longer-term trends without considering the volatility of business cycles, commodity prices, or trade flows. By doing this, we will try to avoid overemphasizing the most high-profile events that happened during the writing of this book. Instead, we will try to capture the bigger picture.

1.6.3 *Backward and forward looking*

Of course, there are challenges ahead, but most longer-term analyses predict that the NEP-9 will return to their longer-term norm of relatively high growth, increase in human indices, and regain the political and institutional stability needed for economic development. Indeed, we often can see that countries tend to move back to their structural and longer-term growth path, but we cannot take this for granted (Sharma, 2020). A pre-pandemic growth path does not guarantee that the same growth will continue post-pandemic. Experience tells us that correlation of growth between different decades is low, and consequently, forecasting is a dangerous business.

The discussion on Japanese growth in the 1970s and 1980s, among others, has taught us that straightforward extrapolation is a big mistake. Ezra Vogel published his book *Japan as Number One* in 1979. He predicted that if Japan continued to grow as it did between 1963 and 1973, it would have a larger GDP per head than the US in 1985 and a larger absolute GDP in 1998. The same has been said about the development of the Soviet economy, for example, in a 1957 article by economist Calvin B. Hoover, in which he declared that Soviet claims of astonishing economic achievements were fully justified. Their economy was achieving a rate of growth *twice as high as that attained by any important capitalistic country over any considerable number of years [and] three times as high as the average annual rate of increase in the United States.* He concluded that it was probable that a "collectivist, authoritarian state" was inherently better at achieving economic growth than free-market democracies and projected that the Soviet economy might outstrip the United States by the early 1970s. Despite these alarmist books and articles, reality proved different. In the next chapter, we will look at why this view of the Soviet economy was incorrect. However, the main conclusion is that a simple projection of past growth rates into the future was likely to overstate actual prospects greatly. Even though it contains hard numbers, the discussions on longer-term trends that follow should be interpreted as painting a plausible scenario, not as a point forecast.

Assuming that previous trends are continuing is dangerous

Finally, this book takes great effort to explain pivotal moments and important choices made in the past, so we will often switch from forward-looking to backward-looking. As Machiavelli put it in his *Discourses*, "Wise men say, and not without reason, that whoever wishes to foresee the future must consult the past." Perspective and context matter because they allow us to understand better the choices the NEP-9 make today. It also enables us to anticipate how these countries will help shape the globalized world.

Chapter 2

Understanding Why Countries Grow

2.1 Measuring Economic Development

In Chapter 1, we considered the relatively strong economic development of the New Economic Powers by looking at their gross domestic products (GDPs). After serious debates in the 1920s and 1930s, delegates of the 44 countries attending the 1944 Bretton Woods conference decided that GDP would be the best indicator for measuring the welfare level of a country. GDP represents the total value of all goods and services produced by an economy over a specific period, usually a quarter or a year. Therefore, GDP is regarded as a calculation of the total size of an economy. The value of domestic production also generates exactly the earned income in the form of wages, business profits, salaries for the self-employed, interest revenues, and other sources of income. Thus, whatever production occurs in an economy, some income is simultaneously (and automatically) generated in the process. Hence, the level of production equals the level of earned income. However, we should remember that this total of earned income is only partly allocated to labor in the form of wages.

Translating prosperity into a single indicator has its pros and cons

---

This equivalence of GDP and national income is why the media sometimes indicates economic growth achieved in a certain period as the growth of GDP and sometimes as the growth of national income. These indicators are mostly identical. GDP and its development enable us to judge whether the economy is contracting or expanding, whether it needs a boost or to deflate, whether the market is growing or shrinking, and whether an economy is seen as advanced, emerging, or less developed. The emphasis on GDP as an indicator of welfare is also driven by the idea that it influences other economic, social, and environmental indicators.

Reducing the measuring of welfare into a single indicator is in clear contradiction with the broader concept of economic development, which purposely involves many aspects. Of course, economic development includes not only material welfare but also purchasing power and human indicators, such as life expectancy, healthcare, and housing. Furthermore, it may involve environmental quality and even socio-psychological factors, such as feeling safe and happy and having political freedom. As we will see throughout this chapter, moving forward from the conference in 1944, economists and policymakers slowly introduced additional, non-economic indicators to capture the entirety of the economic development of countries.

2.1.1 *GDP versus GNP*

GDP measures the value of the goods and services produced in a country. It doesn't matter whether this production (or earned income) is done (or earned) by its citizens. For example, the Chinese GDP is the value of goods and services made in China by Chinese firms and foreign firms. Brazilian GDP is the value of goods and services produced within Brazil, no matter the owner. The earned income of an English soccer player in China is part of China's GDP. Chinese GDP is indicated on the left-hand side of Figure 2.1. It shows the health of the Chinese economy (although translated into a single indicator).

Gross national product (GNP) is another metric used to measure a country's economic output. Where GDP looks at the value of goods and services produced *within* a country's borders, GNP is the value of goods and services produced by *all* its citizens, both domestically and abroad. The Chinese GNP is the production and income earned by Chinese citizens, both domestically and abroad. It means the production of a

GDP   GNP

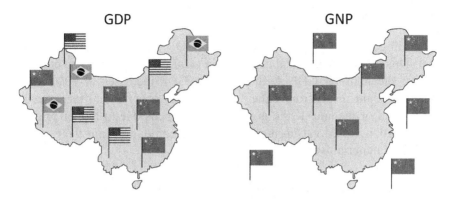

Figure 2.1:   The difference between Chinese GDP and GNP.

Chinese firm and the income received by its Chinese workers in Dubai are included in China's GNP (and, of course, in Dubai's GDP). This GNP approach is shown on the right-hand side of Figure 2.1. GNP can be seen as the yardstick of the health of Chinese and Chinese-based firms.

If many Chinese and Brazilian workers abroad send part of their income back home to their families, it means that, based on these transactions, Chinese and Brazilian GNP is higher than their GDP. As stated before, after 1944, most statistics refer to GDP (although the World Bank, for all kinds of reasons, uses GNP), and for the vast majority of countries, the two values are nearly identical. For example, in the last decade, the difference between GDP and GNP was around 0.2% in China and 0.9% in India (IMF, 2021). The same holds for Brazil, Russia, and South Africa, where, in line with China and India, the GDP is only slightly larger than the GNP. However, some countries show a large discrepancy between GDP and GNP. For example, several Middle Eastern players, such as Bahrain and the United Arab Emirates, have a much higher GDP than GNP, from 15% to 20% higher. Conversely, Pakistan and the Philippines show much higher GNP levels compared to GDP. The same holds for smaller, less developed countries. GDP is very low, but international aid may reduce the burden of poverty slightly. This aid is counted in the same way as remittances from income earned abroad: It contributes to GNP but not to GDP.

2.1.2 *Nominal versus real GDP*

According to the IMF, in 2019, Brazilian GDP was 7.3 trillion Brazilian real. This number is the total economy in local currency, based on current prices: the nominal GDP. If the nominal GDP increases in 2020, this increase could result from either higher prices or an actual increase in production or income. If the growth only happens due to higher prices, this inflation would eat up the increase in income, meaning there is no growth in material welfare.

We want to know real development

To ensure that GDP growth always reflects economic growth due to higher production and income and not as a result of higher prices, the number is always adjusted for inflation. This is called the real GDP growth. To study trends in economic growth, we use real GDP. The 1.4% growth (2019) and the 4% contraction (2020) in Brazil, the 3% decline of the Russian GDP in 2020, and the 6% growth in Mexico in 2021 all refer to development in real terms. Figure 2.2 shows the growth figures of the NEP-9 and several advanced economies in the past decade.

Economic growth	2013	2014	2015	2016	2017	2018	2019	2020	2021*
South Korea	3.2	3.2	2.8	3.0	3.2	2.9	2.0	-1.0	4.3
China	7.8	7.4	7.0	6.8	6.9	6.7	6.0	2.3	8.0
Russia	1.8	0.7	-2.0	0.2	1.8	2.8	2.0	-2.9	4.7
Turkey	8.5	4.9	6.1	3.3	7.5	2.9	0.9	1.7	9.0
Mexico	1.4	2.9	3.3	2.6	2.1	2.2	0.1	-8.2	6.2
Brazil	3.0	0.5	-3.6	-3.3	1.3	1.8	1.4	-4.1	5.2
Indonesia	5.6	5.0	4.9	5.0	5.1	5.2	5.0	-2.1	3.2
India	6.4	7.4	8.0	8.3	6.8	6.5	4.0	-7.9	9.5
South Africa	2.5	1.9	1.2	0.4	1.4	0.8	0.2	-7.0	5.0
United States	1.8	2.5	3.1	1.7	2.3	3.0	2.1	-3.5	6.0
United Kingdom	2.2	2.9	2.4	1.7	1.7	1.2	1.4	-9.8	6.8
Germany	0.4	2.2	1.5	2.2	2.6	1.3	0.6	-4.9	3.1
France	0.6	1.0	1.1	1.1	2.3	1.8	1.5	-8.1	6.3
Japan	2.0	0.4	1.2	0.5	2.2	0.3	0.3	0.4	2.4

(*) IMF preliminary data (November 2021)

Figure 2.2:   Economic growth: NEPs and selected countries.

Source: IMF (2021).

2.1.3 *GDP per capita*

Total GDP does not consider the size of the population. In 2020, the GDPs of Indonesia and Australia were roughly the same. Still, in Indonesia, the total GDP must be divided by 270 million people, while in Australia, production and earnings are divided by only 25 million people. Clearly, GDP per head of the population (GDP per capita) is a better measure of economic welfare than total GDP, as the latter measures the income of an entire country. In previous decades, per capita GDP has increased in most countries because the GDP growth rate was greater than the growth rate of the population. But this is a relatively new phenomenon, as we will see in the next chapter. The same critique for using total GDP to measure development applies to GDP per capita: it is a single indicator to measure the broad and complex concept of development.

2.1.4 *International comparison*

GDP is calculated and reported in the local currency. Brazil's GDP is reported in Brazilian real, India's GDP in rupees, Turkey's GDP in lira, etc. To compare the GDPs of different countries, they are converted into a common currency, typically the US dollar. There are two methods to convert GDP from the local to a common currency. The first is to use the market exchange rate at a specific moment: GDP at market exchange rates (or nominal GDP). For example, in 2019, the Brazilian GDP was 7.3 trillion real: 1.6 trillion US dollars at the 2019 exchange rate. However, this GDP at market exchange rate does not consider differences in living costs between the various countries. Obviously, a drink or meal in a restaurant is considerably cheaper in Brazil, India, or China than in the United States. The same holds for local services, such as the hairdresser, the coffee-to-go, and mending your trousers, which I'm sure you have experienced during your travels.

GDP in market exchange rates versus GDP in purchasing power parity exchange rates: substantial differences

After converting your dollars (or euros) to the local currency, you were able to purchase a lot more in these countries than you would have at home. The low cost of living increases the purchasing power of one dollar (or euro) in these countries. To account for the differences in living costs between countries, we use the purchasing

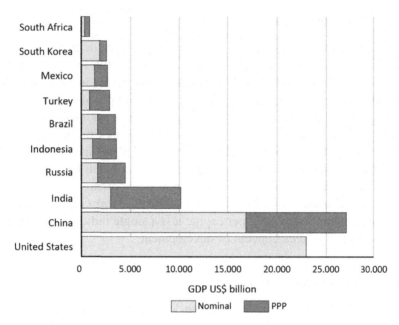

Figure 2.3:   GDP in market exchange rates (nominal) and in PPP, 2021.

Source: IMF (2021).

power parity (PPP) exchange rate for conversion. PPP is the second method of converting local GDP into GDP in dollars. The low prices of local services and locally produced and traded products in NEP-9 countries, such as China, South Africa, Brazil, and India, result in a significant difference between market exchange rate and purchasing power parity GDP, as you can see in Figure 2.3. The size of NEP economies substantially increases when we use PPP GDP.

In terms of market exchange rates GDP, in 2020, China was the world's second largest economy, followed by India in fifth place and Indonesia at 16th. However, by purchasing power parity, China is the largest economy, India the third, and Indonesia the eighth. This comparison is about the size of the economy, but it is clear that for GDP per capita, we also must separate the market exchange rate from the purchasing power parity exchange rate. I often start the International Economics course at Nyenrode Business University with the question: "What is the GDP per capita in China and Brazil?" Answers usually range from low, at around $3,000, to high, at around $11,000. When asked for the motivation behind these answers, students that gave relatively high estimates mentioned, for example, the explosion of the middle class and advanced urbanization, and those who provided low estimates reason that, for example, many citizens of these countries are still living in rural areas. These are all valid replies, but none consider the differences between the aforementioned concepts: GDP per capita in purchasing power parity and nominal GDP based on market exchange rate. As you can see in Figure 2.4, there is a substantial difference between the two. For example, in China, GDP per capita in purchasing power was $19,000 in 2021, while based on market exchange rate, it was "only" $11,800, still considerably higher than expected by my students.

GDP comparisons based on market exchange rates can be inaccurate because of the volatility of currencies. The steep decline of the value of the Turkish lira as compared to the US dollar in 2021 automatically lowered Turkey's GDP in US dollars, but only based on exchange rate fluctuations, not based on lower domestic production or less earned income. Despite this issue, the importance of countries and their impact on world markets through trade or investments is analyzed using the market exchange rate GDP. Exporting countries have to accept payment based on market exchange rates. Likewise, when countries import, they must pay in foreign currency based on market exchange rates. The same holds for international investment flow: again, we use the market exchange rate

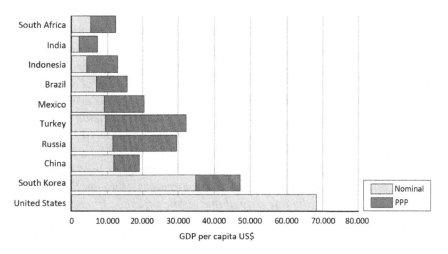

Figure 2.4:   GDP per capita in market exchange rates (nominal) versus PPP, 2021.

Source: IMF (2021).

GDP to determine how vital foreign investments are in the domestic economy.

To compare living standards between countries, we must use GDP in purchasing power parity

---

To compare the development and living standards, however, we must use the GDP at purchasing power parity: we need to eliminate price (level) effects to find out how much purchasing power the average Chinese, Brazilian, and Indian worker has, or to find out how serious the poverty problem in a country is. The size of the economy in purchasing power parity is also essential information for foreign companies producing and selling in countries such as China and India, particularly when they decide to invest their profit in the host country.

2.1.5 *Critical notes on using GDP*

As shown above, GDP facilitates comparisons between countries and provides information about material welfare in a country over time. Although GDP (or GNP for that matter) is widely used, it suffers from certain shortcomings. First, due to its one-dimensional approach, it does not tell us much about the broader health of an economy. This was the key message delivered by Robert F. Kennedy in a speech at the University of Kansas on March 18, 1968:

Our Gross National Product counts air pollution and cigarette advertising, and ambulances to clear our highways of carnage. It counts special locks for our doors and the jails for the people who break them. It counts the destruction of the redwood and the loss of our natural wonder in chaotic sprawl. It counts napalm and nuclear warheads and armored cars for the police to fight the riots in our cities and the television programs which glorify violence in order to sell toys to our children. Yet the Gross National Product does not allow for the health of our children, the quality of their education, or the joy of their play. It does not include the beauty of our poetry or the strength of our marriages, the intelligence of our public debate, or the integrity of our public officials. It measures neither our wit nor our courage, neither our wisdom nor our learning, neither our compassion nor our devotion to our country. It measures everything, in short, except that which makes life worthwhile. And it can tell us everything about America except why we are proud that we are Americans (JFK Library Archives). The quote drives home the point that economic development is a multidimensional concept, which not only includes the economy but also has social, environmental, and emotional dimensions.

Economic and human development is a multi-dimensional concept
---

The same holds for GDP per capita. For a stagnating GDP combined with reduced population due to catastrophe (think HIV in Africa, wars in the Middle East, or the COVID-19 crisis in Brazil), statistics will show rising GDP per capita. Obviously, this rise is not associated with economic development. A fast-growing economy does not automatically positively affect human development indicators, such as healthcare, literacy rate, and education enrollment. And economic progress can also go hand in hand with rising income inequality, environmental damage, and rural poverty. For example, if Russia's GDP goes up because Russian oligarchs, such as Vladimir Potanin and Leonid Mikhelson, are raking in cash, but everyone else's income stagnates, statistically, we will see GDP per capita growth. That does not mean the economy is doing well. Nor is an economy doing well when GDP goes up, but meanwhile, the environment is deteriorating, and resources are depleted. GDP figures should be used carefully and can misrepresent actual living conditions, as we saw with income inequality.

2.2 Inequality and Economic Development

The indicator primarily used for measuring inequality is the Lorenz curve and related to this the Gini coefficient. The Lorenz curve shows the percentage of income earned by a given percentage of the population, illustrated in Figure 2.5. The cumulative percentage of income is plotted (on the vertical axis) against the cumulative percentage of the population, shown on the horizontal axis. The 45-degree line in the diagram represents the perfect equal distribution in a society, meaning that if everyone had the same income, the Lorenz curve would follow the 45-degree line. But of course, this is never the case (and also would not be preferable, as we will see later in the book). Figure 2.5 shows 70% of the people earn 30% of the income. If the highest income group earned all the income, the Lorenz curve would be flat, following the bottom edge of the figure, and then jump to the top of the figure at the very right-hand edge. Greater inequality means that the Lorenz curve will be more "bowed" away from the 45-degree line (the gray curve).

2.2.1 *The Gini coefficient*

The Gini coefficient (named after the Italian statistician Corrado Gini) is an economic indicator measuring (household) income distribution. Once a Lorenz curve is known, calculating the Gini coefficient is straightforward. Look at Figure 2.5, in which we indicated areas A and B. The Gini coefficient is equal to A/(A+B). The more bowed the Lorenz curve is, the higher the Gini coefficient (reaching a maximum of 1), and the greater the income gap in society. Remember the perfect society in which the Lorenz curve follows the 45-degree line. In that society, the Gini index approaches 0, representing complete equality.

What are we measuring with the Gini coefficient?

Note that this coefficient measures what is indicated on the vertical axis of Figure 2.5. In this case, that is the income of the people, but it is

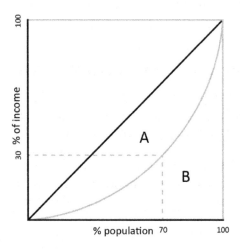

Figure 2.5:   The Lorenz curve.

Source: Ebbers (2019).

possible to use other indicators. For example, we may measure inequality of consumption expenditure or disposable income (after taxation). When plotting the income after tax on the vertical axis, the Lorenz curve may become less bowed, and consequently, the Gini coefficient will fall. We can also put asset ownership on the vertical axis. Inequality of asset ownership is harder to measure but appears to be more extreme in many countries (Piketty, 2014). Because of this and the fact that international statistics on income inequality are based on national statistics, outcomes may differ wildly. For example, in the Russian case, the 2019 Gini ranges from 0.37 (World Bank) to 0.44 (Knoema). Differences can even be bigger. In the case of India, I found Gini coefficients for 2019 ranging from 0.34 (national Statistical Bureau of India) to 0.82 (Credit Suisse bank). Figure 2.6 uses the Gini numbers from the World Bank. The general conclusion is clear: NEP-9 countries are not doing great in reducing income inequality over time.

Some reflections on the use of the Gini coefficient are needed. First, it is possible for the Gini coefficient to rise due to increased income inequality, while the number of poor people living in absolute poverty

Gini	1980	1990	2000	2005	2010	2015	2020*
South Korea	-	0.26	0.29	0.32	0.32	0.31	0.31
China	0.28	0.32	0.39	0.41	0.42	0.39	0.39
Russia	0.26	0.48	0.37	0.41	0.40	0.38	0.38
Turkey	0.49	0.42	0.41	0.43	0.39	0.43	0.42
Mexico	0.48	0.51	0.53	0.50	0.47	0.48	0.45
Brazil	0.58	0.61	0.59	0.56	0.53	0.52	0.53
Indonesia	0.35	0.31	0.29	0.33	0.36	0.40	0.38
India	0.32	0.33	0.34	0.34	0.36	0.36	0.36
South Africa	0.49	0.59	0.58	0.65	0.63	0.63	0.63
United States	0.36	0.38	0.40	0.41	0.40	0.41	0.41
United Kingdom	0.28	0.36	0.38	0.34	0.34	0.33	0.35
Germany	0.30	0.29	0.29	0.32	0.30	0.32	0.32
France	0.36	0.32	0.31	0.30	0.34	0.33	0.32
Japan	0.32	0.31	0.35	0.32	0.32	0.33	0.30

(*) 2020 or latest update (-) no data

Figure 2.6: Gini development of the NEP-9 and several other countries.

Source: World Bank (2021).

decreases. This is because the Gini coefficient measures relative, not absolute, wealth. For example, the Indian Gini coefficient increased from 0.34 in 2000 to 0.36 in 2019, while at the same time, the PPP GDP per capita increased from $2,095 (2000) to $6,995 (2019). The same holds for China. Income inequality increased substantially between 2000 and 2010, from 0.39 to 0.42, while at the same time, per capita GDP in purchasing power parity increased from $2,920 (2000) to $9,250 (2010). This statistic may help explain why many Chinese and Indian citizens do not feel strong discontent with increasing inequality: improved material welfare is seen as much more important than the general rise in inequality.

The NEP-9 are not doing great in reducing income inequality

Another reflection regarding the interpretation of the income distribution is that (social) benefits are not captured in statistics or are difficult to value. For example, subsidized housing, free medical care, and education for the poorest may reduce inequality without showing up in statistics.

2.2.2 *No automatic correction*

Research on the relationship between economic development and income inequality is yielding mixed results. The traditional economic argument says that inequality should promote growth, as it creates incentives for people to work harder and more efficiently. This is what we have seen happening in China since the beginning of its economic reform in 1978. High economic growth created a deeply unequal society in which the Gini increased from 0.28 in 1980 to 0.42 in 2010. Since the liberalization and opening up of the Indian economy, starting in the early 1990s, they have also experienced rising inequality within the context of strong economic growth. The same pattern is visible in each of our NEP-9 countries. They are aware that an equal society may not be optimal for long-term economic development. Countries like China and Russia have experienced destructive egalitarianism, a culture of leveling that rewarded seniority over merit and risk-taking. Still, they understand that inequality got out of hand. At the end of the day, growing inequality creates societal discontent and unrest, even when absolute welfare increases. When a country reaches a certain development level, leaving open how to define that, a further increase of inequality is no longer accepted, not by the poor cohort, not by the middle class, and not by policymakers. That is why in the past decade, the NEP-9 countries have implemented specific government policies aimed at reducing income inequality.

Specific government policies to fight income inequality are needed; the market does not give the solution

This increase in inequality in the early stages of development, followed by a drop due to policy measures implemented by the government in the later stages, is the essence of the Kuznets curve (Figure 2.7). When Kuznets wrote about the movement of inequality in rich countries in 1955, these countries saw a combination of rising welfare levels and substantially reduced inequality at the same time. According to Kuznets, factors such as broadening education, strong increase in wages due to the power of trade unions, and political pressure for greater social transfers (unemployment benefits and state pensions) drove the Gini coefficient down and explained the downward part of his Kuznets curve. So, after the Kuznets turning point, the top of the curve, discretionary government policy will fight inequality with fiscal measures and legislation. This turning point may vary from country to country. In the case of China, the Gini

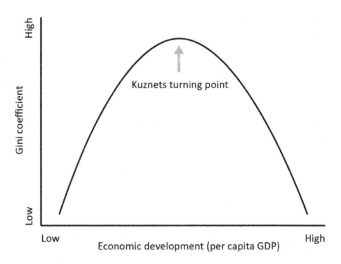

Figure 2.7:   Kuznets curve.

Source: Based on Kuznets (1955).

coefficient reached a peak at 0.42 (at a GDP per capita level of around $9,200 in purchasing power parity) before the government was willing and able to step in. In Mexico, the turning point was at 0.53 in 2000 and $11,900.

Inequality as a necessary price for economic growth sounds plausible. Still, when looking at countries today, there appears to be little relation between the level of economic development and the extent of inequality. Countries with wildly diverging levels of economic development like the United States and China have similar levels of inequality, partly because their governments are not fighting inequality until recently. Therefore, the Kuznets curve gradually fell out of favor because its prediction of low inequality in very rich societies cannot be observed today. Obviously, there are powerful forces that keep on pushing inequality up. Think about the rising share of capital income which is in all rich countries extremely concentrated among the rich (with a Gini in excess of 0.9), growing differences in the labor market and reduction of the power of trade unions, and favorable legislation for rich people.

The disconnect between inequality and economic growth carries within it an essential lesson regarding government policy: policymakers should not rely on any automatic tendency for inequality to drop as their economy develops. Government interference is required through building a social safety net and specific measures for the poorest cohort of society. This emphasis on the role of government is visible in our NEP-9 countries. We see that discretionary policies to fight income inequality are at the heart of the government policies of most of the NEP-9. Some examples are the inclusive growth policy of China, the tax and transfer system of South Africa (among the most progressive of the middle-income countries), Mexico's public social program *Prospera*, and the conditional cash transfer program Bolsa Família launched in 2003 under Brazilian President Lula.

Specific national programs to fight income inequality

Bolsa Família is a cash transfer program that aims to reduce Brazil's poverty and income inequality. To receive financial support, recipients must meet certain strict conditions. Children between six and 15 must go to school and achieve a minimum of 85% class attendance. Children under the age of six must be monitored medically and receive vaccinations before going to school. The program is considered very successful and has raised the welfare standards of millions living in extreme poverty. Within five years of the launch, almost 50 million of the poorest people benefited from the program. Partly due to Bolsa Família, between 2000 and 2015, Brazil's Gini coefficient dropped from 0.59 to 0.52 (before increasing slightly to 0.54 in 2020). However, the Brazilian government that took office in 2019 is actively making it much more challenging to apply for the program and plans to lower the cash transfer considerably to fight budgetary deficits. So the future of Bolsa Família is uncertain.

Knowing the drawbacks of using GDP and income per capita to measure economic development, we can still use them as a starting point to discuss economic development in emerging markets and the NEP. But clearly, a broader concept for measuring welfare is needed.

2.3 Other Indicators for Measuring Welfare

2.3.1 *Human Development Index*

The Human Development Index (HDI) is an effort to replace GDP as the indicator of economic development. Established in 1990, it supplements GDP (income) per capita in purchasing power parity with data on life expectancy and educational enrolment and combines the numbers into a simple index. The three indices are equally weighted because we assume that people value these three dimensions as equally important.

Figure 2.8 lists the countries with the highest HDI, supplemented with the NEP-9 countries. As you can see, the countries with the highest per capita income are also at the top of the HDI ranking. However, we can make some interesting observations. In the past years, the United States was ranked relatively low on the HDI compared to its GDP per capita. On the other hand, several NEP-9 countries, such as Brazil and Mexico, score relatively high on the HDI, even though their GDP per capita is relatively low. We also see that most NEP-9 are climbing up the HDI (e.g., Turkey and China), but measured over two decades, improvement is minimal. The same holds for the lowest HDI rankings: they were and still are found in Africa.

2000		2010		2020	
1	Norway	1	Switzerland	1	Norway
2	Australia	2	Norway	2	Ireland
3	Sweden	3	Australia	3	Switzerland
4	Switzerland	4	Germany	4	Hong Kong, China
5	Unted States	5	Denmark	5	Iceland
6	Netherlands	6	Netherlands	6	Germany
7	Germany	7	Finland	7	Sweden
8	Belgium	8	United States	8	Australia
9	Denmark	9	United Kingdom	9	Netherlands
10	New Zealand	10	Sweden	10	Denmark
27	South Korea	23	South Korea	23	South Korea
55	Russia	56	Russia	52	Russia
88	Turkey	75	Turkey	54	Turkey
63	Mexico	77	Mexico	74	Mexico
70	Brazil	87	Brazil	84	Brazil
111	China	96	China	85	China
108	Indonesia	111	Indonesia	107	Indonesia
99	South Africa	113	South Africa	114	South Africa
126	India	133	India	131	India
174	Countries	169	Countries	189	Countries

Figure 2.8:   HDI rankings for various countries.

Source: UN Development Programme, various years.

2.3.2 *Extending the Human Development Index*

Although the HDI is a broader concept than GDP or national income, it still lacks vital development metrics such as sustainability and income distribution. Furthermore, in the areas of education and healthcare, the HDI emphasizes *input*. In education, for example, input is measured by looking at enrolment numbers. However, this does not take into account the quality of education: *output*. The output approach is evident in the Human Capital Index (HCI), developed by the World Bank in 2018. This index measures educational quality by looking at harmonized test results. Another index that focuses on output is the Social Progress Index (SPI). This index is the result of the 2009 study on alternatives to GDP, an initiative of the Social Progress Imperative, a non-profit organization formed by a group of prominent scholars and business leaders, and inspired by the writings of Joseph Stiglitz, amongst others. The SPI includes more than 50 social and environmental factors, ranging from health, housing, sanitation, equality, inclusion, sustainability, safety, and personal freedom. Its comprehensive nature is exciting and helpful, but it also makes the SPI complex and unpractical for policy-making. The same holds for the Global Prosperity Index (GPI), developed by the Legatum Institute, a conservative British think-tank. It is a mix of more than 100 economic and social indicators, with a heavy focus on measuring the well-being of people through concepts such as personal freedom, reliance on family and friends, and national tolerance for immigrants and minorities. The SPI leans strongly toward measuring happiness.

The trade-off between comprehensiveness and practicality

As stated earlier, GDP cannot identify whether the level of income generated in a country is sustainable. It cannot distinguish between economic activities that increase a nation's wealth and ones that eat into its natural resources and incur (future) clean-up costs. It is clear that measuring the environmental damage of economic growth is complicated, but this metric is at the heart of the Green Gross Domestic Product or Green GDP. Green GDP calculates the financial loss of biodiversity and the impact of climate change resulting from economic growth. The idea is that, while the economy might look like it is growing now, the damages caused by that growth will, at the end of the day, reduce growth potential. China is one of the few countries that experimented with calculating Green GDP to measure its economic development in 2005 and 2006. However, the translation from GDP to green GDP was dramatic. For example, in 2006, the Chinese Green GDP showed that the financial loss caused by pollution in China was more than 3%. Cleaning up the effects of economic development lowered GDP growth from 10% to "only" 7%, which could be why the Chinese statistical bureau stopped official publication of the Chinese Green GDP in 2007 (Rauch & Ying Chi, 2010). Maybe it was too early for this type of radical innovation, but the search for a way to measure a Green GDP is underway in several NEP-9 countries.

In 2015, China revived the Green GDP concept. The "Green GDP 2.0" was implemented in the appendix of the 13th five-year plan. Some years ago, the Brazilian government declared its intention to incorporate the country's ecological heritage into GDP calculations.

The Green GDP concept

A meaningful first step, but the discussion about the methodology for calculating the Green GDP appeared to be difficult, and a Brazilian Green GDP is not yet published. In 2018, the Indian government started a five-year program to calculate Green GDP at the district level, and Indonesia tested a new model that shows policymakers how their decisions help or hinder the green transition: the Indonesia Green Economy Model. The first publications are interesting, but they did not yet arrive at a calculation of a Green GDP.

2.3.3 *Happiness index*

In 1972, Bhutan started prioritizing happiness over other factors such as income and assets: the Bhutanese Gross National Happiness Index. In a speech in New Delhi in 2009, the king of Bhutan explained Bhutan's view on the essence of happiness and economic development:

We strive for the benefits of economic growth and modernization while ensuring that in our drive to acquire greater status and wealth; we do not forget to nurture that which makes us happy to be Bhutanese. Is it our strong family structure? Our culture and traditions? Our pristine environment? Our respect for community and country? Our desire for peaceful coexistence with other nations? If so, then the duty of our government must be to ensure that these invaluable elements contributing to the happiness and well-being of our people are nurtured and protected. Our government must be human (Raonline.com).

From the start, there was intense discussion in the international community about whether money equals happiness. The results of national happiness polls showed mixed results. Rich people were generally happier than poor people in the same country, but citizens in more affluent countries were not always happier than those in poorer countries. And it appeared that beyond a certain income level, rises in income over time fail to increase happiness, a trend also observed in Western labor markets. For

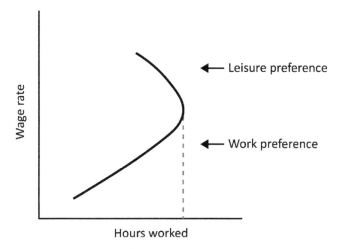

Figure 2.9: Supply of labor based on wage level.

example, a clear paradigm stated that increasing wages result in more people supplying labor, as indicated in Figure 2.9.

However, when they reach a certain level of income, most people are satisfied with their pay and prefer free time instead of more income, which explains the backward bending supply curve of labor. This is the behavior we expect from western workers in advanced countries that earn reasonable wages. In developing countries, emerging markets, and several of our NEP-9 countries, however, it is to be expected that most workers still prefer more money over free time. We can conclude that money brings (or adds to) happiness, but only up to a certain income level.

The United Nations released the first World Happiness Report in 2012. This annual publication ranks the national happiness of countries based on respondents rating their lives. The Happiness index ranges from 0 (not happy) to 10 (perfectly happy) and builds on 33 indicators, like community vitality, ecological diversity and resilience, good governance, health, psychological well-being, and education.

The World Happiness Report of 2020 indicates that the COVID-19 pandemic has led to more mental health issues. However, because this occurred worldwide, we see only modest changes in the overall rankings compared to pre-COVID year(s). As can be seen from Figure 2.10, money makes a person happy, with highly developed countries scoring high on

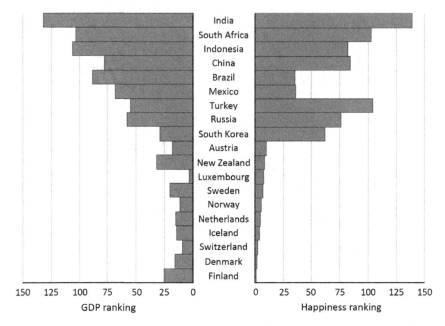

Figure 2.10:   GDP per capita and Happiness Index ranking, various countries, 2019.

Source: IMF (2020) and World Happiness Report (2020).

the Happiness index as well. At the same time, we observe that Brazil and Mexico score relatively high on happiness, while on the other hand, Turkey's and South Korea's happiness ranks are relatively low compared to their development level.

2.3.4 *Combining the UN's sustainable development goals and planetary boundaries*

Kate Raworth started her doughnut economics by attacking the central paradigm of modern economics: the view that a self-interested person's main objective is to achieve endless growth. The aim of economic activity, she argues, should be "meeting the needs of all within the means of the planet [...] Instead of economies that need to grow, whether or not they make us flourish, we need economies that make us flourish, whether or not they grow" (Raworth, 2017). Essentially, it is a continuation of the critique on using current indicators to measure welfare. GDP does not include the natural world, it ignores unpaid work, and inequality is secondary to economic growth. In that sense, Raworth's ideas are not new. However, rebranding this view into the doughnut metaphor attracted the media's attention and created momentum to discuss the much-needed adjustment to this one-sided economic paradigm.

The inner ring of the doughnut represents the minimum resources we need to lead a good life: income, work, food, clean water, housing, sanitation, energy, education, and healthcare (Figure 2.11). These resources come from the Sustainable Development Goals (SDGs), the internationally agreed minimum social standards, as identified by the United Nations (UN) in 2015. The SDGs recognize that ending poverty cannot be done without strategies that improve health and education, reduce inequality, and spur economic growth, all while tackling climate change and reducing pollution. The hole at the doughnut's center reveals the proportion of people worldwide falling short of these SDGs. The outer ring of the doughnut represents the earth's environmental limits, beyond which we will see dramatic climate change, water pollution, and loss of species. This ecological ceiling consists of essential planetary

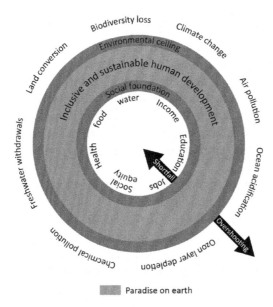

Figure 2.11:   The doughnut.

Source: Raworth (2017).

boundaries, as set out by Rockstrom and Steffen (2009). They estimated how much further humans can go before the habitability of our planet is threatened. Obviously, these calculations are complex and shrouded in significant uncertainties, as they are based on numerous assumptions and complex interactions.

Between the two rings is the bread, the tasty doughnut: a situation in which we can live a decent life where basic social standards are met and in a world that stays within the ecological limits: paradise on earth in Figure 2.12. When we look at countries through this lens, all countries (rich and poor) are developing countries because, as we will see, no country in the world is truly meeting the needs of all of its people. Less developed countries tend not to meet basic social standards, while what we refer to as developed nations fail to live within their ecological limits.

The doughnut sweet spot: paradise on earth

The doughnut metaphor is helpful in many ways. For example, it can be translated into a toolbox to explore the priorities in governmental policies or the investment portfolio of large companies and banks, emphasizing zero-carbon public transport and green investments. Again, this doughnut concept is not a new insight but a transparent framing of the dilemmas every country is facing. However, some elements of economic doughnut thinking can be considered fundamentally new, for example, the way we discuss income inequality. Reducing inequality is done primarily through progressive taxes and subsidies to redistribute income afterward. But you could also start at the cause of income inequality and redesign economic activities so that they share the value at the front end instead of redistributing it afterward. In this case, discussions on how to achieve this are already emerging.

Reframing the discussion on economic development to new ways of thinking was accelerated during the COVID-19 pandemic. Think back to the debates about protecting patents versus sharing knowledge as soon as possible and sharing the technicalities of the development and production process of the COVID-19 vaccine. These discussions are difficult. Emerging markets and most NEP-9 countries say that the protection of patents went too far and blocks the dissemination of innovation and knowledge. In contrast, the governments of the advanced nations (backed by companies) argue that this protection is needed because it is the primary reason for investments in new and necessary products and the

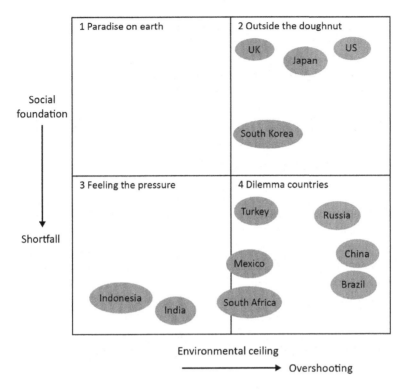

Figure 2.12:   The social-ecological matrix.

Source: Based on research done by Leeds University, good life website.

development of knowledge. The same discussions are happening concerning private ownership and the power of shareholders. This debate is intense in the NEP-9 countries and goes hand in hand with finding the optimum balance between government and market.

Based on Raworth's work and the research done at the University of Leeds, I have translated the doughnut into a matrix based on the two dimensions (Figure 2.12). The vertical axis represents the inner circle, the social dimensions, and the outer ring and the earth's biophysical boundaries are on the horizontal axis. This layout gives us four types of countries (quadrants 1–4) and allows us to place our NEP-9 countries onto this matrix.

1. *Paradise on earth.* The countries in the top left corner of the matrix provide their citizens a decent life where the main social thresholds

are met, without overshooting any biophysical boundaries. This is humanity's sweet spot. This quadrant is empty because no country in the world has managed to achieve this.

2. *Outside the doughnut.* South Korea is the only NEP-9 country in this corner of the matrix. It meets the basic needs of all its citizens (although interrupted by the COVID-19 crisis) while overshooting the planetary boundaries. It has to answer the same question as other high-income nations: how to maintain reasonable living standards while moving back within Earth's biophysical limits.

3. *Feeling the pressure.* Countries like Indonesia and India are hardly overshooting any biophysical boundaries, but they are massively falling short on meeting almost all of the essential needs of their people. Their choices regarding their future trajectory will have a tremendous impact on the world. You can imagine what will happen if they follow the same development path of countries like China and Brazil or copy the industrial course of the current high-income countries such as the US.

4. *Dilemma countries.* Countries such China, Turkey, South Africa, Mexico, and Brazil are falling short on some social dimensions while already overshooting multiple planetary boundaries. These countries are currently making future-defining investments in urbanization, energy systems, and transport networks. The main question is whether these investments will bring them (back) into the doughnut by shifting to the left in Figure 2.12 or whether pressure from society will result in following the advanced nations and moving to the northeast corner of the matrix.

Keeping in mind the various ways we can measure economic development, in the second part of this chapter, we will focus on how countries can generate economic growth to move from poor to middle income.

2.4 Making the Transition

In the 1980s, back when I studied development economics, the views on economic development were based on two pillars. The first: development was a linear path along which all countries travel. The advanced countries had, at various times, gone through the take-off stage, and that is where the developing countries are now. This idea resulted in theories that divide economic development into specific stages or phases. An example is Rostow's theory (1960) which considered developing countries a homogeneous group with similar problems. The second pillar: development was primarily a matter of economic growth, and a fixed set of drivers determined this growth, which is the core of the Harrod–Domar growth model, developed in the 1940s and 1950s.

2.4.1 *Stages of economic growth*

Rostow wrote his classic Stages of Economic Growth in 1960, and in it, he presented five steps through which all countries must pass to become a developed country:

* Traditional society
* Preconditions to take-off
* Take-off
* Drive to maturity
* Age of high mass consumption.

Rostow developed his framework in the context of the assumption that all countries admire the western model. We can illustrate Rostow's five stages with the metaphor of a plane flight. The first phase is the plane leaving the departure gate and taxiing toward the take-off runway. The second phase is gaining speed (the precondition for take-off), followed by the third phase: actual take-off. This phase is the most challenging part of the flight because the pilot must execute every action in a specific sequence and in a relatively short time frame. When the plane is in the air, flying is relatively easy, and only minor adjustments are needed to handle this part of the flight (phase 4: the drive toward maturity). In the final part of the flight, more actions are required in the cockpit to ensure that the plane arrives at its destination (phase 5: age of high mass consumption). In this chapter, we will focus on the take-off stage: how to achieve the status of a middle-income country. In Chapter 3, we will explore what is needed to escape the middle-income trap and achieve the economic development required to become a high-income nation.

The importance of the take-off stage

The traditional society is agricultural, has mainly subsistence farming, and has no international trade. Investments are limited, and there are hardly any productivity gains. In the preconditions to take-off phase, we will see some technological advances in agriculture, based on using more capital in the production process. There is some growth in investments (and the required savings to finance them), although this starts at a very low base level. We will see the beginnings of international trade and the first influx of foreign investment. As stated earlier, the take-off stage relates to the pivotal transition in a country's development process. In this stage, essential structural transformations are happening in the economy, combined with government-initiated reforms. Industrialization develops, and the manufacturing industry becomes dominant, although most people may remain employed in the farming sector. A few "leading sectors" drive industrialization and this stimulates the overall expansion of modern industry. During this stage, the rate of investment increases in such a way that real output per capita rises, complemented by radical changes in production techniques. We will see a substantial increase in investment, above 10% of GDP, and the government focuses on stimulating industrialization. Although agriculture is becoming less important, technological advancements in the agricultural sector are essential to free up people from the farmland so they can move to urban centers and find employment in manufacturing. This phase sees some easy productivity gains, but the required social change toward a more outward-oriented, entrepreneurial, and innovative society is quite difficult to achieve.

2.4.2 *Take-off and the role of the government*

A key learning point for countries going through this take-off stage is that government must intervene in many aspects of society and the economy because market forces do not automatically bring about these shifts. Structural reforms (political, social, and institutional) are needed, and consequently, a strong government is essential. Gunnar Myrdal came to the same conclusion in his soft state concept (1969): the state must have the will or the political muscle to bring about structural changes in the economy and society; otherwise, sustained economic development will not occur. Another lesson we can learn from the take-off experiences of many countries is that a move away from agriculture toward industrialization and diversification of the economic structure is needed but difficult if a country is commodity-dependent. (Chapter 4 shows that excessive dependence on commodities should not be seen as a pillar of economic development.) Rostow believed that the take-off phase is relatively short, around 20 years.

There is no consensus on the precise indicators for delineating a clear take-off period for specific countries. Mainstream research focuses on average economic growth (GDP per capita) of more than 3% over 10 years. Other research focuses on particular indicators, such as the development of the investment ratio and changes in economic structure. The third way of finding out the exact take-off stage relates to sustained economic growth that is considerably higher than the US growth over 10 years. This is the commonly named relative approach. Despite these differences in approach, it is evident that the take-off phase for the NEP-9 started with Mexico and Brazil in the 1950s, South Korea in the mid-1960s, followed by Russia, Turkey, China, Indonesia, and India in the 1980s.

Essential structural transformations are needed

South Africa is a special case that shows how complex defining the take-off stage is. You could argue that the 1930s was the starting point of take-off, as that is when the country started to focus on industrialization and diversification of the economy. However, you could also argue for the early 1970s as the mineral booms of the day created a foundation for industrialization and drove structural reforms in the economy. A case can also be made for the mid-1990s after South Africa opened up to the outside world, welcomed foreign investments, and had a relatively stable political and social climate.

Figure 2.13 combines several concepts of this chapter into one framework. It shows the five phases of economic development. The economic development in the first phases is driven by putting more labor and capital into the production process. This is what we see in low-income countries. They are able to achieve economic development by combining more labor with more capital: a relatively easy way to increase GDP. To achieve a take-off and reach middle-income status, however, more is needed. Productivity growth becomes essential. During *take-off* and the *Drive to Maturity* stages, this productivity growth is relatively easy by mobilizing resources differently in the country. But at the end of the day, productivity growth is only possible through more efficient use of labor and capital: the commonly named efficiency phase, indicated in the figure and discussed later in the chapter. When the transition toward the high-income status fails and the country stays at the

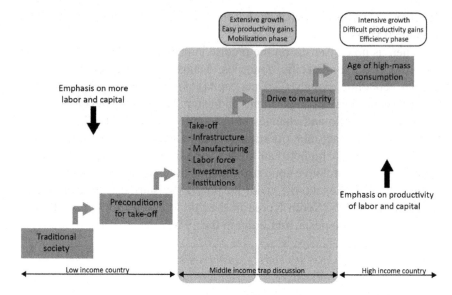

Figure 2.13:   Stages of economic development.

middle-income level for a considerable period, we may refer to the commonly named middle-income trap, the main topic of Chapter 3.

The Drive to Maturity phase can take a long time. As we will see in the next chapter, many emerging markets achieved middle-income status in the 1950s and 1960s and are still in this income cohort. Standards of living and most of the human development indicators are rising only gradually. We see a more diversified industrial base and more emphasis on efficiency and productivity. In the early part of this phase, productivity growth is relatively high as the country is still at the beginning of its development. The *advantage of being backward* (Gerschenkron, 1952) makes productivity growth relatively easy. There is accessibility of import technology from more advanced economies, combined with high absorption capacity in the country due to rising educational levels and market structures that stimulate competition, resulting in the growth of productivity. Finally, in the Age of High Mass Consumption, GDP per capita increases toward high-income status, and we see greater purchasing power, particularly in the growing middle class. The economic structure transforms from industry to services and from low-tech to high-tech production, driven by technological advancements. International trade is growing, and we see inflow and outflow of foreign direct investments.

Although helpful for understanding economic development, some critical notes about Rostow's model must be said. First, it assumes that all countries desire to develop in the same way, with the end goal of high mass consumption.

There is no single universal path to grow

The bias toward a western model as the only path toward development does not consider specific national priorities and choices. Second, we do not necessarily always see every stage of development occur. Countries do not always develop linearly; there is no single universal path to growth, not a one-size-fits-all. Rostow disregards social-cultural and political aspects. You could argue that sometimes, cultural heritage or political red line inhibits reforms necessary for development. Third, if one compares the growth rate across countries for subsequent decades, there is very little correlation. Countries that grew fast for one decade do not tend to grow faster during the next decade.

2.4.3 *Drivers behind long-term economic development*

Rostow's analysis does make clear some critical drivers behind economic development. Think about the role of infrastructure, productivity gains in the agricultural sector that free up workers and enable them to move to the growing manufacturing sector, the increase in investments in leading sectors, implementing market forces, international trade, and a stable institutional system that stimulates the entrepreneurial spirit. Be aware that the analyses until now are about the longer-term development of nations. Short-term fluctuations of the economy are important when they happen but less so in the longer span of history. In the longer term, we may ask ourselves why China was growing over the previous 25 years, how much richer the average Indian worker is today compared to 15 years ago, and why we saw high average economic growth in Turkey during the past 10 years.

The longer-term perspective: a supply-side approach

Rostow was clearly influenced by another model, developed in the 1940s and 1950s. The Harrod–Domar growth model (Harrod, 1939; Domar, 1946) illustrated that economic development was determined primarily by a fixed set of drivers common to all countries, despite differences in culture, history, and politics. From the supply side point of view, the determinants of GDP (growth) per capita in the longer term come from three sources:

1. The size and growth of the working-age population, and consequently, the size and growth of the labor force.
2. The size and growth of the (physical) capital stock, referred to as capital accumulation.
3. The increase in the productivity of physical capital (better machines), human capital (skills of workers), and more efficient institutions. The effect of this technological progress is increased output from a given amount of resources. I should stress that this technological advancement can happen in agriculture, manufacturing, and services. Still, manufacturing has the most significant impact on transition because it is the source of jobs, innovation, and increase in productivity.

2.4.4 *Extensive growth*

Extensive growth (Figure 2.13) is based on quantitative increases in labor and capital (and other factors of production, such as land and natural resources), the first two determinants mentioned above. It is input-driven growth. For example, modern-day workers use excavators to install fiber optic cables in your street. They are much faster compared to their colleagues of 50 years ago that did the same work using shovels. Excavators have increased productivity, but labor is not more efficient; it simply has more capital to work with. The same holds for using more labor in the production process. If a country can increase the participation of women in the labor market, we will see an increase in total GDP and GDP per capita. That helps explain why countries like Italy and Japan, whose populations (and labor forces) are shrinking, have a more challenging time growing their economy than India or Indonesia, where the population is still growing. To a large extent, this demographic dividend is extremely helpful in achieving growth. However, this demographic dividend is only the case when the population is young enough and able to work. Young people (and a large labor force) have been a major source of growth for India. Economic development of the previous decades occurred in part because its demographic transition resulted in its working-age population growing at a much faster rate than its dependent population.

In the 1960s and 1970s, the former Soviet Union achieved growth figures higher than the United States over many years and showed impressive industrialization and increases in income per capita. However, this growth happened solely because of large injections of labor, capital, and natural resources. The Soviets were able to mobilize resources, not use them efficiently. This situation has surprising similarities with the Asian miracle of the 1970s and 1980s, including South Korea. The newly industrializing countries of Asia, like the Soviet Union of the 1960s, achieved rapid growth by massive additional inputs like labor and physical capital rather than by efficiency gains.

Similarly, the Mexican and Brazilian economy after 1981 (the start of the debt crisis) was only able to grow thanks to the expanding labor force and government investments in infrastructure. The economic development of South Africa during the last two decades of apartheid was also driven by more labor and by government investments in infrastructure. Technological progress and increase in productivity were almost absent, but still, reasonable growth figures were possible. The Chinese strategy to increase GDP during 1993–2007 was also mainly based on a growing labor force, combined with capital accumulation of more machines per worker (Ebbers, 2019). The same holds for India. From the 1990s onwards, the country complemented the increase in labor with a growing investment rate. Capital accumulation through government investments mostly drove economic growth between the 1990s and the financial crisis of 2008 in countries like Turkey and Indonesia.

Achieving growth through perspiration rather than inspiration

---

Clearly, all the NEP-9 countries achieved growth based on perspiration rather than inspiration. It is possible to achieve relatively high economic growth (per capita) over a considerable period by putting more labor and capital into the production process. However, there is a ceiling to this input-driven growth because endlessly combining more labor with more capital is not possible. In the end, the added value of (extra) investments drops (the commonly named diminishing returns): simply throwing more capital in the system yields fewer benefits. The roads and machines are there, and new investments hardly create more production. And also, there is a limit to the amount of labor available. As we all know, there is a tendency of working fewer hours, and in many countries, the participation level is already relatively high. Hence, the need to move to a more intensive growth strategy based on productivity growth, the third pillar of the Harrod–Domar model. Of course, we will see some productivity growth during this extensive growth phase, but that is the easy by-product of more labor and capital, not because of technological advancement.

2.4.5 *Intensive growth*

Intensive growth is derived from gains in productivity: the increased efficiency of labor and capital, generally identified with technological progress (Figure 2.13). In this case, the workers taking care of the cables may produce faster and better because they are better managed or have more technical knowledge. It may also result from more market competition, making certain companies in this sector more innovative than others. Both extensive and intensive factors usually support economic growth. For example, intensive growth based on more effective methods of production (new processes, labor-saving devices, better factory layout, and improved quality of products) is usually only possible with additional investments.

Moving from the mobilization phase toward the efficiency phase

---

The easy way to increase productivity, namely, by using more labor and capital in the production process, is essential for going through Rostow's take-off stage and achieving the Drive to Maturity phase, which is associated with the middle-income status as defined by the World Bank. This input-driven extensive growth based on mobilizing resources is called the mobilization phase, as indicated on the left-hand side of Figure 2.14. An example of this is China, where the shift of workers from the agricultural sector (low productivity) to the manufacturing industry (much higher average productivity level) explains post-mid-1990s increased productivity (and economic growth). Another source of productivity gain was the shift of labor from former and outdated state-owned enterprises to the more productive private sectors. In part, this shift was the result of the privatization process that started in the 1990s. The result was a high productivity growth in the manufacturing sector with 14% per year between 1998 and 2007 (NBS).

The same is happening in Russia today, where productivity is growing mainly due to the mobilization of resources. Most of the Mexican

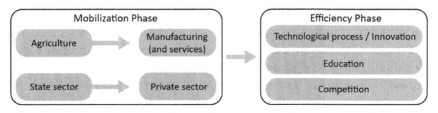

Figure 2.14: Sources of productivity growth.

Source: Ebbers (2019).

productivity growth between 1981 and 2020 can also be attributed to the expanding labor force. The same holds for the productivity growth of Indonesia and Brazil. An important learning point from these cases is that productivity growth during the mobilization phase has its limits. For example, after 2008, productivity growth in Russia decelerated substantially and even declined from 2015 until 2020. Another learning point from experiences in NEP-9 is that, although a country may increase productivity relatively easily by allocating labor from a low productivity sector (agricultural) to a more productive job in manufacturing, this reallocation of work does not happen automatically. People may continue to work in the traditional, often informal sector instead of moving to the more productive manufacturing sector. The South Korean, Indian, Mexican, and South African cases make clear that this reallocation must be guided by structural reforms and government intervention, including establishing productivity gains in the traditional sectors as well.

2.4.6 *Different growth strategy is needed*

To conclude, all NEP-9 must reconsider their growth strategies, as economic development based on more input in the production process reaches its limit. A sense of urgency was built in the last decade, but, as we will see in Chapter 3, fundamentally changing growth strategies appears to be difficult. Although productivity was emphasized, reforms were aimed primarily at the mobilization phase, the period of easy productivity growth, seeking to extend it. This easy productivity growth may continue for many years to come as countries such as India, Indonesia, and China still have the *advantage* of being behind in their development process. The idea is that their industrialization processes can continue with the help of productive machines and new techniques that are easy to import and implement. Of course, workers need some educational basis to operate these machines and apply these new techniques. Still, primary and secondary enrolments in these countries are good enough to absorb the new technology. The situation in countries such as South Africa and Brazil is slightly different because their productivity level is higher, and therefore, the potential for productivity growth is less.

Relationship between productivity level and productivity growth

---

Figure 2.15 summarizes the relationship between productivity level and productivity growth. The lower the productivity level (compared to the most productive countries), the higher the average increase in productivity: the advantage of being backward. China, India, and Indonesia achieved high annual productivity growth over a longer period because of the considerable distance between the most innovative and productive countries. We have also seen this in the Asian Tiger economies. For example, in 1980, South Korea's productivity level was less than 25% of the productivity level of the US (ADBI, 2017). The Asian Tigers witnessed strong productivity growth when they started their reforms and

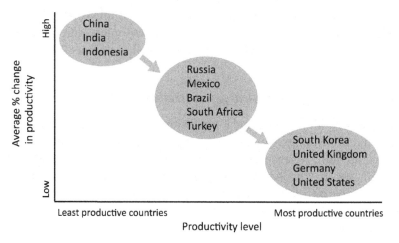

Figure 2.15:   Productivity level versus annual average productivity growth.

Source: Based on OECD database.

early catching-up. But as soon as they approached 60–70% of the productivity level of the most productive countries, annual growth of productivity declined (OECD, 2012). For example, annual productivity growth in South Korea was three times higher in the 1990s compared to the 2009–2019 period. The same can be expected in China. That is partly why longer-term forecasts (up to 2040 or 2050) are so much lower than the 7% annual growth we see today. For the medium-term future, however, productivity growth can still play an important role. Even after 40 years of reforms, the Chinese productivity level of the whole economy compared to the US is still low (around 30%), and we expect relatively easy productivity gains (mainly in the mobilization phase) in the years to come. But at the end of the day, to move into Rostow's fifth phase, the High Mass Consumption phase, and develop into a high income nation according to the benchmark set by the World Bank, they must switch to the efficiency phase including technological advancement and innovation. This final step, leaving the middle-income status, appears to be very difficult, as we will see in the next chapter.

2.4.7 *Finding the optimum balance*

As said, to guide countries through the take-off stage and in achieving middle-income status, the role of the government is essential. Consequently, governments have a clear presence in all our NEP-9 through its interference in the market: subsidizing strategic sectors, protecting local companies, and setting benchmarks for prices and wages. But it should be clear that this interference does not mean that they do not believe in the market. There is a consensus view among the NEP-9 that market forces are essential. Examples in China and India show how important the market is.

NEP-9: the visible hand of government intervention is needed to balance the failures of the invisible hand (market)

The shift in China from a planned to a market economy under Deng Xiaoping and the efforts to dismantle the "License Raj," the intense bureaucracy in India, resulted in an unprecedented boost in welfare. This embracing of the market lined up with the market-driven sentiments of the period that followed the fall of the Berlin Wall in 1989. However, the NEP-9 countries do not see the market and government intervention as being in opposition. They emphasize that combining the two is essential. The visible hand of government interference is needed to balance the failures of the market (invisible hand) if they want to generate sustainable longer-term development. Finding the optimal balance is the new search for the NEP-9. As we will see later in this book, this emphasis on a strong government put the NEP-9 countries into tension with the market, individualist, and liberal view of western economies and the global governance architecture.

2.5 Separating Short- and Longer-Term Growth Drivers

In our discussion of economic growth, we need to make a distinction between short- and long-term developments. Until now, we focused on the longer-term (average) economic growth of the NEP-9 in the previous decades. And in our glimpses of the future, we looked at how much richer the average Indian, Chinese, or Mexican worker will be in 2030 or 2050, compared to today. The answer to this type of question is found on the economy's supply side, which is why we discussed the role of labor, investments, and productivity. The longer-term average growth is conceptually shown on the left-hand side of Figure 2.16. We see that over a longer period, the slope of the line showing the growth in GDP can be steep or flat, driven by the supply determinants in the Harrod–Domar growth model, such as demographics, capital stock, infrastructure, institutions, and technology. In the case of China, the figure indicates an average annual growth of 5% over a longer term while the Netherlands witness a relatively flat development.

2.5.1 *Business cycle*

Governments, households, and companies are also (or mainly) concerned with the short-term ups and downs of the economy. What is the economic growth this quarter compared to a year ago? What is the economic growth next year? To answer such questions, we must focus on the demand side of the economy. Spending is what drives year-on-year economic growth. Expenditures in the economy result in a business cycle with high or low growth of GDP. When we put China's average of 5% growth per year on the vertical axis on the right-hand side of Figure 2.16, periods of booms and recessions appear. Sometimes, growth in one year is substantially higher than the average of 5%. In contrast, in periods of economic crises,

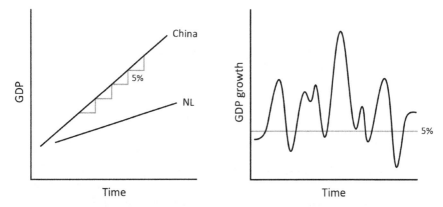

Figure 2.16:   GDP development and economic growth.

annual growth can be much lower and sometimes even negative, as we experienced in 2020. This volatility of annual growth results in the business cycle, shown on the right-hand side of Figure 2.16.

The average economic growth in India between 2000 and 2025 will be around 6%. However, the COVID-19 pandemic hit India hard, resulting in a dramatic contraction of GDP, driven by less spending. According to official numbers, in 2020, the economy dropped by 8%, the first fall in more than four decades. This short-term economic crisis in 2020 with negative growth is happening despite high average economic growth in the previous period and relatively positive longer-term projections, as we saw in Chapter 1. The same holds for other NEP-9 countries. Brazil, Mexico, Russia, South Africa, and Turkey all had negative growth in 2009, the year after the financial crisis erupted, complemented by global problems and falling commodity prices, while at the same time experiencing relatively high average growth over a longer period.

The government as crisis manager

The distinction between long- and short-term drivers to explain economic development also affects the discussion about the role of the government. You could argue that the government is needed as a crisis manager when the economy goes down, as we saw during the COVID-19 pandemic. In this setting, the government is the only entity that can stimulate the economy through its budget. In the absence of a crisis, the role of the government can be more limited, and there is more room for the market. This does not say that the government must be absent during boom periods. Needed transitions, such as the transition toward a more value-added production, may only happen with substantial government interference.

2.5.2 *The iPhone case*

The exported products of most NEP-9 countries are composed of relatively many imported parts. For example, to produce and export a car or a smartphone, both Mexico and China import all kinds of components to be able to export. These exports result from low value-added production processes that simply assemble the final goods, confirming the downstream position of both countries in supply chains. This commonly named processing trade (importing various components, assembling, and subsequently exporting the final product) accounts for a significant share of exports from China and Mexico. Although exports may rise, at the end of the day, assembly by itself does not create a lot of domestic value and economic growth. This processing trade is also blurring international trade flow. Statistically, China is a major exporter of high technology goods, such as the iPhone, but in reality, the product is only assembled in China and then exported. The same applies to Mexico and their export of the latest car models.

The difference between net export and gross export

Figure 2.17 aims to show that the production (and export) of iPhones does not bring so much additional income (GDP) for a country such as China. The analysis was originally based on the iPhone 6S but now includes the iPhone 11, introduced in 2019. The iPhone is assembled in China and exported by Taiwanese-based company Foxconn and included in Chinese production and export statistics. However, to produce the iPhone 6, almost all components are imported, and only the assembly is done in China. Figure 2.17 shows that to be able to produce the iPhone 6, imports are needed for a total of $231,50. Manufacturing itself, meaning the wage costs of the Chinese employees, was $8 and this can be considered as domestic value-added (GDP) or earned income in China.

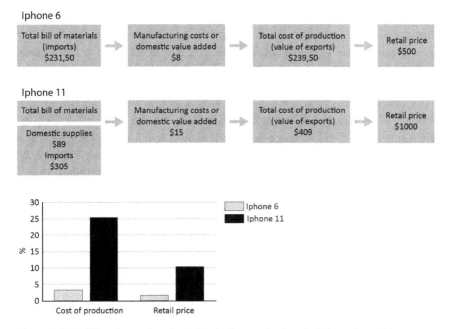

Figure 2.17: China domestic value-added when producing the iPhone 6 and 11.

Source: Ebbers (2019) and Statista (2020).

The traditional (and wrong) way of thinking is that the $239,50 per iPhone 6 is the value of Chinese exports and, therefore, part of Chinese GDP. However, this GDP is based on value added domestically. That means the actual value of Chinese export is only $8 per iPhone, the assembly costs. Assuming the export price is the manufacturing cost, the Chinese domestic added value is only 3.4% of the total manufacturing costs per iPhone (shown in the lower half of Figure 2.17). Essentially, the production and export of the iPhone 6 barely increase Chinese GDP. A key learning point is that growth in GDP is driven by the net export (export minus import) and not by the gross export.

Now, consider the cost of production of the iPhone 11. The impact of Chinese government interference in the iPhone value chain is evident. Because of specific measures, such as subsidies, and preferences, we see growing involvement of Chinese firms in the production of iPhone 11 components. Several Chinese companies are supplying (non-core) components and substitutes for imports. The total value of domestic components was $89, a marked change from the iPhone 6, which shows that the Chinese mobile phone industry as a whole has moved up the iPhone value-chain ladder. Furthermore, we see an increase in labor costs to $15, generating domestic value added of $104. The total cost for the materials of the iPhone X is at $409, of which about 25.4% is contributed by Chinese firms and employees. This Chinese value added of the iPhone 11 is dramatically higher than 3.6% in the case of iPhone 6. The same development can be seen with respect to Chinese domestic value added and the retail selling price at introduction. In the case of iPhone 6, the Chinese domestic value ($8) makes up only 1.6% of the retail price, while this increased to 10.4% regarding the iPhone 11.

Conventional trade statistics gives a distorted picture of trade imbalances

---

There is one more interesting conclusion we can draw from the iPhone case. Since iPhones are assembled in and exported from China, shipments to the US are recorded as Chinese exports, thus becoming part of the US trade deficit with China. However, when bilateral trade flows between the US and China are calculated correctly, namely, by taking only the value added domestically into account and not the gross export, the bilateral trade deficit of the US with China will disappear almost entirely. Clearly, with today's fragmented supply chains, conventional trade statistics provide a distorted picture of bilateral trade imbalances, as we will further discuss in Chapter 6.

2.5.3 *The smiling curve analysis*

As it stands, the production of the iPhone 6 was not of much help to the Chinese economy. Things would be different if a Chinese firm created the iPhone or if most components were developed and produced in China: a shift we already witnessed by looking at the iPhone X. Look at Figure 2.18. It depicts the commonly named smiling curve. The vertical axis shows the value added by important functions of the supply chain, ranging from R&D and components to marketing and after-sales services. In essence, it shows that focusing on assembly activities in the global supply chain (as shown by the iPhone example) does not add much value

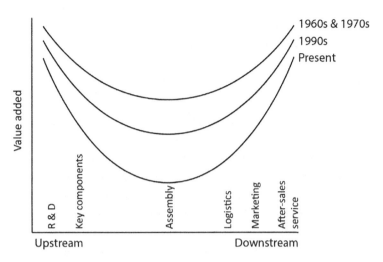

Figure 2.18:   The smiling curve.

Source: Based on Shih (1996) and UN (2018).

(GDP) or profitability for the company. The only reason that Foxconn is willing to assemble the iPhone is to achieve enormous economies of scale.

The smiling curve has deepened over time. (Keep in mind that paradoxically, a bigger smile is bad for developing countries and emerging markets.) This deepening of the curve implies that the value-added gap between, for example, R&D activities and assembly has increased. There are two reasons the smile has become more profound. The first deepening resulted from increased competition between countries in attracting foreign companies. In the 1990s, we saw heavy competition on wages that attract companies and production processes with low added value. Competition has become more intense because more and more countries are opening up and integrating into the world economy (Central and Eastern Europe in the 1990s, African countries in the 2000s, and new Asian markets such as Myanmar after 2010). Automation, robotics, digitalization, and associated technologies such as 3D printing may also contribute to the deepening of the (present) smiling curve, such that the smile gets more pronounced. For example, digitalization and digital technologies such as Big Data emphasize the importance of intangibles in the value chain, creating high added value at the extreme upstream and downstream sides of production.

Higher added value and profitability can be reached by moving left (upstream) or right (downstream) on the smiling curve; moving away from assembly activities.

Deepening of the smiling curve and the implementation of national industry policies

---

This is what we see in today's NEP-9 countries. Specific government policies designed to move the economy toward R&D, innovation, branding, and services are a core element of their growth strategies. These policies may have different names and take many forms, but essentially, they come down to two beliefs. First, the market will not generate the required shift away from assembly, so government interference is needed. Second, this policy is not a substitute for market forces, but they are necessary to overcome market failures. Industry policies executed by the NEP-9 range from the high local content rules in India and Mexico that aim to force foreign companies to buy components from domestic suppliers, to move away from commodities, and to focus on processing as seen in Indonesia and Brazil. The Made in China 2025 program is another example of industry policy. It was launched in 2015 and aims to raise the domestic content of core components to 70% by 2025. The plan indicates the need to transform "Made in China" to "Made by China," moving along the smiling curve, precisely what we witnessed when analyzing the role of Chinese suppliers in the production process of the iPhone. The smiling curve analysis helps understand past and future policy choices made by NEP-9 designed to increase economic development and gain momentum in the catching-up process, which is our subject for the next chapter.

Chapter 3

The Catching-up Process

3.1 A Recent Phenomenon

Despite the perception that the norm is economical and human development, stagnation was the standard until the 19th century (Maddison project database). Prosperity is a recent phenomenon. From the 1st century to 1800, total world output and world population grew only marginally. As a result, the average person's income was almost stagnant for over more than 1,800 years. Although reconstructing GDP per capita over such a long time frame is complex and uncertain, nearly all estimates draw the same conclusion. On average, no visible progress of living standards occurred over an individual's lifetime from the Roman empire until the start of the Industrial Revolution in the United Kingdom in the 1750s, as visualized in Figure 3.1.

Prosperity is a recent phenomenon in world history

Along with stagnating income, daily life also did not change much. A person that fell asleep in the city of Londinium, founded by the Romans in the year 50 AD, and woke up just before the Industrial Revolution took off would have understood the world he saw and would be able to adjust relatively easy. Shelter, food, clothing, and energy supplies stayed pretty much the same for a very long time. Almost everything used and consumed by ordinary people would have been familiar to our ancient Londoner. Naturally, over time, there were some innovations, technological advancements, and increased prosperity, but they lasted only for a

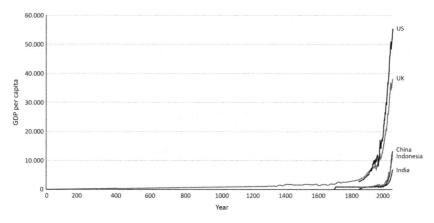

Figure 3.1:   GDP per capita between the year 1 and 2020.

Source: Ourworldindata.org (2021), based on Maddison historical statistics (RUG, 2021).

short time, and progress did not reach the masses. Moreover, technical improvements and innovative ideas often failed to reach other societies, which means that when innovative societies weakened and disappeared, so did their technologies. Furthermore, sporadic technological advancements that temporarily increased food supplies did not create better living standards because the result was that more people survived while the technological improvements stopped. In the preindustrial world, sporadic technological advances produced more people, not wealth. And when population increases, the marginal returns of the land diminish, depressing average living standards and creating famine and human disaster: the commonly named "Malthusian Trap" (Malthus, 1798).

Escaping the Mathusian Trap

In the absence of technological advancement, marked increases in living standards can occur only when the population declines. After famines, the living standards of those who survived increased: In this Malthusian Trap, as we will see in the following, births and deaths determined income. This prolonged stagnation of development was directly associated with a lack of significant technological progress. Britain's Industrial Revolution between 1750 and 1820, a period of rapid technological advancement, broke this long-term stagnation and released people of the Malthusian Trap. This renewed progress resulted in a substantial increase in GDP per capita after 1750, followed by the enormous rise in welfare seen in the 19th and 20th centuries. Note that this is per capita GDP, meaning that the increase in the total output of a country grew even more because both average incomes and the number of citizens increased.

3.2 Divergence, Followed by Convergence

3.2.1 *Growing deviation*

The Industrial Revolution of the 18th century created welfare, but it also created a division: advanced countries versus developing countries. It shifted economic power toward Western Europe and the United States. Perhaps surprisingly, up to 1750, the largest and wealthiest economies in the world were China and India, and even as late as 1820, China continued to reign the global economy. However, the rapid increase in welfare in the West and the post-1800 standstill of China's development resulted in a decreased Chinese share in the world economy. China had close-to-zero growth in per capita GDP from 1800 to 1950, right when the economies of Europe (starting in Great Britain) and North America began to take off. Figure 3.2 shows this fall between 1820 and 1870. While China's share was still above 30% in 1820, it dropped to 17% in 1870.

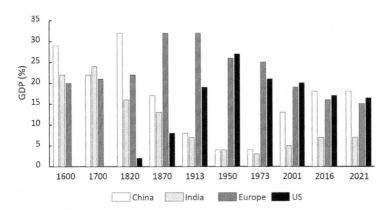

Figure 3.2:   Historical share of global GDP.

Source: Based on Maddison (2001) and IMF (2021).

Still, a power to be reckoned with but considerably smaller than the UK and its colonies. By 1950, China's share of the expanding world economy was down to about 3% and around 2% at the start of the reforms in 1978. India shows the same pattern, as its share dropped from 17% in 1820 to 2% in 1973.

It is pretty remarkable that industrial growth began in the relatively poor Northwestern Europe and not in the more advanced areas of Asia. However, the UK had coal to stimulate energy-intensive industries, combined with colonies such as the US that were a source for the required primary products and the opportunity to specialize in manufactures. While up to 1500, the global economy was Asian-centric, driven by China and India, between 1500 and 1800, it changed to a more polycentric system (Figure 3.3). Asia and Europe shared economic power, and China and India were still the world's largest economies. After 1800, when the Industrial Revolution achieved momentum, the world order shifted and became Eurocentric — dominated by European countries. The 20th century is a Western-centric global order with the US as the dominating economic powerhouse, followed by the European countries and Japan.

A stalled catching-up process

The divide continued to grow until the 1990s. Although from time to time, some Asian and Latin American countries took their first tentative steps in catching-up, the West dominated in both the economic and political sense. The income gap between advanced nations and developing countries grew wider. Explanations for this stalled catching-up process are numerous, indicating the many facets that determine economic development (Popov, 2015). Also, in many cases, it is driven by country-specific characteristics and circumstances. Discussing all possible explanations suggested for the continuation of economic backwardness is beyond the scope of this chapter but can be clustered around four pillars. The first is the role of national culture: The West had the "right" culture, and the rest of the world had "wrong" cultures for taking initiatives, innovative behavior, hard work, and an eagerness to learn. Leaving aside the well-known criticisms of such sweeping cultural generalizations, research has not been able to link cultural differences to longer-term growth variations. If culture were that influential, you would expect the same countries to develop better than others during a longer period. However, the correlation of economic growth between two periods is relatively low, as we will see later in this chapter. The second pillar of explanations centers around the institutional frameworks of countries. The West had the "right" institutions to promote economic growth, and the rest of the world did not. The third pillar to explain continued backwardness relates to the lack of education, and the fourth is the failure to implement market forces. Although these are reasonable arguments, the different chapters of this book clarify that the explanations for backwardness are exceptionally complex.

3.2.2 The convergence process

The catching-up process of developing countries and emerging markets started in the 1960s with the Asian tigers, followed by other Asian countries (including China) in the 1980s and India and Indonesia in the early 1990s. In the 1970s, Latin America also saw boom periods in Brazil and Mexico. Despite this economic development, up to the mid-1990s, economic catch-up was hardly comprehensive and structural. Between 1960 and 1995, the per capita income of most Asian and Latin-American countries either stabilized or fell, as compared to the US and western Europe (World Bank, 2021). This changed after the mid-1990s when economic growth took off across most emerging markets, particularly the NEP-9 countries. As we will see in Chapter 7, increased economic power also translated to political power through multilateral and regional organizations. This development of catching-up is what Baldwin (2016) called the *Great Convergence*. Earlier chapters clarified that we expect this development to continue, resulting in an emerging market-centric world, an emerging market century shaped by the NEP-9. The economic rise of the NEP-9 will end almost four centuries of economic domination by western countries. Figure 3.3 shows this development.

*NEP-9: Brazil, China, India, Indonesia, Mexico, Russia, South Africa, South Korea and Turkey

Figure 3.3:   Changes in economic power.

Source: Adapted from Ebbers (2019).

3.2.3 *Growth rate perseverance*

Despite this catching-up process, which gained momentum in the 1990s, it should be clear that differences in economic growth among countries are not permanent. Only in a few instances do we see the same country performing relatively good or bad decade after decade. This is illustrated in Figure 3.4 that involves the NEP-9 and several other countries. If

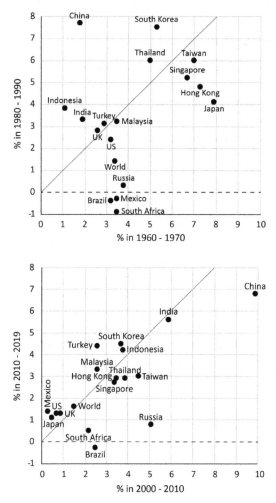

Figure 3.4:   Growth rate persistence.

Source: World Bank growth figures.

country growth rate differences were essentially permanent, the countries would place along the upward sloping line since those with high growth in the first period would also show high growth in the second. However, the upper half of Figure 3.4 indicates there is hardly any relationship between the income per capita growth rates of 1960–1970 and 1980–1990.

If we change periods, we see the same pattern of low persistence, for example, 1990–2000 and 2010–2019 on the lower half of the figure. While Brazil witnessed yearly average growth of 2.5% between 2000 and 2010, it went into recession between 2010 and 2019. The strong growth of the Russian economy between 2000 and 2010 was followed by very moderate growth after 2010. The data show that the Asian countries are an exception to the rule. Countries such as South Korea achieved rapid growth during all periods. This may also serve as a warning for longer-term economic forecasting. Growth performance can change quickly, and consequently, extrapolating forward is dangerous. One reason for this instability of growth rates over time may be that in several NEP-9 countries, commodity prices drove growth, and these have been very unstable over the years, as we will discuss in Chapter 4.

3.3 The Middle-Income Trap

The World Bank assigns the world's economies to four income groups — low, lower-middle, upper-middle, and high-income countries. These classifications, updated on July 1, 2021, are based on income per capita in market exchange rates and presented in US dollars.

- Low income   below US$1,046
- Lower-middle income   US$1,046–4,095
- Upper-middle income   US$4,096–12,695
- High income   above US$12,695

In the past decades, all NEP-9 were able to transition to middle-income status, but except for South Korea, they have not moved further into the high-income position. In 2012, the World Bank upgraded Russia to a high-income country, but today (2022), it is back in the upper-middle-income cohort. Every country will be in the middle-income segment over some time, as this is a transition process. It takes time to implement structural reforms and see the impact of these reforms take shape. According to the World Bank, many developing countries achieve rapid economic growth in the earlier stages of their economic development (to escape the poverty trap). After this phase, they fall into the middle-income trap, which means they spend several decades in the middle-income segment without considerable economic progress. The concept of the middle-income trap can be related to Rostov's five stages of economic development (Rostov, 1960), as well as to the discussion on extensive growth (mobilization phase of increasing productivity) and intensive growth (efficiency phase of increasing productivity), as described in Chapter 2. The trap is visualized in Figure 3.5.

3.3.1 *From poverty trap to middle-income trap*

The poverty trap is the period between points A and B. The countries in this cohort fail to reach middle-income status, and they have missed Rostow's take-off phase. To achieve economic growth and middle-income status, low-income countries can combine more labor and more machines, as indicated by trajectory B–C. However, as we have discussed, this "easy" extensive growth has its limits. As countries reach the

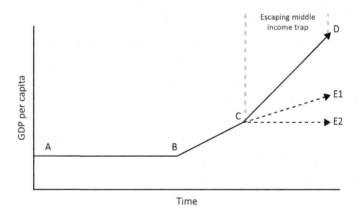

A-B: traditional society, underdevelopment, facing poverty trap
B-C: take-off, escape poverty trap
C: middle-income level
D: growth to high-income level
C-E: middle income trap
E1: high-middle income
E2: low-middle income

Figure 3.5:   Rostov's phases and the middle-income trap.

middle-income level, the surplus of labor will disappear, wages will increase, moving resources to more productive activities becomes problematic, the impact of additional investments becomes smaller, and productivity gains will decrease. These middle-income countries lose growth momentum after reaching a middle-income level, as indicated by C–E segment. Being stuck in the middle-income cohort relates to Rostov's model because the countries cannot escape the fourth phase, the drive to maturity.

Need for structural reforms

After point C, countries may continue to have high growth figures and reach the status of high-income (advanced) countries or the fifth phase of Rostov's development path. This development is only possible if governments implement reforms that stimulate intensive growth through innovation, R&D, and technological advancements. As stated earlier, South Korea escaped the middle-income trap, although it took them more than 75 years to enter the high-income cohort in 1995 (ADB, 2017). The growth experienced by South Korea from the 1960s onwards was staggering. Their economy went from a GDP per capita of around $2,000 in 1960 to $47,000 in 2021 (IMF). Other examples of successful middle-income transitions are Singapore, Ireland, Israel, and Spain, but these are more or less the only examples of the past decades.

Although the discussion on the middle-income trap encompasses the entire middle-income segment, the World Bank distinguishes between lower-middle-income and upper-middle-income. For example, Brazil has been in the lower-middle-income band for 20 years before it became an upper-middle-income country. Similarly, Russia spent 12 years as a lower-middle-income country before it moved to the upper-middle-income section. After 12 years as a lower-middle-income country, China gained upper-middle-income status in 2010 (ADB, 2014). Indonesia made the jump from lower-middle-income to upper-middle-income in 2020, but the impact of COVID-19 saw it fall back to the lower-middle-income cohort. Of our NEP-9, South Korea is statistically the only advanced nation.

The concept of the middle-income trap was made famous by the World Bank report *China 2030: Building a Modern, Harmonious, and Creative High-Income Society* (2013). This report illustrated the concept with compelling graphs, which became even more influential than the report itself. According to the World Bank, of the 101 countries that had obtained middle-income status by 1960, only 13 became high-income economies by 2008. In particular, countries in Latin America showed characteristics of the trap hypothesis, but it was seen worldwide. Several NEP-9 economies reached middle-income status as early as the 1960s and 1970s but have remained there ever since, visualized in Figure 3.6.

3.3.2 *Defining the trap*

Essentially, there are two methods to analyze the middle-income trap: the absolute and the relative approach. One problem in using the absolute benchmark is that at some point in time, all countries will surpass the income thresholds if these thresholds stay unchanged or are adjusted only marginally. The IMF uses the market exchange rate income, and the

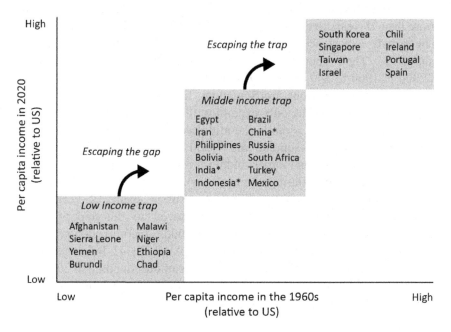

Figure 3.6:   Middle-income trap.

*Countries not considered as trapped due to the relatively short time frame spend in middle-income cohort.

Source: Based on reports by Asian Development Bank (2014, 2017) and World Bank (2013).

Asian Development Bank uses the income in purchasing power parity. Whether one uses market exchange rate or PPP income levels, the absolute approach automatically results in all countries becoming high-income economies when today's benchmarks are used. It makes sense to use this absolute approach if the focus is on welfare analysis. However, to discuss the catching-up process, the relative approach is more suitable.

The absolute and relative approach of analyzing the middle-income trap

---

The relative benchmark approach, or the catch-up benchmark method, focuses on relative income levels. This is the method used in most studies, including the World Bank report of 2013, which uses the US as the benchmark country. The World Bank set the threshold for determining whether a given country is stuck in the middle-income trap between 5% and 45% of the US GDP per capita. Based on this approach, the World Bank concluded that only 13 countries escaped the middle-income trap and became high-income countries by 2008. Countries such as Brazil and Turkey experienced essentially zero growth relative to the US economy, with a per capita GDP between 10% and 40% of the US level between 1960 and 2008. This continues to this day, extending the period countries stay in the middle-income cohort to 60 years.

Some research focuses on the number of years it takes a country to move from one income category to another. The consensus is that if a country exceeds 60 years in the middle-income cohort, that country is classified as stuck in the middle-income trap (ADP, 2017). Brazil and Mexico have operated in the middle-income range for more than 60 years. While Brazil's per capita income increased substantially during the three decades after WWII, due to the debt crisis, it came to a standstill in the 1980s. Today, the per capita income in Brazil is only 13% (in market exchange rate GDP) and 23% (in purchasing power parity) of the level of US per capita income.

As stated before, the World Bank income classification identifies two types of middle-income countries: lower-middle-income and upper-middle-income countries. In a sense, we could also identify two types of middle-income traps: staying too long in the lower-middle-income segment and being trapped in the upper-middle-income status. In general, it is more difficult to escape the upper-middle-income trap than to break free from the lower-middle-income trap. The easy rise in productivity (the mobilization phase) is still an option in the lower-middle-income segment. But, to escape the upper-middle-income cohort and become advanced, the country must transition to the efficiency phase of raising productivity. The focus must shift toward the economy's supply side, such as better education, market forces, intelligent government intervention, investing in R&D, competition to stimulate innovative behavior, diversification of the economy with higher value-added activities, stable institutions, and high-quality infrastructure.

Smart policy mix and smart execution

Some argue that a democratic country will achieve these productivity gains easier than authoritarian nations (Acemoglu, 2019). Typically, a democratic setting sees relatively low levels of corruption, a judiciary system that is relatively free from politics and government influence, and an open society creating an environment that fosters innovation and reforms. There is a certain logic to this reasoning, but as we will see, to achieve these preconditions for escaping the middle-income trap, democratic or semi-democratic structures are not required. (Semi-)authoritarian systems may accomplish them as well. What is needed is a reasonable amount of political longevity. Of course, the system must permit the citizen a voice to make the government accountable. Otherwise, there is a schism between the political elite and the mass of the middle class. The key learning point is clear. To escape the middle-income trap, countries must implement robust structural reforms. They must do so in the correct sequence and on time: a smart policy mix and smart execution, combining the role of the market and government interference. Democratic as well as authoritarian systems may achieve this balance between market and government.

3.3.3 *The South Korean case*

The South Korean experience illustrates the importance of balancing the role of the market and the role of the government in escaping the middle-income trap. In the 1970s, South Korea began shifting to more capital and technology-intensive industries. The government created R&D institutes and started a National R&D Program to support the transition to higher value-added activities. Moreover, it worked closely with private firms to increase the technical absorption capacity of the private firms. According to South Korean policymakers, technological upgrading in the most important industries cannot be left to market forces alone, and government intervention is needed to start the process. Together with Singapore, South Korea is the pioneer of modern state capitalism (Chapter 4), smartly combining government intervention and markets. In many cases, government interference is a precondition for private innovations, a message underwritten by Mazzucato (2021). She says that innovations such as the smartphone would not be possible without government support and tax money. She goes even further by emphasizing that for this type of innovation, government support is more important than a liberal market with an entrepreneurial spirit.

Pro-active government intervention is needed

South Korea did not wait for the market to bring about the required transition to the efficiency phase of raising productivity. Government initiatives, policies, finance, and targeted investments were essential, which lines up with the consensus view that investments must approach 25–30% of GDP over a longer period to enable the step toward an advanced country (Sharma, 2016). That ratio can only be lower (without causing economic disruptions) when the country's level of development is high and stable. Investments in factories, bridges, roads, airports, and 5G broadband cables are essential to building the fundaments for longer-term growth even when it creates (financial) bubbles. Despite the financial crises in the early 2000s, caused by excessive risk-taking, governments running budget deficits, bankruptcies, and banking problems caused by bad debts, at the end of the day, these investments are productive assets, while the companies that did these investments went bankrupt.

Developing countries or emerging markets with an investment ratio below 15–20% over a longer term will witness increasing obstacles to achieving productivity growth. Just look at daily life in these countries with unpaved roads, dilapidated school buildings, large class sizes, and low-quality government services. The above discussion on the investment ratio relates to the question of how much government interference is optimum and what the optimum size is of the government for a specific country. Obviously, successful nations such as South Korea do not have small governments. The same holds for many Western European countries. Nations going through the required transitions, such as Indonesia, Brazil, and China, also do not have small governments. The state needs to be large enough, but not so large as to create inefficient bureaucracy, which we see in Brazil and India, for example. As you will see throughout the book, the conclusion is that the size of government must suit the stage of development of the country. This is the easy answer, based on the South Korean experience. However, the discussion about optimal government size is complex due to the division in central and local governments. Additionally, the role of the government may vary in short-term versus longer-term objectives.

Size of the government must suit the stage of
development of the country

Another learning point of the Korean case is that upgrading the economic structure toward more capital and knowledge-intensive sectors was not always done in line with the country's main sectors of the time. For example, the industries that received strong state support (shipbuilding, automobiles, machinery, and electronics) in the early 1970s were not the sectors where South Korea had a comparative advantage, such as light manufacturing (textile and plastic products). Shipbuilding, automobiles, and machinery were promoted in the early 1970s when the country's per capita income was only 5.5% that of the US. Remarkably, by the early 1980s, the South Korean export structure was nearly the same as the export structure of the US, a transition not easily achieved by market forces alone.

For economies to transition to the efficiency phase of raising productivity, competent government institutions are required. Many countries struggle with this, but it should be clear that the state must address government failures before attempting to fix market failures. Government interference must complement the market and build on a solid foundation of professional, high-quality civil service. Taken from the Korean experience, it is also essential to mention their emphasis on manufacturing. Manufacturing increases productivity more and easier than agriculture and the service sector, a timely discussion in India today. Although for many years the country had an investment ratio of more than 30%, little went into manufacturing, focusing on services instead. Its export structure shows that India is a prominent exporter of services (Chapter 6). In the context of the middle-income trap, the question is now whether

India can switch its focus on low value-added services to more productive, knowledge-intensive activities.

A final learning point taken from the Korean case is the specific role of education in escaping the middle-income trap (and the low-income trap, for that matter). A well-educated labor force that can absorb new technologies is required to make the transition to higher value-added products and processes possible. During the light manufacturing phase, South Korea initially focused on primary education in its education policies. Then they invested more heavily in secondary education and technical training to provide skills for higher value-added industries. With the subsequent move into electronics and knowledge-intensive sectors, investments shifted toward higher education. South Korea designed its educational policies in support of the national development strategy. Increased quality of education automatically results in higher wages (with a time lag) and may motivate the supply side to increase productivity. In this way, education simultaneously increases productivity and purchasing power.

3.3.4 *China: Learning from South Korea*

In general, most NEP-9 are following the Korean example. These countries are eager to transition to higher value-added activities in technology and knowledge-intensive industries. Often they start with rising wages, complemented by investments in education, helping domestic strategic sectors, and limiting the access of foreign companies looking for a low-wage labor force. In line with South Korea, Chinese authorities also believe that government actions are required to initiate the desired transitions. The policy change from "Made in China" to "Created in China" captures this modern state capitalism. For example, the Chinese government stimulates R&D and new technologies through protection, education, and finance, which will boost productivity and help the economy move up in the global value chains. To boost innovation and productivity, the 13th five-year plan (2016–2020) indicated 10 priority strategic sectors, all more or less related to new technologies. The list includes new materials, aerospace and railway equipment, new-generation IT and alternative fuel automobiles, among others. The 14th five-year plan (2021–2025) broadened and intensified this strategy with concrete government support to become a leader in strategically important emerging industries such as artificial intelligence, cloud computing, and quantum science.

3.4 The Urgency of Transformation

In 1954, Lewis introduced the concept of dual economy. The two sectors in this concept are the unproductive and stagnant traditional agricultural sector and the highly productive and dynamic modern industrial sector. In the agricultural sector, we assume a surplus of labor, and consequently, labor productivity is low (or even zero). In the industrial sector, higher productivity leads to increased wages, attracting migrants from rural areas to move into the urban centers to seek employment. This mobilization of labor does not hurt agricultural production because a worker's productivity in the rural sector is low to zero and will continue to be a powerful force behind economic development during the take-off stage.

Making use of the demographic window of opportunity

In Lewis' view, there is significant or even infinite surplus labor, the primary trigger of "easy" productivity gains within the mobilization phase, resulting in an easy expansion of the modern manufacturing sector. In this situation, the country has a commonly named demographic dividend, and it creates a window of opportunity for countries; it facilitates rapid growth based on more labor, in particular, when combined with more machines in the manufacturing sector. However, in the end, the surplus of labor is exhausted because as a country develops toward advanced economic status, it tends to go through a period of demographic change where it loses its demographic dividend. Four interrelated developments usher in this loss of demographic dividend. First, a country's population declines or population growth reduces significantly. Consequently (secondly), the potential labor force (people aged between 15 and 65) will shrink. A third development is the growing older cohort (aging) and, fourth, rising dependency ratios, a term we will discuss later on in this chapter. Several NEP, including South Korea, Russia, China, and Brazil, had a demographic dividend and the population (and labor force) was a key driver behind economic success. However, this positive demographic picture either changed (as it did in Russia) or is changing fast (in China, Brazil, and South Korea). Every single one of these countries is losing its demographic dividend.

3.4.1 *The demographic transition*

Figure 3.7 depicts the demographic transition. First, have a look at the upper half of the figure. In the early stage of development, both birth

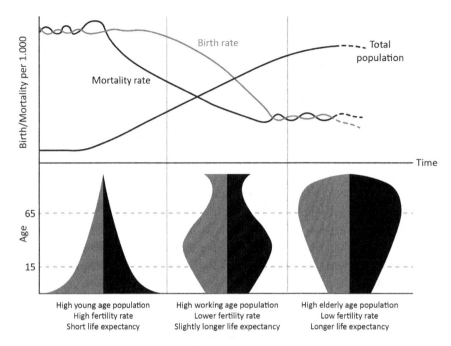

Figure 3.7: The demographic transition.

Source: Ourworldindata.org.

rate (or fertility rates, the number of children per woman) and mortality rate (the number of deaths per 1,000 inhabitants per year) are high. As you can see, the mortality rate is the first to begin its substantial fall, followed after a time by a fall in the birth rate.

Birth rates generally decline as income rises, education improves, and women become more active in the workforce. Better healthcare, hygiene, and improved general living conditions drive the fall in mortality rates. The consequence is clear: population numbers decline or population growth reduces strongly. This demographic change can happen in a relatively short period (World Bank, 2021). For example, in 1950, the Mexican fertility rate was seven children per woman, while the death rate was just below 0.02 (or 2%). The total fertility rate fell to six children per woman in 1975, five in 1979, four in 1985, and, currently, has dropped to 2.3 children. This rapid fall did not happen in Mexico alone. In 1950, all NEP-9 countries had a fertility rate above five (and most above six). Today, the fertility rate in most NEP-9 countries is even below the commonly named replacement rate of 2.1. (South Korea: 1.1, Brazil: 1.6, Russia: 1.6, China: 1.7, and Turkey: 2.0). South Africa is the exception, with a relatively high fertility rate of 2.5 in 2021. We see the same pattern for the mortality rate. Again, this development can happen in a relatively short time frame. For example, in Mexico, the death rate fell from 1% (10 death per 1,000 population) in 1970 to just below 0.6% today (2021), and, with two exceptions, it dropped to approximately 0.6% in the other NEP-9 countries. Although they are also declining, South Africa and Russia have relatively high mortality rates of 1% and 1.3%, respectively. Consequently, between 1970 and 2020, NEP-9 average population growth dropped to less than half the former numbers, from 2.0% in 1970 to 0.9% in 2019, the year before the COVID-19 pandemic. China is one of the countries that will witness a decline in its population in the coming years. Undoubtedly, there was a pressing reason for the government to implement the three-child policy in the summer of 2021, complemented by supporting measures to prevent further declines in the birth population.

---

*Developments in fertility and mortality are changing
the population pyramid forever*

Developments in fertility and mortality generate a change in age structure. This commonly named population pyramid shows the distribution of a population in terms of age group and sex, shown in the lower half of Figure 3.7. The first phase of development corresponds to a "healthy" population pyramid in terms of economic potential. The base, made up of relatively young people, is solid. The cohort of people in their working age is relatively large, while the cohort of older adults past working age is still relatively small, indicated by the dashed lines at the ages of 15 and 65. This is the situation of a democratic dividend. The changes discussed above will reshape the population pyramid into a vase. The drop in birth rate generates a smaller base of young people, and at the same time, the fall in mortality rate generates a growing old-age segment. The middle cohort, able and willing to work, is still significant in size, and the demographic dividend may continue. However, this changes when the population pyramid looks like a diamond, which means an aging population and a relatively small potential labor force. Again, the NEP-9 have followed this general pattern in the previous decades and will continue to do so in the future.

3.5 The Lewis Turning Point

The population pyramid shows the change from a surplus of labor to a labor shortage: the commonly named Lewis Turning Point (IMF, 2013). The Lewis Turning Point is the point in time when labor surplus no longer exists, and labor growth cannot serve as a pillar of the growth strategy of a country. In this case, the demographic dividend changes to a demographic burden: A large share of the population is not working because they are too old (65+) or too young (under 15).

3.5.1 *Labor force decline*

A look at China's working-age population (aged 15–64) reveals a decline in absolute numbers. Between 2020 and 2050, China's potential labor force will decline from 900 million to 780 million: a drop of 120 million people (Figure 3.8). The figure also shows the development of the working-age population in other NEP-9 countries, as well as several advanced nations. The picture is mixed. Because they have a relatively young population, India's potential labor force will grow from 900 million in 2020 to 1.1 billion in 2050. The 15–64 group is also growing in South Africa and Turkey. In contrast, this segment is in decline in absolute numbers in countries such as South Korea and Russia.

In most NEP-9 countries, the labor force is at or near its peak. South Korea reached its peak in the early 2000s, while Russia and China are approaching it within the next couple of years. Brazil, Mexico, Turkey, and Indonesia will feel the pressure around the 2030s. For South Africa and India, it may take a little longer. It is interesting to note that most African countries will not feel the pressure of labor shortage until the end of the century.

When this Lewis Turning Point approaches, governments implement policies to increase the labor force. For example, in the early 2000s, South Korea began to promote extending work permits to foreigners in industries facing labor shortages. China announced that it will raise the pension age in 2023, and Turkey subsidized parental leave and stimulated flexible working hours in the past years. Russia is changing specific labor market legislation to increase the participation of women. There are still former Soviet laws that prohibit women from working in over 400 occupations, designating these jobs as "not possible for women." However, step by step, women are now allowed to do these restricted jobs. For example, in

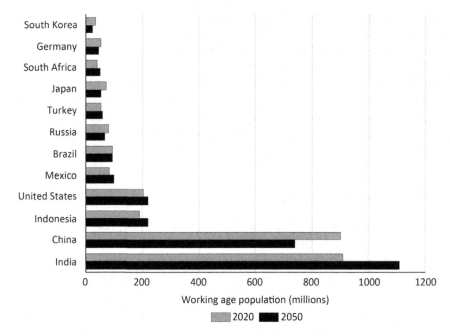

Figure 3.8:   Development of working-age population between 2020 and 2050, specific countries.

Note: The population age 15–64 cohort is referred to as the potential labor force (China: 15–60 years).
Source: United Nations database.

early 2021, the country opened up the job of train operator to women. India is one of the exceptions, as it may continue to enjoy a demographic dividend for several decades to come. One-third of its population is under 14, and its working-age population will grow during the next 30 years. Furthermore, in the coming decade, Mexico and Brazil will also have young populations and consequently a large cohort in the working age. However long countries can reap the benefits of demographic dividend, at the end of the day, it disappears.

3.5.2 *Aging*

By now, it's clear the demographic transition in NEP-9 countries is happening fast. Doubling the population share of those over 60 years old from

7% to 14%, the benchmark of an aging population determined by the US government, took a long time in western countries. For example, in France and the US, this process took over a century and 70 years, respectively, and, in most other developed countries, it took 45–60 years. In the NEP-9, it's taking much shorter. In China, it takes 25 years to double the percentage of the 60-plus cohort to 14% (2000–2025), and the same holds for India, Turkey, Brazil, and Indonesia, although part of this development will take place in the future. For example, in India, this will happen between 2025 and 2050.

Aging is (also) a big problem to emerging markets and the NEP-9

As shown in Figure 3.9, an aging population is not a problem exclusive to western countries. The NEP-9 countries and almost all Asian countries exhibit the same patterns. The 65+ share of the Brazilian population was 6.9% in 2020, which will climb to 20.3% in 2050: an increase of 300% in only two generations. In 2050, the share of the old-age cohort will be the largest in Japan, followed by South Korea, with a 300% rise

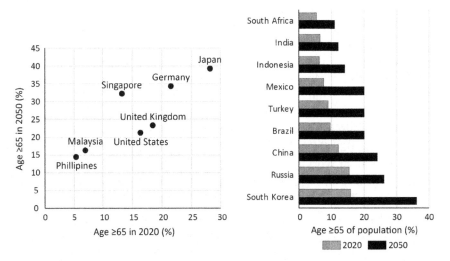

Figure 3.9: Aging.

Source: World Bank database.

from 20% to 60% in just two generations. In 2050, only Japan, Germany, and Italy will have a higher ratio. As shown by the figure, the growth of the old-age cohort between 2020 and 2050 is much higher in NEP-9 countries than in advanced western nations. All the NEP-9, except for South Korea, are growing gray before getting rich, and they all are urgently looking to solve the aging problem and the related social and financial burden. The speed of aging will also affect labor markets; in particular, it will result in labor shortages.

3.5.3 *Rising dependency ratios*

To determine the timing of the "window of opportunity" and recognize the ceiling of economic development based on more labor, we often use the demographic dependency ratio. The dependency ratio is the sum of the number of children and adolescents (aged 0–14 years) and of older adults (65 years and above), who are regarded as the dependent population, divided by the number of people of working age (15–64 years), regarded as being the income-earning population.

Dramatic projections up to 2050

Although dependency refers to population cohorts too old and too young, emphasis is mainly on the aging population's old-age dependency ratio. The old-age dependency ratio is the ratio of the population aged 65 and up to the working-age population. In line with the other aspects of the demographic transition, we see a dramatic change in the old-age dependency ratios of the NEP-9 countries. For example, the old-age dependency ratio in Mexico grew from 5% in 1950 to 10.2% in 2015 and over 13% in 2020 (UN, 2021). In other words, whereas in 1950, Mexico had 20 people of working age for each retired person (assuming a retirement age of 65), in 2020, this was only 7.6 persons. The old-age dependency ratio will continue to rise until 2050 and stabilize at around 30% or three workers to each retiree. In China, the old-age dependency ratio stood at 18% in 2020 but will grow to over 40% in 2050. The growth of the *total* dependency ratio (young and old) will continue steadily from 0.39 in 2015 to 0.43 in 2025 but will accelerate after that, reaching 0.65 in 2050 (National Bureau of Statistics, 2020). In short, the old-age dependency ratios of the NEP-9 were low and stable between 1980 and 2010 but have

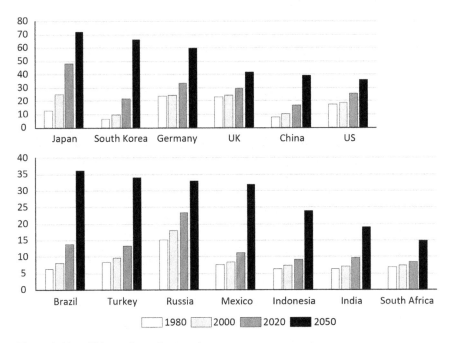

Figure 3.10: Old-age dependency ratio.

Source: World Bank (2021).

started to rise. They are projected to increase dramatically up to 2050, as shown in Figure 3.10.

3.5.4 *Reaching the Lewis Turning Point*

In analyzing whether a country approaches the Lewis Turning Point and is on the verge of losing its demographic dividend, we can combine the indicators we have just discussed. We could, for example, combine the workforce at peak and the growth of the dependency ratio or assess the absolute development of a population with the old-age ratio. This approach involves the interpretation of what can be mixed signals. For example, we evaluated the Lewis Turning Point for China in 2025 in *Unravelling Modern China* (Ebbers, 2019). Most of the criticism I received after writing that book was on this topic. My inbox exploded with emails regarding this assessment, saying I was either too optimistic or too pessimistic about China's Lewis Turning point. Despite these reactions, I decided to assess the Lewis Turning point again, not just for China but for all the NEP-9 countries.

Losing the demographic dividend

Figure 3.11 summarizes the outcome. Although the figure indicates a specific year, keep in mind that the Lewis Turning Point is a period rather

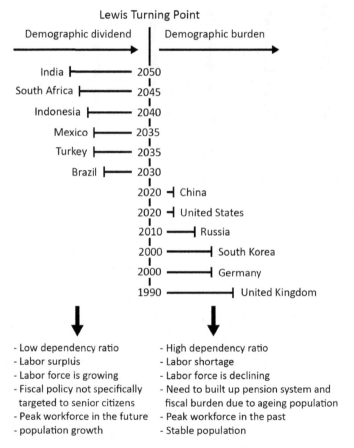

Figure 3.11:   Lewis Turning Point, several countries.

Note: Although the Turning Point is illustrated as a specific moment here, in reality, it is a period that may extend over several years.
Source: Adapted from Ebbers (2019).

than a point in time, and it may extend over several years. As you can see, in Figure 3.11, countries such as the UK, Germany, and Japan have already passed the turning point. They have a demographic burden, and the window of opportunity to benefit from the abundance of labor is gone. All the NEP-9 will experience the same aging patterns as developed countries.

NEP-9 countries such as India, South Africa, Mexico, and Brazil still have demographic dividends, but they have different runtimes. For example, India will reach the Lewis Turning Point around 2050, while the window of opportunity in Mexico will only remain open until the end of the 2020s. Except for India and South Africa, there is a sense of urgency to coping with demographic burden becoming a reality. Reforming an economy may take one or two generations, and consequently, governments must implement the necessary changes today. As stated before, the emphasis in the discussion of the dependency index is usually on the aging population. Still, some research also concludes that a sizeable young cohort may create problems for long-term development. First, the population aged below 14 is inactive. Second, a large share of young people (16–30 years old) may find their ideas and ambitions contradict the ruling authorities, which may cause civil unrest and political instability. According to this stream of research, problems may arise when more than 60% of the population is younger than 30 (Goldstone, 2002; Huntington, 1996). This theory helps explain the problematic transition currently experienced by countries like the Democratic Republic of Congo, Uganda, and Pakistan.

3.6 Overcoming the Middle-Income Trap

3.6.1 *The growth of the Asian NEP-9; implementing the seven pillars of western wisdom*

Escaping the middle-income trap requires robust structural reforms on the supply side of the economy. Kishore Mahbubani reaches the same conclusion in his book: *The New Asian Hemisphere: The Irresistible Shift of Global Power to the East* (2008). He explains why the rise of Asia (and China in particular) has begun only recently. His analysis is that the Asians have finally discovered and implemented the seven pillars of Western wisdom that, after the Industrial Revolution, brought development and welfare to Western countries. His seven pillars of Western wisdom line up with the World Bank view on overcoming the middle-income trap and are summarized in the following, although slightly adjusted for some NEP-9:

- *Free market economy*: Markets are essential because they generate incentives to increase productivity. Markets and opening up the economy were critical elements in achieving economic development in the West. The same is happening in NEP-9 countries. For example, China complemented market forces with government intervention, not to substitute the market but to supplement it and reduce market failures.
- *Science and technology*: Europe was dominant for centuries because it surged ahead in its mastery of science and technology. But extrapolating from what is happening on campuses and colleges today, soon 60–90% of all new PhDs in science and engineering will be held by Asians. Whatever the percentage ends up being, it is a remarkable shift from the past.
- *Meritocracy*: Why is Brazil a soccer superpower? During his presentation at Nyenrode University in 2010, Mahbubani said: "The answer is clear. Because when it comes to soccer, they look everywhere. They search for the best players in cities as well as in favelas. But when they look for business and political talent, they only look to the upper or medium class. This is the main barrier for developing a high-quality government." Asian countries have discovered that the millions of brains that went unused for centuries can generate enormous benefits. Social mobility is one of the many silent revolutions happening in Asian countries today.
- *Pragmatism*: The opposites of pragmatism are idealism and dogmatic thinking. Both do not help achieve economic development. As Deng Xiaoping said: "It doesn't matter if a cat is white or black; if it catches mice, it is a good cat." Most of Asia is abandoning ideological debates, although recently we have seen a resurgence of it.
- *A culture of peace*: The Asian continent was a warzone during the 1950s, 1960s, and early 1970s, but that changed dramatically in the 1970s. The region is now predominantly stable (despite geopolitical disagreements), and this stability is a precondition for economic development.
- *The rule of law*: A rule-based economic system is essential for longer-term economic development. Asia has some work to do here, but most Asian countries are moving in this direction. It is interesting that

Mahbubani only referred to the rule of law and did not mention democracy and political openness.

- *Education*: The hunger for education in Asia is phenomenal, and government investments in education support this desire. Most Asian countries have free primary education for everyone and heavy subsidies for studying at university.

Although Mahbubani focused on Asia, the catching-up process of the NEP-9 as a group will continue, as well as for the individual countries. For example, China is challenging the US in international trade (Chapter 6) and playing an increasingly leading role as a world importer. In contrast, the US is losing its relative share. In 1980, China was the main export destination for 1% of the world's countries, whereas in 2020, that percentage grew to 20%. For the US, those numbers are 28% (1980) and 20% (2020). The field of innovation also reveals evidence of the rise of several NEP-9 countries. Over the years, South Korea, China, and India have been the economies with the most significant progress in their Global Innovation Index ranking (WIPO, 2021). These are only two indicators that show the rise of the largest emerging markets and many will follow throughout the next chapters. We are clearly at the start of the emerging market century, led by the NEP-9 countries.

3.6.2 *The Thucydides Trap*

There have been several catching-up periods in history, during which some of the economically lagging countries joined and sometimes even overtook the economic leader. For example, in the 18th century, France joined Britain as a world power. In the 19th century, Germany challenged the two leading economies of Europe. In the late 19th century, it was the US' turn to catch-up, and by the start of the First World War, it had overtaken most European economies in terms of the size of its economy and income per capita. Today's growing tensions between the US and the EU on the one hand and China (and Russia) on the other have resulted in a new discussion on the commonly named Thucydides Trap.

A peaceful transition of power?

The concept of the Thucydides Trap was developed in 2012 by Graham T. Allison to describe the potential effects of rising tensions between China and the US. Ancient Greek historian Thucydides interpreted the Peloponnesian War as a conflict between the leading power (Sparta) and the upcoming challenger (Athens). Based on this, he analyzed 16 cases similar to the Thucydides Trap from the past 500 years, discovering that only four of them ended in a peaceful transition of power, while the other 12 ended through war. His analysis ends with the growing power of Germany (after German unification in 1992) challenging the United Kingdom and France in the context of the European Union.

Today's catching-up process sees the NEP-9 countries challenging the dominance of advanced western countries and China challenging the US. It is interesting to note that in previous years some policymakers have referred to this concept. For example, Chinese President Xi Jinping stated in 2015 that "we all need to work together to avoid the Thucydides Trap [...] But should major countries time and again make the mistakes of strategic miscalculation, they might create such traps for themselves." Former US President Obama used the metaphor in 2015 and indicated that he "did not agree with the Thucydides Trap notion" and its relevance to US–China relations." There was no reference to the Thucydides Trap during the Trump government, maybe because the former president was unfamiliar with world history (Figure 3.12).

	Period	Ruling power	Rising power	Result
1	First half of 16th century	France	Hapsburgs	War
2	16th - 17th centuries	Hapsburgs	Ottoman empire	War
3	17th century	Hapsburgs	Sweden	War
4	17th century	Dutch Republic	England	War
5	Early 18th century	France	Great Britain	War
6	Late 18th - early 19th century	United Kingdom	France	War
7	Mid 19th century	UK, France	Russia	War
8	19th century	France	Germany	War
9	Late 19th - early 20th century	Russia, China	Japan	War
10	Early 20th century	United Kingdom	United States	No war
11	Early 20th century	Russia, UK, France	Germany	War
12	Mid-20th century	Soviet Union, UK, France	Germany	War
13	Mid-20th century	United States	Japan	War
14	1970s-1980s	Soviet Union	Japan	No war
15	1940s - 1980s	United States	Soviet Union	No war
16	1990s- present	UK, France	Germany	No war

Figure 3.12:   Thucydides Traps.

Source: Allison (2015).

In one crucial respect, this current shift in global economic power toward the NEP-9 will differ from several preceding changes. When in the early 20th century, global power passed from Europe to the US, and when Germany challenged the UK and France in the early 1990s, the ruling and rising nations had similar views on the world, the role of government, democracy, and justice. They also had similar cultural and social heritage. In contrast, the NEP-9 countries have different opinions about political systems, different levels of state control, and different views on the role of the government. The rising powers have a more state-directed model instead of a traditional form of capitalism. They prioritize economic prosperity and deprioritize democratic and human rights, although many of them do have democratic elections.

Does this mean that we are approaching the Thucydides Trap? In my assessment, this is not the case. In the chapters to come, we look at how much agreement there is between the nations. For example, today's problems in the World Trade Organization (Chapter 7) may make it seem like there is a big fight between India, China, and Brazil on the one hand and the US and the EU on the other. However, as we will see, the NEP-9 countries are eager to keep the multilateral design as it is. Obviously, they want to see changes within global governance architecture, but they do not want to change the system. Both the NEP-9 and the advanced countries are aware of the need for such a rule-based system. The same holds for the economic system. One may emphasize the differences between a market versus a planned economy or between private capitalism and state capitalism. However, it appears that this division is not black and white. An esteemed colleague at Renmin University stated that we need to get rid of looking at international trade and economic dominance as a boxing match in which one side must win. According to him, we should look at this competition as an NBA basketball game where a draw is possible and reasonable. Essentially, he suggests going away from the commonly named "gap-thinking."

Too much black and white thinking

Emphasizing the catching-up process may cause us to forget that today's advanced economies will remain the richest and most open for decades to come. However, their economies may no longer be the largest, the fastest-growing, or the most dynamic. Figure 3.13 shows the development of the NEP-9 relative to the US in terms of income per capita in

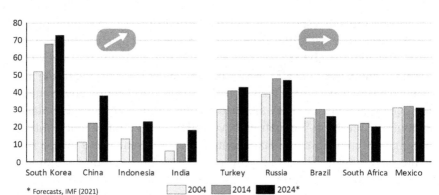

Figure 3.13:   GDP per capita as a percentage of US GDP per capita, in PPP.

Source: IMF (2021).

purchasing power parity. It's clear that most countries are catching-up, certainly when taking a longer-term view, but it is also clear that the previous years were challenging, as well as the short-term forecasts. The catching-up process will cease in the next coming years in NEP-9 countries such as Brazil, South Africa, and Mexico.

The US as a superpower is here to stay. It is the only country that is simultaneously big, young, and highly educated. The US workforce is still relatively large, which may be the case for some decades to come and may even grow. The US is also the most productive economy among the major powers, and it is ranked highly in the innovation rankings. Looking at these aspects, the NEP-9 countries are catching-up to advanced economies on some points, but at the same time, there is a gap they still have to overcome, and some NEP-9 countries are further in the catching-up process than others. Furthermore, there are obstacles to escaping the middle-income trap. These countries should feel a sense of urgency in counteracting these obstacles, as the effects of the easy reforms implemented to increase prosperity are fading. With this in mind, we may look at a more detailed level to the common characteristics and fundamental differences of the NEP-9.

Chapter 4

Common Characteristics and Important Differences

4.1 NEP-9: Homogeneous and Heterogeneous at the Same Time

NEP-9 countries share a set of common characteristics. Generally speaking, these economies are increasingly reliant on industrial manufacturing and services and are moving away from commodities. Furthermore, our NEP-9 countries started to rebalance their economies toward higher value-added manufacturing through technological advancements and innovation. South Korea has finished this process, while South Africa has only just begun. To achieve this rebalancing, government interference is necessary to navigate economies through several transitions. A common characteristic related to this is that the NEP-9 countries combine a large market with a large government. Government intervention must complement market forces because economic transitions are inherently disrupting, and markets cannot protect the people against negative consequences. Moreover, market forces may not automatically bring about the necessary restructuring.

NEP-9: combining large markets with large governments

Similarities between the NEP-9 also exist concerning the middle class and urbanization. Today, each of these countries focuses on a policy mix that considers the impact on the middle class. NEP-9 governments realize that this segment is key in generating the transition toward higher prosperity and escaping the middle-income trap. The NEP-9 also recognize the importance of (organized) urbanization as a complement to the focus on the middle class.

These are fundamental similarities, but on specific issues, the NEP-9 countries are heterogeneous. In certain areas, the differences may even outweigh the similarities. For example, Russia is a resource-rich country, emphasizing energy export, while South Korea depends heavily on imported energy. China and Brazil have large domestic markets, but this is certainly not the case for Mexico or South Africa. India has a growing and relatively young population, while China and South Korea are already aging, and the countries also differ with respect to democracy and economic systems. This mix of differences and common characteristics makes this chapter somewhat of a balancing act. In a way, the same applies to a comparison between China and the European Union. Everyone agrees that the two entities are different. Still, the Communist Party of China bailed out its banking system in the early 2000s, and the EU did the same during the 2008 financial crisis. Government spending as a percentage of GDP is around 45% on average in the EU countries and approximately 40% in China (2021). EU countries protect their strategic industries and national icons, while China protects state-owned companies. These examples show that even between the EU and China there are many commonalities and significant differences. And obviously, we see the same when analyzing NEP-9 countries. One important topic in which countries differentiate is the choice of their economic system and the balance between market and government intervention.

4.2 Economic Systems

Every economic system must answer the fundamental questions of economics: What to produce, how to produce it, and for whom. This is straightforward in a planned or command economy as the government determines the answers. Planned economies are able to adjust rapidly to changing circumstances because the authorities can shift resources away from one industry to another, quickly if needed. However, a planned economy also has critical shortcomings. First, it is exceptionally challenging for central planners to find out and understand what a society needs, and planning mistakes result in surpluses or shortages of products and services. Second, in planned economies, efficiency is of secondary importance. In many cases, it does not matter how companies produce their products as long as they stick to the plan. Third, the system does not incentivize people to work hard or to grab opportunities, creating a motivation problem that negatively affects production and productivity.

<hr>

Flexibility versus efficiency and innovation

<hr>

In contrast, in a market economy, private companies and individuals decide what to produce and what to buy. Supply and demand determine the production of goods and services. An "invisible hand" (the market) coordinates economic activity, and the government does not intervene. When demand for a product exceeds supply, prices will rise, signaling producers to increase production. If supply exceeds demand, prices will fall, signaling producers to produce less. Economic freedom and financial incentives are the basis of a market economy. In general, market economies tend to be relatively efficient and stimulate innovative behavior. The force of competitive pressure keeps prices low, quality relatively high, and promotes innovation.

4.2.1 *Market failures*

The disadvantage of a market economy is that the market can overreact, creating bubbles (e.g., price hikes) and economic crises. For example, due to acute shortages, in April and May of 2021, the price of medical oxygen cylinders exploded in India. And although COVID-19 patients required oxygen, hospitals had run out. The only option was buying oxygen on the market at ridiculous prices. This example clarifies how quickly the market can react to shortages and surpluses, but obviously, this is not the outcome any society wants.

Sometimes, the market is slow to solve an economic problem. Consider the economic crisis of 2020 and early 2021 caused by the pandemic. Wait for the market to react, and the situation drags on and gets worse. Consumers are unwilling to spend, investors are reluctant to invest, and economic recovery will take a while. In this situation, government was more or less the only entity willing to spend money and stimulate the economy.

<hr>

Disregarding externalities

<hr>

Another disadvantage of market forces is that certain goods do not get made, as in a market system, producers do not produce unprofitable goods or services. But sometimes, it may be necessary to produce some (public) goods regardless of profitability. A full-fledged market system will fail in this aspect. The market will also fail to achieve a social optimum because consumers and producers do not consider external effects. A classic example to illustrate this is pollution. The impact of disregarding externalities when buying a plane ticket or returning (for free) a product purchased online is that the outcome of the market forces differs from what is optimal from a social (and environmental) perspective.

Up to the 1980s, Brazil, India, and South Korea were countries with considerable government interference. In Mexico, Indonesia, Turkey, and South Africa, governments were also in the drivers' seat, and China and Russia were still planned economies, also referred to as state capitalism. The West also saw relatively high government interference in the 1970s in France, the United Kingdom, and Sweden, for example. These were considered mixed economies, a system that combines the roles of government and the market. In such a system, the market will do its work (leaning toward capitalism). Still, when required, government may intervene (leaning toward socialism) to stabilize (sectors of) the economy, to achieve social aims (income equality and social safety net) and environmental aims.

4.2.2 *The rise of neoliberalism*

This situation changed in the 1980s with the rise of neoliberalism, based on the paradigm "More market, less government." The election of Margaret Thatcher in the UK in 1979 and Ronald Reagan in the US in 1980 popularized the message that the market is good and government is bad: policy mixes called "Reaganomics" and "Thatcherism."

More market and less government

Simultaneously, several NEP-9 countries, such as Turkey, Mexico, and Brazil, liberalized their domestic economies and embraced a market system. However, sometimes this was forced by the conditions attached to IMF and World Bank loans (as we will see in Chapter 7). In China, it was Deng Xiaoping's program of economic reforms initiated in 1978 that opened the door for market forces. In India, it was the dismantling of the Licence Raj legislation, a set of bureaucratic economic controls, in the early 1990s. The fall of the Berlin Wall in 1989 resulted in (more) market forces in Russia. In this context, Francis Fukuyama wrote his book *The End of History and the Last Man* (1992). He concluded that capitalism and the universalization of Western liberal democracy had brought a history of ideological conflict to an end: capitalism and free markets triumphed in the ideological battle with state capitalism. It is interesting to note that the success of the East Asian model, framed as an opening up success, accelerated the ideological shift toward liberalism and free markets in the 1980s. However, as said in Chapter 2, we can also interpret this Asian miracle as evidence of successful state interference and a system that reduced the power of the market. In countries like South Korea and Singapore, government intervened systematically and through multiple channels to foster development and build strategic industries. We may call this modern state capitalism, or state capitalism 2.0, to separate it from the traditional state capitalism in China and Russia.

The neoliberal era (spanning the 1980s and 1990s) came under attack at the start of the new millennium. Its decline accelerated after 2008 with the sub-prime mortgage crisis in the United States (2008) and the sovereign debt crisis in Europe (2010–2012). These crises demonstrated to the NEP-9 countries (and many western economies) that "too much market" is bad and government guidance is helpful (and even required) in stabilizing irrational market behaviors.

Rethinking the role of markets and governments

This emphasis on market failures resulted in a rethinking of the role of government in both advanced western countries and the NEP-9 countries.

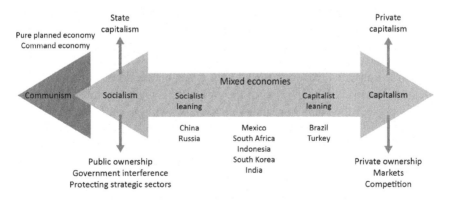

Figure 4.1:   Economic systems.

Today, we see considerable convergence of economic systems. Countries with heavy state interference move toward more market forces just as market systems are choosing to increase the guiding role of government. The Russian, Chinese, Indonesian, European, and US economies are now heavily regulated, subsidized, and taxed (Figure 4.1).

4.3   State Capitalism

Traditional state capitalism or state capitalism 1.0 is often equated with the economic planning system in Russia and China up to the late 1970s. In these cases, the influence of the state was enormous. It owned companies, dictated production, allocated labor, and controlled the economy and daily life.

State capitalism 2.0

Clearly, there was no role for market forces. Starting in the Asian miracle countries, 1950–1980 saw the rise of state capitalism 2.0 (Chatham House, 2010). Here, the government allows domestic private initiatives while continues to protect the domestic economy from international competition. Government still plays a strong role, but market initiatives are possible and sometimes even stimulated. In this setting, state-owned enterprises in strategic sectors are a tool for the execution of government policies. Even where the state does not have an ownership stake, it has a significant influence on decision-making. Exactly how state capitalism 2.0 was put into practice varied, with Singapore and South Korea on one end of the spectrum and Brazil and Mexico on the other. However, in general, the results of this state capitalism 2.0 were quite impressive. Brazil and Mexico saw robust economic growth from the 1960s up to the mid-1970s and substantial improvement in human indicators. Then came the oil and debt crises. These had dramatic economic consequences for fast-growing emerging markets, like Brazil and Mexico. Because the debt crisis of the early 1980s is crucial for understanding the choices the NEP-9 are making today, we will have a closer look.

4.3.1   *The debt crisis*

Figure 4.2 summarizes the international economy of the early 1970s. At that time, the Organization of the Petroleum Exporting Countries (OPEC)

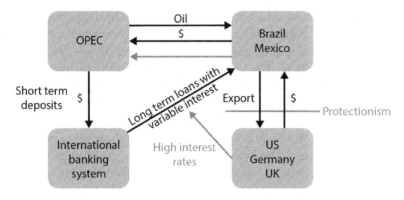

Figure 4.2: The debt crisis explained.

dominated oil exports. Besides OPEC, the world economy and international finance were dominated by fast-growing emerging markets, such as Brazil and Mexico, an international banking sector, and the advanced western nations. The first oil crisis (1973) caused oil prices to skyrocket, rising by more than 300% within six months. Countries with high economic growth, like Brazil and Mexico, required energy to sustain that growth, and the import of oil resulted in a dramatic worsening of the trade balance. The oil market is a US dollar market, which means buyers must pay for oil imports in US dollars. Luckily for Brazil and Mexico, western countries were also experiencing tremendous growth. Consequently, increased Brazilian and Mexican (commodity) exports to the US and Europe partly compensated for the trade deficit with OPEC members. A favorable coincidence was that commodity prices were high, raising export earnings of countries dependent on commodities.

Dollars received by OPEC members increased after the first oil crisis. There were few domestic investment opportunities and even less willingness to invest in western nations. Instead, these countries put their oil dollars in deposits in the international banking sector, mainly for a short duration of three to six months. This enormous inflow of OPEC dollars led to massive liquidity in the global banking sector, which allowed Brazil and Mexico to borrow money at low interest rates. However, these countries wanted to borrow for 20 or 30 years, while the banks received deposits for a period of three to six months. To solve this maturity mismatch, banks agreed to lend money at a long maturity but with flexible interest rates. This solution posed an increased risk for the lending countries, but this was their only option. At that time, a growing economy needed OPEC oil. This first oil crisis and subsequent skyrocketing oil prices resulted in growing public debt in debtor countries but did not harm the economy much. Growth was still relatively high, and although the growing public debt increased inflation, it did not set off any alarm bells. The black lines in Figure 4.2 represent this situation.

Then in 1979, the second oil crisis erupted, and the price of oil doubled within one year. The Brazilian and Mexican economies were still growing but experienced some headwinds as increasing protectionism made exporting to the advanced nations more difficult. This protectionism had two reasons. First, the United States and Europe also dealt with the rising oil price, trade deficits, and rising unemployment. Second, most economists in this period forecasted a dramatic increase in inflation because of increased prices of oil imports and building-up public debt. Hence, American and European central banks increased their interest rates. This combination of events resulted in fewer export opportunities for Brazilian and Mexican companies, a fall in the commodity prices due to the economic crisis in the West, and higher interest rates. And as most of the debt was borrowed at flexible interest rates, the result was dramatic. Indebted countries experienced an economic crisis combined with growing interest payments and difficulties paying back their debts — the start of the debt crisis. Deterioration of their exchange rate with the US dollar worsened the situation because the debt was in US dollars. The gray lines in Figure 4.2 represent the period after the second oil crisis.

Important external factors: too much liquidity and protectionism

---

The narrative used by western policymakers and the IMF in the 1980s to explain the debt crisis was built around domestic governments spending too much and accruing debt: a consequence of irresponsible and incorrect macroeconomic policies. We may question this viewpoint. The factors contributing to the economic and social collapse of the debt countries were primarily external. The falling prices of primary commodities, rising interest rates, and increasing protectionism created a perfect storm for many emerging markets, and for the most part, this was outside their control. Regardless of the causes, the debt crisis helped paint governments of emerging markets as irresponsible spending machines and increased the market's credibility. Global institutions such as the IMF internalized this mainstream of economic thought. In their advice and conditions for credit lines, countries had to follow opening-up policies and reduce government spending because markets and competition would generate the efficiencies required for longer-term development. Interestingly, the debt crisis was solved not by the market but through government intervention. Only after the United States and other European countries conditionally wrote off a substantial part of their debts through the commonly named Brady Plan (1989) did the countries recover.

The paradigm of the early 1980s was more market and less government, not only in the West but also in China, India, Russia, Brazil, and Mexico. This focus on market forces and liberalization resulted from difficult economic circumstances (China and India), political issues (Russia), and country-specific events, such as the debt crisis in Brazil and Mexico.

4.3.2 *The late 1990s*

In the late 1990s, resistance against the negative impact of markets and opposition against the neoliberal doctrine started to grow. Around the change of the millennium, this opposition remained within the margins: the timing and sequencing of reforms. The idea of having the market in the driver seat and functioning as "the invisible hand" endured more or less undisputed. This was certainly the case in western, advanced nations.

State capitalism 3.0

In NEP-9 countries, however, resistance against the effects of market forces was stronger, likely driven by a heritage of accepting a dominant role in society for government. The global financial crisis (2008–2012) has helped bolster the resistance further. During this period, I was teaching in China. Interestingly, in discussions, the Chinese always referred to it as the *western* financial crisis, not the *global* economic crisis. It was a western crisis of capitalism and free markets. This perspective gave rise to state capitalism 3.0 (Nolke, 2014) as an alternative development model for economies that are still in the process of catching-up. State capitalism 3.0 is an evolution of its predecessor and emphasizes the need for market forces and opening up to the outside world. State capitalism 3.0 combines the market and governance intervention and involves a broad set of policies.

- State-owned enterprises are essential players in strategic sectors and are tools for the government to implement and execute policies.
- Multinational enterprises have strong ties to the home country.
- Traditional industrial policy tools are used to favor specific firms or sectors, and governments are leading in building industrial clusters that can innovate and compete internationally.
- The state does not intervene in what is produced, but (entities of) the government may influence decision-making in the private sector.
- Sovereign wealth funds are essential tools for financing domestic investments and are used to establish structural reforms.
- Export is stimulated by elements of mercantilist behavior, such as local content rules, exchange rate manipulation, and taxation preferences.
- International trade and foreign investment environment are relatively open, but safeguard measures must be available. Hence, domestic or national autonomy is essential.

In the NEP-9 countries, the state-guided private enterprise was important. Still, a great deal of initiative was put in the hands of the private sector, as governments recognized the market and the private sector could create prosperity. Even in the depth of the crisis (2008–2009), there was global recognition (advanced western nations and the NEP-9) of the contribution of the market in generating prosperity. This view lines up with what former president Obama declared in 2009: "The question before us (is not) whether the market is a force for good or ill. Its power to generate wealth and expand freedom is unmatched" (inaugural address, January 21, 2009). Therefore, the NEP-9 choosing to reduce the power of the market and use specific elements of state capitalism 3.0 is not a choice against the market or in favor of government intervention. It is a choice for an optimal balance between the market and state. The label state capitalism 3.0 fits all NEP-9 countries. They embrace globalization, open trade, participate in multilateral governance structures, and liberalize markets to a large extent.

This does not mean state capitalism is good for longer-term economic development. Still, it is a helpful system to go through the transition of the middle-income cohort in certain specific periods. It also does not preclude short-term economic crises. The slowdown of growth in Brazil, Turkey, India, China, and Russia in previous years shows that state capitalism 3.0 has its limits in establishing stable development.

4.4   The Middle Class in the NEP-9

As stated earlier, the quality of labor (human capital) and capital (machines and equipment) drives longer-term development. Moreover, technical progress and stable institutions can achieve productivity growth. A sizeable middle class is associated with all these factors. The urban middle class produces increasing numbers of skilled workers who contribute to higher productivity. They invest in education for themselves and their children, and their investments in housing and assets generate demand for stable institutions that protect their rights and ownership. They demand good quality public services.

The middle class is important for short-term as well as longer-term economic development

---

Finally, the urban middle class may also drive growth because it is the source of entrepreneurs and innovative behavior. The middle class also affects the short-term fluctuations of the economy through spending (consumption) and saving, the source for required investments. The middle class becomes increasingly willing to spend money on services such as entertainment, travel, and leisure and tends to spend a relatively large share of its disposable income on imported products. The OECD report *Under Pressure: The Squeezed Middle Class* (2019) says: *A strong and prosperous middle class is crucial for any successful economy and cohesive society. The middle class sustains consumption, drives much of the investment in education, health, and housing, and it plays a key role in supporting social protection systems through its tax contributions. Societies with a strong middle class have lower crime rates, enjoy higher levels of trust and life satisfaction, as well as greater political stability and good governance.*

Considering the essential role of a dynamic middle class, it is remarkable that the NEP-9 waited relatively long before emphasizing specific middle-class measures. Explicit middle-class policies are recent in countries such as China, Brazil, India, and Indonesia, inspired by growing discontent and protest of the urban middle class. Examples are the Brazilian approach to increase real wages in the 2000s and the implementation of large-scale social programs, such as the Bolsa Família.

NEP-9 countries are late in implementing measures targeted specifically to the middle class

A comparison with advanced nations, such as the United States and Germany, shows that the NEP-9 were quite late in implementing institutional and legislative measures to initiate, sustain, and develop a dynamic middle class. Germany introduced social insurance for all workers in the late 1880s at an income per capita lower than the Indian average today (Brookings Institute). Indonesia is more prosperous now than the United States was in 1935 when it passed the Social Security Act. And China is wealthier today than Britain in 1948, the moment they launched the National Health Service. None of the NEP-9 countries has anywhere near a social safety package as well developed as today's advanced countries had at a similar stage of development. They are quickly catching-up on this front in recent years, but most social safety nets are still in the infant stage.

4.4.1 *Measuring the middle class*

Measuring the middle class is complex because there are several ways to go about it. Essentially, there is the income-based method and the sociological method. The latter focuses on education, occupation, and, more generally, social status. The former can focus on absolute income, but it may also adopt the relative approach, using the cohort located in the middle of the income distribution.

The absolute income versus the relative income approach

For example, Brazil uses the relative approach and considers a person that earns two, three, or four times the official minimum wage middle class. India defines the middle class simply as everyone except the richest and poorest, 20%. Mexico defines the middle-income class as the population living in households with incomes ranging between 75% and 200% of the national median and divides the middle-income class into three groups: lower-middle (75–100% of median), middle-middle (100–150% of median), and upper-middle (150–200% of median). This relative approach is helpful for the analysis of a single country. However, because every country has a different median income level, it makes comparing countries difficult.

This difficulty is why international comparisons use the absolute income method and are usually based on income expressed in purchasing power parity, converted into US dollars. There is no international agreement on the definition of middle class. For example, in its report on East Asia, *Riding the Wave* (2018), the World Bank defines the middle class as daily consumption expenditures per capita in purchasing power parity of more than $15. It makes sense to use this specific benchmark for one region, in this case, East Asia. The United States considers households that earn $25,000–$75,000 middle class. But undoubtedly, this benchmark is unsuitable for defining the middle class in India, Brazil, or China, which is why the World Bank uses a specific benchmark designed for the East Asian region. However, applying a single benchmark to a larger region or even a country may blur the picture. An annual income of $7000 may give you a reasonably pleasant life (and middle-income status) in a third-tier city in China, India, or Turkey. Still, it is certainly not enough to live a middle-income life in Beijing, Mumbai, or Istanbul. In most NEP-9 countries, regional differences in the middle class within the country are more significant compared to more mature economies. For example, the Russian middle class (based on income) was approximately 25% of the population in 2020. Still, in the northern oil and gas-rich autonomous district Yamal-Nenets and around the main urban centers, the middle-class population share is around 40–45%. At the same time, the percentage is much lower in the more rural areas. Brazil has the same regional differences. In the country's northeast, the middle class is much smaller than in the cities near the economic centers in the southeast.

Large regional differences within the NEP-9 countries

In previous World Bank publications, the middle class in less developed countries started at a daily income above $2 (PPP), with the two-dollar mark as the absolute poverty line. The problem with this lower benchmark is that during an economic downfall, many people will fall back into poverty, which happened during the COVID-19 pandemic. Due to lockdowns and bankruptcies, millions of people in India, Brazil, and Indonesia lost their (informal) income. The benchmark issue becomes even more problematic when we focus on the global middle class, pooling them all into one segment. Kharas (2017) used the range of $11 to $110 per day in purchasing power parity as the benchmark, which means an annual income for a four-person middle-class household above $16,060.

At the lower end, the $11 threshold makes it less likely for individuals to fall back into poverty (compared to the $2 threshold). At the same time, in this income range, consumers start to have a level of disposable income that allows them to buy luxury goods and services. Figure 4.3 is based on the Kharas research (2017), which uses the absolute income benchmark to measure the middle class in countries.

The explosion of the global middle class

Figure 4.3 illustrates the development of the global middle class and the acceleration of the middle class in NEP-9 countries. The speed at which the global middle class is expanding is dizzying. At just over 3 billion in 2015, the upper half of Figure 4.3 shows that forecasts predict it will grow up to 5.5 billion in 2030. Furthermore, the largest share, both absolute and relative, is located in Asia, which will be home to 65% of the global middle class by 2030. Translated into markets and global consumption, the growth of the middle class shows an interesting feature. In terms of PPP, 43% of the global middle-class spending happens in Asia in 2020.

Middle class Region	2015 Absolute	%	2020 Absolute	%	2030 Absolute	%
North America	335	11	344	9	354	7
Europe	724	24	736	20	733	14
Central and Latin America	285	9	303	8	335	6
Asia Pacific	1.380	46	2.023	54	3.492	65
Sub-Saharan Africa	114	4	132	4	212	4
Middle East and North Africa	192	6	228	6	285	5
World	3.030	100	3.766	100	5.412	100

Consumption Regio	2015 Absolute	%	2020 Absolute	%	2030 Absolute	%
North America	6.174	18	6.381	15	6.681	10
Europe	10.920	31	11.613	27	12.573	20
Central and Latin America	2.931	8	3.137	8	3.630	6
Asia Pacific	12.332	36	18.174	43	36.631	57
Sub-Saharan Africa	915	3	1.042	2	1.661	3
Middle East and North Africa	1.541	4	1.933	5	2.679	4
World	34.814	100	42.279	100	63.854	100

Figure 4.3:   Middle-class development (millions, share in world and spending), 2015, 2020, and 2030.

Source: Kharas (2017).

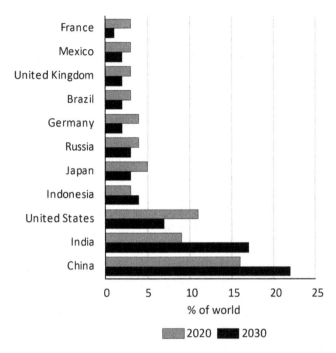

Figure 4.4:   Consumption middle class, share in world, 2020 and 2030.

Source: Kharas (2017).

Forecasts say that in 2030, this share will increase to 57%, as is visible in the lower part of Figure 4.3.

Figure 4.4 shows individual countries and their share in the global middle-class consumption. China was the largest middle-class consumer market in 2020, followed by the US. Forecasts show that by 2030, India will overtake the US and become the second largest middle-class market in the world.

The trend is clear. In 2015, the top 10 middle-class markets in the world were the G7 (except Canada), Brazil, Russia, India, and China. Indonesia will enter the top 10 around 2020, Mexico will join around 2030, and Turkey has the potential to become a middle-class market larger than the UK or France in the mid-2030s. Obviously, this may create ample opportunities for companies, but at the same time, it may put extreme pressure on our natural boundaries and social cohesion.

The earlier analysis is based on income, but we can also measure the middle class by using the sociological method, focusing on education, occupation, and social status.

A middle class life-style

This method says that middle-class people should have at least tertiary education, possibly a professional or white-collar job, own a house and a car, and enjoy a modern lifestyle and consumption patterns. The Russian-based Sberbank uses this method to discuss the Russian middle class. To represent the typical middle-class person in Russia, Sberbank developed a tool called *The Ivanov Index* (Ivanov is the Smith of Russian last names.) By way of a questionnaire, people can indicate if they consider themselves part of the middle class. This research method leads us to an area of concern when studying middle-class statistics: one should always pay attention to how things were measured. For example, based on people's perceptions (The Ivanov Index), Russia has a large middle class, between 60% and 70%. However, considering income, consumption, and a general modern lifestyle, Russia's middle class constitutes only 30–35% of the population (2020). The same holds for Turkey. While the Kharas calculations of 2017 put the middle class in Turkey at 66 million, other sources quote a middle class of less than 10 million (Banerjee & Duflo, 2008). We should also note that the sociological approach by definition excludes farmers from middle-class statistics.

4.4.2 *Middle class and democracy*

Research on the relationship between the middle class and democracy (or democratic changes) shows mixed results, so there is no clarity on the causality between the two. On the one hand, research shows that democracy (mostly a liberal democracy, combined with capitalism) brings economic development and a growing, prosperous middle class. The argument is relatively straightforward: democracy creates stable institutions and the freedom to make your own choices, both economically and politically. It also stimulates innovative and proactive behavior, and consequently, higher productivity and prosperity. And this economic development gives rise to the middle class. Empirical evidence of this causality primarily uses advanced western countries. However, the fact remains that economic development in most NEP-9 countries was not the result of liberal democracy.

No clarity on the relationship between middle class and democracy

---

There is research that turns the previous argument on its head. In short, it claims that where there is economic development and expansion of the middle class, democracy will follow. Economic growth and a rising middle class will force democratic processes to unfold because the middle class demands protection, transparency, clear rules, and stable institutions, the pillars of democracy. This different perspective prioritizes economic rights above political rights in most NEP-9 countries as part of the struggle to escape the middle-income trap. Within this paradigm of economic development (and the rise of the middle class) as a precondition for establishing a stable democracy, research focuses on pinpointing exactly where democracy enters the equation. As indicated by Dambisa Moyo (TED talk, November 2013), we may expect sustainable democracy to develop at a per capita income of $6,000 and a large and stable middle class of 40% of the population. In this context, she referred to earlier research by Przeworski and Limongi (1993, 1997).

Different ways of measuring democracy

You may already suspect that some of the conclusions above are partly the result of the different ways of measuring democracy. As we will see later on in this chapter, there is no consensus on the definition of democracy or how to measure it. The term democracy changes according to when, where, and how it is used, and as a result, there is neither consensus on the definition nor on how to measure it. As the principle of liberal democracies is to uphold the development and well-being of the individual and the system stands on a framework of legitimacy, justice, freedom, and (defined and limited) power, this seems the preferred system. However, in many cases, current democracies do not meet this definition in terms of freedom of speech and freedom to move freely. And even if the middle class achieves a specific income benchmark and demands democratic change, we cannot be entirely sure that demand was the actual catalyst for democratic change. As the middle class accumulates wealth and property, it develops a vested interest in stability and the rule of law, promoting the development of a set of democratic checks and balances on the government. Brazil and Indonesia provide examples of a middle class creating the momentum for change. This was also clearly what happened during the Arab Spring in Tunisia (2011), which resulted in the removal of President Ben Ali. However, at the same time, the middle class prefers stability and may choose to support military intervention (Egypt, 2013) or not to back democratic initiatives (China and, to a lesser extent, Russia).

Insiders and outsiders

How can we explain this passive role of the middle class? In my 2019 book on China, I distinguished between the middle class inside the Party and State establishment and the middle class outside the bureaucracy. The insiders are civil servants and people working in hospitals, education, and middle management in state-owned enterprises. The outsiders are private business owners and self-made entrepreneurs. The establishment insiders make up a considerable proportion of the Chinese middle class, and many officials have seen their living standards upgraded to the middle-class level. They are unlikely to challenge something that they depend on for a living. The outsiders are not eager to change the system either. They are all direct beneficiaries of the government's pro-market and pro-business policies and have close connections with the establishment in one way or another. The same holds for Russia. A large proportion of the Russian middle class depends on the country's vast bureaucracy. These are people working in the state-owned oil and gas sector, the enormous cohort of state officials, including education and legislation, for example, and those that do not work directly for the state but in sectors and functions whose existence depends on connections with state officials. This middle class will opt for stability and the political status quo rather than risk the uncertainties brought about by democratic reforms, which, in the case of the former Soviet Union, is a logical choice. While the demand for change rarely emerges from the middle class, from time to time, there is rising discontent toward the government, ranging from protesting against corrupt local authorities to fighting the environmental problems caused by polluting state-owned companies. But in essence, the middle class wants better governance and a legal system that protects them. Obviously, they would prefer a full Western-style democracy, but other priorities are more important and they are not in a hurry for change.

4.4.3 *Urban middle class and economic development*

When we talk about the middle class, we refer to the urban middle class. Middle-class development directly links to urbanization. As such, urbanization plays a role in economic development and escaping the middle-income trap in our NEP-9 countries. For example, in the late 1960s, Brazil showed a sharp increase in urbanization. The structural shift from rural activities to more productive urban-based industries and services was a key driver of Brazil's success. The same happened in China, where people switching from rural agriculture to urban manufacturing contributed to economic development. The influx of farmers offering low-skilled labor to lower value-added manufacturing activities led to significant efficiency gains. An industrial worker is much more productive in a modern factory than in traditional agriculture. In this way, urbanization helps achieve economic growth but is not enough in itself. For example, the steep rise in per capita incomes in China happened at a low level of urbanization, about half that of the United States. And the Brazilian case in the 1980s and after 2015 clarifies that advanced and growing urbanization alone is not nearly enough to sustain economic growth.

Urbanization plays an important role in economic development

Urbanization relates to economic growth in four ways, which in many cases align with the development process of the countries.

1. The transfer of people from rural agriculture to manufacturing in the cities contributes to economic development through increased efficiency. Industrial workers in modern factories are much more productive than those working in traditional agriculture.
2. After a certain point, urbanization itself contributes to growth because new urban workers need housing, infrastructure, schools, and hospitals. Building urban infrastructures creates new

employment opportunities and increases demand for basic materials and public services.

3. The explosion of the middle class and the urban lifestyle generates growth in private consumption. Part of this consumption impulse translates into higher productivity. E-commerce, for example, can only grow in an urban setting.

4. Urban density facilitates frequent face-to-face contact among employees, entrepreneurs, suppliers, and financiers. Contact in turn promotes innovation and productivity. Proximity also stimulates the growth of other specialized services, such as legal, software, data processing, advertising, and management consulting firms. The results are commonly named agglomeration effects: concentrated urban settings that create (high-skilled) jobs and stimulate innovation.

Figure 4.5 shows the percentage of the total population living in urban areas in the NEP-9 and several other countries between 1970 and 2020. In 2020, the degree of urbanization in countries like Brazil, Mexico, and South Africa was considerably higher than in China. As stated many times, China is full of contradictions, which is also true for their urbanization process. On the one hand, the country boasts several megacities and more than 100 cities with one million people or more. At the same time, looking at these statistics, one may conclude that urbanization in China has only just started and that, compared to other countries, one may even argue that China is underurbanized.

Between 1990 and 2020, countries such as Indonesia, India, and China have also shown relatively fast urbanization. For all these countries, the annual growth in urbanization in the previous 30 years lies between 2.2% and 3.8%. These are nationwide averages, and as such, they obscure regional differences. For example, the regions around Delhi and Goa in India are greatly urbanized, while the urbanization ratio in areas such as Odisha, Assam, and Bihar is below 20%.

Figure 4.6 also shows the rate of urbanization but now projected up to 2050. The tendency is clear: we see a continuation of urbanization in the world.

Despite the positive impact on growth and specific human indicators, discomfort with the urbanization process is growing. During the Shanghai Expo in 2010, I moderated a workshop in the Dutch pavilion. The theme that year was *Better city — Better life*. Unsurprisingly, the audience mentioned urban problems such as a growing income

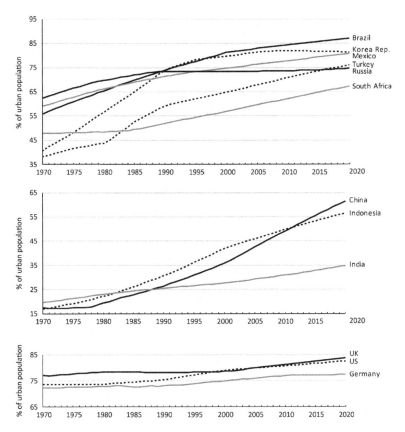

Figure 4.5:   Development of urbanization, 1970–2020.

Source: World Bank (2021).

gap, visible poverty, informal sector employment, and sustainability problems. Many of these urban problems are perceived as failures of urbanization, although they often emerge in the wake of economic success.

Growing discomfort about the urbanization process

Consider the notorious favelas in Brazil, which sprung up around the urban centers. The Rio de Janeiro favelas are home to approximately two million inhabitants, while Brazil and Rio experience increased economic

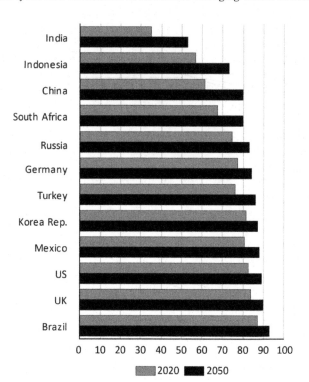

Figure 4.6:   Forecasted rate of urbanization in 2050.

Source: Ourworldindata.org (2021), based on UN forecasts.

success. In a sense, people move to cities well before the institutions that accommodate an orderly urbanization process emerge. Urban problems sometimes necessitate unconventional steps. In the footsteps of Nigeria's decision to replace Lagos with the new capital city Abuja and Brazil replacing their capital Rio de Janeiro with Brasilia (the early 1960s), the Indonesian government plans to change their capital Jakarta (Java), to a new city on Borneo. In 2021, the Egyptian government has decided to do the same with their capital city. The aims are always the same: reducing the urban problems such as pollution and congestion, together with spreading economic activities to backward regions to fight regional income inequality.

Research into the happiness of city folk compared to people in rural areas gives mixed results. On average, the happiness score is slightly higher in cities than in rural areas, but walking through some of Rio's favelas, I found this difficult to believe. Not only because of the living conditions but also because happiness is deeply related to social cohesion, trust, helping each other, and strong social networks, which traditionally is more prevalent in rural areas. A colleague at the University of Rio explained the relatively low happiness scores of rural Brazil in the context of regional monocultures: "Every villager is hurt in the same way, and when income disappears, it's difficult for people to help each other. This will certainly create discomfort and may reduce happiness." So, the general feeling of higher happiness in small, rural regions is not always the case.

NEP-9: official urbanization plans

Several of the NEP-9 have official urbanization plans. In their newest plans (2020), China and India prioritize the development of townships and smaller cities in rural areas, away from megacities, and emphasize the need for satellite cities adjacent to major cities. In addition, through legislation, governments try to allocate new migrants to these smaller cities and generate a planned urbanization process. The same holds for Brazil. In the latest urbanization plan, it uses government subsidies to allocate the migrants optimally. Whether or not they have a formal urbanization plan, the NEP-9 acknowledge that urban conglomerates are essential for long-term economic development because cities are the basis of industrial clusters and agglomeration effects.

4.4.4 *Agglomeration effects*

Agglomeration effects are the benefits that companies generate by locating near each other (NBER, 2007). These effects, such as easier knowledge spillover and innovative behavior, can occur in smaller cities, but they generally require cities of a certain size. The framework often used to discuss agglomeration effects in a concentrated geographical area is the Diamond Model, developed by Michael Porter and used in his book *The Competitive Advantage of Nations* (1989). The four points of the diamond represent the

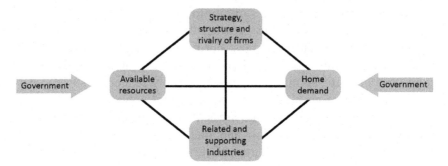

Figure 4.7:   The diamond framework.

Source: Porter (1989).

four interrelated determinants that create competitiveness in domestic and international markets. Figure 4.7 shows these four factors: (1) company strategy, structure, and rivalry, (2) related supporting industries, (3) demand conditions, and (4) factor conditions or available resources. In the following, we will apply this model to special economic zones, and in Chapter 6, we will use the Diamond Model again to explain international trade.

The factor "Firm strategy, structure, and rivalry" summarizes that the intensity of competition forces businesses to increase efficiency and innovative behavior. "Related supporting industries" refers to upstream and downstream industries that facilitate innovation through cooperation and exchanging ideas. It means that vertical collaboration, e.g., between supplier and buyer, may increase efficiency and innovation, and lower production costs. "Demand conditions" points to the size and nature of the market. Of course, every product or service needs customers willing and able to buy them. In his book, Porter emphasized the home market, but today, markets are increasingly global. Some companies go worldwide immediately: the commonly named "born globals," which means their market can be anywhere. The final determinant to achieve innovative behavior and competitiveness is the "Factor conditions" (also: available resources). These are the elements that Porter believes a country's economy can create for itself, such as a large pool of skilled labor, infrastructure, and physical capital goods. Porter argues that these factor conditions, which can be created, are more important in determining a country's comparative advantage than naturally inherited factors, such as land and natural resources.

As indicated in Figure 4.7, governments have a vital role in creating a highly innovative and sustainable cluster. Through direct or indirect measures, government can stimulate all four factors.

The role of the government in creating competitive clusters

For example, specific regulations can promote competition between companies, and subsidies may boost demand for green and environmentally friendly products.

4.4.5   *Special economic zones*

To generate these agglomeration effects, NEP-9 countries are actively developing industrial clusters inside commonly named special economic zones (SEZs). The World Bank broadly defines SEZs as *demarcated geographic areas contained within a country's national boundaries where the rules of business are different from those that prevail in the national territory.* Known under different names, like maquiladoras, free-trade zones, export processing zones, high-tech zones, or industrial zones, they are characterized by more liberal custom procedures, lower administrative costs and taxation, and a more pro-business regulatory environment, including labor legislation.

Although we associate SEZs with emerging markets, up until 1970, free zones were located primarily in industrialized countries, such as Ireland, Denmark, and Germany. The first free zones in emerging markets appeared in the 1980s. The high-profile SEZs created in China during the 1980s (e.g., Shenzhen) became economically successful in attracting foreign investments, stimulating export, and generating jobs, which inspired other NEP-9 countries. However, success is not guaranteed. Investments did not always arrive in the expected amounts, positive spillover effects to the local communities were absent, and the jobs generated by foreign investments were mostly low-skilled jobs at low wages. Furthermore, in many cases, local industries could not link their production with foreign companies, and learning effects were absent. In this context, SEZs are enclaves that, in many aspects, promote a race to the bottom, including taxation and labor regulations, to name a few.

The appetite for developing SEZs differs from country to country. South Korea is very active in building new zones and further developing the existing ones. At the same time, India and Brazil are cautious in implementing legislation to stimulate new SEZs.

Pros and cons of Special Economic Zones

South Korea has a strong sectoral concentration; the various SEZs house specific industries. For example, the city of Gwangju must become an SEZ that focuses on electric car manufacturing and artificial intelligence, and the area around Incheon international airport is dedicated to drone manufacturing. This sectoral concentration is also visible in Indonesia. The Indonesian government designated 30 regions up to 2025, focusing on sectors such as electronics, high-tech industries, and shipbuilding. The current Indonesian SEZs are relatively successful regarding employment and technology transfer because of their proximity to Singapore. The companies in these SEZs benefit from low wages, tax preferences, and liberal regulatory procedures, combined with the efficient logistical hub of Singapore. Although Brazil is not actively developing SEZs, it has some successful examples, primarily related to export. Companies in the zones receive tax benefits if 50% of a firm's gross income comes from export. Turkey is implementing similar legislation to build its export processing zones. Besides its 20+ export processing zones, Turkey has around 100 commonly named technology development zones designed to support R&D activities and attract foreign investments in high-technology sectors.

Among the most famous SEZs are the Mexican maquiladoras, developed in the mid-1960s. Maquiladoras are manufacturing plants in Mexico whose parent company's administration facility is located in the United States. Companies operating in the United States can send equipment, supplies, machinery, raw materials, and other assets to their plants in Mexico for assembly or processing without paying import duties. The finished product is exported back to the United States or a third country. To achieve positive spillover and build up human capital, companies receive a 25% deduction for training expenses for employees in the SEZ. This focus on training is an essential feature of Mexican policy and aims to avoid the SEZs creating low-skilled and low-wage jobs only. Similar to the situation in Indonesia, the most successful Mexican SEZs are located in the north, relatively close to the US border. The success of these SEZs is creating growing inequality between the north and south of Mexico. While the north has attracted considerable amounts of foreign direct investment, developed important industrial hubs, and GDP per capita has increased, economic development in the south is lagging far behind. Consequently, the south has the highest poverty levels, so today, the Mexican policy regarding SEZs is to develop them in the south.

South Africa also uses SEZs to stimulate local development, attract foreign investments, and achieve industrial upgrading. As said, India is not very active in developing SEZs, which may be explained by past experiences and issues regarding land ownership. Additionally, current SEZs are not very successful. The combination of incorrect regulations within the zones, poor infrastructure connections with the rest of the domestic economy, and the absence of forward and backward links to local firms prohibit realizing the potential positive effects. An Indian-specific explanation for the slow development of SEZs is the scarcity of land and protests from local people, asking why land should be allocated to private businesses and taken away from farmers and public purposes. Today, there are growing discussions on the use of SEZs. But, according to one of my Indian colleagues at SP Jain School of Global Management, in the coming years, we will see an acceleration in the development of Indian SEZs to help revive the manufacturing sector. Russia has numerous SEZs and continues to look at investing in more, especially near their far eastern borders with China. Like Indonesia and South Korea, Russia's SEZs have a strong sectoral focus, clustering around logistics, forestry, electronics, and automotive. And like India, Russian SEZs today are unsuccessful in attracting (Chinese) investors and generating positive spillover effects for domestic companies and consumers.

Innovative clusters, agglomeration effects, and SEZs, in general, located near urban clusters, are important drivers behind the rebalancing process. One key objective of these SEZs is industrial upgrading by moving upstream or downstream on the smiling curve (Chapter 2), away from primary commodities, and switching to higher value-added activities.

4.5 Commodity Dependence

When over 60% of the value of a country's merchandise exports is commodities, that country is considered commodity-dependent (UNCTAD). In this context, commodities are energy products (crude oil, coal, and natural gas), raw materials, such as metals (aluminum, copper, rubber, and zinc), and agricultural products (rice, wheat, maize, and soybeans). This minimum threshold for the definition of commodity export dependence is the result of studies that show that almost all countries exceeding 60% achieve only modest or no improvement in human indicators over a longer period. About half of the countries worldwide, mainly developing countries and emerging markets, were commodity dependent in 2021. For 30 of the 48 African nations, a single commodity accounts for over 40% of their exports (UNCTAD, 2021). This commodity dependency is even more problematic if combined with only one or two large export markets because in that case, an economic crisis abroad or geopolitical tensions can dramatically affect commodities' exports.

Dependency on commodity export and import

A country can also be dependent on commodity imports. Commodity import dependence occurs if the share of energy, raw materials, and agricultural products in total imports exceeds 30%. As with export dependency, import dependency is more problematic if it goes hand in hand with a heavy concentration of imports from a small number of countries. Commodity import dependency may also create problems. Price hikes of essential imports can affect the current account (Chapter 6) and fuel inflation to the extent that it hurts sustainable development. For example, in the

Country	Commodity export as % of total merchandise export 2008-2009	2018-2019	Commodity export as % of GDP (2019)	Main commodities*	Commodity import as % of merchandise import 2008-2009	2018-2019
Russia	74.8	67.8	17.7	E	18.5	16.4
Indonesia	60.8	55.6	8.9	A, E	33.3	31.9
Brazil	56.5	66.6	8.4	A, R	27.3	24.1
South Africa	53.3	57.3	14.6	R	32.2	29.6
India	41.7	37.4	4.1	A, R	53.8	53.6
Mexico	25.8	15.9	5.9	A	19.6	17.3
Turkey	21.1	19.9	4.5	A	24.0	29.7
South Korea	12.4	12.5	4.2	R	44.8	40.6
China	6.7	6.6	1.2	R	34.0	40.4
Australia	80.5	71.0	12.9	E, R	26.2	24.2
United Kingdom	24.6	26.1	4.4	E	26.4	30.1
United States	22.6	27.2	2.1	A, E	30.2	19.2
Germany	11.8	11.1	4.4	R	26.7	21.9
Japan	6.6	7.0	1.0	R	50.8	40.4

(*) A: Agriculture, E: Energy, R: Raw materials

Figure 4.8:   Commodity dependency.

Source: UNCTAD (2020).

decade before the global financial crisis of 2008, the prices of many commodities skyrocketed. Between 2000 and 2008, energy prices increased by 150%, metals by 110%, and agricultural products by 60%. In this period, NEP-9 countries accounted for 92% of the increase in metal consumption and 67% of the rise in global energy consumption. As a consequence, these countries faced dramatically higher import bills. The same happened after the Covid-19 crisis. In 2021, we saw rising energy and commodity prices and the forecast is that this price increase may continue for the next years. The export dependence and import dependence of the NEP-9 countries and several other selected countries are shown in Figure 4.8. From these data, we can draw several conclusions.

The NEP-9 are a heterogeneous group when it comes to commodity dependency. The export of countries such as Russia and Brazil are heavily dependent on commodities, while for China and South Korea, commodities are not important export products. From the import side, India, South Korea, and China are important commodity buyers and, therefore, are sensitive to unexpected price hikes for energy and raw materials. From Figure 4.8, it also looks that Brazil became more commodity dependent in the previous years.

4.5.1 *The interpretation issue*

Interpreting the development of commodity dependency should be done carefully: things are not always as they seem. For example, price movements of commodities can distort the picture. Looking at Russia's percentage share in crude oil and gas in total merchandise export, we could conclude that between 2016 and 2021, Russia became more commodity dependent. However, in early 2016, the oil price was around $30 per barrel, while in October 2021, it reached $75. The gas price shows a similar development: it stood at $2 per million BTU in early 2016 and rose to $5 in 2021. Obviously, these price hikes increased the value of oil and gas export and, therefore, commodity dependency. However, this increased dependency is solely due to the price effect. Therefore, the best approach is to analyze commodity dependency at similar points in the (oil or gas) price cycle.

Besides price volatility, there is another interpretation issue regarding commodity dependency. An increase in commodity dependency does not indicate that the growth of other export products is flat. In Brazil, commodities increased from 44% of total exports in 1998–2002 to 62% in 2013–2017. However, non-commodity exports grew by 160%, but this could not compensate for the even more significant increase in agricultural exports, growing by 300%.

4.5.2 *The commodity trap*

You would think that an abundance of resources helps economic development and increases human indicators. Governments can translate wealth in the shape of natural resources, such as oil and minerals, into infrastructure, good quality education, and a stable social safety net, as done by resource-abundant countries, such as Australia, Canada, New Zealand, and the US. When looking at GDP alone, this is also visible in countries like Qatar and the United Arab Emirates. The general view, however, is that commodity dependency is often harmful to economic development. In many cases, resource-rich countries are less successful than their resource-poor counterparts. There are some reasons for this adverse effect of commodity abundance on economic growth. In this context, we may refer to *the Resource Curse, the Commodity Trap,* or *the Dutch Disease.*

After the Netherlands discovered massive natural gas deposits in the North Sea in 1959, longer-term economic growth declined after the discovery. Successful development of a specific commodity sector (natural gas) resulted in a decline in other industrial sectors. For example, massive gas exports caused the Dutch guilder to rise sharply, making exports of all non-oil products less competitive internationally. Furthermore, this booming sector attracted labor, resulting in higher wages. These higher wages spilled over to other industries and were complemented by rising inflation. A third disadvantage was that the booming gas (and chemical) sector attracted investments, pulling them away from other sectors. The Dutch experience shows that natural resource exports may come at the expense of the manufacturing sector, which generates most of the productivity gains and creates the most employment. Essentially, it means that over an extended period, resource abundance may undermine rather than foster economic development.

Resource abundance may undermine rather than foster economic development

---

Besides the negative effect on other industries, as shown by the case of *the Dutch Disease* above, the terms of trade of countries exporting primary commodities tend to deteriorate in the long run due to the decline of commodity prices relative to the price of manufactured goods. Therefore, building a country's growth strategy on commodities alone is not a viable basis for long-term development strategy, the commonly named Prebisch–Singer hypothesis (1950).

4.5.3 *Speculation*

A final problem of commodity dependency is that in the short term, commodity prices are incredibly volatile. This volatility generates uncertainty and creates a barrier to stable, sustainable government policies. Short-term commodity price volatility is caused by changes in supply and demand and is driven by business cycles, weather conditions, or political instability. These general causes apply to most markets, but one aspect adds to the extreme volatility of commodity prices: price speculation. Investors, funds, and traders that use commodity derivatives (e.g., futures and options) as part of their investment strategy can influence prices dramatically.

Destabilizing speculation

Due to their behavior, commodity markets are fundamentally unstable, creating upwards and downwards overshooting of prices. Figure 4.9 shows the impact of speculation on oil price development. The premise of the left-hand side drawing is a fall in oil demand and a subsequent fall in prices, as was the case during the 2020 COVID-19 crisis. The downward sloping D1 and upward sloping S1 represent initial supply and demand. Energy and metal commodities were affected the most by the sudden stop of economic activities. This resulted in a leftward shift of the demand curve for oil to the lower demand D2 with price P2. Now traders and speculators entered the equation. In the first half of 2020, they believed that the global slowdown would intensify. They anticipated a further price decline, exacerbated by uncertainty around production agreements among the Organization of the Petroleum Exporting Countries (OPEC) and between other oil producers. This expectation led speculating traders and investors to reduce demand further to D3 (waiting for a lower price). On the other hand, speculators want to sell as much as possible (why wait for the expected lower price), shifting the supply to the right (S2). This behavior resulted in extreme downward overshooting of the

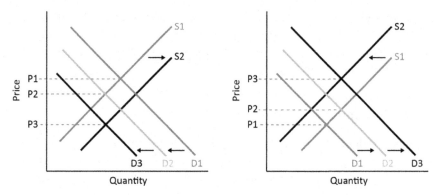

Figure 4.9:   Overshooting of prices.

market toward price level (P3), now much lower than at the initial fall in demand (P2).

In 2021, we witnessed an upward overshooting of the oil market, driven by speculators. Growing economies required oil, and consequently, demand went up. This development is shown on the right-hand side of Figure 4.9 with a demand curve shift to the right (D2), resulting in a rising price level P2. Again, we saw traders and speculators entering the market. Based on the expectation that prices would continue to rise, they reacted with more demand (why wait for a higher price) and less supply (waiting for higher prices). Hence, demand increased (D3), while supply was reduced to S2 because they waited for better prices. The consequence is, once again, overshooting of the price, in this case, upwards to P3.

Between January and May 2020, average crude oil prices plunged 60%, and in 2020, it was only $36 per barrel ($61 in 2019). Specific metal prices also fell in early 2020. The most significant declines were in copper and zinc, which are particularly associated with global economic activity. Also, in these markets, speculation resulted in overshooting, in particular after COVID-19 took off, in early 2020. Upward overshooting happened in 2021 with a price explosion up to 400% for some commodities (Figure 4.10).

It is important to note that the above focus on speculation has significant real-world repercussions. It is disheartening to know that speculation on the price volatility of commodities is enriching traders and speculators, while at the same time, it has such dramatic effects on sustainable development in commodity-dependent countries, mainly in Africa.

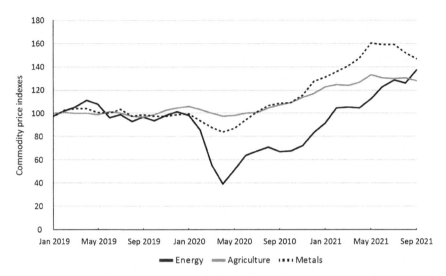

Figure 4.10:   Price volatility commodities.

Source: FXTrading.com (2021).

4.5.4 *Measuring the diversity of exports*

Up to this point, we discussed the NEP-9's dependence on a narrow range of products within their exports. Now, we will extend the analysis to see how diverse their exports are. The range of goods shows the NEP-9 are quite mature exporters. Our data on international trade (here and in Chapter 6) use the commonly named *Harmonized System* (HS), a classification standard of about 5000 different products, to categorize exports and imports. The data show that the United States, the European Union, and China export most of the 5000 items listed in the HS classification. Exports of the other NEP-9 are also highly diversified, and most of these countries have an export structure similar to traditional industrialized economies.

NEP-9: growing export diversity

Over the past two decades, NEP-9 countries have expanded their export diversity. In the early 2000s, China's export diversification increased enormously, and it joined the European Union and the United States as the most diversified exporters. India and Turkey also experienced a rapid expansion in export diversity. In contrast, the export structure of Indonesia shows only a marginal development in the number of exporting products, and Brazil shows none at all. Besides the number of products, we can also measure and analyze export diversification using the *Herfindahl–Hirschman Index* (HHI). The index measures the regional concentration of the destination of exported products and the concentration of exports in specific products. With respect to product concentration, this ratio sums up the squared shares of each commodity in total domestic exports. The index is expressed as follows:

$$\text{HHI} = \sum i = 1 N (xiX)^2$$

- x_i is the nominal domestic export value of commodity i,
- X is the country's total nominal domestic exports,
- N is the total number of export products.

The index ranges from zero (perfect diversification) to one (complete concentration of exports into a single product or to a single country of destination). To differentiate, we will use the following thresholds:

- Diversified (or unconcentrated) exports or markets: HHI < 0.15
- Moderately concentrated exports or markets: $0.15 \leq$ HHI < 0.25
- Highly concentrated exports or markets: HHI $\geq$ 0.25

Figure 4.11 shows that only Russia has a highly concentrated export portfolio driven by mineral fuels and chemicals. The other NEP-9 have a diversified export structure. Development in the past 25 years shows only marginal changes. Note that the indicated concentration ratio measures diversification, not commodity dependency. For example, South Korea may have a relatively high export concentration compared to other developed countries, but unlike developing countries, Korea's exports are concentrated in manufacturing and high-tech, not in commodities.

The concentration ratio in Figure 4.11 concerns the composition of exports (portfolio of products), not market concentration. In some cases, we see significant differences between the two types of concentration ratios. For example, Mexico is heavily concentrated in market concentration and much less in its portfolio. Mexico largely depends on the US market: Almost 80% of Mexican exports go to the US (2021). Both Brazil

Country	1995	2010	2020
Russia	0.26	0.37	0.32
India	0.14	0.13	0.12
South Korea	0.13	0.15	0.17
Indonesia	0.13	0.16	0.13
Mexico	0.12	0.15	0.15
South Africa	0.11	0.14	0.14
Turkey	0.11	0.07	0.17
Brazil	0.09	0.15	0.16
China	0.07	0.11	0.09

Figure 4.11:   HHI for product portfolio NEP-9.

Source: World Bank (2021).

and South Korea are relatively dependent on the Chinese market, but they have a highly diversified export structure. In contrast, Russia has a highly concentrated product portfolio, while its market concentration is low.

Concentration of export products and of export markets

Structural increase of commodity dependency and development based on resource exports only should be avoided. Therefore, diversification of the manufacturing and export sector is an explicit economic objective for all NEP-9. Obviously, this diversification should focus on more value-added activities, as illustrated in Chapter 2 with the smiling curve analysis. The problem, however, is that in many cases, the market alone cannot achieve this. Active government intervention is required.

4.6 Diversification Choices and the Use of Import Substitution Industrialization

By now, we have concluded that diversification away from commodities toward higher value-added activities is required for further economic development. One strategy to achieve this is to diversify *horizontally*: increase the export of related but different types of products. Russia exports natural gas, and consequently, diversifying to more chemical products is relatively straightforward, and targeted government policy and institutional changes are not required. Another strategy is to diversify *vertically:* creating more value domestically and increasing the complexity of the exported products, moving upstream and downstream of the value chain. For example, Chinese companies could choose to get more active in supplying high-tech components to car manufacturers instead of solely focusing on car assembly in China or companies could switch to the export of machines instead of textiles. Brazil combines these two main strategies. For example, the pineapple industry is expanding with apples, grapes, and oranges, and at the same time, we see a developing wine sector and food processing industry.

Horizontal and vertical diversification

The NEP-9 countries have already gone through the horizontal diversification process, what I refer to as the easy diversification strategy, in line with the easy increase of productivity in the mobilization phase of take-off (as explained in Chapter 3). Vertical diversification is about increasing the complexity of the products exported. This strategy is not so easy. Higher value-added production concerns non-resource industries and must be accompanied by institutional and educational changes. This strategy relates to the efficiency phase needed to escape the middle-income trap (Chapter 3).

There is a distinct order of events in the diversification process, starting with horizontal diversification. This step is achieved by connecting to global supply chains, primarily through relatively cheap labor and natural resources. The next step in the process is vertical diversification, and this is the situation in the NEP-9 countries today. South Africa recently adopted measures to move up the diamond value chain by establishing a diamond cutting and polishing industry. Mexico is starting a high-tech manufacturing sector in the south, and Indonesia is trying to move away from unprocessed nickel and bauxite by building smelting plants, thereby increasing its share of the value added to its mineral resources.

4.6.1 *Import substitution industrialization 1.0 and 2.0*

The NEP-9 transformed their economies and export structure by several means. One of these is import substitution industrialization (ISI), replacing foreign imports with locally produced products. As this strategy relates to trade policies, such as increasing tariffs or tax benefits for domestic companies, we will return to ISI in Chapter 6, which dives deeper into trade flows. This paragraph discusses the ISI as it relates to the structural transformation of domestic economies and trade composition.

NEP-9: moving from ISI 1.0 to ISI 2.0

Traditional import substitution industrialization (ISI 1.0) was a remedy for rising poverty levels in the 1950s and 1960s, partly a result of high commodity dependency. The NEP-9 countries chose the import substitution policy for industrial development early in their development process. The focus of ISI 1.0 was on developing the industrial sector, placed behind a high wall of policies to protect them from international competition, and transforming it toward manufactured products instead of raw materials and commodities.

Despite reasonably favorable economic growth results throughout the 1950s and 1960s, the perception of ISI 1.0 turned negative in the 1970s. It was associated with non-efficient and less-innovative companies that, due to government shielding, produced low-quality products at relatively high prices for the consumer. It was also associated with rising inflation and the inability to compete internationally, even after decades of government support. The closed nature of domestic markets created monopolies and reduced competition. ISI 1.0 (as was state capitalism 1.0) appeared outdated and unable to achieve sustainable longer-term prosperity. As a result, the 1980s witnessed a fundamental shift in economic policy, away from import substitution industrialization and toward market forces and trade liberalization. For example, in the late 1970s, Turkey's ISI 1.0 ended in a deep crisis, resulting in the launch of a radical change to the economic program in January 1980. Policies to foster market forces were also implemented in Brazil, Mexico, Indonesia, China, India, and South Korea.

Although import substitution industrialization is generally regarded as bad policy, one might argue that for emerging markets, including NEP-9 countries, the basic features of ISI can jumpstart the required economic transformation. This argument is the starting position for modern import substitution industrialization: ISI 2.0 (IMF, 2019).

ISI 2.0 does not completely abandon the ISI framework but emphasizes opening up and export and is connected to vertical diversification and state capitalism 2.0. South Korea is one of the pioneers of ISI 2.0. Its policies, implemented in the early 1970s, combined export promotion and specific import policies. The temporary shielding of strategic domestic industries from intense competition allowed them to develop and become efficient enough to compete effectively with more mature and efficient foreign industries. After achieving high levels of development and coming under increased pressure from its trading partners, South Korea adopted a more market-oriented policy and reduced protectionism.

We see the same in Indonesia and China, as well as western countries in the early stages of their industrialization. Russia and South Africa also adopted modern ISI 2.0. South Africa, promoted exports as an add-on to the traditional ISI 1.0, and trade liberalization started in the early 1990s. The Russian case clarifies that ISI is not always the result of a clear strategic government plan but may start and develop accidentally. Russia stumbled into ISI 2.0 after the 1998 crisis caused by the devaluation of the national currency, which led to higher prices of imported goods in the domestic market, and consumer demand shifted to domestic production. In reaction to this development, the Russian government started to execute a potent ISI policy mix that targeted specific sectors.

Preconditions for a successful ISI 2.0

A problem with executing successful ISI 2.0 policies is that the focus shifts toward vertical diversification, sectors that are in a sense removed from current comparative advantages and which have weak links to the rest of the domestic economy. As a result, trickle-down effects in terms of socio-economic development can be limited. Also, there is political pressure against protecting large and strategically important domestic companies for too long. Industries that fail to become competitive should not be protected indefinitely. Successful protectionism within ISI 2.0 is possible under the following conditions:

- Protection is limited to a specific time frame.
- Sizeable domestic (or regional) markets are essential. A small domestic market is a barrier to achieving required economies of scale; therefore, countries need to export.
- The ability to identify sectors that can compete internationally. The selected industries should be close to comparative advantages. Industries and sectors must be selected in the correct order.
- Regular assessments to determine if the sector or the specific companies are increasing their competitive advantage.

4.7 Differences and Commonalities Regarding Corruption, Economic Freedom, and Democracy

This paragraph divides the national governance system into three inter-related factors: corruption, economic freedom (separate from political freedom), and democracy. As we saw earlier in the book, good governance is essential for sustained economic development. Corruption weakens institutions and may negatively affect investments, essential for longer-term growth. Research shows that economic freedom positively impacts human development indicators and poverty elimination. And democracy may stimulate creativity and innovative behavior, all vital ingredients for longer-term development.

4.7.1 *Corruption*

Based on empirical evidence, the consensus is that on many fronts, corruption is bad for longer-term social and economic development. First, it lowers domestic and foreign investments because investors are reluctant to pour money into an environment where legal decisions are for sale. Second, corruption is a disincentive for innovation. Specific companies achieve monopolistic power through government help, resulting in high prices for low quality and no need to innovate, as there is no competition. Third, corruption is also associated with excessive expenditures on non-productive projects and low spending on social welfare, leading to low quality of infrastructure and public services. Fourth, corruption may cause a misallocation of human talent. This final point is somewhat ambiguous. One could argue that the talented students in my Chinese, Indian, and Brazilian classrooms are wasting their skills by working for inefficient governments. However, you may also take a different perspective: the best students choosing a career in government are a deliberate step toward more efficient and more credible governments, which we see in South Korea.

Corruption is an obstacle to achieve longer-term economic development

Interestingly, despite the consensus view that corruption is detrimental to longer-term economic development, there are situations in which the opposite is true. For example, corruption may counteract government failure caused by bureaucratic rules and regulations. Another case in which corruption is sort of helpful is when a government requires the assistance of vested interests to push through structural reforms. In this case, the government may limit the fight against corruption because otherwise, these vested interests will stop the necessary restructuring.

Corruption occurs in the public domain (government) and the private domain (individuals and companies). A well-known attempt to measure public corruption is the *Corruption Perception Index*, undertaken by Transparency International. It measures the level of corruption in the public sector, as perceived by experts and business executives. It is the combined outcome of surveys and assessments collected by institutions, such as the World Bank and Bertelsmann Stiftung, based on quantitative data and qualitative expert assessments. Many indicators (e.g., bribery, red tape, excessive bureaucratic burden, and nepotistic appointments) to measure elements of corruption are translated into one value that runs from zero (highly corrupt) to 100 (very clean).

Since its inception, countries like Denmark, New Zealand, Finland, Sweden, Norway, Singapore, and Canada have topped the list as the least corrupt countries. Figure 4.12 shows that progress in tackling corruption appears quite tricky. Countries like Brazil, Mexico, and Turkey have dropped in the ranking between 2010 and 2020, and the other NEP-9 countries have made only a little progress.

NEP-9: implementing effective measures to fight corruption appears to be difficult

---

Within the NEP-9 group, only South Korea is perceived as relatively free of corruption. It is a sad observation that the 2020 report started with the following statement: "This year's Corruption Perceptions Index (CPI) paints a grim picture of the state of corruption worldwide. While most countries have made little to no progress in tackling corruption in nearly a decade, more than two-thirds of countries score below 50. Our analysis shows corruption not only undermines the global health response to COVID-19 but contributes to a continuing crisis of democracy" (p. 4). Obviously, corruption is resilient, and reducing corruption appears to be difficult. Even incremental improvements are difficult to sustain because no single blueprint is available, and achieving results may only be possible if measures are being backed by the political system.

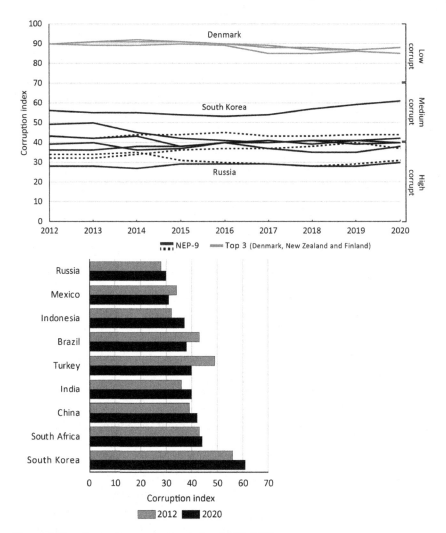

Figure 4.12: Corruption perception index, 2012–2020.

Source: Transparency International (2021).

4.7.2 *Economic freedom*

Economic freedom means removing unnecessary regulations and laws that restrict individual choices. In an economically free society, individuals are free to work, produce, consume, and invest in any way they please, within the boundaries set by governments to protect and maintain individual freedom itself, of course. In this sense, it is about the empowerment of the individual and separate from political freedom. As stated before, the consensus view is that economic freedom generates prosperity because it promotes risk-taking, innovation, entrepreneurship, and a government that makes healthy competition possible. *The Index of Economic Freedom Report 2021* states that "People in economically free societies live longer and enjoy healthier lives. They have access to higher quality "social goods" such as education, health care, and a cleaner environment" (p. 1).

Economic freedom versus political freedom

The most common measurement of economic freedom is the commonly named *Index of Economic Freedom*, published by the Heritage Foundation. It uses 12 quantitative and qualitative factors, all equally important, grouped into four broad categories:

1. Rule of Law (property rights, government integrity, and judicial effectiveness).
2. Government size (government spending, tax burden, and fiscal health).
3. Regulatory efficiency (business freedom, labor freedom, and monetary freedom).
4. Open markets (trade freedom, investment freedom, and financial freedom).

Each of the 12 economic freedoms is graded on a scale of 0 (repressed) to 100 (totally free). The index distinguishes five types of countries, also ranging from "Free" to "Repressed." Figure 4.13 shows that the index labels four NEP-9 countries as "Mostly unfree," Indonesia, Mexico, Turkey, and Russia as "Moderately free," and only South Korea as "Mostly free." In general, the NEP-9 countries show little progress in economic freedom. In fact, in the previous decade, scores and consequently the rankings for India, South Africa, and Brazil dropped.

4.7.3 *Democracy*

As discussed earlier in this chapter, there is no consensus on the definition of democracy, and as a result, measuring democracy is complex.

Figure 4.13: The index of economic freedom.

Source: Heritage Foundation (2021).

Although definitions vary, in most cases we can argue that democracies require a sort of minimum set of fundamental features. Citizen involvement, basic human rights, equality under the law, and government accountability are examples of these minimum conditions for a democratic country. These aspects of democracy are also visible in the two most common attempts to measure democracy: the *Global Freedom Index* by Freedom House and the *Democracy Index* by the Economist Intelligence Unit.

4.7.4 Global Freedom Index

According to Freedom House, the central dimension of democracy is freedom. Political freedom means an electoral process and the ability to participate in the political arena. Freedom is also related to civil liberties: the freedom of expression and belief, freedom to organize, and individual rights. Therefore, the Freedom House organization measures democracy through these two constructs: political rights (based on 10 indicators) and civil liberties (based on 15 indicators). The results translate into a ranking (1–7) that measures the level of democracy, with 1 representing the freest countries and 7 the least free.

Global decline in liberal democracies between 2005 and 2021

Of the 195 countries assessed in the 2021 report, 82 (42%) were rated "Free," 59 (30%) as "Partly Free," and 54 (28%) as "Not Free." The title of the 2021 report is *Democracy under Siege,* and the main message is that democracy and pluralism are under attack. The report shows a decline in global democracy in the past 15 years. After 2005, we see that every year up to 2020, more countries reduced democracy than countries that increased in democracy. The following quote taken from the report speaks of the frustration with this development: "The enemies of freedom have pushed the false narrative that democracy is in decline because it is incapable of addressing people's needs. In fact, democracy is in decline because its most prominent exemplars are not doing enough to protect it."

Figure 4.14 shows the democratic status of the NEP-9 countries. The Global Freedom Index considers China, Russia, and Turkey "Not Free," labels Indonesia, India, and Mexico as "Partly free," and South Korea, South Africa, and Brazil are "Free Nations." I remember teaching this subject in one of the Global Immersion Programs at SP Jain University. Some of my Indian students were shocked that in the index,

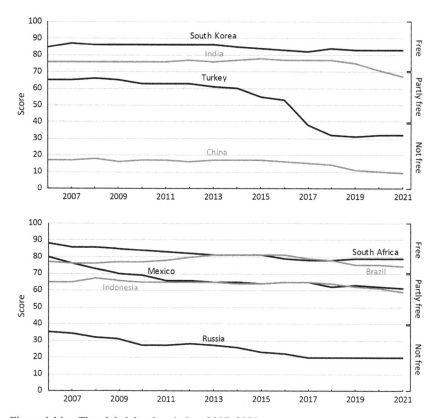

Figure 4.14: The global freedom index, 2007–2020.

Source: Freedom House.

India had dropped from "Free" to "Partly Free." Students emphasized the previous successful elections and the harmonious handing over of parliamentary power, in line with the voters' wishes. Of course, India has free and fair elections, but in other aspects, according to the 2021 report, democratic values are under attack. Consider the handling of COVID-19 that included a ham-fisted lockdown resulting in the dangerous and unplanned displacement of millions of internal migrant workers and growing anti-Muslim sentiment driven by government policies in regions such as Jammu and Kashmir, India's only Muslim-majority state. Freely elected leaders can go hand in hand with neglect of democratic process.

4.7.5 *Democracy index*

The Economist Intelligence Unit uses another way to measure democracy. Their Democracy Index shows substantial overlap with the Freedom House concept, but it puts less emphasis on the idea of freedom. It measures (based on expert's assessments) democracy through five categories: electoral process and pluralism, civil liberties, functioning of government, political participation, and political culture. Based on the score, the Index categorizes each country into one of the four regime types: full democracies, flawed democracies, hybrid regimes, and authoritarian regimes. Out of 167 countries, the Democracy Index 2020 classifies 23 countries as full democracies, including South Korea. They categorize 52 countries as flawed democracies, including India, the US, Belgium, South Africa, Indonesia, Mexico, and Brazil. Turkey is among the 35 countries labeled hybrid regimes, and 57 countries are authoritarian regimes, including Russia (124th) and China (151st) as some of the worst-performing countries. Lectures on this subject always spark lively debate on whether democracy is a western normative concept. Indeed, the Index is a reflection of the perception of what an ideal democracy looks like. In this sense, it is an ideological concept.

Measuring democracy: an input-based approach

During my class sessions on this subject, several students from NEP-9 countries suggest that a more outcome-based approach would be better. This approach asks whether a country effectively delivers what its citizens need and not just whether it follows the format of western democracies. According to them, the Index does not consider whether or not an election-based democracy serves people better in daily life. These students point out that for many countries, putting that much emphasis on elections automatically results in the classification "undemocratic." China would be undemocratic by definition, regardless of how often and how seriously the Chinese Communist Party and government consult think tanks and the public. A government that can increase welfare, healthcare, and education may be better than having a government elected into office that cannot. It is interesting that in recent years, more and more Italian and American students now agree.

Furthermore, under certain circumstances, a political culture that gives overwhelming credibility to elected government representatives that ridicules technocrats and experts may have a damaging effect during a crisis, as seen during COVID-19 in 2020 and 2021. For example, it is precisely this democratic culture that made it so challenging to make mask-wearing the natural thing to do in many democratic countries. Consider what happened in the US and Brazil, but the same holds for many countries in Europe.

Although different from western democracy, most of the adjustments to the governance structure in the NEP-9 relate to increasing accountability and transparency. Some steps have been taken on this issue, even by low-ranked China. The idea that China's economy changed dramatically while its political system remained static is not entirely true. Today's governance system bears little resemblance to how it was in the early 1980s when China was essentially a lawless country. It has established a comprehensive body of laws and regulations, a significant improvement, even if they fall short of the Western ideal of representative democracy and specific elements measured in the Democracy Index. However, the emphasis of reform was on economics instead of robust adjustments in the political system. The Chinese leadership is not alone in believing democracy is a means to an end, not a goal. Consider countries such as Russia, India, Turkey, Indonesia, and South Africa during the previous decade. They emphasize the potential negative effects of a democratic system, such as changes in leadership that contribute to instability and questioning whether ordinary people would know what is good for them (and the country). It is clear that democracy is not necessarily a dichotomous concept, and it is not correct to conclude that a country is either democratic or not. There are varying degrees of democracy, and not every electoral democracy is inclusive or liberal, as the experiences in India or Turkey showed us.

4.7.6 *Democracy and economic development*

As stated before, there is a large body of mainstream research that concludes that economic development requires a democratic environment (Barro, 1990). Nations with a higher degree of economic freedom and a more democratic system prosper because they tend to capitalize more fully on the knowledge and abilities of all individuals in the society. Innovative behavior and modernization, prerequisites for longer-term development, require "free minds," therefore, modernization and sustainable development need democracy. However, other statistical studies yield fuzzier conclusions, showing that the causality is unclear and complex. They conclude that economic development (and a growing middle class) is a necessary condition for the democratic process. Sustained economic development supposedly leads to the emergence of democratic institutions and, eventually, democracy. Economic development may, as its by-product, lead to new political values, such as an enhanced sense of individuality, personal autonomy, and value of personal freedom and choice that in turn support democratic institutions and practices (Dambisa Moyo's message in Section 4.3). The seven pillars of Western wisdom in Chapter 2, as introduced by Kishore Mahbubani (2008), also made clear that, according to Mahbubani, democracy is not a necessary condition for economic progress. And the fact remains that despite increasing wealth, certain wealthy autocracies remain firmly autocratic.

The complexity of the relationship between democracy and economic development

---

Figure 4.15 illustrates this complex relationship between democracy and economic development by showing the relationship between the level of development (GDP per capita) and the level of democracy. The conclusion is clear: there is no strong relationship between the two and the results are mixed.

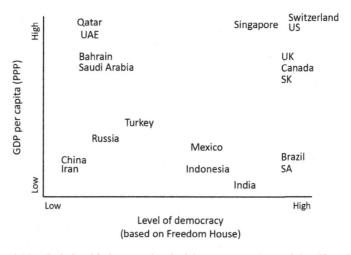

Figure 4.15:   Relationship between level of democracy and material welfare, 2020.

Countries such as South Africa, Brazil (SA), South Korea (SK), Canada, Norway, and the United States enjoy the same level of democracy. At the same time, they show significant differences in GDP per capita. Furthermore, the welfare of Qatar equals that of Switzerland and Norway, but clearly, the levels of democracy are vastly different. The level of democracy differs a lot between China and Russia on the one hand, and Brazil and India on the other hand, while they all witnessed relatively strong economic development in the previous decades. Analyzing specific countries over a longer period may lead us to question the argument that democracy is a precondition for economic development. During their take-off phase and the period after that, the Asian Tigers certainly did not have a democratic system. Still, at the same time, they were able to increase welfare for their population substantially. The same holds for non-democratic regimes like Pinochet's Chile and Franco's Spain.

So, there are mixed results regarding the relationship between democracy and economic prosperity. But when we link economic development to economic freedom and the rule of law, the picture is more homogeneous. The authority of law in a society is regarded as a necessary precondition for longer-term development. The consensus view is that (also) non-democratic countries that could uphold the rule of law achieved relatively high economic development over a longer period. Of course, the political factors that help defend the rule of law may be different in democracies than in autocracies. Still, one core similarity is that the rule of law maintains its effectiveness only when those in power, whether democratically elected or not, are in one way or another placed under certain political constraints. The rule of law is not by definition protected more by elected policymakers.

Democratic institutions may strengthen or defend the rule of law, but the same institutions can also undermine it. Elected policymakers may do so by enacting legislation or politically driven appointments, as we saw in 2020 in the US with appointments to the Supreme Court, the country's highest court of Justice. Democracy does not necessarily say much about the quality of governance, an issue heavily debated, with cause, after the election of Mr. Trump to the office of president and the political situation regarding Brexit. Unfortunately, the democratic process does not automatically lead to reasonable, prudent, and wise governments that make good decisions, and changes aimed at creating more transparency and representation may be needed. Obviously, the same can be said with respect to autocratic systems and governments.

Although the direct relationship between democracy and welfare is not strong, nearly all high-income countries are democracies. Experiences in Western Europe, Japan, Korea, and Eastern Europe (Poland, Hungary, and Czech Republic) suggest that a democratic process is required to achieve sustainable growth after the take-off stage, to escape the middle-income trap. We expect the same to apply to NEP-9 countries, but democracy may look different than in the West.

Chapter 5

Globalization and NEP Viewpoints

5.1 Defining the Concept of Globalization

Globalization is a multidimensional concept, deeply intertwined with our daily lives. Essentially, globalization allows Brazilian residents to consume chocolate from Belgium, buy South Korean cars, and invest in Turkey Airlines on the Istanbul stock market. Italians work for Chinese-owned companies, travel to America for a holiday, and go on Facebook to discuss current events with friends around the world. During a night out, Norwegians see a blockbuster movie by Columbia Tristar, a company owned by Japan's Sony, get a hamburger at Burger King, owned by a Brazilian investment fund, and the next day, they talk Alibaba's customer service, located in India, about the delivery of products bought online. You get the point. Broadly speaking, globalization is the process of integrating nations, companies, and people politically, economically, financially, socially, and culturally, into a global network. Dreher's definition (2006), which introduced the commonly named KOF Globalisation Index (we will discuss this index in Section 5.2), also emphasizes this broader perspective: "Globalization is a process that erodes national boundaries, integrates national economies, cultures, technologies and governance, and produces complex relations of mutual interdependence."

The broader perspective of globalization

Political globalization refers to the development and growing influence of international organizations, such as the United Nations,

International Monetary Fund, World Trade Organization, Group of Twenty (G20), and the World Health Organization. You could argue that this also involves non-governmental organizations, such as the World Nature Fund and Doctors without Borders. These global and regional institutions were essentially established to facilitate or promote globalization. Economic globalization focuses on international trade and international capital flows, particularly international investments. This emphasis on international investments is important because it separates economic globalization from financial globalization. The latter emphasizes the short-term (and often speculative) capital flows that use differences in interest, exchange rates, and prices. Cultural and social globalization is the process that spreads particular cultures, information, and values throughout the world, which intensifies social relations. Stiglitz (2006) mentions specifically the international flow of ideas and knowledge as part of this cultural and social globalization, driven by the Internet, social media, tourism, and global companies and their brands in particular.

Authors such as Bhagwati (2004) identify technology as a separate dimension of globalization.

Technological advancements lead to digitalization and, consequently, digital globalization (Verbeke, 2020). In my view, technological advancement is the primary enabler of globalization and, as such, one of the main drivers behind different types of globalization, not a type of globalization itself. For example, digitalization affects economic globalization. When I order a product from Indonesia through a digital platform, such as Alibaba or Amazon, I can follow the item's journey in real time on a map and, of course, pay via digital transaction. Virtually, every type of cross-border transaction has a digital component. The outcome of these digital activities is the physical transportation of the product, making it part of economic globalization. Five factors drive the process of globalization:

1. Improvements in technology, such as digitalization, resulting in lower costs of communication, transportation, and transactions.
2. Policies that open up countries to the rest of the world.
3. The economic paradigm of more market and less government, which resulted in heavy deregulation and a borderless world for goods.
4. Strategic choices by large multinational enterprises to connect to the global middle class and making use of differences in costs of production.
5. Harmonization of consumer tastes.

5.1.1 *Mixed feelings*

Globalization evokes mixed feelings. I always start the course on globalization by asking my students to illustrate it (not to define it). Their replies divide the group. One half emphasizes those who get left behind: closing industries, the middle class under attack, unfair competition from China, immigration issues, increased income inequality, reduced national autonomy, and multinational enterprises using tax havens to lower tax pressure. They also point out that hyper-connectivity stimulates the waste economy and is (partly) the cause of environmental damage and climate change. The other half of the class calls out the positive aspects. They illustrate globalization through global citizenship, getting to know different cultures, innovations from abroad, employment by multinational enterprises, and SMEs that can become micro-multinationals from the start. These commonly named "born globals" (Rennie, 1993) may scale up quickly and generate prosperity.

The first group labels increased international competition as bad because small local companies may not succeed in competing with large foreign companies. The second group argues that increased global competition is good because it promotes innovation, a better quality of products, and lower prices. The first group claims globalization creates winners and losers, while the second group believes the outcome of globalization is a win-win situation.

5.2 Measuring Globalization

Single indicators, such as trade as a percentage of GDP, are frequently used as a proxy for globalization, but globalization is a multifaceted concept that requires a combination of indicators. The KOF Globalisation Index, published by the KOF Swiss Economic Institute at ETH Zürich (a university), comprises three sub-indices: economic, social, and political globalization. These sub-indices are broken down further into many variables. Figure 5.1 gives an overview of the most important variables and the weights of the sub-indices. While *de facto* globalization measures actual international flows and activities, *de jure* globalization measures policies and conditions that, in principle, enable and facilitate international flows and activities. They reflect a country's willingness to be open.

In the 2020 KOF Index, Switzerland, the Netherlands, Belgium, and Sweden are the most globalized, which makes sense: these countries are

Economic globalization (33.3%)	De facto*	De Jure*
→ Trade globalization	Trade in goods Trade in services Trade in partner diversity	Trade regulations Tariffs Trade agreements
→ Financial globalization	Foreign direct investments Portfolio investments International debt	Investment restrictions Capital account openness Investment agreements
Social globalization (33.3%)		
→ Interpersonal globalization	International tourism	Freedom to visit
→ Informational globalization	International patents	Internet access
→ Cultural globalization	McDonald's restaurants	Human capital
Political globalization (33.3%)		
	Embassies UN peace keeping missions	International organizations International treaties

(*) The overview is not a complete list of all variables

Figure 5.1:   Structure of the KOF Globalisation Index 2020.

Source: ETH, KOF Swiss Economic Institute (2021).

highly developed, well connected, and small. Large(r) high-developed economies, such as Spain and Italy, as well as the United States, are all in the top 30. They are all settled in the middle-lower part of the index. The least globalized countries in the 2020 index were Somalia, Eritrea, and Afghanistan.

The NEP-9 are well integrated in the political landscape but less in economic terms

On average, the NEP-9 are around rank 65, with South Korea as the most globalized at rank 35. The other countries, in particular, India and Indonesia, are substantially less globalized. The 2020 report ranks China in 82nd place (Figure 5.2). This relatively low rank may be surprising, given China's role in international trade, FDI, and its overwhelming number of Internet users, tourists, and students. However, most variables on the list are adjusted to consider GDP and population. For example, in absolute terms, China is the largest exporter globally, but export as a percentage of GDP is much lower than for most (smaller) countries.

Another example of this adjustment is the factor UN peacekeeping missions. The KOF Index measures this by the number of personnel

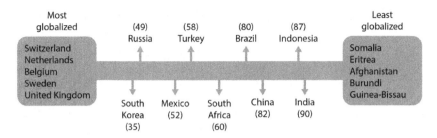

Figure 5.2:   The NEP-9 countries in the KOF Globalisation Index.

Source: ETH, KOF Swiss Economic Institute (2021).

contributed to UN Security Council missions as a percentage of the population. China, as well as other NEP-9 countries are pretty active participants in UN missions. For example, India contributed almost 5,500 people to UN peacekeeping missions (September 2021). Indonesia and China are also in the top 10 contributing countries. South Africa contributes more than France, while the contribution of South Korea is almost the same as the UK.

Figure 5.3 shows, on the left, that except for Mexico, all NEP-9 countries contribute more troops, police, and staff to UN missions than the United States. Furthermore, according to the Lowy Institute's yearly Global Diplomatic Index, which looks at the number of diplomatic posts abroad and the resources associated with this, the NEP-9 are relatively active. The right-hand side of the figure shows that they are all in the top 25 countries with the highest number of international posts (embassies and consulates). This indicator of the KOF Globalisation Index is not adjusted, and the index uses the absolute number of embassies. So, in general, the NEP-9 are relatively well integrated into the global political landscape.

The 2020 KOF Index used data from before the COVID-19 pandemic. But you may expect a COVID-19 effect. For example, the economic crisis in 2020 and early 2021 slowed trade, investments, and financial flows, reducing economic globalization. Furthermore, COVID-19 resulted in a dramatic fall in travel and student exchanges, negatively affecting social globalization. And many governments prioritized domestic objectives instead of putting energy into negotiating international treaties. Hence, a reduction in political globalization.

Rank	Country	#	Rank	Country	#
1	Bangladesh	6447	1	China	276
2	Nepal	5536	5	Russia	242
3	India	5481	6	Turkey	235
4	Rwanda	5263	8	Brazil	222
5	Ethiopia	4856	12	India	186
			13	South Korea	183
7	Indonesia	2818	15	Mexico	157
10	China	2248	21	Indonesia	132
22	South Africa	940	25	South Africa	124
38	South Korea	543			
60	Tukey	151	2	United States	273
63	Brazil	73	3	France	267
64	Russia	72	4	Japan	247
87	Mexico	19			
34	France	618			
35	United Kingdom	605			
36	Germany	563			
83	United States	31			
105	Japan	4			

Figure 5.3: Peacekeeping contributions (left) and global diplomatic posts (right), 2020.

Source: UN (2021) (peacekeeping) and Lowy Institute (2021) (Global Diplomacy Index).

5.2.1 *Development of the NEP-9 globalization index*

Figure 5.4 compares the development of the world globalization index with the progress of the globalization index of the NEP-9. The first observation we can make from this is that except for Mexico, the globalization process of all NEP-9 countries slowed down after 2008, which is in line with the average globalization index worldwide, but the post-2008 slowdown is slightly more pronounced in the NEP-9. The global financial crisis that started in 2008 not only impacted economic globalization through international trade and foreign investments but also reduced the diplomatic network of many countries. Government deficits forced countries to implement significant changes to their workforces and rearrange their diplomatic networks. Second, countries like Brazil, South Korea, Mexico, and Turkey were relatively globalized in the 1970s. For example, South Korea reached the world globalization average in 1975, partly due to its export promotion policy. Indonesia was at the world average in 1990, South Africa in 1998, China in 2000, and India reached this level only in 2007.

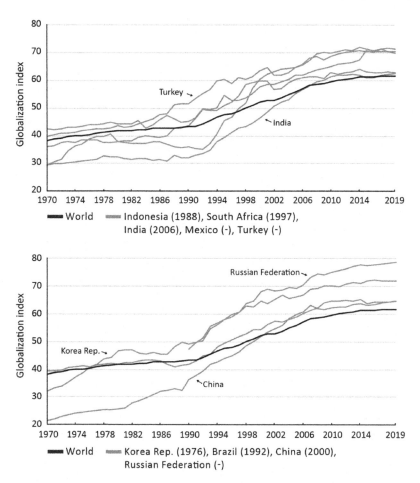

Figure 5.4:   World globalization index versus NEP-9 countries.

Note: The data combine *de facto* and *de jure* into an overall globalization index. (-) means that the country was more globalized than world average over the full period.
Source: ETH, KOF Swiss Economic Institute (2021).

Third, the figure shows there are different periods of acceleration in globalization. For example, Brazil accelerated integration after 1990, losing momentum after 2008. In Mexico, acceleration of integration happened after 2000, continuing up to this day. South Africa accelerated integration from 1992 onwards, while accelerations were visible in China and Turkey in the 1980s.

5.2.2 *A critical note*

Although the KOF Globalisation Index is used widely, there is cause to question some of the selected indicators and the methods used to measure them. For example, trade as a percentage of GDP is a key economic globalization indicator, but it is not always helpful. This percentage is over 300% for Singapore but only 27% for the US (both 2020). This high percentage results from the export processing trade (discussed in Chapter 6). Singapore imports products and later exports the same products with only marginal value added by services in logistics, transport, and insurance. This results from Singapore's entrepot trade and is comparable to the iPhone example discussed in Chapter 2. Calculating globalization this way means that Singapore is 11 times more economically globalized than the United States, an outcome which is obviously debatable.

No separation is made between globalization and regionalism

Another critical point regarding the KOF Globalisation Index is that the index does not take distance into account. For example, the high percentage of trade to GDP in the case of the Netherlands is regionally concentrated. Almost 80% of trade stays within the European Union. From this perspective, we are looking at regionalization, not globalization. A final critique is that the globalization index measures westernization instead of cultural globalization. By using the number of McDonald's restaurants in a country, it focuses on American values, and the same can be said when the index includes the number of IKEA stores.

5.3 Waves of Globalization

Globalization evolves in phases or waves. In his book *The World Is Flat: A Brief History of the Twenty-first Century* (2005), Thomas Friedman divides the globalization process into three phases. Globalization 1.0 started in 1492 and continued up to 1800. This year marks the start of trade and ideas flowing from Europe to America. Of course, this newly "discovered" world was not new at all; it already had civilizations going back thousands of years, but the core message of Friedman is that the discovery of America is the start of globalization. This period was characterized by international transactions organized across and between countries. Deviating slightly from Friedman, Globalization 2.0, the second wave of globalization happened between 1800 and 1990 and was characterized by the globalization of multinational enterprises. MNEs grew and benefitted from the fall in transportation and telecommunication costs and large countries such as the former Soviet Union and China opening up. Deng Xiaoping's program of economic reforms initiated in 1978 (China), and Gorbachev's perestroika policy (USSR) accelerated the fall of the Berlin Wall in 1989 and the subsequent collapse of the Soviet Union. The second globalization wave created the conditions necessary for private enterprises to go abroad. According to Friedman, we reached Globalization 3.0 after 2000. In this phase, individuals can run global businesses and globalize through the Internet.

Globalization 1.0, 2.0, and 3.0: globalization process driven by governments, companies, and individuals

---

Friedman also introduced what he calls *The 10 Flatteners*, the drivers that enable individuals to communicate and collaborate globally. We will not go through all 10 flatteners, but it is clear that the collapse of the Berlin Wall started the opening up of countries in Central and Eastern Europe. Also, companies like Netscape and Google and communities like Wikipedia are flatteners as they made the Internet and information available to people. Technology, like mobile phones, tablets, and other personal devices, made internationalizing the global supply chain possible through offshoring and outsourcing.

The example in Section 5.1 illustrated that globalization today is intertwined with our daily lives. This phase of globalization is worlds away from the situation during Columbus' time and even from the 19th century. Therefore, we must differentiate between internationalization and globalization. Before the start of the 20th century, there was internationalization: the growing importance of trade, foreign capital, and (bilateral) treaties. However, most people had no connection to other parts of the world and, consequently, little interest. Globalization today is very different, with intensive connectivity between nations, companies, and consumers. Indeed, the world is becoming flat. For this reason, we will focus on the era of modern globalization that starts in the early 20th century and its various periods of acceleration.

5.3.1 *The first acceleration*

The period between 1918 and 1950 was a disruptive time for globalization. The two wars were disastrous in countless and unimaginable ways. In an economic sense, it created crises and a rise in protectionism. Most countries looked for internal solutions instead of international cooperation. The first acceleration of globalization occurred between 1950 and 1975 when the United States dominated the world and exported its open global economic order attitude to the rest of the world. We will call this first acceleration phase the *cooperation acceleration*. An essential characteristic of this time frame is that integration happened mainly among the rich countries, driven by multilateral trade liberalization schemes, under the auspices of the General Agreement on Tariffs and Trade (GATT) and regional trading blocs that reduced tariffs and some non-tariff barriers.

---

*Cooperation acceleration: the globalization process without
NEP-9 countries*

In this first acceleration period, most developing countries and emerging markets remained outside the globalization process. Europe, North America, and Japan were leading, concentrating on restoring trade relations. A belief in free trade helped negotiate rules that fostered international trade. This first acceleration was based in part on what Paul Krugman (2009) named containerization: "The ability to ship things long distances fairly cheaply has been there since the steamship and the railroad. What was the big bottleneck was getting things on and off the ships. It is interesting to find out how important the introduction of the container was" (p. 7). When we think about new technology, products, or processes that have a profound impact, we usually think of high-profile innovations. However, for international trade, the invention of the container was the key. When developing countries and emerging markets of this period did engage in export activities, it was mainly primary commodities. They still had their inward-oriented policies. At the same time, western multinational enterprises did not involve developing countries in their global strategies. The exceptions, as we saw in the previous chapter, were some fast-growing countries in Southeast Asia.

5.3.2 *The second acceleration*

The second acceleration of globalization started in the early 1980s and continued up to the financial crisis of 2008. We will call this period the *neoliberal acceleration,* emphasizing the role of the market and the belief that (global) integration generates prosperity. This neoliberal paradigm was the core tenet of UK Prime Minister Margaret Thatcher's and US President Ronald Reagan's policy. We could question whether this policy of more market and less government did anything to help domestic economies, but it was highly beneficial for the globalization process.

Neoliberal acceleration: the globalization rules set by the western nations

---

As stated earlier, the NEP-9 countries went along with this mainstream thinking and also implemented pro-market and pro-opening-up policies. China adopted such reform policies in the late 1970s and early 1980s, and a North American Free Trade Agreement (NAFTA) deal to help Mexico integrate with the US and Canada was signed in 1992. Liberalization packages were formed in India (the early 1990s) and Brazil (early 2000s). China became a member of the World Trade Organization in 2001. Besides the opening up, this second period of acceleration was spurred on by technological advancements in transport and communications. Western companies could exploit low labor costs in emerging markets like Mexico and China. By 2007, factories that assemble imported components for export, owned by foreign multinationals, employed 1.3 million Mexicans. We discussed the maquiladoras in Chapter 4. Technology also launched and stimulated the trend of outsourcing to China by multinationals starting in the early 2000s.

To state the obvious: the 2008 financial crisis negatively impacted several aspects of globalization. The economic crisis resulted in a substantial decline in international trade, and multinational enterprises became hesitant to invest abroad. National governments saw the disadvantages of full liberalization, particularly regarding short-term capital flows and implemented protectionist measures. Political globalization came to a standstill due to discontent about the negotiations in the WTO that started the Doha Round in 2001 (Chapter 7). At the same time, other aspects of globalization flourished, for example, the export of services and the rise in international tourism.

5.3.3 *The third acceleration*

We are at the beginning of the third acceleration period. This period, driven by digitization, started in 2015 with the introduction of the term the *Fourth Industrial Revolution* by Klaus Schwab in an article in the journal *Foreign Affairs*. In 2016, it was also the theme of the annual meeting of the World Economic Forum in Davos, Switzerland. Unsurprisingly, we will call this third acceleration the *digital acceleration*. Digitalization is having profound effects on the economics of globalization. As digital platforms become global, they are driving down the cost of cross-border communications and transactions, allowing businesses to connect with customers and suppliers in any country.

Digital globalization: the acceleration of "born globals"

Globalization was once for large multinational corporations, but platforms reduce the minimal scale needed to go global, enabling small businesses and entrepreneurs worldwide to participate. As a result, new types of competitors can emerge rapidly from every corner of the world, increasing pressure on industry incumbents. This phenomenon is not new. Articles related to the commonly named "born globals" were published as early as the 1990s, but today's globalization has one essential feature: the speed of change. The Fourth Industrial Revolution with technologies like artificial intelligence, quantum computing, 3D printing, nanotechnology, and the Internet of things will increase the speed of many aspects of globalization. The rate of current breakthroughs has no historical precedent. Moreover, it is disrupting almost every industry in every country.

It appears that this latest period of accelerated globalization might be relatively short due to the impact of COVID-19 and the attack on the neoliberal pillar that started in the second phase. A related question is whether the neoliberal pillar is under such heavy attack that it undermines globalization itself. And this question brings us to the pros and cons of globalization. Assessing the balance of the pros and cons is complex. For example, Indonesia implemented specific measures to stimulate investments in oil palm plantations. Between 1995 and 2015, an enormous area of forest was cleared to make way for oil palm plantations, resulting in employment opportunities, increased export revenues, and a positive impact on GDP per capita. However, these oil palm plantations have dramatic consequences for the biodiversity of Indonesian wildlife and the living environment of local people. My students are positive about the impact of international trade, emphasizing the availability of foreign products. However, their perspective on aspects such as the impact of multinationals and immigration is much more negative. A learning point is, therefore, that questions about attitudes on globalization attempt to capture a broad and complex concept, and there are wide disparities between perspectives on the different aspects of globalization.

5.4 Views on Globalization

Various institutions such as the Pew Research Center and Bertelsmann measure attitudes toward globalization. The following is the outcome of the 2020 GED Globalization Survey by Bertelsmann (Figure 5.5). It provides a snapshot of people's perception of the combined dimensions of

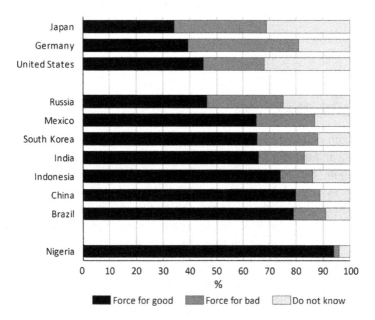

Figure 5.5: Attitudes on globalization.

Source: Bertelsmann (2020, July): Attitudes on Globalization on the Eve of the Corona Crisis.

globalization, the answers to the question: "Overall, do you think globalization is a force for good or bad for the world?"

For decades, believers in globalization lived in countries like the US, the UK, and Germany and thought that globalization was good and that economic openness was positive. In surveys executed in the 1980s and 1990s, western countries (and their citizens) believed in the positive impact of international trade, foreign investments, and cultural exchanges.

Today, the main believers of globalization are the people in emerging markets, including the NEP-9 countries

---

This attitude changed dramatically in the past decade. Today (2020), believers are from countries like Nigeria, Brazil, China, Indonesia, India, and Mexico. In Brazil, 79% of the respondents in the Bertelsmann survey think globalization is a force for good. Citizens of countries such as France, Germany, and the United States are more restrained. In Germany, 41% indicate that globalization is a force for evil. The different views on how globalization affects nation-states can be divided into the following:

- The optimistic view
- The pessimistic view
- The cautious view

5.4.1 *The optimistic view*

A classroom discussion about the pros and cons of globalization is always interesting and usually how I start global immersion programs at Nyenrode and SP Jain. Students who strongly favor globalization motivate their views by saying globalization substantially reduces poverty. There are always some students that note the choice for opening up is a free choice made by countries, and because most countries opt for opening up, it proves the benefits outweigh the costs. The optimistic view sees globalization as highly beneficial to any nation, both advanced and developing economies: the positive-sum game belief. For example, the KOF Globalisation Index is strongly associated with economic development. Research shows that despite some outliers, there is certain robustness to this positive impact of globalization and economic development. In particular, the economic and social dimensions positively impact growth. This positive relationship was already visible in the 1993 World Bank report on the Asian Tigers. In the executive summary, the report says that "openness is associated with more rapid growth" (p. 4).

Bertelsmann (2017) calculated the impact of globalization on the German economy and found that between 1990 and 2014, Germany's real per capita GDP was €1,160 higher in 2014 than it would have been without ongoing globalization. We could question the underlying econometric model and the use of GDP as a single indicator, but the message is clear: globalization and opening up are beneficial to material welfare. It is interesting, therefore, that German citizens have not adopted this reality, as seen in Figure 5.5. Only 39% of the respondents think globalization is a force for good.

5.4.1.1 *The growth-promoting channels of globalization*

Essentially, the growth-promoting effects of globalization and increased opening up are running through several interrelated channels. First, we have the trade channel. Increased trade leads to lower prices for tradable goods and services. Consumers benefit from lower prices since the purchasing power of their incomes increases. Trade also generates access to goods and services for households that otherwise would not be available. The same holds for domestic companies that can acquire the intermediate goods and services they need for their production, mainly at a lower price from producers abroad.

The second channel runs through a larger market. The dismantling of international trade barriers allows companies to produce for a larger market, and this may create economies of scale with lower unit costs and lower prices as a result. Consumers benefit from an additional increase in purchasing power. Third, there is the international competition channel. Domestic companies can compete with competitors from abroad and, when competitive, increase their export and have a positive impact on employment and GDP. If companies want to stay competitive internationally, they must respond to these pressures by innovating and achieving technical advances and, hence, increased productivity.

International competition in many aspects may generate economic development

---

Furthermore, international competition will bring the necessary changes in institutional, political, and business environments and drive structural reforms. Finally, there is the foreign investment channel. Many examples show the positive impact of foreign direct investments in a host country. According to the optimistic view, foreign investments, particularly knowledge transfer, are the main driver behind economic development. This globalization of knowledge entails technical knowledge, new and innovative ideas, management concepts, training employees, and adaptation of institutions. The optimistic view concentrates on the positive impact of foreign companies due to positive agglomeration effects. Therefore, adherents of this view emphasize that global inequality has declined, thanks to relatively strong income growth and expansion of emerging markets and their middle class.

5.4.2 *The pessimistic view*

As you would guess, the pessimistic view is rather negative in evaluating globalization. It does not say that there are no potential benefits, but it is deeply concerned about the negative impact. Amartya Sen (Oxfam Report, 2002) summarizes this view: "Global interaction, rather than insulated isolation, has been the basis of economic progress in the world. Trade, along with migration, communication, and dissemination of scientific and technical knowledge, has helped to break the dominance of rampant poverty and the pervasiveness of 'nasty, brutish and short' lives that characterized the world. And yet, despite all the progress, life is still severely nasty, brutish, and short for a large part of the world population. The great rewards of globalized trade have come to some, but not to others" (p. 3). The adverse effects of globalization relate to five factors:

1. The decreasing power and autonomy of the sovereign nation state
2. Too much market
3. The power of foreign companies
4. The impact on national cultures
5. Environmental impacts

The pessimistic perspective is strengthened by the increasing speed of change generated by globalization and the observation that globalization creates winners and losers. In that sense, the anti-globalist movement sees globalization as a zero-sum game. As we will see in Chapter 6, the commonly named Battle of Seattle, at the start of the WTO meeting in Seattle in 1999, marked the unofficial beginning of the anti-globalist movement. The movement emphasizes the *race to the bottom* in environmental issues, human rights, and labor standards, driven by large companies and governments that gave them unregulated power and continued hyper-globalization.

The Battle of Seattle as the start of the anti-globalist movement

---

In a race to the bottom, nations essentially compete in setting the lowest possible standards, hoping to attract businesses. Globalization pessimists accuse corporations of seeking to maximize profit at the expense of the environment, work safety conditions, and the integrity of national legislative authorities. The pessimistic view criticizes neoliberal policies, the emphasis on profits, individualism, the absence of government regulation, and too much focus on (market) flexibility.

5.4.2.1 *Taking back control*

One of the basic ideas behind the pessimistic view is that globalization is disruptive in many ways, and hence, governments must mitigate the negative impact. Voters, middle class, employees, and employers demand a reasonable level of the welfare state to protect them appropriately. More open countries tend to have larger state sectors and redistribute more (Sharma, 2020). The past years made clear that people blame globalization for many problems, ranging from unemployment, social unrest, disruptive cultural diversity, and environmental damage. They do not feel their government is helping them to counteract the negative impacts of globalization. This has led to a rise in anti-globalist sentiment and the cry to the national government to take back control. There are calls for regaining national sovereignty from EU institutions (resulting in Brexit) or global institutions. "Take back control of the country" was the sentiment shared by former president Trump in the US and former prime minister Johnson in the UK in 2016. It was mostly associated with international trade: imports replace jobs, while exports create them. The US viewpoint (and to a slightly lesser extent also in the UK) is clear. When the US opened its markets, its trade deficits rose as other countries "stole" its jobs, in particular, because of unfair competition from emerging and developing countries.

5.4.2.2 *Race to the bottom*

The race to the bottom is also seen in taxation. Companies, with the help of accountancy firms, reduce substantial taxation payments by concentrating profits in places with the lowest taxation pressure. International firms can shift profits to units set up in tax havens, even though they sell and generate profit all over the world. Countries like the Netherlands, Ireland, and Luxembourg attracted head offices by giving substantial tax benefits; they compete on the lowest taxation rate. China, India, Brazil, and South Africa attract manufacturing operations from foreign companies by promising them no taxation on earnings in the country for a specific period, government subsidies, and even a guarantee that workers are prevented from forming unions.

Multilateral agreements to stop the race to the bottom

After serious discussions in the G7 and G20, in the summer of 2021, the most important countries agreed on a global minimum tax rate of 15% for multinational companies. The agreement aims to stop countries competing against one another by lowering their tax rates to attract investments by companies such as Google, Facebook, Booking.com, and Apple, a process US Treasury Secretary Janet Yellen has called a "30-year race to the bottom on corporate tax rates" (*Reuters*, June 5, 2021). During a meeting of the OECD in July 2021, it was stated that "with a global minimum tax in place, multinational corporations will no longer be able to pit countries against one another in a bid to push tax rates down."

5.4.2.3 *National identity*

The US and the UK's experiences after 2016 also show that protecting the national identity is seen as a legitimate reason to reduce globalization. The pessimistic view fears that globalization is creating a monoculture. A large cohort of people is not satisfied with this outcome of cultural globalization, whether it is McDonald's restaurants and other global brands popping up everywhere or the blockbuster movies from Hollywood and Bollywood. Studies have shown that in sub-Saharan Africa, the poorest people know most Disney characters. Daily life comes to a standstill during lunchtime in several parts of Africa because everyone is watching a Bollywood series, although they may not even know how to read and write, let alone understand Hindi. The same holds for Netflix. I asked my Nyenrode students to write a paper on the impact of Netflix on globalization and the title of their paper was clear: "Netflix and the creation of global monoculture."

5.4.2.4 *Largest companies*

As said, the anti-globalist movement focuses on the size and behavior of multinational enterprises. They fear that the power of MNEs is so big that it substantially reduces the autonomy of national governments, resulting in many concessions which are advantageous for the companies but bad for the country. The largest companies in the world are very large indeed. For example, in October 2021, the stock market values of Apple and Microsoft were $2.3 and $2.2 trillion, respectively. There are only seven countries in the world with a higher GDP in nominal exchange rates than the market value of these two companies. In fact, both Apple and Microsoft have a greater market value than all of Central Europe and the Baltic countries put together. Some research builds on this by adjusting for the number of people in a country and the number of employees in the company, resulting in a comparison of GDP per capita and the company's wealth per employee.

Some companies are larger in size than middle-size countries

Besides stock market value, we can use several other metrics to compare the size and power of companies and countries. All of them show the enormous size of various multinational enterprises. For example, many large corporations have revenues that far exceed most governments. The revenues of companies such as Walmart, State Grid, Amazon, and China National Petroleum exceed the total government revenue (taxes and non-tax revenues) of countries such as Brazil, South Korea, and Mexico (Figure 5.6).

5.4.2.5 *A common mistake*

Another (but incorrect) way to compare the size of companies and countries is by comparing the GDP of nations with company revenues. Walmart's revenue is about the same as the nominal GDP of Thailand and Belgium and an incredible 40% higher than South Africa's GDP. Of course, we cannot say that Walmart is 40% larger than South Africa, a common mistake made in trying to compare businesses and companies. The revenue of a company is turnover, while the country's GDP is a value-added concept. Think back to the iPhone example in Chapter 2. The

	Revenues 2020 (US$ bn)					
1	United States	5923	19	Toyota	257
2	China	3622	20	Mexico	254
3	Germany	1729	21	Volkswagen	254
4	Japan	1666	22	Berkshire Hathaway	254
5	France	1334	23	Mc Kesson	238
6	United Kingdom	966	24	China State Construction	234
7	India	620	25	Saudi Aramco	230
8	Walmart	560	26	Samsung group	201
9	Russia	468	27	Turkey	188
10	State Grid	386	28	BP	184
11	Amazon	386	29	Shell	183
12	Brazil	382	30	Alphabet	183
13	South Korea	363	31	Allianz	136
14	China National Petroleum	284	32	Home Depot	132
15	Sinopec group	284	33	Indonesia	129
16	Apple	275	34	General Motors	122
17	CVS Health	269	35	South Africa	77
18	United Health	257		Company / Country	

Figure 5.6:   100 largest corporations and countries based on their consolidated revenues in 2020.

Source: Fortune, Global 500 (August, 2021) and IMF (2021).

Chinese GDP is calculated using the value added by the assembly of the iPhone and not by the price (turnover) of the iPhone. We want to compare the value added by the company as well as the country, so we need to adjust revenue to added value. Usually, profit is used as a proxy for added value. Another option to calculate the total value added by the company is to add profit to the wages paid. These adjustments will show that multinational enterprises are not as large and dominating as indicated by Noreena Hertz (2002), but they are powerful nonetheless.

5.4.2.6 *Environmental impact*

The pessimistic view also focuses on the impact multinational enterprises (MNEs) have on the environment. Consider outsourcing activities by MNE to bad suppliers, investments in palm oil plantations, child labor in the global supply chain, and cheap flights because the airliners are not paying taxes on fuel and, obviously, not considering the externalities associated with air travel. In that sense, globalization has a dramatic impact on the environment. It is quite depressing that even highly reputable companies act irresponsibly. For example, Norwegian aluminum miner Hydro Alunorte is responsible for repeated leaking of toxic materials into the Brazilian Amazon. This case is significant because its largest shareholder is the government of Norway, the country with one of the highest scores on sustainability and sustainable development. Unfortunately, this case does not seem to be an exception. In July 2021, the European Commission fined Volkswagen and BMW, two of Germany's largest carmakers, accusing them of forming a cartel and illegally conspiring to restrict competition in emission-cleaning technology for diesel cars. The companies agreed they would not use the technology at its full potential and that none of them would aim at cleaning above the minimum standard required by EU emissions standards. Daimler also participated in this agreement but received full immunity because it informed Brussels about the existence of the cartel.

Markets do often not generate optimal outcomes

According to the pessimistic view and the anti-globalist movement, markets do not generate optimal outcomes due to market failures and assumptions behind neoliberal thinking that we do not see in reality, such as the assumption of full competition, despite oligopolistic behavior as in the German automotive sector.

5.4.2.7 *Growing discontent*

Disbelief in the market started with the Asian crisis in the late 1990s and accelerated strongly during the global financial crisis of 2008. According to the pessimistic view, the financial and economic crisis that followed the Lehman bankruptcy in 2008 resulted from too much market and too little government. The help given to the financial sector was seen as using tax money to bail out an irresponsible sector and its extremely well-payed employees.

NEP-9 countries view on capital convertibility is clear: watch out for opening-up too early

---

One specific element of this free-market paradigm that received enormous criticism was the liberalization of short-term capital flows. Surprisingly, the IMF still defended capital market liberalization, even at the early stages of the East Asian crisis in 1997, and as a precondition for receiving financial help, strongly advised capital account convertibility for countries like Thailand, Malaysia, and Indonesia. It did this in the face of mounting evidence suggesting that capital account convertibility would generate economic instability with adverse consequences, especially for the poor in these countries. For example, the influx of short-term capital in the real estate sector surely crowed out more productive domestic investments, and capital liberalization managed capital outflow. This capital flight from domestic investors is dramatic because it diminishes growth and lowers the currency's value, generating inflation and falling purchasing power of the people. Globalization, with its free-market paradigm, has facilitated such outflows and resulted in an economic and human development crisis in Asia in the years after 1997. Furthermore, globalization and the rise of interdependencies make the world economy more vulnerable to systemic shocks. For example, COVID-19 caused dramatic overshooting up and down in commodity prices and shocks to healthcare prices, as discussed in Chapter 4. The volatility of commodity prices and exchange rates is clearly linked to global trade and global capital and, hence, to globalization.

We cannot blame globalization for all these problems. Shifts in the labor market and unemployment in specific sectors are primarily the results of domestic developments such as labor market policies influencing flexibility, economic cycles, the educational system, and the absorption of new technology. It is not true that globalization alone generates labor market problems, and in many cases, globalization is only a secondary cause of domestic problems. For example, 86% of manufacturing job losses in the US between 1997 and 2007 resulted from a rise in productivity, compared to less than 14% lost because of trade (Housemann, 2018). Despite some mixed outcomes (Scott, 2015), historically, technology has been a net creator of jobs, but new jobs do not necessarily materialize quickly or in the same locations, a view shared by Paul Krugman. New technology has also consistently increased labor productivity and created new and better jobs. However, almost 50% of US jobs are at risk of automation because machines will also become better at cognitive tasks instead of only physical ones. What seems to happen is that old jobs in government-protected industries disappear before new jobs are created. In this sense, technology is much more important in explaining job losses than globalization.

The same holds for income inequality, stagnation of purchasing power of the western middle class during the last two decades, and lower pensions. Domestic policies are also more important than the effects of globalization. But globalization may accelerate the already visible development of these issues. In an increasingly competitive and globalized world, the levels of social spending on pensions are hard to maintain, independent of globalization.

Despite some important disadvantages of globalization,
most of domestic problems are the result of domestic policy mistakes;
not due to globalization

Still, the anti-globalist movement emphasizes that globalization leads to a more competitive environment and, hence, the need to increase the pension age and cut the value of pensions. Again, globalization may accelerate developments but cannot be blamed as the key cause although many anti-globalists feel this is the case.

The discomfort with change is fueled by globalization because globalization accelerates change: new products, new technologies, and different lifestyles. It is precisely this progress, and the speed with which it is unfolding that scares many people, employees, companies, and governments. Rejecting globalization in this sense can be seen as a continuation of the commonly named Luddite movement that called for the destruction of machines during the Industrial Revolution.

This discomfort with change is illustrated in Figure 5.7. The vertical axis indicates the rate of change, and the horizontal axis gives the time frame. The figure shows two upward sloping curves. The steepest curve relates to the speed of change due to economic and social globalization, spurred by technological progress. The pace of change has not only quickened but is now happening on a global scale, including in emerging markets. After the Industrial Revolution and after 2000 in particular, the speed of change increased, and the curve in Figure 5.7 became steeper.

Discomfort with change if the speed of change accelerates

Greater connectivity also makes our rapidly changing world flat, to use Friedman's words. To use our example mentioned in Chapter 3, if a person in 1970 fell asleep and woke up today, they would no longer recognize the world.

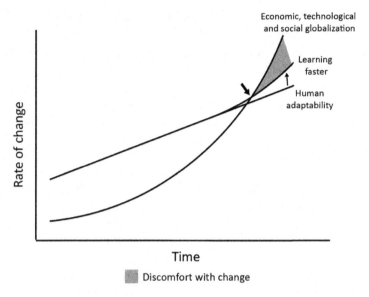

Figure 5.7:   The area of discomfort.

Source: Ebbers (2019) (based on Friedman, 2016).

The second line in Figure 5.7 is human adaptability. The curve is flat in the beginning. In *A People's History of the United States* (2015), Howard Zinn shows how long it took before people accepted that slavery is wrong and that all are created equal. It also took considerable time to accept gender equality as a human right. Over time, the curve becomes steeper. People became more flexible and accepted changes more easily. For example, people adapted relatively fast to social changes such as changing views on the employee–employer relationship and the relatively short time it took to get used to non-smoking policies in public buildings, schools, and public transport. In the past 15 years, we adapted fast and smoothly to the mobile revolution. The human race is adaptable and is learning faster (thanks to more knowledge and experiences with change), and the above examples show the rate at which we have to adapt has accelerated greatly in the past 30–40 years.

As long as the human adaptability curve stays above the speed of change in the world, there is no great uneasiness in society. Still, as soon as the lines cross, a period of discomfort follows, which is happening today. In this period, people feel disoriented. We cannot adapt to the world as fast as it is changing. We feel out of control and see globalization as an important driver behind this development. We could try to increase adaptability through education, traveling, and cultural exchanges, but the point is that the human adaptation line will stay relatively flat. This area of discomfort becomes more problematic as changes come faster and faster.

Watch out for giving away too much national autonomy

According to the pessimistic view, globalization has reduced the leeway that national governments have to make policy choices. In many cases, this reduced leeway is linked to the deterioration of social welfare and protection. This situation occurred in a worldwide neoliberal trend and supply-side economics toward smaller government, less support for redistributive measures, and greater deregulation of markets, including the labor market. In the 1980s and 1990s, many industrial nations have weakened social security mechanisms (protection against dismissal, unemployment compensation, social transfers, and pension levels) in order to improve the international competitiveness of domestic businesses. Governments are now less likely to compensate those who lose due to globalization, even though globalization increases uncertainty and the demand for social insurance.

5.4.3 *The cautious view*

The third view on the impact of globalization shares its concerns about adverse effects. Still, it concludes that the nation state and its government have sufficient room for optimal national policies and institutional choices to control the negative impact of globalization. So, globalization may bring inclusive and sustainable growth but not necessarily. It may lead to severe negative consequences but not necessarily. Therefore, countries must manage globalization by taking advantage of the benefits while minimizing the downsides. Essentially, NEP-9 countries are in the process of finding the optimal balance between market and government, and between opening up to and isolating from the globalized world.

5.4.3.1 *The bird in the cage*

To discuss globalization, we will apply a metaphor: a bird in its cage (based on Ebbers, 2020). The bird represents market forces, and the cage is the rules set by national governments, including government interference. The hyper globalized world that began in the 1990s and continued up to the global financial crisis of 2008 more or less freed the bird from its cage. In some cases, the cage was thrown away all together. Western countries let lose market forces and goods and capital flowed freely, without regulation or barriers. Countries like China, South Korea, Indonesia, India, and Brazil kept the bird caged but did give it a bigger cage. These countries combined a strong market with decisive state intervention. The disruptive effects of globalization require caging while these countries go through periods of intense transformation. A Chinese saying goes: "Crossing the river by feeling the stones," which means to seek stability before you take another step. In a sense, this fits our metaphor of caged globalization: make the cage larger to give the bird more freedom if needed and reduce the size of the cage when the bird gets disruptive.

I should explicitly point out that although the NEP-9 cage markets and globalization, it does not mean that the NEP-9 are globalization pessimists. They are not. Their view is that globalization by itself may be advantageous to economic development and the rise of human indicators. However, the market can be disruptive and needs government interference. That is why China is opening up to the outside world regarding international trade and foreign direct investment. At the same time, we know that the (local) government is intervening heavily in specific sectors. Consequently, in many aspects, China is still relatively closed off to the rest of the world. Substitute China with one of the other NEP-9 countries and the story is the same: opening up should be done cautiously when the country is ready for it.

Finding the optimal balance: adjusting the cage in which the bird can fly

In this case, active industrial policy, export promotion, and subsidizing of local firms and industrial clusters are part of the instruments governments have to modify the cage. In NEP-9 countries, the visible hand of government (and therefore the cage) was never gone and is back in fashion after the 2008 crisis and surely after the COVID-19 outbreak in 2020.

The cautious view recognizes that measuring the impact of globalization on development and human indicators is incredibly complicated, and assessing how international trade affects employment is exceptionally complex. There are just too many factors influencing both variables. This is one of the reasons why we often see a pragmatic approach toward international trade and foreign investments. There is a problem today, and it requires a reaction (e.g., trade barriers). In this sense, there is no principled viewpoint like the conviction we hear in the US saying that globalization and the resulted trade deficits (import is higher than export) mean that China and other countries are "stealing our jobs." As Figure 5.8 shows, this statement is hardly provable. On the contrary, high trade deficits are usually associated with low unemployment. High economic growth will increase imports, and at the same time, it may raise prices, resulting in lower export. In this case, high economic growth (with low unemployment) is linked to higher trade deficits. So, according to NEP-9 countries, globalization that creates a trade deficit is no problem.

The cautious view sees the potential dangers inherent to the race to the bottom, but at the same time, understands that western companies may have relatively high internal and external standards. And if poor working conditions exist in foreign companies, the commonly named CNN effect may lead to better circumstances in high-profile foreign companies. The NEP-9

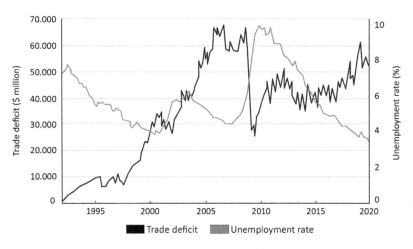

Figure 5.8:   US trade deficit and unemployment rate, 1992–2020.

Source: Urata (Ed.), Globalization and its economic consequences, 2021.

countries realize the dangers of a global monoculture, but greater attention and efforts to maintain ethnic identities may provide a counterbalance. Some even argue that globalization reinforces local cultures.

NEP-9 countries: opening up should be done cautiously, step by step in the correct sequence, when the country is ready for it

---

In India, for example, satellite TV has given Indians access to an increased number of regional channels, many of which can and do broadcast Indian content. This provides the audience with new opportunities to identify with regional ties. Within the same context, as societies integrate, they become more culturally diverse in many respects: IKEA has brought Swedish design to Chinese, which co-exists with Chinese design. McDonald's has popularized chicken tikka and hamburgers in Britain, which co-exist with fish and chips. An important learning point is that "good" globalization requires specific policies.

5.5 NEP-9's Views on Globalization Today

As shown in Figure 5.5 earlier in the chapter, most people and policymakers in NEP-9 countries still have faith in globalization and the positive impact it may bring. As long as globalization is caged, and the government has the autonomy to make the cave bigger or smaller, cautious globalization is a force for good. We can summarize the NEP-9 views on globalization in three points:

1.   Away from the commonly named Washington Consensus
2.   Toward the Beijing Consensus
3.   Smart globalization

5.5.1 *The Washington Consensus*

The world was a pretty dark place right after World War II, characterized by growing ideological divisions between countries, unimaginable destruction in Europe and other parts of the world, economic crises, and protectionist attitudes. At that time, the United States was the new economic superpower, and its economy was by far the largest in the world. Undoubtedly the largest exporter, it had considerable political sway over

European countries, unquestioned dominance in high-tech manufacturing, and large American companies ruled the world markets. From this position of undisputed political and economic dominance, the US decided to push for trade liberalization.

US domination of multilateral institutions that set the global rules

---

In doing so, they accepted, somewhat unenthusiastically, global rules as long as it was (also) in the interest of the United States. Their position of global power made it logical that the US dominated multilateral institutions such as the GATT, IMF, and the World Bank and that these institutions all followed the paradigm of neoliberal thinking, open markets, and competition. This dominant paradigm became a synonym for the commonly named Washington Consensus.

The Washington Consensus denotes a set of policy prescriptions that forms the standard package deal offered by the IMF and the World Bank to countries in crisis asking these Washington-based institutions for help. In Chapter 4, we pinpointed the Latin American debt crisis of the early 1980s as the start of the Washington Consensus. The debt crisis resulted in an enormous demand for IMF loans from, for example, Brazil, Mexico, and Argentina. Countries received financial aid from the IMF and World Bank under certain strict conditions. These conditions were later labeled by John Williamson as the Washington Consensus in 1989.

The conditionality of the IMF: one sizes fits all

The core of the Washington Consensus is the neoliberal paradigm of a free market economy with more market and less government. In the Washington Consensus, markets, not states, has the upper hand and can be summarized with the following conditions.

1. Fiscal discipline (responsible government spending)
2. Redirection of public spending toward education, health, and infrastructure
3. Tax reform (broadening the tax base and cutting tax rates)
4. Property rights protection
5. Market-determined interest rates
6. Stable, market-driven exchange rates

7. Trade liberalization (eliminating quotas and tariffs)
8. Openness to foreign direct investment and other capital flows
9. Privatization of state-owned enterprises
10. Deregulation

Recommendations such as fiscal discipline, more social spending on education and healthcare, broadening the tax base, and property rights protection are the consensus view; few people will argue these are not needed for development. However, there is a lot of disagreement regarding the other six prescriptions. It is doubtful whether deregulation, privatization, and trade liberalization are in the interest of every country at any time, and following the recommendations of the Washington Consensus has not proved a precondition for success. In 2002, Williamson stated his Washington Consensus label was misused and that the term was high-jacked by "market fundamentalism" and the "narrow-minded neoliberal agenda": "I of course never intended my term to imply policies like capital account liberalization (I quite consciously excluded that), monetarism, supply-side economics, or a minimal state (getting the state out of welfare provision and income redistribution), which I think of as essentially neo-liberal ideas" (PIIE, November 6, 2002).

The neo-liberal free-market paradigm is under attack as well as the Washington consensus that is built upon it

---

The Washington Consensus is under attack. Not only its neoliberal free-market paradigm but also Washington-based institutions like the IMF and the World Bank. The first major blow to the Washington Consensus came with the East Asian financial crisis of 1997 discussed earlier in the chapter. The second shock to free-market economics was the global financial crisis that started in 2008, driven by the US sub-prime mortgage crisis. This crisis hit the heart of the pro-market paradigm and consequently the Washington Consensus. As many industrialized economies undertook far-reaching state interventions, it became harder to make a credible case to emerging economies that the market should be the guiding principle in the domestic economy and politics because the market alone can generate welfare and prosperity. Again, privatization and free trade did not cause the crisis but certainly made it possible. NEP-9 authorities know how important the market was, in its various forms, in generating prosperity globally as well in specific countries. They also recognize the positive impact of a rule-based system, guided by the WTO as part of the Washington institutions. But rising powers face a dilemma in their orientations toward global governance. On the one hand, the NEP-9 countries are dependent on the existing institutional frameworks of global governance. On the other hand, their interventionist policies (and disbelief in the Washington Consensus) put them into tension with the doctrines of global governance, as we will see in Chapter 7.

5.5.2 *Beijing Consensus*

Unease was growing among many emerging markets and developing countries about laissez-faire market economics as the driving force behind IMF conditionalities. In the 1990s, for the first time, there was an alternative to achieving economic development without following the Washington Consensus. This new and possibly better growth model for achieving economic and social progress was developed and implemented by China. Joshua Cooper Ramo introduced the term Beijing Consensus in his 2004 article *The Beijing Consensus*: "China is marking a path for other nations around the world who are trying to figure out not simply how to develop their countries but also how to fit into the international order in a way that allows them to be truly independent, to protect their way of life and political choices in a world with a single massively powerful center of gravity. I call this new center and physics of power and development the Beijing Consensus."

A new alternative for achieving longer term prosperity

According to Ramo, China's model for economic growth is achieving economic prosperity precisely because they do not apply all aspects of the IMF rules. The words "all aspects" are important here. In many areas, China has followed several of the IMF recommendations. However, China has also convincingly demonstrated that deregulated, market-based decision-making is not the only path to economic growth and successful integration into the global economy. China's success is an example of economic development that combines the advantages of free trade under the auspices of the WTO but at the same time makes clear that sometimes government intervention is needed to smooth the transition process.

It shows that avoiding neoliberal reforms *and* growing human development is possible. It offered an alternative to the strict and fixed one size fits all formula dictated by the Washington institutions.

Earlier in the book, we discussed that imitation of a successful growth model does not necessarily work. Imitating Argentinean soccer star Leoni Messi to become the best soccer player in the world is easier said than done! The same applies to the Beijing Consensus and countries. Strategies that work for some countries may not work for others. The economic, social, and political characteristics which shape the context in which growth development strategies are implemented are, in many cases, unique to China. The "Chinese model" is not a simple recipe for other countries to follow. However, we can undoubtedly translate elements of the Chinese growth model to today's emerging markets and developing countries. Following the Beijing Consensus policy package goes hand in hand with discontent about IMF conditionalities and failures of structural adjustment policies and poverty reduction strategies subscribed by organizations such as the World Bank and western donors.

An essential element of the Beijing Consensus is that it sees government intervention, resulting in some protectionism and replacing the market, as an important tool for increasing welfare. In this sense, the Being Consensus is selective globalization, instead of fully fledged open globalization prescribed by the Washington Consensus. A second important element of the Beijing Consensus is the prioritizing of economic rights and de-prioritizing of political rights. Therefore, China does not prescribe a specific government policy and sets no rules for good governance, a condition often imposed by the IMF and the World Bank. It does not interfere in domestic issues and emphasizes sovereignty. This attitude does mean that China also supports undemocratic regimes: financial aid without political conditionalities. As seen in Figure 5.9, flexibility, pragmatism, and gradualism are key features of the Beijing Consensus. This gradualism or evolutionary change gives domestic policymakers the freedom to develop their optimal development process.

NEP-9 countries: selective globalization is the road to prosperity

---

We discussed the different forms of state capitalism in Chapter 4. Fukuyama's book, published in 1992 after the collapse of the Soviet Union, predicted the triumph of capitalism and the universalization of

Washington Consensus	Beijing Consensus
Fiscal discipline and broadening the tax base More social spending/social safetey net Spending on education, health and infrastructure	
Market determined interest rate and exchange rate	Replacing the market for more government intervention
Trade liberalization	Gradual opening-up and restructuring
Privatization & deregulation	Pragmatic choices and flexibility
Open globalization	Selective globalization
Prioritizing human rights	Prioritizing economic rights

Figure 5.9: Differences between the Washington and Beijing Consensuses.

Western liberal democracy as the optimal economic system, and we concluded that is not the reality of today. As private capitalism came under attack, revised state capitalism emerged, summarized by the Beijing Consensus: an economic system embraced by many emerging markets, including the NEP-9 and many of today's developing countries.

The Beijing Consensus has important implications for the future of globalization. China and some other Asian miracles achieved growth by not following the recommendations of the IMF and WTO and mainstream economic theories. For example, capital restrictions, which are against the IMF rules, proved to be a significant advantage. Furthermore, China showed that subsidies and government support are sometimes helpful and needed to become a prosperous trading nation. State intervention, protecting essential industries, and gradualism are crucial reasons for China's success.

Moreover, every country that has successfully caught up employed some (or all) of these tactics, including Germany and the United States. Obviously, protectionism is terrible for longer-term economic development and should be avoided as a structural feature of an economy. However, opening up should be done gradually. This is what I have labeled smart globalization (Ebbers, 2019).

5.5.3 *Smart globalization*

The above analysis provides us with the third element of the NEP-9 viewpoints on globalization: smart globalization. We will combine this concept with the argument made by Dani Rodrik (2011), who said that it is not possible to combine full-scale globalization, political democracy, and nation state sovereignty. At most, you can have two out of three. He called this impossibility the Globalization Paradox or the Impossible Trilemma.

Figure 5.10 visualizes this fundamental incompatibility between hyper-globalization, democracy, and national sovereignty. We can combine any two of these but never have all three simultaneously and fully. Consequently, there are three possible worlds: the Washington Consensus, global governance, and smart globalization. We may adjust the framework in Figure 5.10 slightly by narrowing "democratic policies" down to "listening to the majority of the citizenry." This adjustment is logical because it reduced the gap between democracy and no democracy. Obviously, this listening to your citizens is impossible to measure in a non-democratic country, but we can use proxies such as trust in the government, transparency, and accountability.

- *Washington Consensus:* The combination of hyper-globalization and nation state sovereignty on domestic issues precludes following the people's wishes. For example, a government may lower profit tax for foreign companies operating in the country because it fears they will leave when taxation is high. This move may be against the wishes of the majority of the people. Despite heavy opposition, the policy measure is

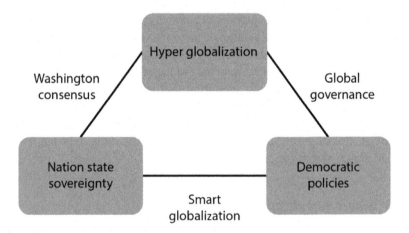

Figure 5.10:   The Globalization Paradox.

Source: Ebbers (2019) (based on Rodrik, 2011).

implemented. Obviously, elected policymakers are not willing to do this structurally and even non-democratic regimes would be hesitating to implement these sorts of measures against the will of the public.

- *Global governance:* If a country chooses democracy and hyper-globalization, decisions must be made and enforced at the supranational level, such as the WTO, IMF, or European Union. In this case, you cannot give nation state autonomy in policymaking. Essentially, you even do not need the nation state. All relevant decisions must be reached within the global platform(s), directly or indirectly elected. As we will see in Chapter 7, the NEP-9 countries are unwilling to surrender that much autonomy to global and regional institutions. The same holds for Western countries, for that matter.

Smart globalization means flexibility, pragmatism and prioritizing domestic objectives

---

There is only one world relevant for NEP-9 countries: a world in which hyper-globalization is transformed into smart globalization. This "Globalization Lite" is a nation-based paradigm of combining market forces and opening up, with government interference and closing down.

- *Smart globalization:* Combining political democracy with nation state sovereignty precludes hyper-globalization. Implements of higher minimum wages and higher profit taxation to pay for a robust social safety net by a nation state's government (in listening to its citizens) will automatically result in capital leaving the country. To counteract this, the government can implement capital controls and, in doing so, act in opposition to hyper-globalization.

The NEP-9 countries choosing smart globalization fit the view that there is no one way to prosperity. Countries differ in economic structure, cultural heritage, and social dimensions and consequently have the right to implement specific, country-based measures. This freedom of choice also applies to non-democratic countries. In this sense, smart means flexible. Room and flexibility for national policies ensure policymakers will feel comfortable and do not feel threatened. The future of globalization will continue to progress toward smart globalization because the NEP-9 have the power to mold the global architecture of tomorrow, including the trade environment, which we will discuss in the next chapter.

Chapter 6

International Trade and the Role of the NEP-9

6.1 Large Exporters

The NEP-9 are significant exporters. In 2020, China was the largest exporter worldwide. In the same year, South Korea, Mexico, Russia, and India were all in the top 20. Figure 6.1 shows the transfer of export power from the advanced nations to the largest emerging markets between 1985 and 2020. On one side are the G7, the Netherlands, and Belgium because in 1990, these were the largest western traders. On the other side are the NEP-9 countries. The focus is on total export and import: there is no differentiation between merchandise trade and trade in services. Between 1990 and 2020, the share of NEP-9 in world export increased from less than 10% to almost 24%. The same pattern can be seen with respect to import. In 2020, the NEP-9 export was already 58% of that of the largest nine exporting nations, changing mutual relationships dramatically.

As we saw earlier in the book, under specific circumstances, it is beneficial for a country to open up and to compete in international markets. We discussed the long-term drivers behind economic development and linked factors such as productivity and innovation to international competition and hence, international trade. The conclusion was clear: international trade can stimulate economic development. The export-led growth strategy implemented by some Asian nations in the 1960s and 1970s "proved" this positive connection. By following the World Bank report "The East Asian Miracle" (1993), we labeled these Asian countries as

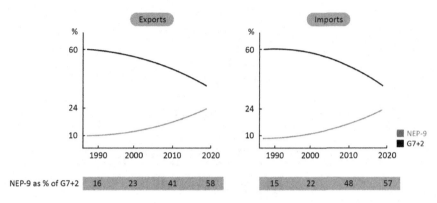

Figure 6.1:   Importance of NEP-9 in world trade; world export and import, 1985–2020.
Source: Based on WTO Database (2021).

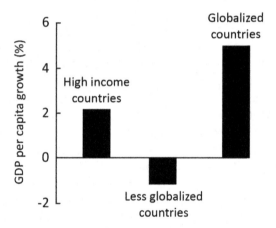

Figure 6.2:   The difference in economic growth (annual growth between 1980 and 1990) between globalizers and non-globalizers.

Source: Dollar and Kraay (2001), based on World Bank (1993).

globalizers, contrasting with the non-globalizers. Figure 6.2 shows the advantages of being a globalizer.

I put "proved" between quotation marks because it appeared that at that time, these Asian countries were hardly open economies. They were open regarding international trade, but at the same time, there was heavy government inference. Earlier in the book, I called this trade policy smart and responsible.

1990	% share in total	2020	% share in total
Clothing	9.9	Consumer electronics	27.4
Miscellaneous manuf. art.	9.2	Machinery (incl. computers)	17.0
Leather	8.2	Furniture, lighting, signs	4.2
Non-edible agricultural prod.	7.4	Plastic articles	3.7
Crude oil	6.8	Medical apparatus	3.1
Carpets	5.4	Vehicles	2.9
Knitwear	5.3	Miscellaneous textiles	2.9
Yarns fabrics	3.3	Toys and games	2.8
Consumer electronics	3.2	Articles of iron or steel	2.7
Plastic articles	2.5	Clothing and accessories	2.4

Figure 6.3:   China's export structure, 1990 and 2020.

Source: Worldstopexports.com, based on WTO (2021).

The Asian countries showed us also that export expansion alone is not sufficient to escape the middle-income trap. It should be complemented by a change in export composition. During the first session of the International Trade course, I ask my students to explain the export structure of China in, for example, 1990 and 2020 (Figure 6.3).

The answers regarding 1990 are always straightforward. Most students link the export structure of that time to natural resources (cotton and oil) and related products. They also note the labor-intensive features of several 1990 export products associated with China's labor surplus and low wages at that time. The export structure of 2020 causes much more discussion in the classroom. How to explain the rise in machinery, medical equipment, or vehicles? We will find out in the next section.

6.2 Explaining International Trade

Over the years, economists have developed several theories to explain trade flows. One mainstream of ideas explains international trade from the perspective of a country. Country-specific features are the basis for explaining trade flows. These country-based theories are called traditional trade theories. By the mid-20th century, these began to shift toward explaining trade from the perspective of companies, away from the country's perspective. These are the modern trade theories. They explain international trade executed by companies through government interference, consumer tastes, and companies' choices to invest (and export from) abroad. Traditional and modern trade theories are summarized in Figure 6.4.

Traditional (country-based) trade theories	Modern (firm-based) trade theories
Absolute advantage	Country similarity
Comparative advantage	product life cycle
Factor-proportion theory	Strategic trade theory
(Heckscher-Ohlin paradigm)	(Infant industry argument)
	Diamond model
	FDI-induced trade

Figure 6.4:   International trade theories.

We will start our discussion by explaining trade flows with the economic theory and policy of mercantilism. Many textbooks consider mercantilism the first international trade theory and part of the traditional trade theory because it focuses on the whole country and not on specific companies. However, others argue that mercantilism is part of modern trade theories because it emphasizes the vital role of the government in intervening in international trade. I decided to exclude mercantilism from the overview of trade theories in Figure 6.4 because it does not explain a country's export structure but only the size of its export and import.

6.2.1 *Mercantilism*

The mercantilist view emerged in the 16th century and flourished well into the late 1800s when gold and silver were used in trade between countries. A country could earn gold and silver by exporting goods while importing countries saw an outflow of gold and silver. Mercantilism said that the amount of its gold and silver holdings determined the wealth of a country. Therefore, the policy recommendation was clear: a country should promote and increase exports and discourage imports. The aim was to achieve a trade surplus, a situation where the value of exports is greater than the value of imports.

Growing mercantilist behavior in NEP-9 countries
as well as in the West

The basic assumption of mercantilism is that trade is a *zero-sum game*: A gain by one country results in a loss by another. In general, most economists today reject the basic elements of mercantilism, but this doctrine is still seen today. Neomercantilism guided the US trade policy after

2016 with its emphasis on "America First." Under the Biden administration, many US policymakers also see international competition as a fight
producing winners and losers. Industrial and export-promoting policies
and protection of domestic industries all fit with the neomercantilism
model of state intervention. Also, the NEP-9 countries use a mix of these
measures to promote exports. For example, China and South Korea's
export success resulted from protecting their domestic industries from
foreign competition and providing substantial subsidies. South Korea's
industry policy meant government support for *chaebols;* large business
groups were able to compete internationally after receiving government
support for some time. During a visit to my university in the Netherlands
in 2012, Kishore Mahbubani (discussed in Chapter 3) stressed that the rise
of neomercantilism does not mean that belief in free trade has disappeared: "In general, large emerging markets believe in the advantages of
free trade. However, sometimes it is needed to help domestic sectors to
prepare for international competition. It is all about the correct sequence."
Neomercantilism can also be a response to the competitive and disruptive
consequences of free trade, particularly if the other party is perceived to
engage in neomercantilist strategies.

NEP-9 countries in the Global Mercantilist Index

The ITIF Global Mercantilist Index 2019 ranks China as the most
mercantilist nation. The Index of this information technology think tank is
based on the number and intensity of distortive trade policies, such as
restricting market access, export subsidies, forced localization, currency
manipulation, and government involvement. NEP-9 countries such as
India, Brazil, Indonesia, Russia, and Turkey also engaged in mercantilist
practices, placing them in the report's "moderate-high" category. Mexican
and South African governments also intervene in trade, but less so, which
puts them in the "moderate-low" cohort. South Korea is the only NEP-9 in
the "low" category. The range of government interference used by the
NEP-9 is broad. China, Indonesia, and Brazil's industry policies aim to
protect strategic sectors in the economy. India uses the local content rule
a lot to make sure that domestic suppliers can grow, parallel with foreign
investors, and Russia favors state-owned companies like Gazprom to
achieve control over energy supply and distribution. These neomercantilist strategies are not for free. As we saw in earlier chapters, international

competition and opening up may increase productivity. From this point of view, neomercantilist behavior can reduce this competitive force, resulting in lower productivity growth.

6.2.2 Traditional trade theories

6.2.2.1 Absolute and comparative advantages

In 1776, Adam Smith questioned the leading mercantilist theory in *The Wealth of Nations*, saying that trade between countries must result from market forces and government should not interfere. From this market perspective, bilateral trade between two countries is based on the so-called *absolute advantage:* the ability of a country to produce a good more efficiently than another nation. If India can produce much more cotton per worker than Brazil due to climate and natural resources, India has an absolute advantage in cotton. If Brazil needs fewer resources to produce the same amount of soybeans as India, Brazil has an absolute advantage in soybean production. Taking these examples further, we can say that India specializes in cotton production, while Brazil focuses on soybeans. Exchanging these products through international trade generates a win-win for both countries. In this case, trade is a positive-sum game, creating net gains for both countries, in contrast to the zero-sum game paradigm within (neo)mercantilism. Be aware that we only consider the productivity of the production process and do not take costs into account. However, it is logical to assume that a country with an absolute advantage can sell the goods for less than a country with no absolute advantage.

Absolute and comparative advantage theories: international trade is a positive-sum game

---

David Ricardo took Smith's theory one step further by exploring what might happen when one country has an absolute advantage in the production of all goods. What if India produced both cotton and soybeans more efficiently than Brazil? In that case, it may not make sense for India to engage in international trade. Ricardo introduced the theory of comparative advantage in 1817 to prove that even in this case, India would gain from international trade. This may seem counterintuitive but let's look at an example from daily life. In my classroom sessions, I use PowerPoint or Prezi. I'm quite handy with these: I know what I want and can develop slides quickly, faster than a student assistant who has problems reading my handwriting and difficulty understanding my graphs. In this case, I have an absolute advantage in teaching and making slides. Unsurprisingly, I like teaching much more than developing slides, and teaching is much more profitable. Every hour spent on making slides could have been used to teach a class. This lost teaching time is the commonly named *opportunity cost*. In general, my productivity (and income) is highest if I focus on teaching and hire the most qualified student assistant to work on the slides efficiently, even though they might be slower than me. By concentrating on our respective tasks, the overall productivity as a team is higher. Although simplistic, this example demonstrates the basics of the comparative advantage theory. Although Brazil (or the student assistant) is less efficient in the production of soybeans (or the slides) compared to India (the professor), it can produce that item better and more efficiently than cotton (or teaching). If each country specializes in the products where it is comparatively more efficient, total production (and consequently income and consumption) is higher compared to the situation without trade. The difference between an absolute and comparative advantage is that a comparative advantage focuses on the relative productivity differences, whereas the absolute advantage looks at the absolute productivity.

Many assumptions behind the positive-sum game paradigm: the real world is much more complex

Of course, the world economy is much more complex and consists of more than two countries and products. Trade barriers may exist, and goods must be transported, stored, and distributed. The result is that this theory of comparative advantage only works within the context of many quite strict assumptions. For example, it is assumed that resources can move freely from the production of one good to another without switching costs within a country. In reality, this is not always the case. The same holds for the assumed absence of transportation costs. The cost of shipping goods from China to Europe has increased dramatically in 2020 and 2021 as the COVID-19 pandemic disrupted trade. At the beginning of 2020, it cost around $2,000 to ship a 40 ft container from China to Europe. In June 2021, that increased to $17,000, with slight variations between regions. A country may have a comparative advantage, but when high transportation costs make distance crucial, this comparative advantage will not translate into high and growing exports.

6.2.2.2 *Comparative and competitive advantage*

Before diving further into the concept of comparative advantage, it is essential to distinguish between *comparative* advantage and *competitive* advantage. Competitive advantage refers to factors that allow a company to produce goods or services better or more cheaply than its rivals. This competitive advantage is related to a company and is driven by brand loyalty, reputation, distribution network, and relationships with suppliers. In contrast, comparative advantage is a country-based concept based on opportunity cost and efficiency. Therefore, the title of Michael E. Porter's book, *The Competitive Advantage of Nations* (1990), was a puzzle of sorts, mashing up competitive and comparative advantage. Obviously, it was done by purpose. Porter believes that the comparative advantages of countries rely heavily upon the competitive advantages of the enterprises and industries of that country. For example, the fact that the Netherlands can export flowers is based on the competitiveness of companies operating in this sector and less on the comparative advantage of the Netherlands regarding climate and availability of land area. Therefore, Porter's theory is an example of the modern trade theory, which we will discuss in the next section.

Watch out for specializing too much

The positive effects of international trade based on comparative advantages are pretty straightforward. Countries specialize in areas that they are naturally good at and benefit from this specialization. That means the average cost of producing the goods falls to a certain minimum level because more goods are made. Similarly, countries can benefit from increased learning due to specialization. They are more skilled at making the product because they have specialized in it. The result is increased efficiency in those countries, producing more goods at lower costs and prices. So, whenever a country has a comparative advantage in production, it can benefit from specialization and trade. However, specialization can also have adverse effects on a country's economy. For example, there is a danger of overspecialization. A sudden fall in demand or an available substitute product may dramatically impact the industry. Another negative effect of specialization is the high dependency on other countries, as seen in 2020–2021 during the COVID-19 pandemic. It became clear that the US imports 90% of its antibiotics used from China. The same was true for face masks, medical gloves, and healthcare equipment. Governments intervened to counteract this dependency. For example, in 2020, the Japanese government announced they planned to award subsidies to Japanese companies to produce medicines and healthcare products domestically.

6.2.2.3 *Abundance of resources*

The absolute and comparative advantage theories also provide straightforward explanations of trade structures. First, countries can have an advantage because they are richly endowed with particular natural resources. For example, countries with plentiful oil resources can generally produce oil inexpensively. It is also logical that oil-producing nations such as Russia have a comparative advantage in producing and exporting chemical and other oil-related products because the locally produced oil reduces the cost of production in the chemical sector. Blessed with an abundant supply of sunshine, soil, and water, Brazil is the top producer and exporter of beef, coffee, soybeans, and sugar. South Africa is a large producer and exporter of gold, silver, platinum, and diamonds due to the availability of these resources. Related to the first point, a second explanation for having a comparative advantage is based on the quantity of labor and capital. India has a comparative advantage and exports labor-intensive commodities and services (such as ICT) based on its relative abundance of cheap labor. This is the starting point of the commonly named *factor proportions theory* or the Heckscher–Ohlin theory (Heckscher, 1919; Ohlin, 1933).

The focus is on the relative abundance of resources

According to this theory, countries with a comparative advantage will export those goods that make intensive use of locally abundant factors while importing goods that make intensive use of locally scarce factors. For example, South Korea is relatively well endowed with capital. The typical worker has plenty of machinery and equipment to assist with their work. Therefore, the price of capital is relatively low

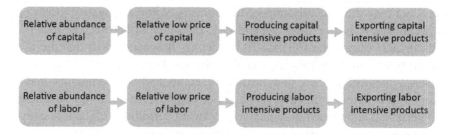

Figure 6.5:   Factor proportions theory.

compared to the price of labor, resulting in comparative advantage in those goods that require much capital and only a little labor, such as automobiles and chemicals. At the same time, the relatively high price of labor results in high production costs of labor-intensive goods, such as textiles, sporting goods, and simple consumer electronics, compared to countries with plentiful labor and low wage rates, such as Indonesia or India. Countries with abundant labor will specialize in and export labor-intensive goods and import more capital-intensive products (Figure 6.5).

The above example clarifies that in the Heckscher–Ohlin theory, it is not the absolute amount of capital that is important. Instead, it is the amount of capital per worker. South Korea has less total capital than China but more capital per worker. Furthermore, the factor proportions theory shows that it is better to focus on the availability of labor (or capital for that matter) instead of referring to specific products. For example, it shows that China has a comparative advantage in assembling the iPhone, not on the iPhone as a complete product. Although most textbook examples of comparative advantages are about goods, we can also use the concept for explaining the service exports (call centers, banking, and entertainment) of India or Turkey.

6.2.2.4 *Latent comparative advantages and government interference*

The success of the Indian service sector is attributable to key government policies that favor ICT industry development. These include government investment in high-speed internet connectivity for software parks, keeping hardware and software imports duty-free, and public investment in technical education. So, here government intervention may explain the comparative advantage and a large part of the export success. This role of the government is also important in explaining the comparative advantages of South Korea. The South Korean and Indian cases are interesting because they show the government can create comparative advantages, while the theory emphasizes that market forces should do this. If South Korea had specialized according to its comparative advantages in the 1960s and 1970s, it would have concentrated on exporting primary goods and raw materials. We know through the smiling curve analysis, explained earlier in the book, that this is not a sound basis for further development and escaping the middle-income trap.

Industry policy is needed to free the latent comparative advantage

---

The critical point is that a trade liberalization policy that solely focuses on taking advantage of the existing comparative advantage may not deliver the promised sustainable economic growth. It is essential for the government of middle-income countries, like India, China, South Africa, Brazil, Mexico today, or South Korea in the past, that industrial upgrading and development support of specific industries is based on the country's latent comparative advantages, not on current comparative advantages. The upgrading process will not be initiated by market forces alone.

However, selecting sectors with latent comparative advantages is not easy. For example, it would be unwise to prioritize sectors too far away from the country's comparative advantage, as these industries cannot compete internationally, even after substantial help.

6.2.2.5 *Measuring comparative advantage*

As stated above, we may have ideas about a country's comparative advantages, but economists always want to measure. One way to do this is to use actual trade flows, the essence of the commonly named revealed comparative advantage (RCA), or the Balassa index, developed by Balassa in 1965. RCA is defined as the ratio of two shares. The numerator is the share of the country's total exports of the commodity in question. The denominator is the share of the world exports of the same commodity in total exports. In this case, the world is the benchmark group. Besides world export, we can also use another benchmark group if applicable. Essentially, we compare the competitiveness of each country in the export of a particular commodity group. If the RCA index is 1 for a given product, the percentage share of that product in a country's total exports is the same as in the benchmark group. When the RCA index is above 1, the export of a specific product is relatively large, and the country is said to have a comparative advantage in that product. For example, the export of mobile phones was around 5.7% of total Chinese exports in 2020. The share of mobile phones in total world exports is approximately 1.1% in the same year. With 5.2, the Chinese RCA of mobile phones is far above 1. Hence, China has a (strong) comparative advantage in mobile phones.

The formula of the revealed comparative advantage is:

$$RCA = \left(\frac{x_{ij}}{x_{ik}}\right) / \left(\frac{x_j}{x_k}\right),$$

where: RCA is the revealed comparative advantage of product *i*, from region relative to a reference zone *k*; X_{ij} is the value of exports of product *i* from region *j*; X_{ik} is the total value of exports of product *i* in reference zone *k*; X_j is the total value of all exports from region *j*; X_k is the total value of all exports from reference zone *k*.

RCA 13 - 58	RCA 6 - 20	RCA 3 - 6
South Africa	**India**	**China**
42 - Silver & platinum	16 - Rice	5 - Silk
41 - Ores	11 - Spices	5 - Lighting fixture & fittings
16 - Cereal & flour	10 - Pearls & precious stones	4 - Baby cariage & wheel toys
13 - Wool	9 - Textile fibres	3 - Telecom equipment
Brazil	**Turkey**	**South Korea**
29 - Oil seeds & oleaginous fruits	20 - Wheat products	6 - Polymers & styrene
18 - Tobacco	16 - Floor coverings	6 - Ships & boats
16 - Aluminium ores	9 - Stone & gravel	5 - Synthetic fibres
15 - Sugar	8 - Iron & steel	4 - Machine parts
Indonesia	**Russia**	**Mexico**
58 - Briquettes	9 - Ingots of iron & steel	7 - Road motor vehicles
51 - Vegetable faits & oil	7 - Wheat	6 - Radio-broadcast receivers
32 - Tin	6 - Fertilizers	6 - Television sets
31 - Natural rubber	6 - Coal	4 - Vegetables

Figure 6.6:　RCA indices above 1 for the NEP, selected products, three-digit, 2020.

Source: UNCTAD Database (2021).

6.2.2.6 *Interpretations based on the revealed comparative advantage concept*

The overview of some of the comparative advantages in NEP-9 countries shown in Figure 6.6 points to a clear connection with natural resources. Brazil's advantages lie in specific agricultural products, while Russia's comparative advantage is oil and related products. However, the mobile phone example shows that the RCA is an indirect proxy for showing comparative advantages in manufacturers. Does the RCA of 5.2 mean that China has a comparative advantage in mobile phones? China exports many smartphones, but partly because China has a comparative advantage in the assembly of, for example, iPhones. Just because a country is the final exporter of a good does not mean that it is responsible for the majority of that good's production. Obviously, because of the worldwide fragmentation of the production process, global supply chains change our understanding of comparative advantage. To illuminate the true comparative advantage of a country, we must isolate how much added value a country contributes to the production of a good.

Sensitivity to statistical disaggregation

In line with what was said about the export concentration indices used in Chapter 4, the Balassa index is also vulnerable to the level of aggregation. The broader the product group in the Harmonized System (see the following), the lower the indices. When we focus on a detailed level, we see incredibly high indices. For example, the share of agricultural products in the Brazilian export is not much different from the world average. Still, if we zoom in on certain narrowly defined products, we may see significant differences, and, therefore, high RCA indices, for specific products, such as poultry, soybeans, and sugar. We see the same happening with respect to Chinese mobile phones and telecom equipment export. The mobile phone is a four-digit item, while it is aggregated into telecom equipment on the three-digit scale.

Within trade statistics, we can analyze export and import through the commonly named Harmonized System of product classification (HS), ranging from one to six digits. One is the most aggregated clustering, and six is the most specific. Figure 6.7 gives an example of the classification. It shows the main export of Mexico in 2020. The export of "vehicles and their parts" (two digits) is divided into product groups, such as "cars,"

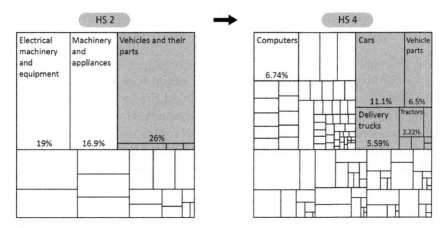

Figure 6.7:   Mexican exports, 2020, two- and four-digit Harmonized System, percentage of total.

Source: UN Comtrade database.

"vehicle parts," "tractors," and "delivery trucks," among others, on a four-digit scale. "Computers" is a four-digit product group and part of "Electrical machinery and equipment" on a two-digit scale.

Be aware that a high Balassa index does not automatically translate into an important export product. For example, the RCA index of the Dutch flower export is exceptionally high (30), but this sector makes up less than 1% of total Dutch exports. A final warning for using the Balassa Index is that government interference influences export and import. Therefore, the assumption that actual trade flows can be a proxy for comparative advantage is not always correct. It is not new that actual trade patterns are different from what you would expect, based on the factor proportions available in the country.

Actual trade flows are often not in line with the theory of comparative advantage

---

As early as the 1950s, economist Leontief observed that the United States was relatively well endowed with capital. Therefore, according to the factor proportions theory, the United States should export capital-intensive goods and import labor-intensive ones. However, Leontief found that the opposite was the case. US exports were generally more labor intensive than the type of products that the country imported.

Because his finding was the opposite of those predicted by the Heckscher–Ohlin theory, it became known as the Leontief paradox (Leontief, 1956). Although later research questioned his methodology, what remains clear is that actual international trade flows are impacted by numerous factors and not always driven by comparative advantages alone. Therefore, measuring comparative advantages through actual trade flows is dangerous.

6.2.3 *Modern trade theories*

As shown in Figure 6.8, both China and Mexico export and import the same products. For example, these countries export electrical machinery and equipment, while at the same time, they also import these products.

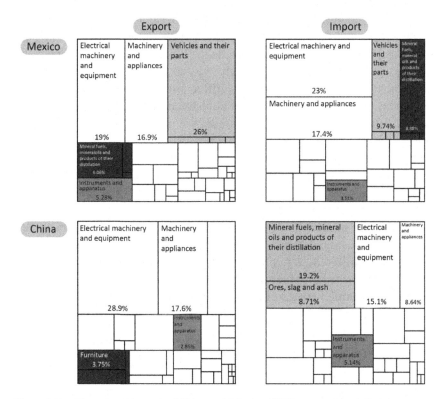

Figure 6.8:   Export and import of China and Mexico (HS2), percentage of total.

Source: UN Comtrade database.

The same holds for machinery and appliances. This is a puzzle within the traditional trade theories. These can only explain the export and import of different products but cannot explain China and Mexico exporting and importing identical products. Differences between countries in productivity (as predicted by the Ricardian model) or factor endowments (as predicted by the Heckscher–Ohlin model) can only explain exporting and importing different products. For example, Brazil exports agricultural products and imports cars from South Korea.

6.2.3.1 *Intra-industry trade*

Exporting and importing identical products is also called intra-industry trade. Of course, "identical" is a broad term. Intra-industry trade may arise because many different types of products are aggregated into one category or industry: exporting a machine used in agriculture and importing a machine that can produce computer chips. Although statistically, they are both machines, they are different products. If we disaggregate China's and Mexico's export and import enough, we see that within machinery and equipment, the exported products differ from the imported products. However, even after this statistical adjustment, traditional trade theories cannot fully explain intra-industry trade. We need the additional explanations provided by modern trade theories. In contrast to the traditional, country-based theories, modern trade theories were primarily developed by business school professors, not economists. The consequence is that international trade is explained through company and government actions and driven by consumer behavior.

One early modern trade theory is Linder's country similarity theory (1961). It is demand-based instead of supply-based theories involving international differences in productivity or factor endowments. According to the country similarity theory, manufactured goods trade occurs between countries in parallel stages of development with similar domestic demand conditions.

Implementing consumer preferences in trade theories

This means that consumers in these countries have comparable preferences, associated with product differentiation, quality issues, and brands, based on similar income levels. A German consumer may prefer the design and power of an Italian car, while an Italian consumer favors a solid and trustworthy German one. The result is that both Germany and Italy export and import the "same" product. This also holds for consumer goods, such as smartphones, clothing, and household appliances. The country similarity theory helps explain part of today's trade, even between developed and developing countries that do not have similar income levels. For example, in many aspects, the urban middle class in emerging markets has the same consumer patterns as their peers in the West.

6.2.3.2 *Strategic trade theory and the infant industry argument*

The second modern trade theory emphasizes that government intervention may increase exports and associated economic development. This is the commonly named *strategic trade theory* and related to this is the *infant industry argument*. The starting point is that state intervention and protectionism in one form or another are helpful. In the case of South Korea, important industries were developed behind protectionist walls and with substantial government support. The same can be said for countries such as Germany, France, and the Netherlands in the 1950s and 1960s. According to the strategic trade theory, the use of trade policies, including tariffs, subsidies, and government procurement, is needed because of imperfect competition and economies of scale. Following Paul Krugman (1986), economies of scale make it very difficult for newcomers to enter a market.

Overcoming the barrier of economies of scale

For example, Volkswagen and Boeing both benefit from economies of scale. The larger the production, the easier it is to reduce costs. Goods such as automobiles or planes require large, mechanized production lines and substantial capital investment. It is challenging for a new entrant to compete with an established company, even though a newcomer could be even more efficient if they achieve the same level of production. From this angle, strategic trade policy is closely linked to the *infant industry argument*, developed by List in the mid-19th century. The *infant industry argument* is used to justify the protection of emerging industries from international trade. An infant industry is an industry (company) in its early stages of development, which can potentially compete internationally (List, 1841). However, because it is new, it needs some form of protective measures to survive before it can compete with (foreign) mature competitors successfully. This is necessary because of the mature competitors' heritage of high market share and large economies of scale.

The infant industry argument makes intuitive sense. Boeing was founded in 1916 and achieved superiority through economies of scale because of its monopolistic power. This superiority arises solely from having begun earlier than other companies, not because of Boeing's competitiveness in terms of innovation or quality. The same can be said of western automotive or pharmaceutical companies. Had it been left to the market, Airbus, the European aerospace company, would not have been established in 1970. At the start of its operations, it was only able to produce a few planes, and consequently, the (average) cost of production was much higher than for Boeing, only due to the absence of economies of scale. Hence, only with government support (subsidies and procurement) could Airbus start and develop. Precisely the same happened in South Korea. The government designated automobile and electronics as important infant industry sectors. Companies such as Samsung, LG, and Hyundai would not succeed if they were left to fend for themselves against market forces.

Government interference to achieve "strategic autonomy"

The discussion about the infant industries (or industry policy) is also relevant today. European initiatives to develop a battery sector for electric vehicles come to mind. In 2021, 73% of all batteries were produced in Asia (mainly China), and it is forecasted to increase to 87% in 2025. The same holds for computer chips used in smartphones and electric cars, of which Asia is by far the largest producer and exporter (Cap Gemini, 2021). The Asian region, including China, has almost monopolistic power and dominates the market, resulting in discomfort in the West about this dependency on such vital strategic sectors. This discussion gained relevancy because of the COVID-19 crisis. The pandemic shed light on the dependence of many advanced countries on a limited number of suppliers (again, mainly China) for critical pharmaceutical and healthcare products. Therefore, increased calls are heard in the EU and the US to localize the production of such essential products and achieve a sort of "strategic autonomy." This discussion is done within the context of the infant industry argument.

6.2.3.3 *Comac C919 versus Boeing B737*

The same is seen in the efforts of the Chinese authorities in establishing a Chinese aerospace or computer chip sector. Since 2000, the Chinese government has been supporting the emerging domestic semiconductor industry with tax breaks and subsidies. "Made in China 2025" aims to fill 70% of domestic demand with Chinese chips by 2025. The rationale behind protecting the Chinese aerospace sector is also based on the infant-industry argument and part of the same "Made in China 2025" plan. The economies of large-scale airplane production are so powerful that latecomers such as China (through China-based Comac) have difficulty establishing such industries. I have translated the infant industry argument into Figure 6.9, where the downward sloping learning curve represents the economies of scale. In the long run, economies of scale lead to a fall in the average cost of production as the output of a company increases. At first, this reduction of average costs is substantial the more one produces, but it may become more complicated as the production scale grows, represented by the curve's flattening. We can assume that average costs will fall, not only because of higher production but also because of learning effects in the production. Increased familiarity of workers and managers with production processes leads to improved efficiency and additional lower costs.

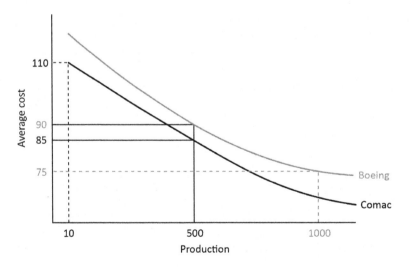

Figure 6.9:   Learning curve analysis, Boeing versus Comac.

214 The Rise of the New Economic Powers and the Changing Global Landscape

Figure 6.9 shows curves for the economies of scale of Boeing B737 and Comac C919. These planes compete for domestic and regional routes, flying approximately 5000 kilometers and carrying around 170 passengers. The curves clearly show that if these companies had the same production scale, the average costs of the Comac C919 would be less than the Boeing B737. At 500 planes per year, the average costs are $85 million for Comac versus $90 million for Boeing. Let's assume that Boeing can produce and sell 1,000 planes per year, while start-up Comac can produce and sell only 10 planes. This difference has a profound impact on the cost of production. In Figure 6.9, the average costs of the Boeing 737 fall to $75 million, while the Comac comes in at $110 million. In this case, if we assume competition on price alone, Comac cannot compete due to the latecomer effect, and Boeing continues to dominate the market solely as a result of being the first company to start production (with the help of the US government at that time). Hence, in this case, based on the infant industry argument, government protection and help is needed.

The NEP-9 countries are active in using the infant industry argument

---

When they were in the catching-up positions, almost all western countries adopted some form of infant industry promotion strategy, and the same is happening today in NEP-9 countries. For example, India, Brazil, and China employ tariffs to protect domestic industries during their infancy. Other countries such as South Korea and Indonesia primarily target specific industries with subsidy packages that protect them from international competition. Obviously, there is a thin line between helping promising companies in strategically important sectors and subsidizing and protecting inefficient (state-owned) companies instead of preparing them for international competition. From the late 1970s until about 1990, Brazil regarded its computer industry as an infant industry. In an attempt to establish an internationally competitive computer industry, Brazil essentially banned imports of computer products for several decades. Despite substantial help, the result was increased domestic sales for Brazilian computers, low quality, and high prices for consumers. And even after many years of financial support, in the 1990s, Brazilian companies still could not compete internationally.

6.2.3.4 Pre-conditions for success

The above case shows that for infant industry protectionism to be successful, important conditions must be met. First, the protection of infant industries should be temporary with regular assessments to determine if the infant company can compete internationally. In Korea, in the 1970s and 1980s, it was common practice to link protectionism and subsidies for infant companies to their success in foreign markets. When export sales rise, the infant industry is successful, and the government can phase out its protection. When export sales do not rise, the infant industry policy has failed, and the government can phase out its protection. Either way, protectionism is temporary. The Brazilian experience shows that political realities such as labor market considerations and vested interests mean prolonged protection.

Protectionism should always be temporary; making companies ready for international competition

---

This is closely linked to the second condition for a successful infant industry policy: the government must oppose political pressures to protect industries that lack competitive potential. In many countries, industries have failed to attain international competitiveness even after 15 or 20 years of operation and might not survive the removal of protective tariffs. In this case, protection hinders instead of improving the competitiveness of these industries. Third, in practice, it is difficult for policymakers to assess which industry warrants special treatment, but selected industries should not be too far removed from the (latent) comparative advantage. Fourth, the term infant industry should apply to a narrow set of industries, not to the economy as a whole. Otherwise, the consumer pays for protectionism through higher prices and lower quality across the economy. A final learning point is that infant industries must be able to depend on a large domestic market or be able to export; otherwise, they cannot achieve economies of scale. Going back to the Brazilian case: even the Brazilian domestic market was not large enough to generate the necessary economies of scale.

The lower competitiveness, the more protectionism is needed to compensate for this

---

The infant industry argument justifies import substitution. Today, all NEP-9 countries have import substitution policies in one form or another or industry policies complemented by opening up if the context is right. In principle, this smart globalization does not point to distrust in globalization or does it mean a step away from international free trade. However, it may substantially disrupt global trade. For example, if an Indonesian or South African company is much less efficient than its western competitor, both Indonesia and South Africa need to impose relatively high tariffs and other obstacles to counteract this difference. Therefore, applying the infant industry argument to sectors with much lower efficiency than western competitors may result in high protectionism.

6.2.3.5 *International Product Life Cycle theory*

The third modern trade theory is the International Product Life Cycle (IPLC) theory. This idea, developed by Raymond Vernon in 1966, says that the life cycle of a product has three distinct stages: (1) new product introduction, (2) the maturing stage, and (3) standardization stage. Wells expanded this theory in 1972 with the effects on trade of a product progressing through its life cycle. Essentially, this IPCL theory answers why a particular product is initially exported (or imported) and finally imported (or exported) by advanced (developing) nations. Figure 6.10 illustrates the trade patterns associated with the product life cycle. This concept was developed in the 1960s, and to fit the period, we

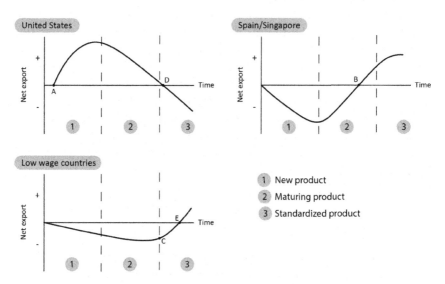

Figure 6.10:   Product life cycle and the trade effects.

will use the television as an example. The horizontal axis indicates the three phases of the product life cycle. The vertical axis gives the net export (export minus import).

The first practical television sets, an American invention, were produced and consumed as early as 1939. These first models were costly, so it took until the 1950s for sales to take off. The production process was highly capital intensive, and skilled labor was essential. In its introduction stage, the US was the only country able to produce and consume the product. After point A in Figure 6.10, we see the beginnings of the export of televisions from the US to other advanced economies. Despite the relatively high price, consumers in these countries could buy television sets. As the product moves into the second stage, the maturing product stage, the basic technology becomes more widely known, and the need for skilled labor in its production declines. Consequently, the production capability of TV sets in the other advanced countries snowballs, driven by newly founded companies or subsidiaries of US companies. At the end of the maturing stage, production in and export from the US were no longer profitable, and US-based companies looked for other locations with lower wages. Since, in this stage, producing television sets required a certain level of skilled labor, production first moved to other relatively advanced economies, such as Spain, Italy, Taiwan, Japan, and Singapore, where wages were still relatively low. They could produce the product but continued to be net importers until point B when the product reached the end of the maturing stage. At this point, they exported more televisions than they imported. Developing countries show the same pattern. At point C, the developing countries begin their domestic production, although they continue to be net importers. Meanwhile, the lower cost of production from these growing competitors turns the United States into a net importer at point D. When the television became a standard product, production moved again, this time from second-tier advanced countries to low-wage developing countries. The product is now relatively mass-produced and requires increasingly less skilled labor: the comparative advantages of manufacturing television sets shifted toward developing countries, and from point E onwards, they become net exporters of the product. This pattern is observed in many industries and products, such as copy machines, smartphones, tablets, or the newest chargers for our electronic devices.

The IPLC theory suggests that developed countries first export innovative products to less developed countries. Over time, less developed countries become more advanced in imitating developed countries.

Trade flows are driven by multinational enterprises and their foreign investments

---

Once they have managed to adopt the technology and produce it at lower factor costs (typically labor costs), they eventually become exporters of these products. We can explain this shift of production to other countries in three ways. First, a company may invest in a non-domestic production facility. If in the new venue they retain management control, this is called a foreign direct investment, the topic in Chapter 8. A second possible explanation for the relocation of production is that the innovative company gives the company in the low-wage country the license to produce the product under the original brand name. The third option is that a new local competitor produces the mature product, particularly after certain patents expire.

The IPLC theory was an additional critical explanation of international trade flows because it clarified them through international investments. Not only did the theory recognize the mobility of capital across countries (breaking the assumption of factor immobility in traditional trade theories) but also it shifted focus from the country to the product and the company. The emphasis in analyzing trade patterns was on the role of multinational enterprises. Furthermore, the theory highlights the impact of the demand side. IPLC explains parts of global trade flows. As they mature, technology-based products show us product life characteristics through changes in the production process. Other products, either resource-based (such as minerals and other commodities) or services, are not so easily characterized by stages of maturity. Furthermore, the IPLC theory assumes inventions and innovations all originate in advanced countries. However, today, innovation and manufacturing occur all over the world. Global companies conduct R&D activities in emerging markets where highly skilled labor and facilities are usually cheaper — advanced R&D activities in China, India, and Indonesia spring to mind.

6.2.3.6 *International supply chain fragmentation*

Essentially, the IPLC theory focuses on final products, such as televisions. However, the discussion in Chapter 2 concerning the iPhone showed that internationally operating companies produce and source components in a worldwide and fragmented global supply chain. The iPhone's components, including the flash memory, the DRAM, and the applications processor, are sourced (and imported) by China from various suppliers like Samsung (Korea) and AKM Semiconductor (Japan). Taiwanese firm Foxconn assembles the iPhone in a plant in China before it is exported from China to the rest of the world.

Global sourcing is a key determinant behind trade flows

Obviously, the global supply chain, which is based on the choices of companies, results in trade flows. In general, New Economic Powers in their initial stages of growth connect to global supply chains through assembly, but as we saw in Chapter 2, this does not generate a lot of added value. The smiling curve analysis showed that the NEP-9 try to increase the share of domestic content in their exports. Instead of importing them, some iPhone components are now produced in China, increasing the value added domestically and domestic production. These developments will substantially impact trade flows (related to the iPhone) between China, South Korea, Japan, and the US.

6.2.3.7 *The diamond framework*

A final addition to the theories that attempt to explain international trade was Michael Porter's, who emphasized that the competitiveness of specific industries drives national competitiveness: his national diamond concept. In Chapter 4, we discussed Porter's diamond analysis and the agglomeration effects: the benefits that companies obtain by locating close to each other. Then we linked that to the policy choice of NEP-9 countries to develop industrial clusters in special economic zones. The diamond model is also helpful in explaining international trade patterns. Strong clusters (or diamonds) in a country result in international competitiveness, and consequently, in export flows. Export is not done by countries but by (industrial) sectors. Porter identified four determinants that together explain successful clusters. The four determinants described in Chapter 4 are (1) local market resources and capabilities, (2) demand conditions, (3) local suppliers and complementary industries, and (4) local firm competitive strategies. Successful clusters are those that find the optimum balance between competition and working together to achieve innovative behavior and higher efficiency. The government is not part of the diamond, but its policy choices significantly impact every single determinant of the diamond. For example, the government may stimulate competition through competition policies. The diamond partly explains the German automotive export of the Baden-Württemberg region, US export of high-tech export (Silicon Valley), and Dutch flower export. Porter's Diamond is seen as a modern theory because it is not based on a country's perspective and costs. Export flows are generated through the competitiveness and choices of companies, government interference, and foreign investments.

Combining characteristics of the traditional and modern trade theories

---

There is an overlap with other modern trade theories, for example, the emphasis on the role of the demand side. Porter believed that a sophisticated home market is critical for ongoing innovation, creating a sustainable competitive advantage. That makes sense: you need a demanding consumer that "forces" companies to innovate continuously. When Porter wrote his book in the late 1980s, domestic demand was the most important. Today, we must consider the global consumer and global demand in the application of Porter's Diamond.

Porter's theory also links to the worldwide supply chain. He emphasizes the advantage of vertical cooperation within the value chain and the external economies of scale that arise when important players are concentrated in a small geographical area. At the same time, he is also influenced by traditional trade theories. For example, the diamond framework considers the value of the factor proportions theory, which states a nation's resources (e.g., natural resources and available labor) are key factors that determine which products a country will import or export. To these primary factors, Porter added a list of created assets, such as skilled labor, education, technology, and infrastructure.

Policymakers in the NEP-9 believe in the advantages of international trade. At the same time, this trust in free trade does not mean they feel trade is beneficial under all circumstances. They believe in managed trade, cautious reform, and industry policy rather than a fully fledged trade liberalization agenda, as evidenced by their trade policy behaviors. Facilitating trade by improving customs procedures while also supporting domestic companies with subsidies. They are lowering tariffs, while at the same time, several sectors are not open to foreign investors. An additional rationale for government interference related to international trade is that opening up and leaving things to the market disrupts societies already going through many transitions. Therefore, governments must interfere to ensure opening up and (trade) reforms are done without causing significant disruptive consequences. What the West sees as protectionist strategies are important tools for managing economies to minimize social disruption. This process takes time, in particular in countries like India and Indonesia, which are focused heavily on agriculture. The desire to counteract the potentially dramatic impact on parts of the economy drives their trade policy and protectionist behavior.

6.3 Protectionist Measures

There are several ways for governments to influence international trade flows, affecting imports and exports. Essentially, these tools fall into two categories: tariffs and non-tariff barriers. A tariff is taxation imposed when products cross the border. A non-tariff barrier is any measure other than a tariff that acts as a barrier to international trade.

6.3.1 *Tariffs*

An import tariff or import duty is a tax levied on imports to protect domestic producers from foreign competition by raising the price of imported goods. Specific tariffs are levied as a fixed amount. For example, the importer pays $1,000 per imported car. *Ad valorem* tariffs are levied as a percentage of the imported good's value, for example, 20% of the value of every imported car. We will focus on this *ad valorem* tariff.

The success of GATT and WTO: reducing tariffs

It is difficult to measure the effect of increasing a tariff because how import demand responds to changes in tariffs (and prices) depends on numerous factors. For example, the reaction of domestic consumers to a more expensive iPhone due to a higher import tariff might be negligible. In contrast, the same consumer might switch to a domestic furniture maker instead of buying imported products when prices of foreign furniture rise due to the tariff. As we will see in Chapter 7, the GATT and WTO have

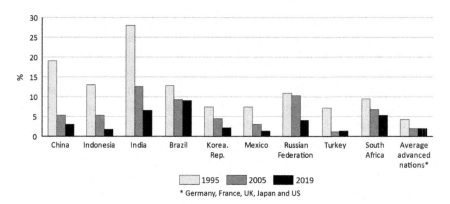

Figure 6.11:   Tariff development, NEP-9 and selected countries, 1995–2020.

Note: Applied tariff on manufacturers.
Source: World Bank database.

successfully reduced tariffs. Today, tariffs, binding for all WTO members, are relatively low, particularly for manufacturers. Figure 6.11 illustrates this success. Average tariffs have been declining since the early 1990s. For example, India's applied tariff has been reduced from 28% in 1995 to less than 7% in 2020. Indonesia lowered its tariff from 13% to 1.8% within the same period. Advanced economies tend to have lower average tariffs than the NEP-9 countries, but the largest decline in tariffs is observable in most NEP-9 countries.

The impact of a tariff depends not only on how domestic consumers react to a price increase but also on whether the tariff is imposed on final products (like cars) or raw materials (like steel). Although a tariff on imported steel will protect domestic steel producers, it will also increase production costs for domestic car manufacturers using steel. Therefore, we have to distinguish between the *nominal* and *effective* protection rates (Figure 6.12). The nominal protection rate is the tariff imposed on a product as it enters the country. For example, if 20% of the value is collected on cars entering the country, then the nominal protection rate is that same 20%. The effective rate of protection is a more complex concept. Let's assume the car costs $10,000 on international markets, and the imported materials (including steel) used to produce the car sell for $6,000. In a free trade situation, a domestic firm can charge no more than this $10,000 on the domestic market because of heavy international competition with so many similarly priced cars (ignoring transportation costs). If the import value is

$6,000, the car manufacturer can add a maximum of $4,000 for labor and profit. This $4,000 (price minus the material inputs) is the added value.

Nominal versus effective protection rate: explaining tariff-escalation

---

Now imagine a situation with a tariff of 20% on cars and 10% on imported (raw) materials and parts. The 20% tariff on cars raises the domestic price by $2,000 to $12,000, while a 10% tariff on steel increases material costs for the domestic producer by $600 to $6,600. In this case, protection gives the company a value-added margin of $5,400 — the difference between the domestic price of $12,000 and the material cost of $6,600. The difference between the $4,000 value added without tariff protection and $5,400 is an extra margin of $1,400. This means the effective rate of protection for domestic firms (the ratio of $1,400–4,000) is 35%, substantial greater than the nominal rate of 20%. This extra protection happens whenever the tariff rate on the final product is greater than the tariff on inputs. That is precisely the reason that, in general, countries do levy higher tariffs on final products than on inputs, the commonly named tariff escalation.

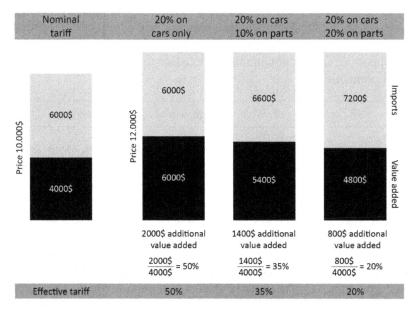

Figure 6.12:   Nominal versus effective tariff.

Note: The nominal rate equals the effective rate if 100% is domestic value added.

The earlier example shows that tariffs are generally pro-producer and anti-consumer. Tariffs on imported products help domestic producers compete domestically and internationally but increase prices on the domestic market. That, in turn, reduces the spending power of the consumer. A tariff on imported steel increases costs for carmakers, which spills over toward the market price. Also, when a tariff is levied on foreign cars, domestic carmakers can also increase their prices. Against this loss of purchasing power by consumers, there is an obvious benefit for the government because tariffs are part of their revenues. The example also shows that even with high tariffs of 20%, foreign carmakers can still sell their cars abroad. From this perspective, the market is still functioning. But, this is not always the case when non-tariff barriers are used.

6.3.2 *Non-tariff barriers*

Lower tariffs do not indicate that trade is free. Tariffs are already relatively low and under WTO rules, which means they are difficult to increase. Countries have given away an important tool to protect domestic producers. As a result, we see the growing use of the commonly named non-tariff barriers, such as subsidies, cheap loans, quotas, voluntary export restraints, local content requirements, and administrative policies. The COVID-19 crisis accelerated this trend, as domestic companies asked for support from the government, including protective measures from import competition.

The other side of the success: growth of non-tariff barriers

Subsidies for domestic producers help them compete with foreign competitors, and consequently, they reduce imports and gain export markets. There are myriad forms of subsidies: for farmers in the EU and the US, supporting inefficient domestic agricultural producers in Japan and South Korea, assistance for inefficient industrial producers in Brazil, China, and Mexico, and government support through cheap loans and tax breaks in China and Indonesia. Sometimes, the rationale for supporting specific companies is built upon the infant industry argument, but in many cases, governments take other considerations (employment, knowledge) into account.

Another non-tariff barrier is the import quota: a direct restriction on the number of imported products, through a direct block at the border but primarily by issuing import licenses to specific foreign companies. A variant of the import quota is the voluntary export restraint (VER). A VER is a voluntary quota imposed by the exporting country itself, but obviously at the strong request of the importing country's government. You may have guessed that voluntary is not entirely the right word for it. For example, between 2012 and 2018, Brazil "asked" Mexico to voluntary reduce the export of vehicles several times. Mexico agreed because it feared Brazil would impose more damaging protectionist measures.

Another example of a non-tariff barrier is the local content requirement. As the name implies, this rule requires that a certain percentage of a good must be produced domestically (either in a country or region). For example, the 2020 trade agreement between the US, Mexico, and Canada (United States–Mexico–Canada Agreement, USMCA) that replaced the NAFTA agreement of 1994 contains a local content rule for vehicles. Vehicles must meet a 75% required value content to be considered a local product that can cross borders without tariffs. NEP-9 countries often use this local content rule. For example, in 2012, the Indian government introduced a law determining that foreign retailers wanting to set up a retail outlet in India had to source 30% of their products from domestic suppliers. In 2020, the government relaxed this rule slightly, but in many sectors, a required minimum level of domestic sourcing still applies. This local content requirement may help the transition toward a more value-added domestic economy.

Non-tariff barriers are not so much about trade but about domestic rules and regulations

---

Our final example of a non-tariff barrier is the impact of bureaucratic procedures or red tape, making exporting to another country complicated and costly, such as mandatory documentation (certificates and licenses) and customs procedures. For certain products, speed is essential. If border control takes two weeks on a container transporting vegetables, export is strongly constrained. Completing the required documentation and customs procedures of an import transaction takes only two days in Singapore and two months in Venezuela, and China, Brazil, Indonesia, and Russia are somewhere between these two extremes. Besides administrative barriers, there are also barriers to making the product itself in compliance with the requirements of countries, for example, regulations regarding product content and manufacturing process. These are examples of

Non-tariff bariers	Actual regulation
Sanitary and phytosanitary measures	Plant and animal regulations Certificatian procedures Quarantine rules
Technical barriers to trade	Content regulations Manufacturing process procedures Labelling rules
Border controls	Administrative procedures Restricted ports of entry
Rules of origin/local content rule	Use of national suppliers Use of specific importer Locally produced content rule and related administrative burden Data localizing policies
Financial measures	Foreign exchange regulations Access to foreign exchange for imports Payment procedures
Business restrictions	Distribution restrictions (e.g. use of local transporter) Restrictions on post-sale services such as repair services must be done by a local firm Government procurement restrictions
Export-related measures	Trade embargo's Restriction on exporting specific products

Figure 6.13:   Non-tariff barriers.

technical trade barriers. Figure 6.13 provides an overview of the most important non-tariff barriers.

Intervening in international trade flows is based on the assumption that government must play a role in facilitating the structural transition of the country and that this transition cannot be left to the market alone. Market forces may drive a country to specialize in commodities with low added value, while this is not the optimum basis for long-term development. Hence, government intervention is required to boost sectors away from today's comparative advantage and toward latent comparative advantages with more value-added activities. This government intervention affects international trade, as seen in the *flying geese model*.

6.4 The Flying Geese Model

The flying geese model intends to explain the process of latecomer economies, such as Japan in the 1960s, in catching-up with industrialization.
This model was developed by Akamatsu in 1961 and popularized by
Kojima and others in the 1970s and 1980s. In my previous (Dutch) book
on globalization (2016), I discussed the flying geese model within the context of foreign investments. But the concept also fits the setting of government intervention and its impact on international trade. Figure 6.14 starts
with the original graph used by Akamatsu when Japan was still a follower
economy in the catching-up process and has the time horizon on the horizontal axis and volume (or value) on the vertical axis.

The first curve (A) represents the import of a product or product
group. During the first stage, the follower economy begins to import foreign products, being consumer goods or machines. Step by step, import is
replaced by a growing domestic industry (B). The second curve shows the
start of the production of the imported manufactured goods in the domestic economy. Over the years, domestic production (B) overtakes imports
(A). This transformation may be driven by selective government intervention (the import-substituting industrialization strategy). This substitution
can be the result of local competitors which are now able to produce the
product and of western multinational enterprises that invest in production
facilities when the product reaches maturity status. The third curve (C)
indicates exports, which starts when local production can compete

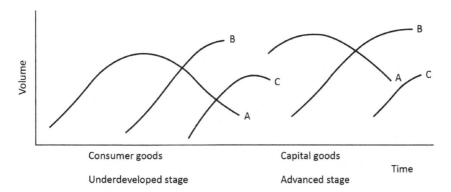

Figure 6.14:   The original flying geese model.

Source: Akamatsu (1961).

internationally, and exports grow. Essentially, these three curves summarize the development of the competitiveness of a specific sector. The graph looks like geese flying in formation, each forming an inverse V. We can link the series of curves to a particular product, product group, or, more broadly, an industrial sector. In this model, the International Product Life Cycle theory is obvious.

Automatic changes in comparative advantages versus specific industry policy

---

The flying geese framework shows the gradual development of industries within a national economy, based in part on changes in comparative advantages. For example, if wages increase and the working force becomes more productive, the comparative advantage automatically shifts from lower value-added labor-intensive products to higher value-added knowledge-intensive products. Consequently, export patterns also change. This sequence of domestic development can also be initiated and stimulated by specific government interventions, such as import substitution policies, the infant industry argument, or specific industry policies. In this case, the government takes the lead in promoting the production and export of industries in which the country has latent comparative advantages. At the end of the day, the result is the same. Over time, a country's comparative advantages change (with export as a result), and comparative advantages between countries in the same product change. Figure 6.15 summarizes these developments.

The flying geese framework has been adjusted and expanded several times, but the above reflects the basic argument. However, one change is worth mentioning: the introduction of the *reverse import phase*. Exporting companies will be confronted with higher production costs and competition from abroad, mostly from countries less advanced in the development process. These issues may spell the end of the export of this particular product, but not of domestic companies in this industry. We see these companies investing in lower-cost nations, producing products abroad under their ownership, and importing them back to the home country: reverse import. The flying geese model needs one important note. It should be clear that it focuses on industries, such as automotive and electronics, but this does not always correspond with the phase of development of a specific country. For example, China exporting iPhones is not

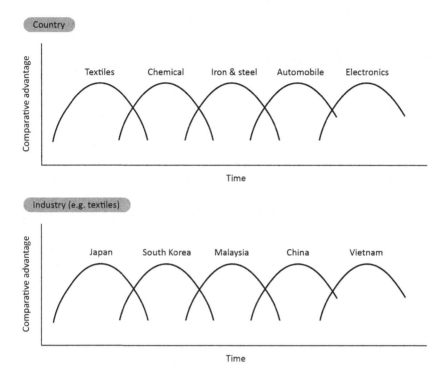

Figure 6.15:   Flying geese model for a particular country and industry.

Source: Ebbers (2016).

an indication of how developed the country is. Still, it is a sign that China has a comparative advantage in the assembly of the iPhone (but not in electronics).

6.4.1 *Selective government intervention*

In the 1960s, South Korea began a structural transformation from producing and exporting textiles, chemicals, iron, and steel to heavy industry and shipbuilding in the 1970s, to semiconductors and biotechnology in the 1990s, and to mobile devices and software games today. They achieved this through selective government intervention aimed at developing industries, even if these industries were counter to South Korean comparative advantage at that time. In this case, such government interference makes sense. The latent comparative advantage would not arise if left to market forces alone, particularly when international competition is not fair. This Korean experience of implementing protective measures for infant industries before fully exposing them to international competition is also seen in other NEP-9.

NEP-9 countries: different names for industry policy

They have different names: Manufacturing Innovation Strategy 3.0 (South Korea), National Strategy for the Internet of Things (Brazil), Made in China 2025, Make in India strategy, Making Indonesia 4.0, Industry 4.0 Roadmap (Mexico), National Industrial Policy Framework (South Africa), and Medium-term Development Plan (Turkey), but they are all examples of industrial and technological upgrading strategies with decisive government intervention. The same happens in more advanced countries. For example, the German National Industrial Strategy 2030, France's Industries du Future, and Italy's National Industry Plan 4.0.

6.4.2 *A decline in the appetite for reform*

The attitude of NEP-9 on trade issues is evident. First, fully fledged outward orientation with instant opening up, driven by market forces, is too disruptive. This view is not new. In the past, today's advanced nations felt the same. These countries opened up and gave way to market forces in international trade only *after* they achieved high levels of development (and came under increased pressure from their partners). Second, the NEP-9 trade authorities know that in the long run, trade protectionism does not work. It may help domestic companies and stabilize the labor market for a short time, but in the end, protectionism hurts a country's competitiveness. It allows inefficient producers to continue operation and forces consumers to pay higher prices for domestic goods.

NEP-9 countries: a cautious view on liberalizing international trade

---

Despite this, we have seen a considerable decline in the appetite for reforms related to international trade (and globalization in a broader sense, for that matter). Brazil has had little to no trade liberalization or structural reforms since the late 1990s. Trade liberalization in Russia stopped when President Putin's second term ended (2008). The situation in India is mixed. Trade liberalization and related structural reforms have stalled since the Congress-led government took charge in 2004. However, between 2017 and 2020, the Modi government took steps to change its complex system of import duties (and exemptions) and relaxed investment regulations. China is the same mixed bag. On the one hand, certain sectors are opening up. For example, automotive companies such as Tesla can now have full ownership over the investment instead of using the joint venture as an entry mode. And they have the freedom to import and export as much as they like. On the other hand, there are more restrictions on exporting services to China. The past few years also saw a slowdown in trade reform in Indonesia. Although overall protection has not increased between 2017 and 2020, government is growing its support for state-owned enterprises. The same is happening in Turkey, South Korea, and South Africa. Mexico is the only outlier in this overview. In the previous decade, Mexico's trade liberalization agenda continued to focus on further opening up. However, Mexico's problem is its inability to reform domestic regulatory barriers to complement its trade liberalization. To conclude, despite following the paradigm that longer-term development requires free and fair international trade, relatively strong government intervention in trade relations continues in the NEP-9 countries. However, this does not mean the NEP-9 are closed countries. In fact, they are quite open.

6.5 Trade Openness

In 2018, I was teaching in Seoul in South Korea. I started my lecture on international trade by asking if South Korea is an open or closed country in international trade. The outcome was remarkable. Half of the class thought the county had an open and outward economy, but for the other half, South Korea was an example of a semi-closed economy with a lot of government intervention. Clearly, openness is a multidimensional concept, and consequently, there is no consensus on how to best measure economic openness. In Chapter 5, we discussed the KOF Globalisation Index and saw many indicators we can use to measure how globalized a country is. Part of the KOF Index was devoted to trade, and again, we saw that several factors are used to measure trade openness, including tariffs. However, as stated before, tariffs may not provide a correct picture of trade openness. For example, if high non-tariff barriers complement low tariffs, it may seem export is easy. However, as soon as the product enters the market, it must compete with domestic firms, which may receive subsidies and tax reductions.

Measuring a multidimensional concept is complex

There are many ways to try and capture trade openness into one indicator. The most basic measure of trade openness is a country's exports and imports relative to the size of the economy: exports plus imports divided by GDP. This measurement has several variants, such as exports divided by GDP. The general assumption is that through actual trade flows, we may assess the importance of tariffs and non-tariff barriers. Low barriers result in high export (and import), and high barriers result in low export (and import). In general, small countries usually have a larger trade sector than big countries because of the limitations of a small domestic market. That does not mean trade flows from larger countries are small. They are small relative to their domestic markets.

As shown in Figure 6.16, over the years, China's trade openness is far greater than that of, for example, the US and Japan. The ratio of trade to GDP for the US fluctuated around 17% during the post-war period up to the mid-1980s and increased to 28% in 2007, just before the financial crisis. In Japan, which is well known for its export competitiveness, the trade to GDP ratio is less than 34% (2019), lower compared to China's ratio of 37% in 2019. In a way, China (and the other NEP-9 countries) is more integrated into the world through trade than the US and Japan ever were. A declining trade-to-GDP ratio after 2008 shows the impact of the financial crisis. However, the 2008/09 financial crisis made several countries look more open simply because of its disproportionate effect on GDP. The Brazilian, Mexican, and Turkey trade openness ratios are considerably higher in 2019 compared to 2007. On the other hand, the trade-to-GDP ratio has declined in China, Indonesia, and India. Among the NEP-9, Brazil is the least sensitive to changes in the global trading economy, with the lowest trade-to-GDP ratio of 28% in 2019. South Africa has a relatively high trade-to-GDP ratio, as do Mexico and South Korea.

Interesting to note is the openness of India and Turkey. India's trade-to-GDP ratio has grown rapidly from below 23% in 2000 to over 40% in 2019. The same development is seen in Turkey (42% and 63%, respectively).

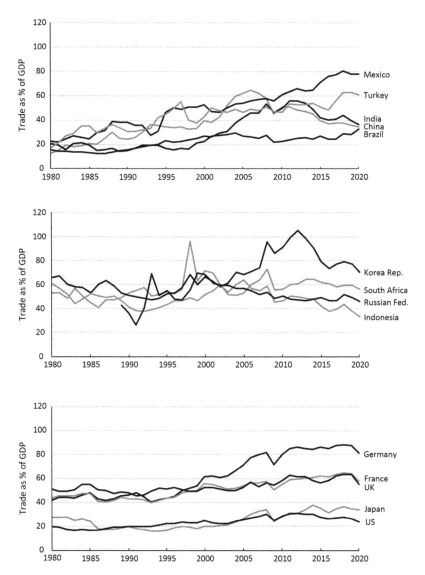

Figure 6.16:   Trade as % of GDP, NEP-9 and selected advanced nations, 1980–2020.

Source: WTO Database (2021).

6.5.1 *Transforming world trade: Digitalization*

Digitalization and digital technologies such as artificial intelligence, the Internet of Things, 3D printing, and Blockchain will dramatically impact the size, growth, and composition of trade flows. New technologies may help reduce trade costs. It also facilitates the coordination of global value chains and may change countries' comparative advantages.

New technologies can positively affect trade. First, digital technologies increase the effectiveness of communication and logistics in global supply chains. Second, online platforms facilitate the search for products, help verify quality, and initiate innovations in cross-border payments through blockchain technologies that further lower transaction costs. New technologies can also reduce transportation and storage costs. In December 2020, I asked one of my Dutch students why he wasn't making any progress on his thesis, the final step in finishing his master's program. He said that he was too busy building his company, selling Chinese products on the global market. It has never been easier to engage in international trade. Today, small businesses, even sole proprietors, engage in international trade through inexpensive digital tools that allow them to source, ship, deliver, pay, and collect online — all the operations related to buying and selling a product abroad. E-commerce also has a significant impact on the trade-in services.

Changing the traditional sources of comparative advantages

Providers could offer previously non-tradable activities such as research and development, cloud computing, and telesurgery through e-commerce. The importance of services in the composition of trade is expected to increase. In 2020, the share of services in total world trade was already 22%. It is growing relatively fast compared to physical products although the new technologies blur the distinctions between goods and services. For example, a smart fridge requires market access not only for the product but also for the embedded service.

The above shows that digital technologies and e-commerce stimulate international trade. However, there is another side to this story. Digital technologies may also negatively affect the international fragmentation of production. For example, to some extent, 3D printing could substitute traditional manufacturing methods, reducing the need for assembly abroad, inventory, logistics, and packaging. And if 3D printing reduces global value chains, it will also reduce international trade. New technologies and digitalization will change the traditional sources of comparative advantage, such as the availability of labor as a basis for a comparative advantage in labor-intensive products. When robots and computers increasingly substitute labor, labor-intensive developing countries lose their comparative advantage. Countries with high quality physical infrastructure may lose their comparative advantage in logistic-intensive activities to countries that have invested in high-quality digital infrastructure since reliable and fast network access is becoming a prerequisite for doing business. Furthermore, geographical factors might become less relevant, reducing the comparative advantages of countries, such as the Netherlands and Singapore, which are important in global supply chains trade flows. The regulations of intellectual property rights, data flows, and privacy are likely to become important sources for comparative advantages, which is why all NEP-9 countries have implemented a digitalization agenda.

NEP-9: struggling with how to deal with the digital disruptions

---

The impact of digital technologies is developing, but one thing is sure, it is disruptive to economies and societies, sparking several concerns, including market concentration, loss of privacy, and security threats. Governments in NEP-9 countries are struggling with these issues. For example, in 2020, China considerably increased its regulatory powers over large tech firms, not only by changing customs regulations or laws regarding intellectual property rights, data privacy, monopolistic behavior, and consumer protection but also by concerning the impact these companies have on society as a whole. The same can be seen in Turkey, Indonesia and Russia.

6.5.2 *NEP-9 transforming trade flows*

Until now, we sought to explain trade patterns, including those of the NEP-9, and discussed why international trade and protectionism might be helpful to development. Both explicitly and between the lines, I presented some learning points regarding NEP-9 behaviors and how they transform world trade. The following overview attempts to summarize key conclusions.

First, the NEP-9 strongly increased their share in manufactured exports, resulting in a share of almost 27% in 2020. The disaggregation into the specific NEP-9 countries is shown on the right-hand side of Figure 6.17. Diversifying exports, away from primary commodities and

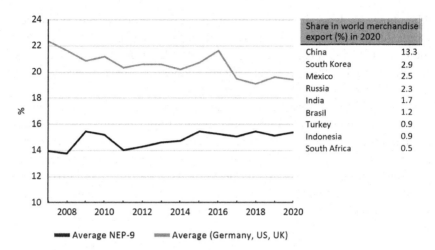

Figure 6.17: Share of high-tech exports as a percentage of manufacturing exports (left) and share of NEP-9 in world merchandise export, 2020 (right).

Note: Both the terms "manufacturing" and "merchandise" exports refer to the exports of goods.
Source: Based on WTO Database (2021).

toward manufactured goods, was a key objective of these countries. Essentially, this transformation has been accomplished by government intervention and specific industry policies, using the infant industry argument, the cluster framework, and the adjusted import substitution strategy. Specific strategic sectors spearheaded this transformation; these industries received government support. This government interference was successful when these strategic sectors were not too far removed from the latent comparative advantage of the country. This success can also be measured through the share of high-tech products in total manufactured exports, as can be seen on the left-hand side of Figure 6.17.

Second, although tariffs in the NEP-9 are still higher compared to more advanced western countries, there was an impressive reduction in tariffs in the NEP-9 during the previous decades. Because tariffs are already low and difficult to increase under the WTO, the NEP-9 are using substantial non-tariff barriers to protect domestic sectors, and it looks like reducing protection through non-tariff barriers is much more complicated than lowering tariffs.

Third, all traditional and modern trade theories partially explain the trade patterns of the NEP-9 countries, but it looks like the role of the

NEP-9 in the global supply chains is the most important. This connection to the worldwide supply chains, not only for products but also for trade in services, such as banking, retail, wholesale, transport, and telecommunications, was established by attracting foreign investments and through the steep learning effects achieved by domestic firms.

Fourth, in line with the demand side of explaining international trade, the growing middle class in NEP-9 was and will continue to be the most important force behind trade flows of products and services. These range from automobiles and consumer durables to education, health, and international tourism. With the explosive growth of the middle class in the NEP-9, these countries will become increasingly important export partners to each other. This commonly named South–South trade is set to grow substantially.

The need for good multilateralism or the fast track through trading blocs

---

Finally, the NEP-9 countries are actively participating in regional trading blocks. As said before, the NEP-9 believe in the advantages of global free trade under the auspices of the WTO. Still, if good multilateralism is not achievable, regionalism might provide an acceptable alternative for them. We heard this combination of multilateralism and regionalism in the speech South Korean President Moon Jae-in gave in 2020 at the signing ceremony of the Regional Comprehensive Economic Partnership (RCEP) in Asia: "We note that the RCEP Agreement is an unprecedented mega-regional trading arrangement that comprises of a diverse mix of developed, developing and least-developed economies of the region." He also emphasized multilateralism: "We believe that RCEP represents an important step forward toward an ideal framework of global trade and investment rules."

6.6 A Surge in Trading Blocs

The past three decades have witnessed a proliferation (and deepening) of regional trading blocs, and the NEP-9 are active participants. Trading blocs aim to reduce or abolish trade barriers between the participating countries. Sometimes, the emphasis is on reducing tariffs, while other trading blocs also reduce several non-tariff barriers. They can focus on trade alone, but in several cases, agreements are reached on foreign investments and harmonization of government policies.

As we will see in Chapter 7, trading blocs are essentially against the WTO principle of non-discrimination. Still, they are allowed under WTO rules and, therefore, comply with multilateral legislation. In essence, the WTO seeks to reduce trade barriers, which is also the essence of trading blocs, reducing trade barriers between the members. Although in compliance with WTO rules, the organization has mixed feelings about trade blocs, as they may not only reduce trade barriers within the bloc but also implement discriminatory measures for non-participants. Therefore, on the one hand, a trading bloc is a step toward trade liberalization, while on the other hand, it may be a step away from global free trade.

The WTO and its ambiguity about trading blocs

Trading blocs may speed up the trade liberalization process. Regional and bilateral trade agreements could yield quicker results than multilateral agreements under the WTO system. Furthermore, trade agreements may allow parties to achieve higher levels of liberalization than the multilateral agreements in which a staggering 164 countries must reach an agreement (early 2022). Negotiating with neighbors with similar cultures or comparable views on the role of government makes the process easier. However, it is harder for non-participating countries to export to the countries within the trading bloc. Groupings such as the G7, G20, and partially cooperative agreements between countries are not seen as formal trading blocs but as coalitions without strong cooperation and often without an administrative body.

6.6.1 *NEP-9 are active in many trading blocs*

Interestingly, since the 1990s, globalization and multilateralism under WTO auspices and regionalism through trading blocs have grown in parallel. Countries such as China, Indonesia, Turkey, India, and Mexico implemented far-reaching trade liberalization policies under the umbrella of the WTO and, at the same time, became very active in regional trading blocs. In addition to a trade agreement with the European Union, Turkey has bilateral agreements with 22 countries, including Israel, Macedonia, Tunisia, Kosovo, Morocco, Egypt, Albania, and South Korea. In 2021, three more agreements (including with the UK) were in the negotiation phase. India participates in 17 trading agreements (2021), while South Africa joined seven trading blocs. A more detailed overview is given for Brazil and Indonesia (Figure 6.18). For the NEP-9, it is a way to take advantage of larger markets and economies of scale in production and move up the value chain without opening up immediately to competition with the most advanced exporters in the world.

The spaghetti or noodle bowl problem

All these treaties have different regulations, coverages, and exceptions, which makes for a complex trade environment: the commonly named spaghetti or noodle bowl problem.

NEP-9 countries participate in many trading blocs and are, in a sense, shaping them. However, there is no fixed template for these blocs. For example, China has signed many trade agreements with different degrees of depth and coverage. Some have included goods, services, and investments, while others cover only goods, and some have started with goods

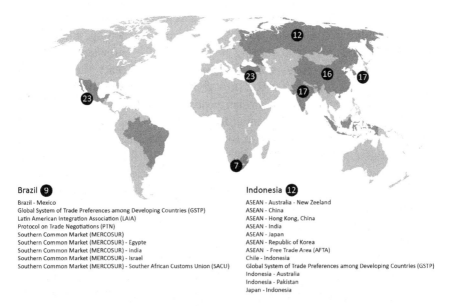

Brazil 9

Brazil - Mexico
Global System of Trade Preferences among Developing Countries (GSTP)
Latin American Integration Association (LAIA)
Protocol on Trade Negotiations (PTN)
Southern Common Market (MERCOSUR)
Southern Common Market (MERCOSUR) - Egypte
Southern Common Market (MERCOSUR) - India
Southern Common Market (MERCOSUR) - Israel
Southern Common Market (MERCOSUR) - Souther African Customs Union (SACU)

Indonesia 12

ASEAN - Australia - New Zeeland
ASEAN - China
ASEAN - Hong Kong, China
ASEAN - India
ASEAN - Japan
ASEAN - Republic of Korea
ASEAN - Free Trade Area (AFTA)
Global System of Trade Preferences among Developing Countries (GSTP)
Indonesia - Australia
Indonesia - Pakistan
Chile - Indonesia
Japan - Indonesia

Figure 6.18: Trading blocs with NEP-9 participation, early 2022.

Source: WTO database.

liberalization, intending to add services and investments later. In general, national sovereignty still has major appeal to NEP-9 countries, and clearly, there is a limit to ceding autonomy. In this way, regional integration in Latin America, Africa, and parts of Asia has a different meaning than the European integration process.

Another feature of these trade blocs is that the NEP-9 countries are still active in multilateral discussions. For example, in Brazil and India, regional policy is subordinate to multilateralism. South Korea has traditionally prioritized multilateral trade negotiations under the auspices of GATT/WTO. In fact, until the 1990s, South Korea had no interest at all in participating in regional trading blocs. Korea's largest trading partner, the United States, was not a proponent of regionalism until the 1980s, and Korea's neighbors did not show much interest in regional trade agreements. At that time, sensitive historical issues such as Japanese occupations before 1945 and past military fights within the region still hampered Asian integration. South Korea signed its first free trade agreement (FTA) with Chile in February 2003.

NEP-9 countries: not giving away too much national autonomy

The Russian case shows that geopolitical and security considerations can be the main driving force behind establishing, deepening, and participating in trading blocs. According to the West, the Eurasian Economic Union (EAEU) as well as the Collective Security Treaty Organization (CSTO) are both vehicles for Russia's geopolitical objectives. The CSTO was used by Russia to send Russian peacekeeping troops to Kazakhstan to help the Kazakhstan government to repress the street protests, in early 2022. Russia's primary interest in Eurasian integration is to strengthen its global influence. The other members of the EAEU focus on geopolitical instead of economic integration in a regional context. The EAEU accounts for only 5% of Russia's trade, and the union continues to fall short of its economic objectives. Still, politically, it is successfully controlling the region after the collapse of the Soviet Union.

As the number of trading blocs increased, so did their percentage in world trade. In 2020, more than half of world trade happened through trading blocs. I should emphasize that trading blocs are mostly regional. Geographical distance equals cultural distance, and a mutual understanding plays a growing and key part in international trade relationships. However, there are exceptions, the South Korean–Chilean trade agreement, for example, so academic literature usually calls them preferential trade agreements instead of regional trading blocs. Again, they are not free trade agreements: they discriminate against non-member states. It should be clear that asymmetry always exists, both within the WTO negotiations and in a trading block with a neighboring country. But this asymmetry is often more visible in trading blocs. For example, when Mexico and the US negotiated on the US–Mexico–Canada free trade deal, it was clear that the US dictated the agenda, and Mexico could only follow.

6.7 Types of Trading Blocs

There are several types of trading blocs with different levels of integration, from least integrated to most integrated. We will discuss the following:

1. Free trade area or free trade agreement
2. Customs union
3. Common or single market
4. Economic and monetary union
5. Political union

The organization's name is often a dead giveaway about the type of cooperation. For example, the ASEAN Free Trade Area (AFTA) is obviously a free trade area. The EU–Turkey customs union and the Southern African Customs Union (SACU) are customs unions. The EU-27 and the Southern Common Market (Mercosur) are common markets, although the latter, in reality, did not reach the goal until today. The focus will be on the first three types (Figure 6.19).

6.7.1 *Free trade area*

The most common trading bloc is the free trade area. Although it removes all internal tariffs and quotas, its members can put their own external

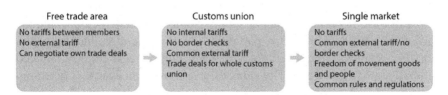

Figure 6.19:   Three types of trading blocs.

tariffs and trade restrictions on non-members. Because members do not cede much autonomy, it is a reasonably easy negotiation process. There is, however, a big disadvantage to this type of trade bloc.

Border controls are needed in a free trade area

The differences in external tariffs mean customs must check every truck crossing borders within the FTA. Imagine Mexico has an external tariff of 20% on cars and import duty for cars imported into the US is 35%. Japanese, German, and Chinese automotive companies will export their cars to Mexico first and then to the US, choosing Mexico's 20% and avoiding the higher US import tariff. The provenance of products is checked at the Mexican–US border to counter this practice. If they are Mexican, they can continue their journey to the US without paying the tariff. If the product is deemed foreign, it will have to pay the additional 15% import duties at the border. It means that exporters within the trading block experience additional administrative barriers. They must prove where different inputs have come from. Rules regarding origin essentially constitute a non-tariff barrier because the higher this benchmark, the more difficult it is for exporters to sell their products in the trading bloc. For Mexico, stricter rules on origin for the automotive industry may result in more automotive suppliers relocating to Mexico to profit from the lower tariff, which could help upgrade the manufacturing sector.

Rules of origin in an FTA require clarity: when is a product, in this case, Mexican? Defining these rules of origin is part of the negation process and can differ from one FTA to another. Products produced entirely in Mexico (or the US or Canada) are subject to preferential rules of origin within the trade agreement. There are no import duties when exporting to the participating countries.

Determining the local content as part of the local content rule is a complex process

---

But the emergence of global supply chains has made determining the origin of a product complex, particularly within the manufacturing sector. Is a car assembled in Mexico, using components mainly sourced globally, a Mexican car? The rules of origin must answer this question. Under NAFTA (1994), the former trade agreement between the United

States, Mexico, and Canada, 62% of materials or components of a product had to come from these three countries to meet rules of origin standards. Today, according to the new USMCA, 75% of car content must be made in these three countries, with 40% of that content made by workers earning at least $16 per hour. The local content rule varies among trading blocs. For example, most items under the Comprehensive Economic and Trade Agreement (CETA) between Canada and Europe require only 50% of a product to come from the originating country. Under the EU–South Korea free trade agreement, a car arriving in the EU from South Korea must be 55% "Made in Korea" to qualify for tariff-free access. The example above, about workers earning $16 per hour, shows that within FTAs, commitments may go further than existing WTO agreements (as we will see in Chapter 7). In the USMCA, it is not only about labor rights but there are also some rules on environmental protection. The Comprehensive Economic Partnership Agreement between India and Korea, signed in 2009 as a free trade agreement, includes some provisions regarding sanitary measures and customs cooperation.

6.7.2 *Customs union*

A customs union has all the characteristics of a free trade agreement, but in addition, members adopt a standard external tariff with non-member countries. Obviously, this eliminates the need for internal border controls on (the origin of the) products, resulting in a substantial reduction in transaction costs. Handing autonomy on external tariffs to the union means participating countries cannot negotiate their own trade deals with other countries. Therefore, FTAs are much more common than customs unions. Globally, as of March 2021, 16 individual customs unions are listed at the WTO, substantially less than the 340 free trade agreements in force.

Ceding national autonomy is a politically sensitive issue, as evident in the post-Brexit negotiations between the UK and the EU. The political situation made it impossible for the UK to establish a customs union with the EU. Such a union would mean the UK would not have the freedom to negotiate trade deals with other countries, directly opposing the pro-Brexit slogan *taking back control*. Because in a customs union, national governments give up substantial national autonomy to the union, most customs unions tend to be geographically proximate, in contrast to FTAs that occasionally include long-distance partners. Many customs unions have struggled to agree on and implement a standard external tariff regime. For example, the Andean Community suspended the implementation of a standard external tariff, and parties have instead opted for a less rigid "common tariff." The Caribbean Community (CARICOM) and the Central African Economic and Monetary Community (CEMAC) both have a standard external tariff in place, but with many exceptions, postponements for certain members, and freedom for countries to adjust it. Where the EU's customs union covers all goods, the South American Mercosur does not cover motor vehicles and sugar, and Turkey's customs union with the EU does not cover primary agricultural goods, transport services, or steel products.

A customs union liberalizes trade but does not create frictionless trade as it does not remove the need for customs documentation and transport documents. These border controls are needed because, in many aspects, national rules do not work in harmony. Think about regulatory and taxation checks that result in traffic congestion at the border between two countries participating in a customs union.

6.7.3 *Common market*

The third type of trading bloc is the single or common market. It has the same features as a customs union, but in addition, there is close cooperation between the member states in many aspects. A common market has free movement of goods, labor, and capital. There are no structural border controls, and workers have the freedom to work in any of the member states. Companies within the common market have the freedom to invest in any of the member states. A common market also has a set of shared rules and regulations. Think about harmonized legislation on product specification (e.g., emission levels on cars or permitted artificial additives to foods) and the rules on competition (e.g., a fair tender system in government procurement).

EU integration: a difficult format to follow

Harmonization is also evident in taxation such as value-added tax (VAT) and regulations regarding the labor market. Again, it is one step further in creating a frictionless or borderless region. The main disadvantage of the common market is ceding national autonomy and sovereignty to a central entity. There is limited room for national policy discretion. On paper, there are several common markets notified to the WTO. Still, except for the EU, other common market agreements made only a few steps toward fully implementing free movement of goods, capital, and labor and developing deeper economic integration between its members.

6.7.4 *Even more intense types of cooperation*

Cooperation between member states can extend beyond a common market by creating fixed exchange rates between the member countries' currencies or a single, shared currency — the essence of an economic and monetary union. A fixed currency system or a single currency has apparent consequences for the fiscal and monetary policies of member states. In essence, governments hand over their monetary policy tools and a substantial part of national fiscal policy discretion to the union. In general, a single currency needs a shared macroeconomic policy, and hence, it reduces the autonomy and sovereignty of the member states considerably. The Eurozone and the Southern African Customs Union (SACU) are examples of economic and monetary unions. When cooperation, coordination, and harmonization move into the convergence of macroeconomic policies, we refer to it as a political union or moving toward unification or a federal state. This involves a central government, shared rules, regulations, and fiscal policies, and centralized monetary policy.

6.8 Trade Creation and Trade Diversion

Trading blocs change trade patterns. In the short to medium term, we distinguish two changes: *trade creation* and *trade diversion*. The following example uses the customs union with its standard external tariff, but trade creation and diversion also happen in other types of trading blocs. In the example, we assume no transportation costs and international competition is entirely based on the cost of production, while due to market forces, the cost of production equals the (export) price of this product.

6.8.1 *Trade creation*

Trade creation occurs when domestic consumers in member countries import more goods from other members when import prices fall due to a fall or removal of tariffs. Essentially, production will shift to the lowest-cost producer in the trading bloc. In Figure 6.20, the trade creation effect is shown with the help of three countries. Imagine countries A, B, and C produce an identical product. In the initial situation (on the left-hand side), there is a tariff between all the countries of 20%. The most efficient and competitive producer is in country C and can make the product at $85. The other producers in countries A and B can make the same product for $100 and $90, respectively. In this situation, there are no trade flows between the three countries, not even from the most efficient producer in country C. When it crosses the border, the 20% import duty increases the products price from $85 to $102, and it cannot compete (on price) with local competitors in countries A and B. The same holds for countries A and B; they cannot export either.

Now imagine countries A and B establishing a trading bloc, shown on the right-hand side of the figure. In this new trading bloc, internal tariffs are zero. The original external tariff of 20% now applies as a standard tariff for non-participating countries, including country C. The effect is clear: consumers in country A buy the product from country B at $90, substantially lower than the relatively high domestic price. Consumers now obtain the product within the trading bloc. This example is for one product, but country A may also have other sectors that can now export to country B. In this setting, the most efficient producer worldwide is situated in country C, which is not part of the customs union. Hence, the most efficient producer is (still) unable to export. As that was already the case beforehand, we could say that the new situation is not hurting country C. Therefore, if they create trade, the WTO is in favor of trading blocs.

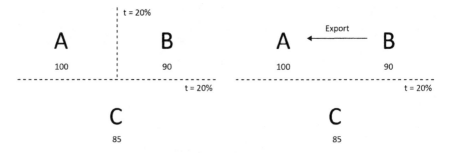

Figure 6.20:   Trade creation.

6.8.2 *Trade diversion*

However, there is also a possible negative impact on country C. When a customs union results in trade flows shifting or diverting from a lower-cost producer outside the trading bloc toward higher-cost producers within the trading bloc, it is called *trade diversion*, as visualized in Figure 6.21. The initial situation is the same as before, countries A, B, and C with external tariffs of 20% between them. I made one minor adjustment compared to the previous case. The cost of production of country A's producer is now $105 (instead of 100).

As you can see on the left-hand side, despite the tariff of 20%, the most efficient producer in country C can export its product to country A. Its selling price after paying the import duty is $102, which is lower than the $105 of the domestic producer in country A. Again, we will imagine a customs union between countries A and B, shown on the right-hand side of the figure. In this case, consumers in country A will buy the product at $90 from country B and shift away from the producer in country C. Trade diverts from country C (outside the trading bloc) to country B (inside the trading bloc). Total trade has not increased, but the most efficient producer in country C can no longer export. The lower price benefits consumers in country A, but domestic producers in country A may be negatively impacted, so will country A's government, due to lower tariff revenues. As with trade creation, trade diversion also increases the trade within the trading bloc.

Trade creation and diversion both increase trade within the trading bloc

---

This trade diversion effect explains why countries decide to join any type of economic cooperation at the same time as their neighbors and

Figure 6.21:   Trade diversion.

competitors. For example, Spain and Portugal jointly entered the EU in 1986, and the same holds for Eastern and Central European countries in 2004. This is also known as a snowball effect. Indonesia made the same assessment when it joined the ASEAN free trade agreement and, more recently, the RCEP. It entered these trade agreements to prevent trade diversion not because it expects major gains from membership. According to Indonesian policymakers, welfare gains from the trading blocs in which Indonesia participates are relatively low compared to the effects of liberalization under the WTO. Be aware that the concepts of trade creation and diversion can also apply to investment flows; foreign direct investments (discussed in Chapter 8) may result from a trading bloc, but we may also see FDI diversion.

6.8.3 *A complex assessment*

Naturally, governments will assess the pros and cons of regional cooperation by evaluating the effect on trade flows, investment flows, and competitiveness and, therefore, the disruptive impact of a trading bloc. Trading blocs can be negotiated relatively quickly, certainly compared to the extended talks in the WTO, and liberalization may go too fast for certain sectors in the society. If disruption is deemed potentially considerable, governments may decide not to participate in a trading bloc and accept the potential negative impact of trade diversion. India chose not to participate in the RCEP signed in November 2020. Apart from the 10 ASEAN members, it includes China, Japan, South Korea, Australia, and New Zealand. According to the Indian authorities, rapidly dismantling tariff barriers between the member states would create significant problems for many Indian industrial enterprises that are not globally competitive, in particular, not able to compete with Chinese companies. In its assessment, the Indian government deemed the trading bloc and swift opening up of the country's markets to foreign agricultural products would wipe out the numerous small, family-owned farms. Australia's and New Zealand's decision to join the trading bloc also happened only after serious discussions. Some economists emphasized the lower prices for consumers for goods imported from China and Indonesia as a consequence of the trade deal. Other economists noted that this advantage of lower prices might not be enough to counteract the potential negative impact of the trading bloc on actual wage rates in Australia and New Zealand due to increased competition from China and Indonesia. This is the essence of the commonly named Samuelson critique of trading blocs. Being able to purchase groceries 20 percent cheaper at Walmart (due to international trade) does not necessarily make up for the wage losses (in America).

6.8.4 *Open regionalism*

If a trading bloc causes net trade diversion, the WTO is against it and is actively trying to reduce the trade diversion effect. One way to do this is to ask member states to reduce the external tariff for non-participating countries.

Bridging globalization and regionalism

Look at Figure 6.21 again. If countries A and B reduce the external tariff toward country C from 20% to 10%, the producer in country C can still compete in market A. This is the essence of the "open regionalism" concept aimed at bridging globalization and multilateralism on the one hand and trading blocs and regionalism on the other. Besides lowering external tariffs, another way to reduce trade diversion is open membership: any country indicating a credible willingness to accept the organization's rules is welcome to join. Economists like Bhagwati that are against trading blocs and advocate reliance on the multilateral process primarily refer to this trade diversion effect. According to these economists, in most trading blocs, the net result is trade diversion. And even if trade creation offsets trade diversion, in principle, trade diversion is bad and should be prevented.

Moreover, they argue that countries may lose interest in the multilateral system when they actively engage in regional initiatives. Finally, according to the criticasters of trading blocs, these agreements always involve asymmetrical power. For example, the US is leading in the negotiations with Mexico and bilateral trade deals with small countries such as Costa Rica (2009) or Singapore (2004). This disequilibrium in economic and political power is also visible in the SACU trading bloc, which South Africa heavily dominates.

On the other hand, the proponents of regionalism like Hoffbauer and Bergsten (1994) emphasize that trading blocs promote multilateralism, which is why the WTO explicitly permits regional agreements and thus acknowledges their compatibility with the multilateral trading system.

According to the proponents of trading blocs, trade creation has generally exceeded trade diversion in most regional groupings, if not in the short term, certainly in the medium term. This is motivated by the growing income effect inside the trading bloc. The economic impact of the trading bloc is so significant that economic growth automatically increases the need to import products from both inside and outside the trading bloc. Furthermore, trading blocs can be negotiated much faster than global pacts, and they may stimulate or lock in domestic reforms. Sometimes domestic reforms are challenging to implement, and international cooperation may help. This was the case in Mexico after the NAFTA agreement. Domestic reforms achieved momentum due to the trading agreement with the US and Canada. The same happened in Central and Eastern Europe when these countries became EU members.

Whether at the end of the day trade creation is more significant than trade diversion is an empirical discussion. Research outcomes are mixed because the effect depends on many influencing factors. As you may have observed, the discussion on trade creation and diversion is about short-term impact. Proponents of trading blocs say there may also be medium- or longer-term effects due to evolving dynamics in the regional grouping. Getting a picture of the longer-term impact of a trading bloc on its members and non-participating countries is even more complex and uncertain because it is the result of choices made by producers and consumers. For example, we do not know how companies react to the larger market. The trading bloc may stimulate economies of scale and increase competition, but it may also involve large takeovers and the emergence of oligopolistic behavior.

NEP-9 countries: multilateralism under WTO guidance can work alongside regionalism

---

As indicated so often throughout this book, we can summarize the NEP-9 attitude on international trade as combining the two worlds: opening up with closing down, the market with government interference, and multilateral trade with regional trading blocs. According to the NEP-9, multilateralism under WTO auspices can work alongside regionalism. The concern that these regional arrangements are likely to undermine the multilateral trading system is, therefore, too one-sided, as we will see in the next chapter.

Chapter 7

Global Governance and NEP-9

7.1 The Many Faces of Global Governance

Global governance or political globalization covers international institutions through which countries cooperate and their policies, values, and procedures. In Chapter 5, we examined the existing paradigms behind the globalization process and introduced institutions under which auspices globalization takes place. The basic argument of this cooperation between sovereign states in an intergovernmental organization, whether bilateral or multilateral, is that an umbrella (global) organization yields better outcomes than individual nation states.

Membership is only open for governments

A characteristic of multilateral institutions is that their members are always governments. Besides the number of governmental participants, multilateral institutions differ in many ways. For example, we have global institutions, such as the United Nations (UN), the World Health Organization (WHO), and the World Trade Organization (WTO). But we also see organizations in charge of *regional* coordination, such as the EU institutional framework. Besides regional perspectives, institutions such as the North Atlantic Treaty Organization (NATO) focus on sectoral cooperation. Essentially, all these multilateral institutions have specific goals and a set of rules that order the relations among those states. For example, membership in the UN means the acceptance of the

UN Charter that stresses international peace (under the umbrella of the UN Security Council), human rights, and economic development. In 2000, the UN broadened its mandate with the adoption of the Millennium Development Goals, such as eliminating extreme poverty, primary education for all, and the substantial reduction of child mortality by 2015. UN members pledged to consider these goals in the implementation of domestic policies. In 2015, the UN added the commonly named Sustainable Development Goals, focusing on human and sustainable development, to ensure that, by 2030, there is no poverty, zero hunger, and gender equality. As stated above, the idea is that these goals and the shared vision will become reference points for policy debates and practices worldwide. The UN is also the global institution regarding climate change. The 2015 Paris Agreement, under the auspices of the UN, meant that countries are legally bound to the agreement, and the main objective is to limit global warming to 1.5 degrees Celsius. The latest UN climate conference, held in Glasgow in November 2021, was disappointing. The only result was a statement saying that going forward, UN members will be more transparent and forthcoming in reporting their progress toward achieving the Paris objectives. During the final session of the Glasgow summit, Patricia Espinosa, then Executive Secretary of the United Nations Framework Convention on Climate Change (UNFCCC) said: "Negotiations are never easy. This is the nature of consensus and multilateralism" (UN, November 13, 2021).

Organizations such as the International Monetary Fund (IMF) rely on specific and formal rules. At the same time, governance relies on looser norm-setting forums, such as the World Economic Forum or the G20 and G7, that include the world's largest economies. These institutions do not set up treaties but discuss ideas, align policies, and set non-mandatory norms. Outcomes of discussions in these forums are often adopted by more formal institutions, such as the IMF and the UN. For example, the flat taxation rate for multinational enterprises was first discussed in the G7, followed by an agreement in the G20. In September 2021, more than 130 countries declared they would join the agreement. The dramatic situation of evacuees fleeing Afghanistan to escape the Taliban in August 2021 was first discussed and coordinated in the G7 before the UN took over coordination. Obviously, in many cases, we see differences in power within multilateral institutions. For example, NATO is dominated by the US, while the Belt and Road Initiative is initiated and led by China. Although formally, countries have equal rights, informal power is often asymmetrical. The WTO operates on a *one country, one vote* principle, but at the end of the day, the economic power of member states drives negotiations. This chapter assesses the role of the NEP-9 countries in the most important multilateral institutions and discusses how they might change the design of global governance in the future.

7.2   The Pillars of Multilateral Institutions

As shown above, the architecture of global governance is made up of many different and overlapping multilateral institutions and is, therefore, rather complex. Clearly, we cannot discuss every major institution here. We will focus on two multilateral institutions because they connect to our discussion on globalization: the WTO and the IMF. The WTO is in charge of international trade in goods and services, and stabilizing the monetary system is the scope of the IMF. Both organizations are essential for global free trade and investments and hence, globalization. The rule-based trade system was created in 1947 through the foundation of the General Agreement on Tariffs and Trade (GATT). In 1995, GATT was incorporated into the WTO. The use of GATT and WTO in the following text is based on the period: GATT before 1995, and WTO after that. The IMF started operations in the 1940s and was established (together with the World Bank) at Bretton Woods (US) in 1944. The main objective was to provide credit to countries with payment difficulties. These credits are essential in smoothening trade flows. When international trade generates a deficit, creating financial problems, protectionist measures should be prevented, and this requires liquidity.

Established in the mid-1940s, the international economic system was built on three key characteristics that are still visible today. First, the United States shaped global economic rules and dominated multilateral institutions. This was the heritage of US domination in world economics and politics after WWII. Second, and related to the first point, the economic system of the United States (and other western industrialized countries) was the template for the international economic system, including the emphasis on free trade, free capital movement, and free markets. Third, the US dollar has been the cornerstone of the international monetary system. Today, despite several adjustments, the US dollar is by far the most important currency for trade transactions, foreign investments, and international loans.

7.2.1   *NEP-9 viewpoint: An introduction*

The world economy is very different today than it was 60 years ago, not in the least because of the emergence of the NEP-9 countries. The NEP-9 countries are not satisfied with today's global governance architecture. Current structures reflect the power that countries had when these institutions were formed, but this may not fit modern practices. Changes in the decision-making process are needed. In this context, there is a trade-off between legitimacy and efficiency: Ensuring representation for all legitimate countries while at the same time trying to keep numbers down to facilitate efficient decision-making.

NEP-9 countries are not satisfied with the global governance structure

---

Another criticism heard from NEP-9 countries is that the economic paradigm *more market, less government* is too one-sided and not applicable to many countries. This specific criticism gained momentum after the sub-prime crisis in the US in 2008 and the global economic crisis that followed. It undermined the neoliberal model because it was a crisis at the heart of the pro-market paradigm and, related to this, the Washington Consensus (Chapter 5). As many industrialized economies undertook far-reaching state interventions, it became harder to make a credible case to emerging economies that only markets generate welfare and prosperity, and the market alone should be used as a guiding principle in the domestic economy and politics. NEP-9 countries question the advantages of free trade and free capital flows and believe that government intervention in trade and investments is sometimes helpful and needed. The NEP-9 countries demand an adjusted architecture of multilateral institutions and ask for consideration of domestic development priorities that require government interference and respect for cultural and political heritage in the development of policy packages by these institutions.

A related critique focused on the IMF and World Bank advice and conditionalities are discussed in Chapter 5. Obviously, these did not cause the 1990s economic problems in Asia or Europe during the 2008–2012 financial crisis. And the WTO's focus on opening up to international trade did not create the Brazilian economic crisis of 2015. However, perceptions were different. In Asia, IMF credibility declined substantially after the mid-1990s. In particular, free capital flows, part of the IMF policy mix, were seen as a major cause of economic crisis and volatility. The IMF package deal was also poorly received by Greece, Italy, and Spain and perceived as the reason the crisis deepened in the short term. The credibility of the WTO is also under attack because many emerging markets are frustrated that the US and EU agricultural sectors are still protected, and advanced nations drive the WTO agenda.

Confrontation and cooperation

The NEP-9 countries face a dilemma in their orientation toward global governance. On the one hand, these countries are increasingly dependent on the existing institutional frameworks. On the other, their interventionist policies put them into tension with the doctrines of global institutions. There are two views on this issue. The first view emphasizes confrontation. In this *confrontation view*, the NEP-9 threaten the present rule-based world order. This idea is supported by the more aggressive bargaining, coalition building, and growing regional initiatives, resulting in a standstill in the WTO discussions. The second view accentuates cooperation. This is what I call the *collaboration view* (Ebbers, 2019) and is, in my opinion, the correct way to look at the present situation. From this perspective, the NEP-9 use the existing global governance order. Although they will seek incremental adaptations of the current rules and institutions, they do not want to change the system fundamentally because they have been the chief beneficiaries of globalization. They are as dependent as the West upon the smooth functioning of an open global economy for their economic success and political stability. They want to see changes in the worldwide architecture but are not system changers.

7.3 The Principles of the WTO and the Role of the NEP-9

After the Great Depression of the late 1920s, the world saw increased protectionism. The response of many countries to domestic economic problems was to restrict imports by way of tariffs and quotas. Obviously, one country's imports are another country's exports. The 1930s were a classic example of the *beggar-thy-neighbor* policies, which had dramatic consequences. Therefore, the rules of a new international trading system had to prevent a return to this era of protectionism. The result was the founding of the GATT in 1947 with its aim of reducing trade barriers and promoting free and fair trade. The motivation behind this was not solely economic. Intensive trade relations and international cooperation help promote peace. These are the four basic views behind the multilateral trading order under the guidance of the GATT:

1. Countries are sovereign and have control of their domestic goals and choices.
2. The best policy is to enter into binding agreements with other states and voluntarily limit sovereignty.
3. Free trade is a win-win context.
4. Acceptance of asymmetry in power but recognition of mutual self-interest and the need for additional advantages and preferences for developing countries.

The above still holds for the WTO, which in 1995 replaced GATT as the presiding body for the multilateral trading system. The basic principles are the same, but the WTO is much more powerful, meaning it has a profound impact on the daily lives of ordinary people worldwide.

The deepening of global rules intervenes with domestic priorities

---

At the birth of the WTO, the rules were extended and deepened to include several areas previously outside the GATT system, notably agriculture, textiles, trade-in services, and intellectual property rights. Also, WTO rules on disputes between countries are much stricter than under the GATT. In addition, to reduce trade barriers and promote free and fair trade, the WTO operates under three basic principles.

1. Non-discrimination
The non-discrimination principle is enforced through the commonly named most favoured nation (MFN) clause and the national treatment rule (Figure 7.1). The MFN clause dictates that countries cannot discriminate between trading partners. If one country grants another country a special favor, such as a lower tariff for one of their products, it must also unconditionally give the same favor to all other WTO members. For example, if Brazil reduces tariff rates on machines from China, this new rate should apply to all other WTO members. Brazil cannot ask for reciprocal treatment to extend the tariff reduction to WTO members other than

Principle of non-discrimination	
Most favored nation	National treatment
Non-discriminatory treatment between products of WTO-members	Non-discriminatory treatment between imported and domestic products

Figure 7.1:   Non-discrimination in the WTO.

China. The principle of reciprocity, a nation benefitting from a tariff reduction from another country must reciprocate by making a similar tariff reduction itself, holds in this case only for Brazil and China. This MFN principle sounds like a contradiction. It suggests special treatment, but in the WTO, it actually means non-discrimination: treating virtually everyone equally. If a country improves the benefits that it gives to one trading partner, it has to give the same "best" treatment to all the other WTO members so that they all remain "most favored."

The principle of national treatment also guarantees non-discrimination. Imported and locally produced goods should be treated equally after the foreign goods have entered the market and compete with the local products on the same shelf. The same applies to foreign and domestic services, trademarks, copyrights, and patents. The goal is to ensure governments do not protect domestic producers through regulation, taxes, and other government actions. For example, if in China the VAT on locally produced tablets is 5% and 10% for Indian tablets, this violates the national treatment obligation. The same holds for information on the packaging. If foreign producers must disclose all the ingredients of a food product on the packaging while domestic producers do not, this violates the national treatment rule.

2. Bound tariffs and the prohibition of quota's
The WTO aims to lower import duties or tariffs as much as possible. Once a tariff of a specific product is fixed, the WTO member is obligated not to apply customs duties above the bounded fixed rate. When a government feels an increase above the fixed tariff is needed, it should negotiate this within the context of the WTO. Quantitative restrictions, such as quotas, are more disruptive than tariffs. While tariffs may discourage trade, quantitative restrictions are prohibitive since they prevent foreign goods from entering the market. That is why the prohibition of quantitative restrictions or quotas is one of the fundamental principles of the WTO. As we will see in this chapter, as an exception to the rule, members

can maintain quantitative restrictions in specific circumstances and for a short period.

3. Trade rounds and the single undertaking

Trade liberalization, in particular through reducing tariffs, has been achieved through a series of multilateral negotiations known as "trade rounds." The outcome of these trade rounds is a single bill or undertaking. Decisions in the WTO are made by consensus and must be ratified by all national parliaments. In general, there is no opt-out option, and it is either "yes" or "no" to the single bill. The à la carte approach, accepting some agreements but not others, was possible in the 1970s under certain circumstances. However, this was no longer allowed after the founding of the WTO in 1995. Since 1947, there have been eight rounds of trade negotiations, and the ninth (Doha) is underway. Figure 7.2 shows the main characteristics and achievements of each trade round.

In its early years, the GATT trade rounds concentrated on reducing tariffs, driven by the US push for trade liberalization, followed by the European countries. The US dominated the world economy and the GATT trade agenda during the first rounds. In this setting, tariff reductions were relatively easy to negotiate. It helped that membership was relatively low. Brazil, South Africa, China, and India were among the

Name	Start	Duration	#countries	Main topics and achievements
1. Geneva I	April 1947	7 months	23	
2. Annecy	April 1949	5 months	13	
3. Torquay	September 1950	8 months	38	Lowering tariffs on manufacturing products
4. Geneva II	January 1958	5 months	26	
5. Dillon	September 1960	11 months	26	
6. Kennedy	May 1964	37 months	62	Tariffs and anti-dumping measures
7. Tokyo	September 1973	74 months	102	Tariffs, non-tariff barriers (subsidies and technical obstacles to trade) and framework agreements
8. Uruguay	September 1986	87 months	123	Tariffs and non-tariff barriers (agricultural subsidies), acccess for textile and clothing from developing countries, intellectual property rights, dispute settlement body and the creation of the WTO
9. Doha	November 2001	Continues	141	New elements such as labor issues, environmental and foreign investment rules

Figure 7.2:   The trade rounds.

Note: The Geneva trade round started in 1947, while the GATT officially began on January 1, 1948.

Source: Based on WTO (2007).

23 founding members of the GATT but with low negotiation power. Over the years, membership grew to 164 members (2022). Indonesia and Turkey joined in 1950 and 1951, respectively. South Korea became a member in 1967, while Mexico's membership started in 1986. Russia was one of the latest countries to join the WTO (2012) and is the only NEP-9 country that was never a GATT member.

The early trading rounds were dominated by the US and Western Europe

---

7.3.1 *Kennedy Round*

In the 1960s and early 1970s, European integration gathered steam, and the United States started to feel the discriminatory effects of European integration. To mitigate these effects, the US pushed strongly for reductions in tariffs during the Kennedy Round that started in 1964. You may argue that the US' main reason for undertaking multilateral trade negotiations in the 1960s was the European integration process. Besides reducing tariffs further, the Kennedy Round discussed the negative impact of dumping, which led to the first anti-dumping agreement. Most developing countries were largely passive in the early GATT rounds, effectively not participating in the discussions. However, they asked for (and received) "special treatment," a form of non-reciprocity or legal free-rider behavior, meaning preferential access to foreign markets and, at the same time, the option to protect themselves from international competition.

7.3.2 *Tokyo Round*

In the early 1970s, the rise of Japan and the Asian Tigers caused nervousness in the US and Europe. The strong growth of the Japanese economy and export was the context of the start of the Tokyo Round in 1973. According to American and European governments, it was driven by government support for its export sector, generating unfair competition. The result of this unfair practice was a growing trade deficit and problems for US and EU companies. Therefore, the focus of the trade talks shifted from tariffs to non-tariff barriers (discussed in Chapter 6) to tackle this government support. Furthermore, countries agreed they could protect themselves if the disruption from Japan got too high, the commonly named safeguard measures to restrict imports of a product temporarily. As shown in Figure 7.2, negotiations were challenging, as the trade round took over six years.

A broader agenda

There are several reasons negotiations were drawn out. For the first time, several larger emerging markets and developing countries became more vocal. India and Brazil demanded the incorporation of their domestic objectives into the negotiations. In addition to changing economic circumstances and the increased number of member states, the Tokyo Round was also complex due to its ambitious agenda, focusing on broad heterogonous non-tariff barriers. Members agreed on further tariff reductions, but the Tokyo Round failed to achieve consensus on these non-tariff barriers. In most cases, only a relatively small number of (mainly industrialized) GATT members subscribed to these agreements. Because they were not accepted by the full GATT membership, they are often informally called "codes" or "frameworks."

The GATT was successful in reducing tariffs. For example, the average tariff on manufacturing products was only 4.7% in the mid-1980s compared to 14% in the mid-1960s. But this low average tariff on manufacturing goods had a negative side effect. As countries could no longer use tariffs to protect domestic industries, the use of non-tariff barriers increased. The economic recessions of the early 1980s drove governments to intervene and protect sectors facing increased international competition. Using these non-tariff barriers resulted in an upswing of protectionism in the 1980s. Furthermore, we saw the emergence of trade in services and the start of fragmented international supply chains through foreign direct investments that changed the character of trade flows. GATT rules, based on the treaty signed after the Tokyo negotiations in 1979, did not cover these issues. Emerging markets and developing countries grew frustrated about the continued protection of agriculture in advanced nations. GATT had a dispute settlement system, but numerous loopholes hindered the process. Because of this, the Uruguay Round agenda, which started in 1986, was extensive in an attempt to tackle the demands from emerging markets, developing countries, rising powers, and advanced countries combined.

7.3.3 *Uruguay Round*

The 1990s was a decade of growing prosperity in many parts of the world. The export-led growth model in Asia created the belief that the countries that prosper the most are those that are the most integrated into the global system. The 1994 World Bank report on globalizers versus non-globalizers (Chapter 6) showed that their trade openness drove the rise of the Asian Tigers. Earlier in this book, we discussed several critical notes on the outcome of this report. Still, in the 1990s, there was a strong belief that opening up to international trade was a precondition for prosperity, so countries pursued the WTO agenda of trade liberalization.

Achieving global efficiency

The most important countries were willing to spend diplomatic capital to reach that goal. Simultaneously, several large trading blocs emerged in the late 1980s and early 1990s. We discussed this development in the previous chapter. One could argue that these regional initiatives substituted multilateral GATT negotiations. However, countries saw these regional initiatives as complementary to the multilateral trading system and as an additional way to lower trade barriers further.

The Uruguay Round is considered successful. At the treaty's signing in 1994, industrial countries' tariff rates on manufacturing goods were less than 4%. And although tariffs on agricultural products were still considerably higher, one of the achievements of the Uruguay Round was to

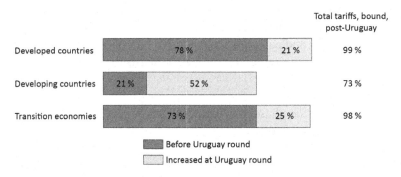

Figure 7.3:   Uruguay Round impact on tariff bindings.

Source: Congressional paper, October 2021.

increase the volume of trade under binding commitments. For example, as shown in Figure 7.3, almost 100% of all products had bound tariffs in developed countries. Furthermore, the treaty also covered services (GATTS agreement) and rules to govern intellectual property protection (patents, copyrights, and trademarks), the TRIPS agreement. For the first time, the US and the EU promised to reduce agricultural subsidies and allow more market access to emerging markets and developing countries exporting agricultural products. It also established a new dispute settlement system to strengthen the organization's monitoring and enforcement mechanism. And finally, the WTO was created during the Uruguay Round.

The start of the WTO in 1995 was also the start of a more rule-based system and stricter enforcement. Countries could no longer take the à la carte approach, accepting some agreements but not others. The Uruguay Round produced a fixed menu for all participants. Furthermore, although the WTO operates on consensus, as the GATT did before, member states can no longer block decisions in dispute settlement.

A fixed menu to liberalize trade for all countries

7.3.4 *Dispute settlement body*

In case of disputes within the WTO, its Dispute Settlement Body (DSB) establishes the commonly named "panels of experts" to investigate the matter. Officially, the panel is advisory, but because members can only reject its reports by consensus, its conclusions are difficult to overturn. Furthermore, the DSB monitors the implementation of its rulings and recommendations and can authorize punitive measures for non-compliant countries. The dispute settlement process consists of three phases.

1. Consultation phase
2. Panel phase (this phase also includes the option to appeal)
3. Implementation phase

During the consultation phase, before taking any action, the disputing countries have to talk to each other to see if they can settle their differences. This may be enough to come to a solution. The parties can also decide to stall the case for a certain period and start the official consultation phase at a later date. If consultations fail, the complaining country can ask for the convening of a panel: this is the start of the panel phase. The defending country can block the formation of a panel only once before the DSB decides on the final makeup of the panel. After the panel decision and the official DSB judgment, the implementation phase starts. The priority at this stage is that the "losing" country brings its policies in line with the panel's and DSB's ruling. Specific time frames are not given because of the heterogeneity and complexity of the cases. Still, "prompt compliance with rulings of the DSB is needed," and the member has a "reasonable period" to implement the required changes (WTO website). The three phases are indicated in Figure 7.4, including the specific time frames.

The WTO dispute settlement process, with its fixed time frames, is a significant improvement compared to the GATT. During the first years of the WTO, most cases were settled within the given time frame, but that changed over the years. Today, it takes much longer. There are different reasons for this. First, WTO cases have become more legalistic with a growing role for private lawyers, complicating the process and increasing the need for technical (and academic) evidence. Second, the panel phase

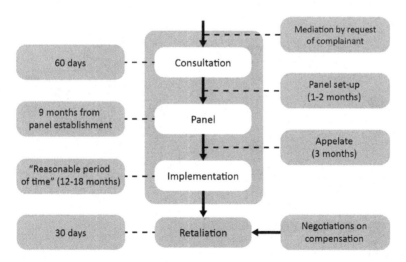

Figure 7.4: The phases of dispute settlement process.

Source: Based on WTO (2022).

takes more time because the parties do not agree on the panel's makeup. Third, the panel process relies on panelists enlisted on an *ad hoc* basis, mainly from the international trade law community. Most panelists already have full-time jobs. There is talk within the WTO about establishing a standing body of panelists rather than recruiting on an *ad hoc* basis, but this remains undecided.

Figure 7.5 summarizes NEP-9 involvement in the WTO dispute settlement process from 2010 to 2021. Brazil, China, India, Indonesia, South Korea, and Mexico are very active, each engaged in at least 10 cases as a complainant and another 10 or more as a respondent. Russia was the complaining country for eight cases, Turkey had six cases as a complainant,

---

A prominent role of the NEP-9 countries in the dispute settlement process

---

while South Africa had zero cases as a complainant. The same pattern can be seen with respect to the NEP-9 countries as respondents. The prominent role of the NEP-9 in the dispute settlement process is easy to explain through the size and growth of their trade, active government involvement

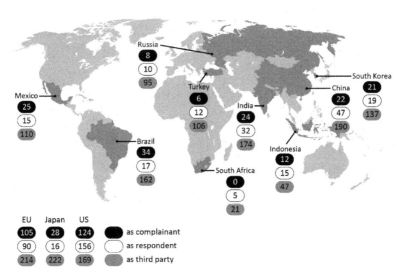

Figure 7.5:   NEP-9 countries' involvement in the DSB process, 2010–2021.

Source: Based on WTO (2022).

in business, and the fact that advanced nations expect more from the NEP-9, including respect for intellectual property, fair international competition, equal treatment of domestic and foreign firms, and keeping their markets open.

7.4 Some Exceptions to the Non-discrimination Rule

Although the WTO is a rule-based system based on non-discrimination, some exceptions exist. For example, the prohibition of quantitative restrictions is one of the organization's fundamental principles. Still, countries can maintain quantitative restrictions in specific circumstances, both on the export and import sides. For example, blocking the import of specific products is allowed when there are serious safety issues and temporary export restrictions are permitted to prevent critical shortages of essential products. We saw this during the COVID-19 crisis when countries like China, India, and Russia decided to use the vaccine domestically instead of exporting it to other countries. The key to using exceptions is balancing domestic values and interests and avoiding abuse. Exceptions to the non-discrimination rule happen in the following situations:

- Safeguard against the disruptive effect of trade due to unfair practice
- Dumping
- Environmental, cultural, health safety, and social considerations
- National security
- Trading blocs

Imposing restrictions is allowed as a safeguard measure when the large-scale import of specific products disrupts the local economy. Of course, in itself, the failure of domestic companies due to international competition is not reason enough for protectionist measures (although the speed of opening up could also be the reason). But if the dramatic inflow results from unfair competition created by government support that enables foreign producers to compete internationally on unequal grounds, this exception to the non-discrimination principle is permitted. For example, imagine a Brazilian producer and exporter of heavy equipment receiving subsidies from the local government. This allows that producer to reduce their international price without creating financial problems and quickly build up market shares abroad. In this case, other countries can protect themselves.

It is even possible that due to this government support, the price abroad is lower than the domestic price or that the international price is even below the cost of production. This practice is called dumping and is considered a second motive for an exception to the non-discrimination rule. Within the WTO context, dumping occurs when a company in a specific country exports its products at a price lower than its domestic price, harming companies abroad. The fight against dumping is based on the view that the only objective of dumping is to increase market share in a foreign market by driving out competition and thereby creating a monopoly. The exporter can now unilaterally dictate the price and quality of the product. Dumping enables consumers in the importing country to buy imported goods relatively cheaply, but at the end of the day, monopolistic behavior and higher prices are bad for that same consumer.

The dumping-assessment: difficult to proof and complex

Dumping is considered unfair as companies can only lower their prices because they receive government support. The WTO demands sufficient proof dumping has happened before members can take counteracting measures such as increasing tariffs on these imported products: the anti-dumping duties. In the following, we will discuss a few points linked to the NEP-9 attitude to the WTO in general and dumping specifically.

7.4.1 *NEP-9 on dumping*

In general, internationally operating companies, including state-owned enterprises, may have different price points in different countries. This practice is called international price differentiation. When a Chinese producer sells a bicycle at a lower price to a German importer compared to what they charge a local Chinese distributor, it is generally seen as dumping. But, we could also consider this price differentiation. Dumping means the Chinese bicycle producer receives government support to lower their international price. However, it is price differentiation if the lower price in Germany results from differences in the willingness to pay for the bicycle and the intensity of competition. For example, the intensity of competition in international markets may be much higher than in the Chinese domestic market and consequently depress the international selling price. In this case, it makes sense that the Chinese bicycles have a lower price outside China. The same holds if the bicycle company tries to sell excess unsold inventory to avoid price wars in the home market. In these cases, the selling price abroad is lower than the domestic price, but this may be labeled as price differentiation and not dumping.

A non-market status and the surrogate country method

A big issue surrounding dumping is whether the price results from market forces of demand and supply. If this is not the case, the country under investigation is labeled a *non-market economy*. These are countries in which the government sets prices, not the markets. Often, this government interference in prices goes hand in hand with currency manipulation and strong government support for domestic firms. In 2021, most WTO members labeled China, Vietnam, and many former Soviet Republics non-market economies. This has important repercussions. While a dumping case is under investigation and there is no reliable home market price, a fictional domestic price is set through the *surrogate country method*. The price and value of the potential dumped goods from a *non-market economy* are translated to a "normal" market economy. Obviously, one should select a country with similar economic development levels and cost structures. In the case of China, that is usually countries like India, Pakistan, Indonesia, Turkey, and the Philippines, but sometimes also Brazil, Mexico, or even Canada have been selected. As China is classified as a *non-market economy* by the EU and the US, the *surrogate country method* is applied to Chinese exports in anti-dumping investigations. The Chinese feel this method is inaccurate and arbitrary because, by definition, surrogate countries are unsuitable for comparison. The problem with the surrogate method was evident in a case involving China dumping concentrated apple juice exported to the US. The surrogate country used to determine the *normal value* of the imported product was India. However, India was not a significant producer of concentrated apple juice, and the WTO had relied on information from a private market study. After Chinese complaints, the WTO changed its surrogate country to Turkey, a major producer of apple juice concentrate. However, at the time, Turkish wages were substantially higher than those in China. These issues render *the surrogate country method* debatable.

When China entered the WTO in 2001, members agreed the country would be treated as a *non-market economy* for 15 years until the end of 2016. If it fulfilled the requirements, China would then receive market economy status. This status is important because the WTO will no longer apply the surrogate country method. According to Chinese authorities, the Chinese economy is a market economy, despite the influence of state-owned enterprises and specific strategic sectors being closed to foreign investments. Today, the US and the EU are still blocking this request for market economy status. According to them, China is not doing enough to ensure fair competition for EU and US companies. This may partly explain China's investments in infrastructure in Africa and Latin America. Through this infrastructural diplomacy, it hopes to receive enough support from countries in the WTO to obtain the preferred status. Several countries have indeed recognized China as a market economy. For example, Brazil and China established a bilateral trade agreement explicit indicating this in 2004. The same holds for several Asian countries.

Chinese dissatisfaction about its non-market status

A third area where exceptions to the non-discrimination rule are allowed is environmental, cultural, health safety, and social arguments. The commonly named tuna–dolphin case was a high-profile dispute between the United States and Mexico and revolved around the national treatment rule. Although the tuna–dolphin case received the most attention, the same has happened regarding shrimp, sea turtles, whales, and genetically modified food. There are also numerous examples related to health issues, such as the ban on Argentinian meat by the EU because of animal diseases in that country or India stopping a cargo flight with Dutch flowers at the border because of insects that may hurt domestic species.

7.4.2 *The tuna–dolphin case*

In the past few decades, US consumers have become aware that many dolphins were killed due to tuna fishing. As they often prey on tuna and swim near them, dolphins become collateral damage. In response to this growing awareness, the US fishery sector developed a commonly named "dolphin-safe standard," which includes a "dolphin-safe" label, and granted it to its fishing fleet. It denied tuna products caught by Mexican tuna fishers this label, even though new fishing techniques have helped reduce the number of dolphins dying in Mexican tuna fishing significantly over the years. Furthermore, all boats in Mexico's tuna fleet have independent observers on board to ensure no dolphins are killed.

WTO: consumers must decide on buying a product, not governments

Although the label is not mandatory for tuna products sold in the US, denying Mexico the label created a clear advantage for US firms. Unsurprisingly, US consumers preferred domestic products carrying the dolphin-safe label over imported tuna from Mexico. According to the Mexican government, foreign (Mexican) products sharing a supermarket shelf with US products were competing on an unfair playing field. The tuna–dolphin case continued for a decade and was formally closed in 2018 (WTO Case DS 381). At first, the WTO ruled that US labeling rules unfairly penalized the Mexican fishing industry and, therefore, should be stopped. However, after several appellate procedures and some changes in US legislation, the WTO panel concluded that the US import ban was justified, and it stayed in place. Mexico accepted the outcome because its fishing sector received financial support from the US government to comply quickly with US rules. Another factor to consider is that the Mexican authorities also took the deal because of asymmetrical power; it is challenging to keep up the fight against a more powerful neighbor.

Exceptions to WTO rules give its members the right to step back from their commitments in the WTO, recognizing the legitimacy of certain social values and national security concerns. Because national security is at the core of sovereignty, security concerns take precedence over trade concerns, which is why members can implement trade-restrictive measures if they are necessary to protect essential security interests. The crux is how to determine when national security is at stake. It is an easy claim to make. Governments can say domestic steel companies need protection because they are key in producing military materials, but this may be overshooting the WTO rule. And even if national security or health issues are at stake, a blockade is always detrimental for exporters, particularly when the timing is wrong. Cast your mind back to the Indian border control and Dutch flowers earlier in the chapter. A delay of several days at the Indian border means the flowers wilt before they can enter the Indian market. Imagine this happens days before a nationwide Hindu festival, always flower-filled occasions. Domestic producers will now supply these flowers, so WTO agreements only permit these exceptions under strict conditions and solid (academic) proof. If a country cannot prove the necessity of border control, the WTO forbids it. But this process did not help Dutch exporters when the border incident happened. They could not sell their flowers, possibly increasing the market share for domestic Indian suppliers in the short, as well as in the longer-term.

The final context in which exceptions to the non-discrimination paradigm are allowed is regional trading agreements between countries. For example, governments can set up a free trade agreement that applies only to goods traded within the group and, therefore, discriminate against goods from outside the group. While permitted by WTO rules, these trade deals are technically a violation of the non-discrimination principle. As we saw in Chapter 6, the WTO allows trading agreements because such agreements may further liberalize trade and promote economic openness.

7.4.3 *The start of the Doha Round*

The result of the Uruguay Round was essentially a compromise between the US and the EU. The other participants, the NEP-9 included, were forced to accept the package as a *fait accompli*, and members signed the treaty in 1995. After years of talking about the agenda for the new trading round and a false start in Seattle (1999), the Doha Round started in 2001 and remains ongoing. The fact that it is still not completed after 21 years means that the multilateral agreement signed in the mid-1990s as the result of the Uruguay Round is the last single undertaking. It also means that today's trade flows are guided by a treaty signed nearly 30 years ago.

Today's trade flows are guided by a treaty, signed in 1994

To make sure that the rule-based system can cope with the issues of today's world, the WTO decided to focus on partial deals, stepping away from consensus, for example, regarding foreign direct investments (FDI) and the field of e-commerce. In 1997, there was already a partial deal concerning FDI aimed at opening the telecommunication markets to competition, allowing foreign operators to purchase ownership stakes in domestic telecommunicator providers and establishing a set of standard rules for fair competition. In the same year, an agreement was reached to liberalize cross-border trade in financial services. It was implemented in 1999, and 102 countries promised to open (to varying degrees) their banking, securities, and insurance sector to foreign competition. Current discussions in the field of FDI use the same format.

The WTO also had to react to the rise of digital technologies and the explosion of e-commerce because both dramatically impact many aspects of international trade flows. For example, through lower transaction costs and easier entry, international competition will grow. Besides the increased intensity of competition, the patterns of comparative advantages will change, affecting the complexity and length of global value chains. The regulatory system must move with these changes to create a level playing field and avoid unnecessary disruptions to trade. One of the most controversial aspects of the negotiations within the WTO is the application of customs duties to electronic transmissions, like e-books or online video games. A moratorium currently prohibits WTO members from imposing customs duties on electronic transmissions. The EU and the US want to make the moratorium permanent, while several NEP-9 countries, led by India, want to phase it out. This division is also visible in the discussion on the freedom of data transit. Countries like Japan and the US strongly favor allowing international flows of data, while several NEP-9 countries argue that there are good reasons to restrict the free flow of data.

There is also disagreement about the status of some NEP-9 countries. Within the WTO, several countries have received the status of developing country, which gives them more time to implement necessary legislation, lower tariffs, and scale down protectionism. All countries can request this special status, and it does not expire. When China entered the WTO, it asked for this status to buy time to implement all the necessary legislation to comply with WTO rules. Member countries can request fellow members to waive this status if they think the developing country has matured into a developed economy. For example, the United States feels that China should give up its position as a developing economy and has expressed its discontent. In response, China points to its low income per capita as evidence that it is still underdeveloped in many aspects.

Growing discontent among the NEP-9 countries

The 1990s saw growing activism from the larger emerging markets. Countries like Brazil and India demanded more emphasis on trade issues of central interest to them, such as textiles, agriculture, and voluntary export restraints. They were unwilling to discuss issues important only to the advanced nations, such as trade in services and property rights. Furthermore, there was growing discontent among the advanced nations regarding the role of NEP-9 countries, pushing the edges of the rule-based system. Add to that uncertainty about the impact of digitalization and e-commerce and the attitude that ceding autonomy to the WTO will substantially decrease the power of national governments. Quite a challenging context to start the negotiations. The WTO launched the broad agenda of the Doha Round in November 2001, just two months after the attack on the World Trade Center.

7.5   The Doha Development Round and the NEP-9 Countries

The new WTO negotiation round was scheduled to start in 1999 in Seattle. It is interesting to note that a few months before the WTO meeting in Seattle, the Group of 77, which includes developing countries and NEPs such as Indonesia, India, Brazil, and South Africa, issued a document to use in the negotiations. In this discussion paper, they expressed their continued support for the liberalization of international trade under WTO rules. However, they also noted the significant asymmetrical benefits, particularly the barriers to market access for agricultural products from less developed countries and emerging markets. The document also stressed that trade should strengthen human indicators instead of only increasing efficiency. Many authors (Bleier, 2002; Levi & Osland, 2006) argue that the Seattle conference collapsed due to the anti-globalist protest on the street. However, the Battle of Seattle also took place inside where NEP-9 countries, smaller emerging markets, and developing countries fought with the more advanced nations of North America and Europe. The NEP-9 views on the current trade negotiations and the future trade governance are summarized in the following.

7.5.1 *Frustration*

The Uruguay Round was expected to open up sectors such as agriculture and textiles, important products for the NEP-9 and developing countries. However, these sectors remained closed many years after the Uruguay Round ended, causing growing frustration among the NEP-9.

You may argue that reducing barriers to the agricultural market barriers, although it may have domestic repercussions, is relatively easy, but that isn't entirely the case. For example, the EU has long-standing agreements with the African Caribbean and Pacific (ACP) countries that ensure their agricultural products have tariff-free access to the EU market. So, if the EU reduces its agricultural tariff for a country like Brazil, which has a large agricultural sector, the ACP producers would be wiped out by Brazilian competition on the European market. Therefore, the EU is hesitant to reduce said obstacles. Unlike the EU, the US has no incentive to make the same concessions on agriculture but has problems phasing out government subsidies to its domestic textile sector. In both situations, the NEP-9 countries feel discontent with the slow process of reducing barriers. This discontent can be summarized in four points.

The end of western domination of setting the trade agenda in the WTO

Asymmetrical power structure. Despite the *one vote, one country* principle, in practice, a small group of rich countries drives the agenda and outcomes of WTO negotiations. That small group is the commonly named *Quadrilateral group* or *Quad*: the US, the EU, Canada, and Japan. They and a small number of other countries, a different mix every time, hold Green Room meetings, during which all the main agenda topics of the new trade round are decided. The Green Room is still important today, but in the Doha Round, the NEP-9 no longer accept this power to set the agenda and lead the discussions. The Doha Round is the first trade round in which the NEP-9 (aligned with smaller emerging markets and developing countries) actively take their share in the negotiations. For example, when the US and EU came to a joint agreement at the Cancun meeting in 2003, a group of developing countries led by Brazil, India, and South Africa (informal backed by China) blocked the proposal. While the Seattle meeting marked the start of NEP-9 power in the WTO, Cancun showed irreversible changes in trade diplomacy, ensuring developed countries no longer set the terms and conditions of negotiations or can they dominate the trade talks.

Human development. Countries such as Brazil, Indonesia, and India want to see an explicit normative shift from trade liberalization as the objective to trade liberalization as a means to promote economic development. Consequently, for the first time in the history of trade negotiations, the Doha Round was explicitly declared the Doha Development Round.

Shifting balance. In the Doha Round, trade negations became more complex right from the get-go not only because of the broad agenda but also mainly due to China's accession to the WTO in 2001.

International trade as tool to achieve economic and human development

---

According to Michael Moore, the then Director-General of the WTO, this was a "defining moment in the history of the multilateral trading system." With China's membership, Moore added, "The WTO will take a major step toward becoming a true world organization" (WTO press release #243, September 17, 2001). At the same time, it shifted the balance much more toward emerging markets and the NEP-9, which created more tension. To comply with the WTO, China revised and abolished over 3000 of its national laws and regulations. In this sense, WTO membership was an important driver behind China's structural reforms in the 1990s. But at the same time, China's government is present in many aspects of trade, investment, and business. According to the advanced nations, China's transition to a full market economy was incomplete, the basis for discontent in the US and the EU as they feel this creates unfair competition.

Heterogeneity of the members. The broadness of issues covered by Doha has made it difficult to assemble a package agreeable to all 164 WTO members. The single undertaking format, which says negotiations can only revisit an issue until everything on the agenda is agreed upon, blocks the actual reaching of an agreement. The same goes for the heterogeneity of the countries involved. For example, the difference in economic structure between South Korea and Russia or between Mexico and Indonesia is substantial. Therefore, they may have different perspectives on the optimal outcome. The same holds for the United States and Europe on the one hand and the largest rising economic powers on the other. The US and China agree on some topics, such as reducing barriers for manufacturers but have intense confrontations on others, like opening up the service sector.

Disagreement among the NEP-9 countries

7.5.2 *The WTO is no longer about trade*

Can established powers accept an international trade regime based on rules that are no longer tailor-made to their interests and concerns, and will the NEP-9 accept that further compliance to a rule-based system is needed? The willingness to cooperate in the WTO is even more complicated today because WTO discussions no longer revolve around trade; more and more, they are about domestic legislative rules.

Tariffs on manufacturers are already low and binding, and countries can no longer protect themselves by increasing tariffs, so negotiations are shifting toward non-tariff barriers. Think back to the dolphin-free tuna or the EU wishing to block the export of genetically modified (GM) food from the US. The US claimed the latter is not in compliance with WTO rules, and the WTO dispute settlement body decided in favor of the US. The EU must accept the inflow of these products. Through transparent labeling, consumers can make their own choice: GM soybeans from the US or non-GM soybeans from EU producers. According to the WTO, consumers should decide, not governments. The same holds for the foreign investments debate. The discussions on this topic in the WTO are not actually about trade in the supply chain but about countries complying with the WTO rules on protecting foreign companies. In this case, the WTO has a direct impact on domestic legislation. WTO rules are about domestic regulations on food safety, environmental issues, and investments. It means that a multilateral institution in Geneva (which has not been elected by the people and is made up of bureaucrats) decides on Dutch, US, Mexican, and Brazilian domestic rules and legislation, reducing the autonomy of the nation state to make their own laws.

Interfering with domestic and local rules

In a period (starting in 2008) in which government intervention is back in fashion, it is far from clear if governments, including the NEP-9, are prepared to give up further discretion in policymaking. Again, giving up control in setting your own tariff is one thing, but ceding autonomy in setting domestic rules is another matter. There is a limit to how much autonomy governments are willing to give up.

7.5.3 *The future of the trade system*

Despite its shortcomings, the NEP-9 countries want to improve the current trade regime, not replace it. The same holds for advanced nations: if changes are needed, they should be made within the context of the basic principles of the WTO. Indeed, the rule-based system has its advantages.

An individual country negotiating bilateral trade deals with over 160 countries takes considerably more time than a worldwide agreement under the WTO umbrella. Moreover, without a multilateral regime, the more powerful countries would be freer to impose their preferences on smaller trading partners unilaterally. At the same time, smaller countries would have to deal with each of the major economic powers individually, which may be detrimental to their interests. It is the same as what we will see with respect to the IMF: if the WTO did not exist, countries would be eager to establish such an institute.

The rise of the NEP-9 complicates the WTO negotiations considerably

---

In general, building a rule-based system is becoming more difficult due to the emergence of the New Economic Powers. Essentially, the reason for GATT's success in liberalizing trade after World War II was that the US had such a dominant position. It could, and did, perform the role of initiator and promotor. Also, it could count on receiving the largest share of the benefits of free trade. Another constellation that would support an open, rules-based system is one with many small countries that are open and built upon the paradigm of market forces and global free trade. However, today, we see the emergence of the NEP-9, a small number of large economies, larger than the many small ones but not large enough to dominate the system. This complicates the negation process considerably. It is safe to assume that within this constellation, continuing to move further toward a fully fledged, market-driven, rules-based system is hard to imagine.

Although it varies per country, the NEP-9 countries generally want WTO reform in three broad aspects. First, they want the economic paradigm of the WTO to shift from the Washington Consensus toward the Beijing Consensus and from hyper globalization to smart globalization (Chapter 5). They want to achieve this by giving national governments more discretionary power to decide the sequence and speed toward WTO compliance. In this case, more emphasis should be given to domestic development goals instead of conforming to international efficiency rules. The NEP-9 believe in the advantages of free trade and the positive-sum game paradigm, but market failures and the potential for disruption to the local economy require intervention.

The second type of reform relates to the running of the institution. As Joseph Stiglitz said, "The problem is not with globalization but with how it has been managed" (Stiglitz, 2002, page 214). In principle, all WTO members have equal representation and influence within the organization, but the reality proves different. In theory, any country can take trade disputes to the DSB. In practice, the asymmetry between countries makes sanctions an ineffective tool. For example, South Korea's dependency on the US economy makes it difficult for South Korea to fight with its most important trading partner within the DSB. This means the DSB is used mainly by the largest countries and rarely by the smaller countries. The NEP-9 conclude that the rule-based system looks fine on paper, but in reality, it is not. And this should be tackled.

NEP-9 countries are demanding reforms

Third, reform should address the consensus issue and the single undertaking principle. Both cause talks and negotiations to a grinding halt, and there is growing frustration about the slowness of the process. In principle, the decision-making triangle of WTO consists of three pillars:

1. The single undertaking
2. Consensus
3. National-centric membership

To speed up the negotiation process, one of these pillars must go. For example, partial agreements that focus on important sectors, like government procurement and e-commerce, can replace the Single Undertaking principle. Qualified majorities may be a workable alternative for the consensus. Finally, efficiency would increase if the WTO secretariat conducts the negotiations instead of member states driven by domestic considerations. Again, it is difficult to assess the NEP-9 as a group on these issues, but it is clear that they are not keen to give away decision power to WTO bureaucrats. However, giving up the Single Undertaking and the consensus policy is, under specific circumstances, negotiable for them.

7.6 The IMF and the New Economic Powers

What we have said about the creation of the GATT in 1947 also holds for the founding of the IMF. The economic, social, humanitarian, and political crises resulting from the Great Depression and WWII created a window of opportunity for such an institution. The interbellum was a period of much distrust and national self-interest with heavy protectionism as a result. The world needed an institute to guarantee open borders (GATT) and another to help countries during periods of financial imbalance to avoid closing borders. The IMF was founded in 1944 after a month-long conference with delegates from 44 countries at Bretton Woods, New Hampshire (US). The outcome of WWII was US domination of the world economy, and as a consequence, the IMF based its financial structure on the US dollar.

The origin of the IMF: based on US ideology and currency

Article 1 of the IMF agreement clearly states its objective: "To facilitate the expansion and balanced growth of international trade [...] with the opportunity to correct maladjustments in their balance of payments without resorting to measures destructive of national or international prosperity." In other words, the primary purpose is to ensure the stability of the international monetary system, which consists of exchange rates and international payments. A stable system ensures international transactions (trade and investments) can continue without obstacles and promotion of economic growth. Mexico, China, India, and South Africa joined the IMF at its official start on January 1, 1945, followed one year later by Brazil and in 1947 by Turkey. Indonesia and South Korea took up membership in 1954 and 1955, respectively. Russia joined in 1992. Although the Soviet delegation to Bretton Woods agreed with the IMF objectives, its domestic parliament did not ratify membership. To understand the NEP-9 views on the IMF, we first need to spend some words on its functioning, choices, and evolution.

7.6.1 *The Bretton Woods system: A fixed exchange rate system*

At Bretton Woods, delegates decided on a system of fixed exchange rates, tying every convertible currency to the dollar, itself exchangeable for gold at \$35 per ounce. The US guaranteed that it would convert dollars into gold. The hope was that the credibility of the US and the IMF system would encourage countries to hold dollars as their primary reserve currency. After all, if dollars were freely convertible into gold at a fixed price, they were as good as gold. Fixing the exchange rate to the dollar (within a small margin) was made possible by the dollar reserves held by countries, intended for intervention in the currency market to establish this stability. If a country lacked the liquidity to stabilize its currency's value, the IMF would provide the necessary money. However, borrowing from the IMF for stabilizing exchange rates was only possible if the lender followed the IMF prescriptions, the commonly named *IMF conditionalities*. IMF money came from mandatory deposits from member states based on their economic size and share in global trade. These quotas also determined voting rights.

7.6.2 *Too much liquidity*

The world economy and international trade recovered fast after WWII, and more and more currencies became fully convertible for trade and investment purposes. This development resulted in more volatility of exchange rates and, consequently, the need for more liquidity to intervene in the currency market to stabilize currencies toward the dollar. Furthermore, more intense US involvement in the Vietnam War in the 1960s and early 1970s, combined with a sizeable increase in US domestic spending, resulted in significant dollar holdings outside the US, such as France, Germany, and Japan. Discomfort withholding such large dollar reserves to fight currency volatility grew. Governments feared that eventually, the US would be forced to suspend convertibility for gold. This fear created a self-fulfilling prophecy. Indeed, as many countries exchanged dollars for gold, the US was forced to stop convertibility, signaling the demise of the Bretton Woods system (1971) and the start of the era of flexible exchange rates.

The IMF had to adjust to dramatic changes in the world economy

---

7.6.3 *The Cold War and decolonization*

The Cold War significantly reduced IMF membership as almost all Central and Eastern European countries withdrew in the 1950s. Essentially, the IMF became a western grouping that only supported market-oriented economies. The fall in membership changed fundamentally when decolonization in Africa achieved momentum. Independent African countries joined, and by 1969, 44 of its 115 members were African. By 1990, all

African countries were IMF members. Because most of these countries had structural instead of financial-macroeconomic problems, the World Bank, founded in parallel with the IMF, was in charge of the discussions and helping these countries.

7.6.4 *Growing capital flows and the IMF as a catalyst*

The range and importance of capital flows exploded in the early 1970s during the first oil crisis and the rise of petrodollars by oil-exporting countries. This intensified due to the second oil crisis of 1979. As we discussed earlier in Chapter 4, the second oil crisis took place just when economic thinking underwent a paradigm shift. In the 1960s and 1970s, the mainstream economic theory was Keynesian: government interference is required to fight an economic crisis. This economic model was also the paradigm endorsed by the IMF. However, that changed quite dramatically in the early 1980s, with the rise of supply-side, neoliberal economics in most countries, and the IMF discussion rooms.

Previous international crises, such as the oil shocks of the 1970s, intensified the demand for IMF lending without fundamentally changing how the IMF worked. The 1980 debt crisis was different because the range and diversity of creditors involved made it unlikely to be resolved without the active involvement of other institutions. Remember, when the IMF was founded, the scope and importance of private sector financial flows were limited. In the early days of the IMF, countries facing financial crises in their balance of payments could often solve it solely by borrowing from the IMF. From the 1980s onwards, IMF power was marginal compared to private capital flows. After the mid-1980s, the Fund evolved into a catalyst for other capital flows instead of lending itself. Countries borrowed relatively small amounts from the Fund and implemented IMF conditions. This convinced other creditors that the country was credible enough for loans. The IMF still has this catalyst function today. In 2020, IMF lending capacity was US$1 trillion. This lending capacity consists primarily of IMF quotas and multilateral and bilateral borrowing arrangements negotiated with member countries and institutions to provide the commonly named second and third lines of defense. While this sum may seem enormous, it was equivalent to about 0.4% of total global debt and 1.2% of world GDP. It is a relatively modest sum, adequate for dealing with a handful of crises in a few middle-income countries, but if larger countries are involved, the IMF can only act as a catalyst.

7.6.5 *IMF voting power*

Quotas are the IMF's primary source of financing. Upon joining the IMF, countries must contribute financially, a sort of membership fee. This contribution is called a quota. It is based on the IMF quota formula, shown in Figure 7.6. Typically, 25% of this is paid with widely accepted foreign currencies (such as the dollar, the euro, the yen, or the pound sterling) or the commonly named Special Drawing Rights (SDRs). The remaining 75% is paid in the country's own currency. SDRs are part of countries' international reserves. An SDR is not a currency, but a unit for bookkeeping that member states can use to settle international accounts. The IMF does all its accounting in SDRs, and commercial banks accept SDR denominated accounts. The value of the SDR is adjusted daily against a basket of currencies, which currently includes the US dollar, the Japanese yen, the euro, the Chinese renminbi, and the British pound.

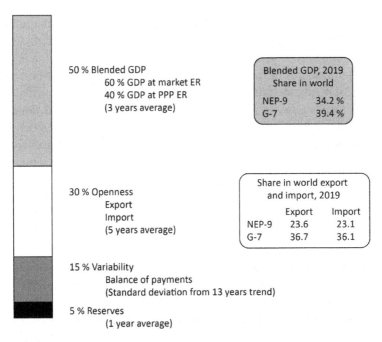

Figure 7.6: The IMF quota formula, March 2021.

Note: A compression factor applies after the quota has been calculated.
Source: IMF.

The quota, in turn, determines the voting power and the access to finance for every country. The conditionality attached to a loan becomes stricter as its size (relative to the borrower's quota) increases. So, the higher the loan, the tougher the conditions. The decision-making process within the IMF is based mainly on a majority vote, but an 85% majority must approve the most important decisions.

GDP is the most crucial variable in the quota formula, with a share of 50%. It is a combination of the size of the economy in market exchange rates (60%) and in purchasing power parity exchange rates (40%). Within the GDP blend variable, GDP at PPP exchange rates favors emerging and developing countries. In contrast, GDP at market exchange rates works to the advantage of developed countries, as we saw earlier in Chapter 2. The openness metric (30%) reflects a member's integration with the global economy through international trade and capital flows. It benefits small and well-integrated economies. The variability measure (15%) is the volatility of the balance of payments. It is seen as a proxy for a country's vulnerability to the balance of payments shocks and, consequently, the need for financial help. The reserves, accounting for 5% of the quota formula, indicate a country's ability to contribute to the Fund and its share in global capital flows. The commonly named compression factor is a way to limit quota shares of the largest countries, given the positive correlation between GDP and the other variables included in the formula. Effectively, it brings some gains to smaller countries and medium-sized developed countries. In Figure 7.6, I calculated the blended GDP for the NEP-9 and G7 to show their relative position. The same holds for the share in export and import. Obviously, you may expect that this relative position is being translated into the current voting shares.

NEP-9 countries: discontent about the division of voting power

---

Figure 7.7 provides an overview of the actual quotas and voting shares (as of 2021) and the theoretical quotas these countries would have if the IMF's formula had been applied. The US has the largest voting share of 16.5%. Because of the 85% majority rule for important decisions, this essentially gives them veto power. The US is followed by Japan (6.2%), China (6.1%), and Germany (5.3%). The difference between actual and theoretical voting share is striking and is part of why the NEP-9 are unhappy with the IMF decision-making process. Because the IMF doesn't use its quota formula, the NEP-9 are dramatically underrepresented.

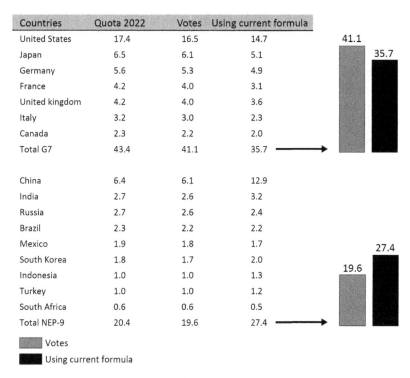

Countries	Quota 2022	Votes	Using current formula
United States	17.4	16.5	14.7
Japan	6.5	6.1	5.1
Germany	5.6	5.3	4.9
France	4.2	4.0	3.1
United kingdom	4.2	4.0	3.6
Italy	3.2	3.0	2.3
Canada	2.3	2.2	2.0
Total G7	43.4	41.1	35.7
China	6.4	6.1	12.9
India	2.7	2.6	3.2
Russia	2.7	2.6	2.4
Brazil	2.3	2.2	2.2
Mexico	1.9	1.8	1.7
South Korea	1.8	1.7	2.0
Indonesia	1.0	1.0	1.3
Turkey	1.0	1.0	1.2
South Africa	0.6	0.6	0.5
Total NEP-9	20.4	19.6	27.4

Votes
Using current formula

Figure 7.7: Members quota share and vote share, including the NEP-9.

Source: Based on IMF (2021) and European Parliament briefing, April 2019.

If they did, voting power for the NEP-9 countries (most notably China) would increase substantially from 19.6% to 27.4% at the expense of the US, Japan, and European countries, and the US would lose its veto power.

Advanced countries defend not adjusting the voting power of fast-growing emerging markets is based on three viewpoints. First, they see the quota formula as a guideline, not a rule. Second, they feel that the formula should change to emphasize opening up and de-emphasize GDP. And third, some adjustments were made in 2016, so there is no need to rush additional adjustments any time soon. Quotas and voting shares should be reviewed every five years. However, this is not a strict rule, and the process can be delayed substantially. The latest adjustments in the voting shares, implemented in 2016, were primarily based on numbers from 2008. The advanced nations say the latest redistribution of quota shares brought significant gains in voting power to emerging market and developing economies (about 6%). However, several NEP-9 countries argue that this increase is marginal compared to the growth of their shares in the world economy. They also criticize the continued US veto power. In October 2019, the IMF decided to leave quotas (and voting power) unchanged until the end of 2023. The NEP-9 as a group, however, are not fully aligned on this issue. For example, India agrees with the US in opposing substantial reform of the quota and voting system. According to the Indian authorities, too much power for China in the IMF is dangerous. And they want to keep the status quo in which the US dominates the IMF.

NEP-9 countries: heterogeneous views about the functioning and future of the IMF

7.6.6 *IMF conditionality*

As a creditor, you want to be sure that the debtor can repay the loan, and, therefore, you want to know what they will do with the money. The same holds for the IMF. When a country borrows from the IMF, its government agrees to follow the conditions set by the IMF to ensure that the country will be able to repay the loan. The conditions set by the IMF focus on structural adjustments:

- Increased (foreign) competition through deregulation and the opening up of domestic markets.
- Promoting a smaller role for the state, achieved through privatization and limits on the ability of governments to run fiscal deficits and accumulate debt.

These conditions for structural adjustment refer to the Washington Consensus. We discussed the Washington Consensus in Chapter 5, and it became clear that this economic model is heavily under attack, as is the conditionality of the IMF (and World Bank) loans. The IMF is criticized for ignoring the short-term adjustment costs associated with its conditionality regarding increasing openness and fiscal discipline. Indeed, as the former UK prime minister and Chancellor of the Exchequer Gordon Brown noted in 2001: "The assumption that just by liberalizing, deregulating, privatizing and simply getting prices right, growth and employment would inevitably follow, has proved inadequate to meet the emerging challenges of globalization" (speech at Federal Reserve Bank, New York, November 16, 2001). It is interesting to note that googling the IMF brings up pictures of protests against the institute and banners saying the IMF acronym means "It's Mostly Fiscal" or "I'M Fired." Indonesia illustrates the adverse consequences of the IMF conditionality. In 1997–1998, the Indonesian government had to solve its fiscal deficit and needed to implement spending cuts and increased taxes as part of the IMF loan. The austerity meant cutting food and fuel subsidies for the poor and reducing spending on free public transport. Increasing the tax revenue helped to reduce budgetary problems but reduced purchasing power of the poor and middle class. And although privatization resulted in some additional government revenues, it had a short-term negative impact on the labor market. From a longer-term perspective, the IMF conditionalities make sense. Liberalization, opening up, and privatization will increase productivity which is essential for longer-term development (ensuring the country can repay loans).

IMF: losing credibility in emerging markets and developing countries

However, liberalization, opening-up and privatization may negatively impact the situation in the short term, for example, when a privatized company must reduce its labor force to compete in the market, resulting in higher unemployment.

7.6.7 *The South African case*

The IMF loan to South Africa (with a maturity of five years) in the summer of 2020 shows there are not always strict conditionalities. The IMF approved a US$4.3 billion loan at 1.1% interest for South Africa to manage the impact of COVID-19 on the economy. The loan carried no conditions, as long as the money went to fighting the adverse effects of the COVID-19 crisis. The South African government asked for the loan because of an economic contraction of about 8% in 2020, a steep budget deficit, and low credibility in the capital market. Credit rating agencies downgraded South Africa, which complicated the government's efforts to finance the (growing) deficit. It would have had to pay around 7% interest on government bonds of comparable maturity (2020). The South African government indicated that it would improve the governance of state-owned enterprises, improve competition in specific sectors, and introduce reforms targeting the poorest of its population. But again, these were promises made by the South African government, not formal conditionalities imposed by the IMF. Besides cheap finance, another potential benefit is that the IMF loan will increase credibility, inspiring other investors to invest in South African debt. The most significant downside is that the loan is denominated in foreign exchange. Thus, South Africa has to bear the risk that if the local currency, the rand, depreciates, the loan and the associated interest will become more expensive. It is important to remember that the IMF denominates the loan and the repayment obligations in SDRs, which are based on a mix of currencies. The values of these currencies tend to fluctuate: some appreciate while others depreciate. This helps mitigate the foreign exchange risk.

In the South African case, the IMF did not apply strict conditionalities, but this is an exception to the rule. Although, in many cases, conditionality affects the economy negatively in the short term, there are examples in which the IMF financing and conditionalities created a positive impact on the country that had to operate within the IMF straitjacket. For example, a key driver behind Turkey's economic success between 2002 and 2007 was the IMF loan and its conditions. The structural reforms imposed under the IMF (and World Bank) umbrella accelerated the required reforms and helped achieve economic development.

Balancing short- and longer term impact of conditionality: taking domestic culture and politics into consideration

---

The one size fits all policy, emphasizing austerity programs and reducing budget deficits, is changing slightly. This makes sense: academics heavily debate the optimal fiscal policy during and after a financial and economic crisis, and the IMF discussions and outcomes reflect academic opinion. For example, in 2008, at the start of the global financial crisis, the IMF called for fiscal stimulus to solve the financial and economic problems. This marked the first time the IMF advised increasing spending during an economic crisis. However, the fiscal austerity attitude returned during the European Euro crisis in 2010–2012, heard, for example, in a speech by former IMF Director Christine Lagarde: "Everyone should recognize that there is no alternative to the structural reforms and fiscal adjustment needed to get back on the right path" (Speech at the Peterson

Institute, September 24, 2012). During the COVID-19 pandemic in 2020 and 2021, the IMF once again became very active in giving financial support. Between March 2020 and September 2021, more than 90 countries asked the IMF for financial aid. In some cases, like the South African loan, conditionality was absent, but in general, we see that the IMF holds to its main conditions but in a slightly indirect manner. The focus is still on whether the borrowing country's debt is sustainable (and whether it will be able to repay that debt), but this does not go hand in hand with strict conditions on how to achieve this. Furthermore, the IMF gives the countries more time to achieve this sustainable debt situation, and hence, they accept fiscal stimulation to fight a short-term crisis.

7.6.8 *IMF critics among the NEP-9*

From the above, it is clear that the criticism of the IMF falls into two clusters of arguments. First, the specific format of the conditionality is based mainly on the Washington Consensus and the one-size-fits-all policy. Second, the US and European countries still dominate the IMF governance structure and voting power. Let us complement the above discussion with some final thoughts.

The IMF policy prescriptions that focus on market forces are built upon the experiences of advanced market economies, and according to the NEP-9, these policies are often unsuitable for emerging markets and developing countries. Speculative capital movements, political heritage, and cultural differences come to mind. Therefore, the IMF's one-size-fits-all approach is unacceptable to the NEP-9 countries. A related critique is that the structural adjustment policies imposed by the IMF affect the lives of millions of the world's poorest people who have no voice in these institutions.

The most visible way in which the governance of the global monetary system no longer reflects the actual global economy is the allocation of voting power in the IMF, as the majority of this power is still with the United States, Japan, and European countries. The voting power issue is not easy to solve because it is a *zero-sum game*. A higher vote share for one country automatically means another country loses some share because the combined voting stays at 100%. After the adjustments of 2016, China is still unsatisfied with its new share and claims a substantial increase in its voting power is warranted. The same holds for New Economic Powers, such as India and Brazil. Unsurprisingly, the US wants to retain its current veto power, and the EU countries want to keep their combined share as high as possible. There is more criticism of the management of the IMF. For example, rules stipulate that the Managing Director is always a European (and the President of the World Bank is always an American). China's share in the IMF eclipsing the US' would start an interesting discussion, as IMF statutes prescribe that its seat should be in the country with the largest quota. That implies the IMF would eventually have to move its headquarters to China.

Despite these critical notes, it is clear that if the IMF (and World Bank) did not already exist, we would be eager to create it. However, the system must urgently reform to remain legitimate in the eyes of the NEP-9. Several structures and institutions have already emerged that complement the IMF and World Bank in international finance, for example, the Asian Infrastructure Investment Bank (AIIB), a Chinese initiative. In October 2021, this China-centered institution had 104 participating countries, including the UK, Germany, and France. Another Chinese initiative is the BRICS Development Bank. Its purpose is to fund infrastructure and sustainable development projects in BRICS countries and other emerging and developing countries. Its goal puts it in direct competition with the World Bank. One could argue this is a negative development because it further reduces IMF and World Bank's credibility. However, the world is big enough to accommodate different types of multilateral institutions. Competition in this field may not be so bad. The same happened with credit agencies. New competitors in the field of credit rating agencies, such as China-based Dagong, are challenging the monopoly of US credit rating agencies like Moody's, Fitch, and Standard & Poor's. In many aspects, breaking up this monopoly is positive, considering their behavior in past decades.

7.6.9 *The legitimacy problem*

We haven't talked much about the World Bank, even though it is also considered a key institution created during the Bretton Woods conference in 1944. Although important, the World Bank is less relevant for most NEP-9 countries. The World Bank allocates most of its loans to poor, developing countries, which still receive loans from the World Bank through its International Bank for Reconstruction and Development (IBRD). The IBRD obtains most of its funds by borrowing from the capital market through the issue of bonds. These bonds carry an AAA rating because World Bank member governments guarantee repayment. This process is helpful if the country can only borrow from the same capital market by paying a much higher interest rate. In the past decade, most NEP-9 countries borrowed directly from the capital market at low-interest rates or received bilateral loans from other countries. And although the World Bank is still helpful for India, South Africa, and Indonesia, forecasts show that the role of the World Bank will shrink further after 2030, transforming the institution into an African Development Bank.

The World Bank is less relevant for most NEP-9 countries

Another reason to focus on the IMF and not on the World Bank is that they both have the same basic view on the importance of structural reforms when a country receives financial support. For the IMF to help Brazil establish a stable currency and a sound exchange rate system if, at the same time, Brazil's main sectors cannot export because they are sheltered from competition and receive a level of government support that holds them from creating competitive advantage would be illogical. At the same time, the World Bank may finance a project to increase agricultural production in Brazil, but that does little good if the country's balance of payments position and the volatility of the currency are so chaotic that no foreign buyer will deal with them.

Three pillars hold up the Washington Consensus or, more broadly speaking, the western ideological system: private capitalism (Washington Consensus), liberal democracy, and prioritizing political rights. However, as discussed, the NEP-9 have different views on these issues, and the same holds for many emerging markets. Instead of private capitalism, they see the advantages of modern state capitalism. Of course, citizens in emerging markets want political influence but based on their current daily lives, they prefer economic freedom and economic prosperity. The Beijing Consensus has some critical implications for the design of globalization and the functioning of multilateral organizations. China and other Asian countries achieved economic development by not following the recommendations of IMF and WTO. Furthermore, China and South Korea showed that subsidies and government support are sometimes helpful and required. State intervention, protecting essential industries, and gradualism are critical elements of their success. This gradualism also holds for opening up the economy. Some see this as the opposite of the free-market paradigm. However, a gradual approach to opening up is not the same as protectionism. It is the search for an optimal way to open up. The view is that globalization and opening up are disrupting in the short term. Hence, a strong government is needed to counteract these potential disruptions.

The ideological schism between state and private capitalism is mostly driven by differences in economic development

---

From the earlier summary, it is easy to overly emphasize the differences between state versus private capitalism and the Beijing versus Washington Consensus. However, this is often an ideological schism instead of reality. The NEP-9 do not intend to rebuild the multilateral system completely, but they do demand more influence on important international economic decisions and more voting power in multilateral institutions. Granting these is the only way current multilateral organizations can retain their credibility. In his speech at the World Economic Forum on January 25, 2021, President Xi Jinping called for a return to multilateralism and cooperation: "to slip into arrogant isolation will always fail," and countries should not try "beating each other like a wrestling area." He continued by saying that the world is at risk of falling "back into the world of the jungle if multilateralism is abandoned" (Xinhua).

7.6.10   *G7, G8, and G20*

The legitimacy problem of the WTO, IMF, and World Bank also relates to the Group of Seven (G7). The G7 is an inter-governmental political forum founded in the mid-1970s by the world's seven largest advanced economies of that time. The discussions between France, (West) Germany, Japan, the United States, Italy, Canada, and the United Kingdom in the 1970s and 1980s were predominantly economic and financial. In 1998, after the fall of the Berlin Wall, the G7 grew to the G8 with the addition of Russia, and discussions expanded beyond economics and finance. (In March 2014, the G8 suspended Russia indefinitely following the annexation of Crimea.)

The trade off between representation and legitimacy

In the late 1990s, representation and legitimacy of the global governace design came under pressure, and the NEP-9 countries demanded more representation in global governance design, leading to the creation of the G20 in 1999. The G20 comprises 19 countries, the European Union, and all NEP-9. With much broader representation than the G7 and the G8, the G20 fills an essential gap in global governance, creating coalitions that cut across advanced and developing country lines. The NEP-9 favor the G20 mechanism for international economic governance, and step by step, the G20 grew more influential. For example, the G20 took collective action against the global financial crisis and recession in 2008. Its growing role was also evident in the implementation of a flat 15% profit tax for multinational enterprises in 2021 and meetings regarding the Afghanistan humanitarian, migration, and economic crisis after the Taliban takeover in the summer of 2021. While the G20 summit has become a powerful mechanism for international economic decision-making, it is not a formal international organization. For example, there is no permanent secretariat, and until now, the G20 is an entity that utilizes existing international institutions, such as the IMF, to implement its important policy decisions.

7.7 Soft Power

According to Joseph Nye (2008), soft power is the ability "to affect others to get the outcomes one wants through attraction rather than coercion or payment" (p. 94). Soft power is associated with a country's image. This image is influenced by factors like the national culture, political values, economic performance, technological capabilities, and how a government acts in foreign policy. Soft power is the opposite of hard power, which Figure 7.8 involves military power and (hard) money. The separation between hard and soft power is understandable, but in many cases, there is some overlap between the two. Several developing countries choose to follow China's development path based partly on the perception that this

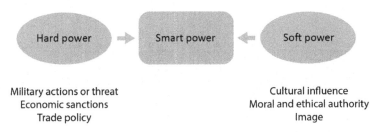

Figure 7.8:   Smart power.

Source: Nye (2011).

is the best choice by looking at economics and social stability. Still, they may also base this on large investments and substantial soft loans from China. In his book *The Future of Power* (2011), Nye also discusses the commonly named "smart power" (Figure 7.8) to refer to the complementarity between hard and soft powers. Combining hard and soft powers is required to achieve the results countries hope for: going for either one or the other will not.

7.7.1 *Why is soft power important?*

Soft power delivers all kinds of benefits for countries, their governments, their people, and businesses. Figure 7.9 summarizes the benefits, both domestically and internationally. A strong nation image and positive soft power perceptions allow a country to promote itself as a place for people to visit, invest in, study, and build a reputation for the quality of goods and services. The latter relates to the commonly named *country of origin effect*.

Countries (and regions and cities) induce strong emotional reactions, and companies can use these in branding their products abroad. This is evident with German automobile manufacturers that regularly leverage the nation's reputation in quality and high standards to differentiate their cars. The same holds for high-quality clothing from Italy (Milan) and, as everyone knows, the best watches are Swiss. In some cases, the country and the company complement each other. Singapore Airlines, for example, has become an ambassador for Singapore while it is making use of its stellar reputation. As shown in Figure 7.9, a strong nation brand and high soft power can also deliver better outcomes at home. It encourages domestic tourism, the consumption of nationally produced goods and

Domestic	International
Domestic tourism	Attracting investments and tourists
Local products and services	Business abroad
National pride and engagement	Political influence
Happiness	Talent attraction
Talent retention	International cooperation

Figure 7.9:   Positive aspects of soft power.

Source: Based on Brand Finance (2021).

services (rather than imports), and, less tangibly, makes people feel better about their country, which increases happiness.

7.7.2 *Soft power rankings*

There are several annual rankings of soft power. The world's most comprehensive assessments of global soft power and used the most in international research are the Portland Soft Power 30 index and the Brand Finance Global Soft Power Index. The Portland annual index combines objective data and international polling (subjective) data to build a picture of global soft power. The weighting of the main categories for 2019 is shown in Figure 7.10. Government and international engagement (related to foreign policy) are the two most important indicators. Companies and the quality of education are also important factors that determine the country's image. Although a ranking is useful, the perception of the image may be different from country to country.

Soft power is perceived differently from country to country

A country may possess soft power in one country and not have any credibility in another. The perception of China is very different among my Indian students at SP Jain than among my Indonesian and Korean students. Furthermore, the image and reputation of an illiberal democracy could easily be unfavorable in a liberal democracy. In contrast, the same country may have a favorable image in other parts of the world. For example, Russia enjoys a strong reputation in former Soviet nations. Turkey has high credibility in certain Middle Eastern countries and North Africa, while China's image is much better in developing countries, mainly in Africa than in Western Europe and North America.

In 2019, France had the most soft power, followed by the UK and Germany. France's strengths lie in its vast diplomatic network and membership in multilateral and international organizations. Obviously, French cuisine is also a substantial help. The UK is helped by its reputation in education. Most of my students at the London-based Academy of Diplomacy and International Governance are Chinese. Clearly, they believe that getting an education in the UK will improve their job prospects abroad, as well in an increasingly challenging Chinese job market. British soft power also benefits from the BBC. It is interesting that despite four years of Trump, the United States is still ranked high in the Portland

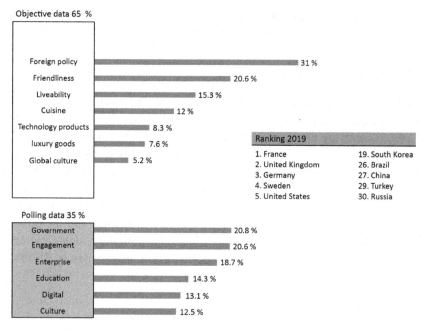

Figure 7.10:   Categories of measuring soft power and the ranking in 2019.

Source: Portland (2019), Soft Power 30 index.

Soft Power Index. In a sense, there is not much mobility over the years. A five-year period is relatively short for substantial changes in education, government effectiveness, and reputation. The US is still unrivaled in indicators such as higher education, movies and music, culture, and technological innovation. Countries with high soft power stay at the top, while it is difficult for other countries to increase their soft power substantially. Specific NEP-9 countries are analyzed in the Portland report and their ranks are indicated in the figure.

A critical note on the concept of soft power is that it tends to be used in a normative manner, for example, "liberal democracy is good." Increasing soft power is therefore quite complicated for authoritarian countries, whether that is China, Russia, or Turkey. At the same time, in the past decade, China has gained some soft power. You may argue that this rise in soft power results from the problems in democratic countries, such as the UK and the US. For example, China's soft power accelerated in 2017 when Trump announced stepping away from the 2015 Paris Climate Agreement. Suddenly, China (through a speech by Premier Li

Keqiang) became visible as a global leader in the fight against climate change. Furthermore, you could question whether the outcome of a democratic procedure is better than a decision by a non-democratic government. Another issue is that the Soft Power Indices looks at government as a homogeneous body, but it does not question the balances of power hidden behind this concept. We have many governments, and for sure, the credibility of these different governmental layers may differ substantially.

NEP-9 soft power is growing but lies substantially below western
liberal democracies

Figure 7.11 summarizes some of the factors that contribute to the soft power of NEP-9 countries, ranging from economic success and multilateral engagement to pop music and entertainment. An important pillar of Brazil's soft power is its active participation in multilateral institutions. One of my colleagues said Brazil has soft power because it doesn't have enemies, giving the country a unique advantage and the ability to build bridges in international negotiations. However, the credibility created by the Lula and Rousseff administrations is crumbling through the actions of the Bolsonaro presidency. India's soft power is driven by its democratic tradition, spirituality, and Bollywood and complemented by high economic growth rates since the liberalization in 1991. India is an example of a country that is not pro-actively praising its soft power, while, for example, China is actively promoting it. This is the difference between defensive and offensive soft power. President Xi Jinping said in 2014, "We should increase China's soft power, give a good Chinese narrative, and better communicate China's message to the world" (18th National Congress CCP archive). The Chinese government has been developing an international media network and establishing cultural study centers (Confucius Institutes) worldwide. The Beijing Consensus and the One Belt One Road (OBOR) initiative are concrete vehicles promoting soft power. The results are mixed. The OBOR initiative, with its international investments in railways, roads, pipelines, ports, and telecommunications infrastructure to promote economic integration, is increasing China's soft power in some countries but not in others. Countries like Myanmar and Sri Lanka have expressed their discomfort toward China's growing presence. Ultimately, China's (tightening) authoritarian political system is the biggest obstacle to the positive image the country and government are looking for.

Country	Aspects of soft power		
Brazil	Engagement in global and regional institutions Lifestyle and sports Diverse cultures National beauty	Indonesia	Democratic and modernization, combined with islam Asian Games Scenery and tourism Asian connections
India	Democratic process Spirtuality / yoga Bollywood Economic succes	Turkey	Democratic islam Model for several MENA countries
		Mexico	Heritage and culture Investment stability Relationship with the US Participation in miltilateral institutions Mariachi
China	Bejing consensus and economic succes OBOR and infrastructure diplomacy Confucius institutes Panda dimpomacy		
Russia	Alternative to US model Health diplomacy and Covid-19 help Space program	South Africa	Democracy after Apartheid Voice of African continent Wine-sector Tourism and nature Free press
South Korea	Hightech society K-pop and movies Sport events (Olympic games)		

Figure 7.11:   NEP-9: Aspects of soft power.

COVID-19 has created some opportunities to increase soft power through international help programs. China's help to other countries received some international attention. The same holds for Russia. On March 22, 2020, 104 Russian military doctors and health workers arrived in Italy with ventilators and other medical equipment, their boxes and vehicles decorated with stickers reading "From Russia with Love." The reactions in Italy were mixed, ranging from gratitude to naming it a "Russian propaganda offensive." One important aspect of Russia's soft power in the West is Moscow's image as the primary opponent of US unipolarity and "normative imperialism."

Besides its reputation as a high-tech country, South Korea is famous for using cultural elements in its public diplomacy. Korean pop music (K-pop) has successfully introduced the country to the international community. It also included sports diplomacy during the 2018 Pyeongchang Winter Olympics and the 2019 Oscar-winning movie *Parasite* helped to understand the South Korean way of living. Due to corruption and incidents of (Islamic) terrorism, Indonesia currently has some features that block the rise in soft power. However, it is also known as one of the largest countries able to combine democracy and Islam. The same can be said about Turkey. After the Arab Spring of 2011, several countries in the

Caucasus and North Africa saw Turkey as a model. Turkey presented as a secular model of modernization for Muslim-majority nations. In the West, the "Turkish model" gained popularity after the early 1990s, driven by its desire to enter the EU. In line with China and Russia, Turkey's soft power policy is offensive in nature as they have numerous programs abroad that promote Islam. As we saw with Brazil, soft power is not a linear process but comes in waves. Turkish soft power fell after the election of Erdoğan in 2014.

Soft power development is not a linear process, it fluctuates

---

Mexico's soft power also declined quite dramatically over the past decade. I vividly remember a presentation on this topic by one of my Mexican students at Nyenrode in 2013. He referred to the commonly named "Pact for Mexico," a governmental initiative that served as an

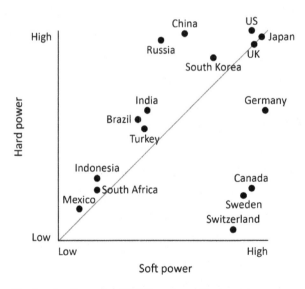

Figure 7.12:   Hard and soft powers, NEP-9, and specific countries.

Note: Because the Portland Soft Power 30 report put substantial weight on government and foreign policy, we used the Brand Finance annual report to analyze soft power. Hard power combines military strength, economic influence, and international alliances.

example for the other Central American countries of civic engagement in politics and consensus between political parties, quite different from today's situation with human rights violations and drug wars and in stark contrast to *Marca País* or "Nation Branding" campaign.

It is clear that before 1994 (the end of apartheid), South Africa could not increase or use its soft power. Today, its soft power is based on the peaceful transformation into a democratic state and South Africa's first democratically elected president, Nelson Mandela. South Africa's active and robust engagement of civil society as well as a sophisticated and thriving private sector are also elements of the country's attraction. South Africa's pillar in foreign policy today is African-centric, and it sees itself as one of the leaders of the "South." In many multilateral settings, like the G20, South Africa is the only African voice.

Obviously, the COVID-19 pandemic influences soft power. Think about how different South Korea and Brazil or China and India are dealing with the coronavirus. Despite the impact of this *black swan event* (Taleb, 2007), we can still focus on the fundamental factors that influence soft power. Figure 7.12 is the result of the analysis of several reports that measure the soft and hard powers of countries. Those countries to the northwest of the line have soft power below their weight in hard power. This cohort includes all NEP-9 countries. The countries in the Southeast corner have soft power above their weight in hard power. This is the case for most of the smaller western nations.

We saw in this chapter the growing importance of the NEP-9 within the political globalization process and its growing power in multilateral institutions. This development may continue and it is to be expected that this is also visible (with ups and downs) with respect to soft power. Another dimension in which we see the growing importance of the NEP-9 is foreign investments: the topic of Chapter 8.

Chapter 8

Foreign Direct Investments and the NEP-9

8.1 Management Control

Foreign direct investments (FDIs) are cross-border investments made by a company to obtain a long-term interest in a foreign company. *Direct* refers to the direct management control over the foreign subsidiary resulting from the investment. Foreign investment and putting the new subsidiary under the umbrella of the mother company result in a multinational enterprise (MNE). Until recently, theories and discussions on MNEs concentrated on companies from the US, Europe, and Japan. However, today, FDIs by emerging market companies, mainly from the NEP-9 countries, are growing exponentially.

There are many ways to invest abroad, but for FDIs, it essentially comes down to the preferred level of control. Wholly owned subsidiaries through greenfield investments (building a new plant from scratch) and mergers and acquisitions (M&A) are high control modes and, therefore, labeled FDIs. The same counts for majority holdings in a foreign company. A joint venture, in which the two mother companies invest in a new entity, is an intermediate control strategy. In principle, the two parties share control based on equity or contract, but as we will see in this chapter, joint ventures are also often considered part of FDI flows. Other modes of entry that do not involve equity are not considered FDIs and consequently not part of this discussion.

Examples of FDIs are the takeover of Volvo Cars by China-based Geely and US-based Intel, which invested in a new, fully owned plant in

Costa Rica. Korean carmaker Kia invested in an owned-dealership network in the United States, and fast food chain KFC opened a new full ownership restaurant in China.

Ownership does not always create management control

These examples are relatively straightforward: the new owner has complete control over the operations abroad and is in charge of its strategy and strategic choices. You could argue that an equity share of more than 50% automatically gives management control, but equity is not always the most crucial factor behind power and control within an organization. Imagine a collaboration between a western and a Russian company. The western company has an equity share of 20% and brings essential and innovative knowledge to the table. The Russians bring in 80% of the financial capital. Based on equity, the Russians have the majority share. In reality, the Russian company will likely have little say in strategic decisions, with the western company taking the lead.

Another example that shows ownership is not always leading to the level of control: A brewery buys a 49% share in a metal container plant abroad. This minority share may not give them control over management if the other 51% is in the hands of one single owner. However, even if the same brewery gains a minority interest of just 20%, and 80% of equity is in the hands of millions of small shareholders that operate through the stock exchange, it could have management control. The same holds for a joint venture. A 20% stake in a joint venture may give management control, while a 49% stake does not, depending on the structure of the venture.

8.1.1 *FDIs versus portfolio investments*

Management control is what distinguishes FDI from an investment portfolio. Statistics consider a transaction an FDI when the party in question obtains, at minimum, a 10% stake in a foreign company (UNCTAD). A 10% share in equity is assumed to result in substantial management control. Ownership of below 10% is considered an international portfolio investment and not included in FDI statistics. Besides this benchmark of 10% ownership, the nature of the FDI is entirely different from the portfolio investment. Because FDI implies a controlling stake in a business abroad, it connects to physical assets, such as buildings, real estate, and machines. Therefore, companies with management control are not footloose. It is not easy for the owners to leave the country. Because of this, FDI flows are considered relatively stable, long-term capital flows. Portfolio investments are much more volatile because they only relate to financial assets. The short-term capital enters and leaves countries in a short space of time, generating dramatic swings in the availability of capital. A large part of the portfolio investments is speculative capital.

FDI flows are considered as relatively stable compared to portfolio investments

---

As said, statistical overviews regard every ownership of more than 10% as FDI, with its associated direct control over management. This also holds for minority holdings. However, in explaining FDIs from the NEP-9 countries, we will focus only on FDI flows with actual management control: takeovers, mergers, greenfield investments, and majority joint ventures. FDIs are both inflow and outflow. China-based SAIC's investment in the construction of its Indonesian plant is outflowing FDI from China and FDI inflow for Indonesia. You would expect data on FDI inflow and outflow to be equal, but due to differences in administrative procedures for FDI flows, there might be some statistical differences.

FDIs are horizontal, vertical, or conglomerate in nature. Horizontal FDI means a company invests abroad in the same businesses they operate in its home country. For example, SAIC automotive starts a new production facility in Indonesia or State Bank of India opens a new office in Singapore. FDI is vertical when a company invests in a foreign country in a different but related business, moving up or downstream in the value chain, for example, Kia building a dealer network in the US or Brazilian brewery Ambev investing in a metal container plant abroad. This type of FDI is heavily associated with slicing up the value chain and locating various stages of production in different countries and regions. Finally, FDI is conglomerate in nature when an MNE invests in a business unrelated to its existing business in its home country, for example, China-based Ping An Insurance starting foreign operations in the field of healthcare or mobility.

8.2   FDI Data of NEP-9 Countries

As stated in Chapter 1, I always begin my course on FDIs in the different Global Immersion Programs by asking: "Which country is the largest investor in Africa?" Students get four options: the United States, China, France, and the United Kingdom.

Not a clear black or white answer

The consensus is overwhelming: Over 90% choose China. It is not China, though, despite anecdotal evidence published by the media or presented by politicians. The answer is also much more complex than it may seem at first glance, a returning learning point throughout the book. The world is not black and white, and there are many ways to interpret data.

8.2.1   *Stock and flow concept*

My question about the largest investor is purposefully vague. Are we referring to this year? Or last year? Or since the start of the globalization era? The answer relates to the difference between the flow and the stock of FDI. A Chinese company investing in a South African mining company in 2021 is part of the FDI inflow of South Africa and FDI outflow from China in that year. This is the flow concept of FDI. The sum of all investments from China into South Africa between 1979 and today is the stock of Chinese FDI in South Africa. Western companies from the US, the UK, and France have been investing in Africa for many years, as early as the beginning of the 20th century. In contrast, Chinese investments in Africa started only in the past decade. Hence, the US, the UK, and France's stocks of FDI in Africa are substantially larger compared to China's, even though in some years, Chinese investment topped the ranking. Based on owned assets in 2021, China ranks 5th place (UNCTAD, 2021). The difference between the flow and stock of FDI is shown in Figure 8.1. The upper half of the figure indicates the development of FDI flows between 1990 and 2020. Despite the decline after 2017, we see the explosion of FDI that started in the 1990s. The result of this acceleration of FDI flows is that the value of inward stock in 2020 was almost 2,000% higher than in 1990.

	1990	2005-2007*	2017	2018	2019	2020
FDI inflow	205	1425	1647	1437	1530	999
FDI outflow	244	1464	1605	871	1220	740
FDI inward stock	2196	⟶				41354
FDI outward stock	2255	⟶				39247

(*) Pre-financial crisis average

	% of global inflow, 2020	% of global outflow, 2020	% of global inward stock, 2020	% of global outward stock, 2020
United States	15.6 %	12.6 %	26.1 %	20.7 %
China	14.9 %	17.9 %	4.6 %	5.9 %

Figure 8.1:   Flow and stock of FDI in billion US$ 1990–2020 and share in global FDI, 2020.

Source: Based on World Investment Report (2021).

In the lower half of Figure 8.1, the share of worldwide flow and stock of FDI is shown for the Unites States and China. While China's share in FDI outflow in 2020 was 17.9%, its share in total outward stock was only 5.9%, substantially lower than the US (20.7%).

Another issue regarding the largest investor in Africa is whether we refer to the total value of FDI or the number of FDI projects. In the African context, the largest investors by the number of projects were, again, the US, the UK, and France, while China was the largest investor in terms of total value and jobs created between 2015 and 2019. This difference is closely associated with the main types of FDI. Greenfield investments are often relatively small in value, while mergers and acquisitions are relatively small in number but have a more considerable average value.

8.2.2 *Financial centers*

One more complicating factor within FDI statistics is knowing who the real investor is. You would expect this to be obvious, but it is not.

If South Korea-based Doosan Infracore, one of the world's largest companies in the heavy equipment manufacturing sector, invests in Brazil because of the market potential, it is clear that we measure South Korean FDI outflow. But what if Doosan uses financial centers such as the Cayman Islands to invest in Brazil? In that case, statistically, the FDI outflow relates to the Cayman Islands. However, this is clearly the intermediate, while South Korea, the ultimate investor, does not show up in the statistics. Financial safe havens such as the Cayman Islands, the Virgin Islands, and countries like the Netherlands, Ireland, and Luxembourg blur FDI statistics. Consequently, it is pretty complex to find out the precise investor position of countries. Brazil is the only NEP-9 country that provides (partial) information on FDIs on an intermediary and ultimate investor basis. The difference is remarkable. For example, China's FDI stock in Brazil ranked 25th in 2017 but 9th if considered on an ultimate investor basis. Conversely, the Netherlands ranks only 5th on an ultimate investor basis but is top ranked on an immediate investor basis (World Investment Report, 2020).

As the Chinese case makes clear, FDI is only part of the total capital flows between countries

---

A final issue with FDI statistics is that these investments make up only part of the total flow of capital between countries. For example, China's financial support to African countries has mainly taken the form of loans to governments (often part of a foreign aid package), complementing the FDI from state-owned enterprises and private firms. Let's return to my question to the students. From the FDI point of view, it is a misperception that Chinese companies are making massive investments in Africa despite high-profile infrastructure investments and M&A deals in the energy and metals industries. However, it is clear that this is only a part of the full flow of capital from China to Africa. FDIs are complemented by an enormous debt-generating flow, such as bilateral loans and project financing.

Now that we are aware of the statistical caveats, let's look at some interesting FDI figures, of course emphasizing the New Economic Powers. Most of the figures used in this section are based on UNCTAD statistics: The World Investment Report (WIR). Due to statistical issues, they may differ slightly from figures published by the OECD and the IMF–World Bank. Those will complement the WIR data when needed.

8.2.3 *Four phases*

We can divide the role of New Economic Powers in FDI flows into four phases. The first phase started in the 19th century and continued until the First World War. I call this period the *resource phase* (Ebbers, 2016). There was a massive wave of western multinational investment in Russia, China, India, Brazil, South Africa, and Indonesia, among others. Multinationals sought access to resources, and national governments frequently gave them exclusive contracts and favorable deals. In this phase, the primary management challenge was to overcome logistical obstacles. During this period, FDI flow was one-sided; we did not see investments from these emerging markets to the western advanced countries.

The second phase runs from 1914 to the early 1980s: the *withdrawal phase*. The investment flows changed dramatically up to the point that by 1980, levels of FDI in countries such as Russia, China, India, Brazil, and South Africa were zero or close to zero. Obviously, this disruption in FDI flows was the effect of the first and second world wars, combined with the Great Depression of the 1930s, which resulted in protectionism. The spread of nationalist, anti-foreign sentiments in many countries sharply raised political risks during the 1930s. For example, the Communist Revolution in Russia in 1917 resulted in the expropriation of a large amount of western FDIs. The spread of communism to China and Eastern Europe after 1945 shut off even more countries from direct investments and other types of capital flows.

NEP-9 countries reduced restrictions on FDI inflow considerably in the 1980s and 1990s

The third phase is the *acceleration phase*. Foreign investments in NEP-9 and other emerging markets started to accelerate in the 1980s, driven by China's adoption of market-oriented policies in 1979, followed by opening up in India in the early 1990s. This opening up came in parallel with the rise of free-market economics in the West. The victories of right-wing, free-market governments in Britain and the United States, in 1979 and 1980, respectively, and the collapse of the Soviet Union in the early 1990s helped break down barriers to foreign investment. The arrival of the Internet and technological advancements gave this a further massive push. In NEP-9 countries, restrictions on foreign ownership, the mandatory use of joint ventures with local firms, trade barriers, and

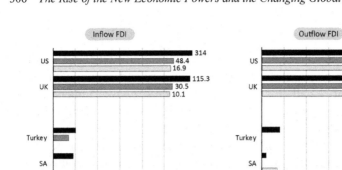

Figure 8.2:   Inflow and outflow between 1980 and 2000, billions US$.

Note: Russia: 1992 instead of 1990.

Source: World Investment Report (2021).

exchange controls disappeared or were significantly reduced, at least until the start of the new century. This acceleration can be seen in Figure 8.2. While FDI inflow and outflow were (almost) absent in 1980, countries such as China, Brazil, South Korea, and India witnessed dramatic increases in FDI inflow up to 2000. The same pattern, although less distinct is visible with respect to FDI outflow between 1980 and 2000.

At the beginning of the new millennium, we entered the fourth phase of FDI: the *reversing phase* involving foreign investments from companies originating from NEP-9 and other emerging markets. In particular, after 2010, we saw an explosion of NEP-9 companies that became active in foreign markets through takeovers, greenfield investments, and controlling equity stakes in western companies (Figure 8.3).

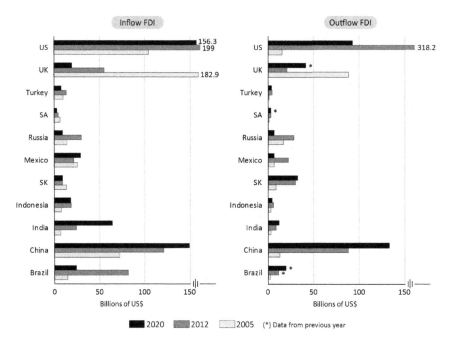

Figure 8.3: Growing FDI inflow and outflow, NEP-9 countries, 2005–2020.

Source: World Bank Database (2021).

8.2.4 *The COVID-19 effect*

In 2020, COVID-19 affected FDI flows and will continue to repress the longer-term trend slightly in the years to come. The sudden and simultaneous interaction of supply- and demand-side shocks, combined with policy reactions by national governments, affected FDI through various channels. The immediate effect was the result of the strict lockdowns. For example, the closure of construction sites to contain the spread of the virus immediately caused delays in the implementation of investment projects. Another short-term effect of COVID-19 was the lower margins for businesses. Reinvested earnings are an essential source for financing FDI projects, and, therefore, the lower margins resulted in lower foreign investments. In the longer term, COVID-19 may negatively affect FDI flows through rising uncertainties and policies executed by national governments to protect domestic companies and employment.

Finally, the pandemic may accelerate the longer-term development of restructuring global supply chains, including reshoring and divestments.

8.2.5 *The role of NEP-9*

The analysis of FDI data uncovers some interesting trends. First, FDI inflow and, in particular, outflow from the NEP-9 countries are growing. NEP-9 companies (private and state-owned) are important investors in foreign markets, and the share of the NEP-9 in total FDI rose substantially between 2000 and 2020 (Figure 8.4).

This growing role is also visible when concentrating on 2020. Some of these countries are in the top 20 of the most important home and host

	FDI inflow				FDI outflow		
Rank	Economy	2019	2020	Rank	Economy	2019	2020
1	United States	261	156	1	China	137	133
2	China	141	149	2	Luxembourg	34	127
3	Hong Kong SAR	74	119	3	Japan	227	116
4	Singapore	114	91	4	Hong Kong SAR	53	102
5	India	51	64	5	United States	94	90
6	Luxembourg	15	62	6	Canada	79	49
7	Germany	54	36	7	France	39	44
8	Ireland	81	33	8	Germany	139	35
9	Mexico	34	29	9	South Korea	35	32
10	Sweden	10	26	10	Singapore	51	32
11	Brazil	65	25	11	Sweden	16	31
12	Israel	19	25	12	Spain	20	21
13	Canada	48	24	13	UAE	21	19
14	Australia	39	20	14	Sweden	-44	17
15	UAE	18	20	15	Thailand	8	17
16	United Kingdom	45	20	16	Taiwan	12	14
17	Indonesia	24	19	17	Chili	9	12
18	France	34	18	18	India	13	12
19	Vietnam	16	16	19	Italy	20	10
20	Japan	15	10	20	Belgium	2	10

Figure 8.4:   Top 20 host countries (left) and home countries (right), 2019 and 2020, billions US$.

Note: A negative FDI outflow means that the value of direct investments made abroad was less than the value of repatriated direct investments from abroad.

Source: World Investment Report (2021).

economies in 2020. Important to note is that the FDI flows can show large fluctuations from year to year due to one or two large takeovers.

A second development is the growing economic importance of FDI for the NEP-9 countries, shown in Figure 8.5. China's outward stock of FDI grew from a mere 2.8% of GDP in 2005 to 15% in 2020. The same development goes for the other NEP-9. Brazil's outward FDI stock as a percentage of GDP grew from 8.0% in 2005 to almost 14% in 2020. Although the importance of outward FDI stock for the NEP-9 is clearly increasing, it is still relatively low compared (with the exception of South Africa) to advanced economies such as Japan (37%), the US (39%), Germany (51%), and Belgium (114%). The picture is slightly different for inward FDI stock as the ratios of the NEP-9 and the more advanced countries are closer together. Ratios of countries such as Mexico, Brazil, and

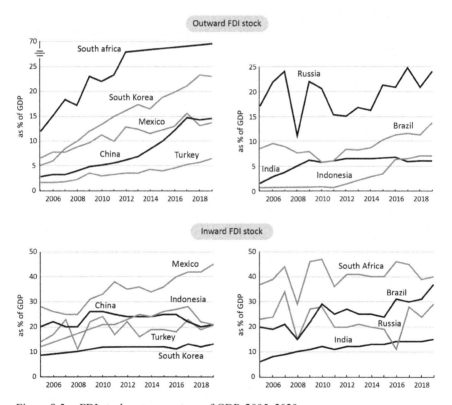

Figure 8.5:   FDI stock as a percentage of GDP, 2005–2020.

Source: OECD Database (2021).

Russia are similar to Germany and France. Two extremes among the advanced countries are Japan (4%) and the Netherlands (313%).

Despite the growth of FDI flows over the previous decades and the growing importance of foreign investments in the domestic economy, the share of the NEP-9 in the global FDI stock is still relatively low. This is visible in Figure 8.6 in which the share of the NEP-9 in global FDI stock is compared to the combined share of the US and the UK.

The share of the NEP-9 countries in the global FDI stock is still relatively low

---

As shown in the Figure 8.6, the share of the UK and the US in global inward stock in 2020 was 32%, considerably higher than the combined share of the NEP-9 countries (12%). The same pattern can be seen with respect to outward FDI stock.

The data do not detail the type of investor involved in the transaction. It may be a private company or a state-owned enterprise. Clearly, this is a big difference in the perception of the public and policymakers. A foreign

Country	Inward FDI stock, 2020	Outward FDI stock, 2020
Brazil	608	277
China	1918	2352
India	480	191
Indonesia	240	88
South Korea	264	501
Mexico	597	179
Russia	447	380
South Africa	137	250
Turkey	212	52
NEP-9 as % of world	12 %	11 %
United Kingdom	2206	2055
United States	10802	8128
UK and US as % of world	32 %	26 %
World	41354	39247

Figure 8.6:   Inward and outward FDI stock, billions US$ and share in world, 2020.

Source: World Investment Report (2021).

private firm getting a majority share in a well-known domestic firm may be acceptable, but this may not be the case if the foreign firm is a state-owned enterprise (SOE). Things become even more problematic if this foreign buyer is a sovereign wealth fund.

8.3 Sovereign Wealth Funds

Sovereign wealth funds (SWFs) or state funds are a heterogeneous group of institutional investors, directly or indirectly linked to the government, managing a pool of domestic and international assets to achieve national (political) objectives. Diversity is large, ranging from large public pension funds to oil state funds. Oil funds are derived from oil export revenues, while pension funds are the imposed savings of employees. Besides these two sources, SFWs are also funded by revenues from privatization (Malaysia and Australia), fiscal surplus (Korea and New Zealand), or the balance of payment surplus, translated into central bank reserves (China and Singapore).

Independent of the source of capital or the direct ownership, if an SWF invests substantially in a foreign company, the government (directly or indirectly) is partly in charge of all decisions made by the company. This structure creates discomfort in many countries, and this exacerbates if the investments are in strategic sectors, such as mining, energy, and high-tech. Although SWFs are present in advanced nations, they are used primarily as an investment vehicle by emerging market governments. Some research on SWFs statistically includes SOEs in which the state has significant control. However, in our discussion, we separate SOEs from sovereign investors. Also, we decided not to include pension funds in the discussion on SWFs, although we will implement them in some statistics.

SWFs of NEP-9 countries: large,
growing, and globalized

Emerging markets actively use SWFs to invest abroad. If the foreign stake is more than 10% of the company's assets, this investment falls into FDI statistics. If the stake is below 10%, the investment is regarded as a portfolio investment. Most SWFs (75%) are from the Middle East and Asia and are gaining importance. It fits with the narrative of changing power: the shift from net foreign debt to net foreign asset positions or the transition from a debtor country to a creditor country. Although the financial crisis of 2009–2010 and COVID-19 (2020–2021) led to falling oil prices and rising fiscal deficits, sovereign investors will likely remain essential sources of investments worldwide, besides traditional players, such as companies, large investment banks, prominent asset managers, and hedge funds.

8.3.1 *Discomfort*

In 2007, I attended my first conference on SWFs in Costa Rica. In the same year, China launched its first SWF, China Investment Corporation (CIC), with a registered capital of $200, established as a vehicle to diversify foreign exchange holdings by investing part of its assets abroad. One of the sessions asked how to access this type of investor. I can only describe the mood as profoundly skeptical of CIC and other SFWs from emerging markets. Attendees regarded such funds as products of authoritarian regimes, having only political objectives. Their conclusion was near unanimous: the West should protect itself from these investors. As we will see, indeed, several countries created screening mechanisms to assess the potential dangers of such investments proactively.

The SWF model is not new. For example, the Kuwait Investment Authority was created in 1953 to deal with the country's oil revenue, and in 1970, Singapore's Temasek Holdings was founded. SWF momentum grew after 2001. In 2008, the International Forum of Sovereign Wealth Funds (IFSWF), together with the IMF, developed guidelines to increase transparency and governance quality, the commonly named "Santiago Principles." However, these only apply to countries that volunteer to follow them, and even today, many SWF lacks transparency about their international activities.

8.3.2 *Largest sovereign investors, 2021*

Figure 8.7 shows the largest sovereign investors, led by the Government Pension Fund Global of Norway, with $1,400 billion in assets, primarily sourced from oil sales, and followed by SWF from the Middle East and Asia. The asset allocation of SWF differs substantially, but it looks like equity securities in listed corporations and fixed income securities are

Rank	Name SWFt	Assets under control, bn. $
1	Norway Government Pension Fund Global	1400
2	China Investment Corporation	1220
3	Kuwait Investment Authority	738
4	Abu Dhabi Investment Authority (UAE)	698
5	Hong Kong Monetary Authority	586
6	Government of Singapore Investment Corporation	578
7	Temasek (Singapore)	484
8	Public Investment Fund Saudi Arabia	480
9	National Council for Social Security Fund (China)	447
10	Qatar Investment Authority	367
11	Investment Corporation Dubai (UAE)	302
12	Turkey Wealth Fund	294
13	Mubadala Investment Company (Abu Dhabi)	243
14	Korea Investment Corporation	201
15	National Welfare Fund Russia	183

Figure 8.7:   Largest sovereign wealth funds by ranking of total assets, early 2022.

Source: SWF Institute (2022).

most important. Most SWFs in NEP-9 countries are explicitly involved in national industrial diversification strategies and domestic infrastructure. These funds make international investments in western, industrialized countries, developing countries, and countries in transition when domestic investment opportunities are non-existent or when international investments stabilize risk. In this sense, in line with other investors, SWFs seek balance between security and profitability.

8.3.3 *SWF strategies*

It is interesting to note that step by step, sovereign investment funds are becoming more active as venture capitalists. A substantial part of the money needed by Uber, Alibaba, and Spotify to broaden their international presence came from sovereign investors. For example, Korea Investment Corporation (KIC), founded in 2005, plans to allocate a fifth of its portfolio to high-tech start-up ventures in 2020–2025. In 2015,

I visited the small office of KIC in San Francisco and was impressed with their plans regarding investments in Silicon Valley ventures.

SWFs: not a fixed format

As stated earlier, most NEP-9 sovereign wealth funds were developed for domestic purposes. For example, the primary objective of Brazil's SWF, created in 2008 and funded through the current account surplus, was to provide funding for domestic projects. In 2010, the fund was allowed to buy US dollars in the foreign exchange market in an attempt to stop the rise of the Brazilian real. The Brazilian government closed the fund in September 2019 to solve budgetary problems and pay off its national debt. On the other hand, the aim of KIC was more outward-driven and heavily focused on helping Korean firms go abroad.

From its beginning in 2004, the Russian Reserve Fund aimed to finance domestic industry policy. The Russian government claimed this SWF was needed to insulate the government budget from the volatility of the oil market by providing a source of funds that could supplement the budget in case of declining oil prices. From 2006 onward, international investments were possible through the Russian Direct Investment Fund, an SWF specifically for investments abroad. Interestingly, the Russian SWFs financed a substantial part of the research costs of the Sputnik V COVID-19 vaccine in 2020.

The Turkish Wealth Fund also invested in Corona-related projects, when, in 2021, it assisted private and public domestic companies hit by the coronavirus outbreak. Examples are Turkish Airlines, Turkcell, and Türk Telekom. In line with Russia, the Mexican SWF, founded in 2015 and sourced from oil revenues, aims to finance required transformations in the domestic economy. The same holds for the fairly young South African SWF, founded in 2020 and funded from mineral royalties and current account surplus. Its main aim is "stimulating domestic development." In line with Russia, it serves as a countercyclical fiscal tool. Indonesia is also quite late in the game, launching its SFW in early 2021. Due to Indonesia's current account deficit and low international reserves, the SWF, which focuses mainly on domestic projects, is funded by the state budget.

Combining domestic and foreign investments, based on economics and (geo)politics

---

In line with Russia and South Africa, the Indian SWF is also an extra-budgetary fund operating outside the normal annual governmental budgetary processes. Again, its domestic objective is to invest in strategic sectors and infrastructure. The state manages the National Investment and Infrastructure Fund, owning 49% of the assets. Domestic and international parties finance the other 51%, for example, the Abu Dhabi Investment Authority and the Canada Pension Plan Investment Board. CIC is China's sovereign wealth fund, founded in 2007 with $200 billion of registered capital. Its assets grew to $1.2 trillion in early 2022. Its objective is to diversify China's foreign exchange holdings. Like "normal" investors, high returns are not always guaranteed, which was undoubtedly the case with CIC's investment in private equity firm Blackstone. In 2008, CIC had a stake of almost 13% in Blackstone. In March 2018, CIC sold its stake in Blackstone with a significant loss. The exit from Blackstone resulted from growing trade tensions between China and the US government, wishing to block investments from Chinese parties as much as possible. This distrust toward SWFs from China, Russia, and other NEP-9 countries is also apparent in Europe and Australia. And this discomfort is related not only to SWF but also to takeovers by state-owned companies. That is why some statistics cluster both entities. The number of countries that feel concerned about SWF investments is rising. Some have issued specific regulations to supervise or restrict operations of and investments by such government-linked entities. NEP-9 authorities try to counteract this negative sentiment by emphasizing that their SWFs has no intention of buying strategic stakes in big western companies and that it is a passive investor with a small stake, helping promising companies to grow.

8.4 Explaining FDIs

Most research attempts to explain FDIs using theories developed in the 1960s and 1970s with western companies in mind. Therefore, after a summary of the mainstream theories, we will explore how to apply these theories to companies from NEP-9 countries.

8.4.1 *Transaction costs*

The study of FDI is rooted in the *transaction costs approach*, developed by Coase (1937) and expanded further by Williamson (1975). Companies choose to keep all activities within the boundaries of the firm (internalization) because this is cheaper compared to using the market. For example, searching for a trustworthy external supplier, negotiating, monitoring, and resolving disputes comes with various costs. An integrated or internalized supplier comes with much lower costs as coordinating *within* the company may be much more cost effective than finding, checking, and monitoring external parties. Integration or internalization keeps transactions inside the company's hierarchy, and from this perspective, integration or internalization leads to a multinational enterprise. Besides lower transaction costs, control over pricing, branding, technology, and knowledge may also make internalization preferable.

8.4.2 *Liability of foreignness*

Hymer (1976) explained FDIs through the competitive strength of companies. He claimed that foreign subsidiaries experience the commonly named *liability of foreignness*; they have a competitive disadvantage compared to local firms because they have a better understanding of the local culture and consumer behavior. They also have links to the (local) government. Therefore, according to Hymer, companies must have some specific resources and competencies so substantial they compensate for this *liability of foreignness*. These resources or competencies are, in many cases, intangible assets, such as knowledge and brands. Only when these competitive advantages counteract the *liability of foreignness* can a company succeed in the foreign market.

8.4.3 *The eclectic paradigm or the OLI model*

So, internalization aspects (Williamson) indicate that companies may prefer full control through an FDI, while the *liability of foreignness* (Hymer) emphasizes prerequisites for success in foreign markets. John H. Dunning combined the main elements of these partial explanations into one broad (eclectic) model: his OLI framework (1980). He uses the internalization aspect of Williamson, and he borrowed some elements from Hymer. According to Dunning, companies will undertake FDI if the company possesses certain ownership advantages to overcome the *liability of foreignness*, the host country possesses certain location advantages, and the internalization in itself holds benefits for the company.

1. Ownership-specific advantages (O-advantages)
2. Location-specific variables (L-advantages)
3. Internalization advantages (I-advantages)

Explaining FDI starts with the notion that a company seeking to go abroad must have powerful tangible or intangible assets (or advantages) specific to that company (O-advantages). These advantages compensate for the liability of foreignness and are, for example, brand recognition, technology, patents, know-how about the market, and sufficient resources. Note that these O-advantages must compensate for the disadvantages in the *foreign* market. Having a strong domestic brand name is not enough, as it must help the company abroad. Although Nyenrode Business School is a powerful brand name in the Netherlands, with a reputation for high-profile professors, this in itself does not give Nyenrode an O-advantage. Only if the brand is known internationally and its faculty has an international reputation will this give the school a competitive advantage abroad. The same holds for commercial brands. China-based Xiaomi is a well-known brand in China but not in many foreign markets. Consequently, their brand recognition in China is not an O-advantage for Xiaomi.

Many large and domestically well known emerging market companies are still lagging O-advantages

---

Location-specific advantages (L-advantages) of the host country tell a company *where* to invest, which is why, for example, Philips chose to invest and produce medical equipment in China and why China Minmetals invests in Peru. Of course, location advantages are heterogeneous but, in principle, have to do with the political and institutional environment, including political stability, level of corruption, bureaucracy, public service quality, laws and regulations, and FDI incentives. These factors determine whether a location is attractive (or not) to foreign investors. Laws and regulations that influence the choice of FDI location also include the government's attitude toward foreign capital and companies. Chinese FDI in Peru increased dramatically in the mid-1990s, driven by the Fujimori administration, which stimulated the inflow of foreign investors in the mining sector. This positive attitude regarding foreign investors increased Peru's L-advantage in the eyes of Chinese companies.

Another important L-advantage is the size and growth of the market. Companies invest abroad because there is a large and increasing purchasing power in the country or the neighboring countries if the host country is part of a larger trading block. In that case, the foreign company may not have to set up entire operations or supporting offices in each country but can use a regional office for further expansion in the trading block. China's integration into Asia through the ASEAN or the One Belt One Road initiative increases China's L-advantage considerably. A final L-advantage relates to Porter's Diamond (1990) and its agglomeration effects. Strong clusters may generate high L-advantages and attract investments from abroad, significantly impacting inward FDI.

Finally, internalization advantages (I-advantages) tell investors *how* to invest abroad — choosing the optimum entry mode. A company has several options for how to enter a foreign market. High I-advantages signal a need for a high level of control, which leads to expansion through a takeover or greenfield investment by internalizing activities. For example, if Hilton wants to start a new hotel in Indonesia, it may decide to keep control over its daily operations because it is of utmost importance to keep quality at a high level. The high I-advantages drive the choice for full control. The same holds for Philips investing in R&D in China. Again, its high I-advantages result in the choice of a full control mode of entry, hence, a greenfield or takeover. If the I-advantages are not high, a company may decide to use non-control modes of entry, such as strategic alliances. For example, fast-food chain KFC invests in new outlets in Brazil through franchise instead of full control. In this case, speed maybe more important than control and there are no important I-advantages at stake. Obviously, the OLI framework is clearly closely related to the motives for going abroad.

L-advantages are strongly related to the motivation for going abroad

---

8.4.4 *Motives*

Based on the OLI paradigm, Dunning (1998) distinguished four types of FDI motives:

1. Market-seeking
2. Resource-seeking
3. Efficiency-seeking
4. Strategic asset-seeking

Companies that are looking for new markets (*market-seeking*) will focus mainly on location factors related to the market of the host country

FDI Type	Description
Resource-seeking	Investing abroad to acquire (part of) natural resources and raw materials. Foreign resources can be interesting due to lower costs of production
Market-seeking	Investing abroad to take advantage of the current (or potential) market. The various reasons relate to follow suppliers or customers, to adapt products to local needs and avoiding transportation (and serving) costs
Efficiency-seeking	Investing abroad to take advantage in differences in availability and costs with respect to labor and capital. It includes the possibility to achieve economies of scale and scope
Strategic asset-seeking	Investing abroad to acquire (part of) new technology, knowledge and building up brand-image

Figure 8.8:   Motives for and types of FDIs.

Source: Based on Dunning (1998).

or region when deciding on a specific investment location. They will look at L-advantages, such as market size, market growth, income level and development, and urbanization rate of the potential country or region. The urbanization rate is important since cities are large consumer markets in relatively small geographic areas. This concentration makes logistics and marketing fairly easy (think about the development of e-commerce). In *resource-seeking* FDI, the company tries to secure scarce resources like raw minerals at lower costs.

Efficiency-seeking FDIs will occur when companies search for opportunities to lower their costs of operations, for instance, by reducing labor costs. In the 1990s and early 2000s, reducing production costs was the primary motive for western companies to invest in NEP-9 countries. Finally, strategic assets are the resources and capabilities within a company that give it a competitive advantage compared to its rivals. *Strategic asset-seeking* FDI occurs when a company wants access to unique capabilities, such as knowledge, technological skills, or brands. Takeovers of high-tech and knowledge-intensive companies abroad by NEP-9 companies are examples of strategic asset-seeking FDIs (Figure 8.8).

The literature mentions additional (firm and sector-specific) motives besides these four. For example, heavy domestic competition, to avoid high tax rates, or as a reaction to moves from competitors. According to the *oligopolistic reaction theory* (Knickerbocker, 1973), companies tend to follow their (primary) competitors when investing in foreign markets. If a leading company in a specific industry invests in a foreign market, other companies within the same sector tend to react by investing in the same market: *follow the leader theory*. Within the same line of thinking, investing abroad is also provoked by customers and suppliers.

8.4.5   *Global challengers*

In *Unravelling Modern China* (2019), I used the commonly named *filter approach* to determine the type of Chinese companies we can expect to engage in foreign investments. We can also apply this approach to NEP-9 companies. For example, you may expect that specific industry features such as industry concentration or government support may act as an accelerator for companies operating in these markets to go abroad. Another method to develop an understanding of international competition and the development of FDI flows from emerging markets is the methodology used in the Boston Consultancy Group report "Global Leaders, Challengers, and Champions" (2016). BCG gives an overview of the leading emerging market companies that can become world-class competitors in the not too distant future. The report is an annual publication to determine which emerging market companies are on the verge of challenging western companies in international markets. The assessment uses numerous objective data such as global presence (indicated by the number of foreign subsidiaries) and significant international investments over the past five years. BCG complements these data with a (subjective) scoring based on criteria, such as the depth of the company's technologies, its intellectual property portfolio, and the international appeal of its products. The 2019 BCG report, published in 2020, focused on high-tech companies specifically. Figure 8.9 presents some of these future global players from our NEP-9.

We attribute this impressive list of companies to factors such as strong government support, creating economies of scale on the home market, flexibility to adjust products and processes, more quality at reasonable prices, and cheap sources of capital. These factors are the growing O-advantages of emerging market companies. The conclusion is clear. The presence of NEP-9 companies in western markets is growing, and we can expect to see much more of them.

> *NEP-9 companies: growing internationalization but still considerably less internationalized than western international operating companies*

Although NEP-9 companies' speed of internationalization increased during the past decade and despite the fact that they are also now

Country	Company		
China	Baozun	South Korea	Coupang
	BYD-electronics		Kakao
	Didi Chuxing		Ticket Master
	JOYY	Russia	Tinkoff Bank
	Nxin		Yandex
	Oppo electronics		
	Shongshu AI	Turkey	Getir
	Vivo global		
	Xiaomi	India	Byju's
			Practo
Brazil	Creditas		Udaan
	Nubank		Zomato

Figure 8.9:   Global challengers, selected companies, high-tech sector.

Source: Boston Consulting Group (2019).

internationalizing at a faster rate than their western peers, they are less internationalized than their western competitors. Researchers have suggested a wide range of variables to measure internationalization, but the most used is the *Transnationality Index* (TNI) developed by UNCTAD. The TNI is the unweighted average of three ratios: (1) foreign to total assets, (2) foreign to total sales, and (3) foreign to total employment. The number of foreign subsidiaries and the number of countries with operations sometimes complement these three ratios (Ietto Gillies, 1998; Muller, 2004). On the right-hand side of Figure 8.10, it becomes clear that certain sectors in the economy are, by its nature, more international than others.

The fall in the TNI, shown in Figure 8.10, is in line with the gradual decreasing trend of the TNI in the previous decade. This is explained by geographical and industry compositional effects, and not so much by the reversal of internationalization of individual MNEs. For example, the number of MNEs from emerging markets in the global top 100 increased from eight in 2015 to 15 in 2019. Their lower internationalization levels automatically affect the aggregate TNI of the largest global MNEs.

	Global MNEs		Emerging Market MNEs	
	2018	2019	2018	2019
Foreign assets as % of total	58	54	31	31
Foreign sales as % of total	60	57	46	42
Foreign employment as % of total	53	47	37	33
TNI	57	53	38	35

High
TNI

Publicers
Mining
Industrial equipment
Electronics

Low
TNI

Construction
Telecom

Figure 8.10:   TNI of the top 100 largest companies, 2018 and 2019.

Source: Based on World Investment Report (2021).

Saudi Aramco and China State Grid entered the global league with a TNI of 15% and 4%, respectively. Such low internationalization figures clearly affected the TNI of the 100 largest companies. There is also an industry compositional effect. The fall of the TNI is partly the result of digitalization and the rise of digital companies. Digitalization allows MNEs to penetrate foreign markets without establishing a large physical presence there: digital companies break the relation between revenues gained abroad and the physical presence in the host economy and tech and digital companies have gained growing relevance in the top 100 MNEs ranking by foreign assets since 2010.

8.5   Adjusting the Theory to Fit Companies from New Economic Powers

The eclectic approach or the OLI paradigm was developed in the 1970s and early 1980s when western companies dominated global markets and FDI. Specific characteristics brought them domestic and international success. Today, NEP-9 companies are expanding abroad. Should this development lead to a revision of the FDI theory? In 2017, while lecturing on globalization at Renmin University Business School in Beijing, I debated said question with colleagues in the MBA department during a round table meeting. Some opined that although minor modifications are required, in essence, the OLI model is still relevant in explaining FDI from China and other NEP-9 countries. Others stressed the need for an entirely new framework to explain the internationalization of emerging market companies, as they consider the OLI framework insufficient. The analysis that follows is mostly based on this discussion. As we will see in the following, this difference in viewpoints, adaptation versus replacement, is a bit artificial.

NEP-9 companies: modifications of the three pillars behind the eclectic approach are needed

---

Our golden mean is to use the three components of the OLI model but discard the OLI as the comprehensive framework because it cannot explain the internationalization behaviors of emerging market companies. The first modification to the OLI model relates to different O-advantages.

8.5.1 *Different ownership advantages*

The O-advantages concept requires adjustment because, in many aspects, the nature of the O-advantages of emerging market companies is quite different from those of western firms. Examples of western competitive advantages are proprietary technology, powerful brands, marketing power, and other managerial capabilities. The emerging market companies' O-advantages are found in their ability to adapt existing technology to develop products suited to the unique needs of local customers, making the products cheaper and more affordable. This ability to design products without unnecessary bells and whistles is then exploited internationally. African, Asian, and Latin American mobile companies developed flexibility and adaptability to survive tough home market conditions, like infrastructural constraints, policy changes, local protectionism, and unclear legislation. Flexibility and adaptability are indispensable O-advantages when aiming to conquer new, challenging, and rapidly changing markets. Utilizing these advantages made them world leaders in areas such as mobile banking and mobile health monitoring. When we talk about companies, we also talk about their managers: they often are more flexible and adaptive than their western counterparts.

China-based Haier is famous for redesigning its washing machines to add a "potato and vegetable" option for its target group in rural China. This adaptability is also visible in the United States where Haier introduced innovative niche refrigerator designs for student rooms. The creative avoidance of formal regulations on its South African home market became a managerial strength in SABMiller's overseas expansion. Russian enterprises have a competitive advantage in relational assets or networking skills, generating an O-advantage different from western companies and their managers. Flexibility as an O-advantage may also explain so many NEP-9 companies investing in risky places in the past decade. Perhaps they do not hesitate to invest in relatively dangerous regions because their home markets are institutionally complex environments. They have mastered the required competencies not only to survive but also to thrive.

The difference between country specific advantages and firm specific advantages

---

There is another way to discuss the different O-advantages of companies from the larger emerging markets. Rugman (1981) divides the competitive advantages of a company into firm-specific advantages (FSA) and country-specific advantages (CSA). In general, western companies such as Unilever, Philips, and Walmart possess firm-specific advantages, driven by technology, knowledge, and innovation exclusively to the company. In contrast, the success of Chinese, South African, and Russian firms abroad relies on the specific advantages of their home countries: cheap labor, national resources, cheap money, and government support. They may have a competitive advantage, but it is country-specific. As soon the market is opened to foreign companies, these may also obtain those advantages. Consequently, the competitive advantages based on country-specific advantages shrink and disappear, and building firm-specific advantages becomes essential. According to Rugman, companies can make this switch in several ways. For example, through collaboration with foreign firms, competition on the domestic market, reducing government support, and buying specific advantages through M&As.

8.5.2 *A lack of O-advantages*

The above fine-tunes the O-advantages concept for NEP-9 companies; it does not deviate from it. The concept presupposes that an investing company has O-advantages. So, how do we explain FDIs from emerging market companies that do not have O-advantages? The OLI model states clearly that a company or organization must have an O-advantage *before* conducting business abroad. However, many MNEs from the larger emerging markets invest abroad to acquire strategically created assets such as technology, brands, distribution networks, R&D facilities, and managerial competencies (buying O-advantages) to offset their competitive shortcomings. For example, China-based Lenovo took over IBM's PC division in 2005 to acquire the ThinkPad brand and reputation in the B2B market.

The lack of O-advantages is an important reason to engage in FDIs by emerging market companies

---

A lack of O-advantages (instead of *having* O-advantages) driving FDI from emerging market companies is the essence of the *Linkage-Leverage-Learning Model* (LLL model, Mathews 2006). This model is based on the observation that firms have three ways to build knowledge-based and firm-specific competitiveness:

1. Linkage: Connecting to an existing network that holds essential sources of advantages.
2. Leverage: Using access to new resources or knowledge to upgrade and diversify the product portfolio.
3. Learning: Successfully exploiting newly acquired knowledge requires integration into the company's existing knowledge portfolio. Through learning, the company increases its technological capabilities.

8.5.3 *Different I-advantages*

The I-advantages of the eclectic approach flow from control over technology, knowledge, and the ability to control strategic choices. Choosing internalization and assessing I-advantages is different for emerging market companies. For example, the absence of sophisticated suppliers that can provide quality intermediate inputs makes it necessary for the company to internalize these supplies. The same holds for finance. If the company cannot rely on necessary loans under reasonable conditions due to an immature financial sector or government intervention, it makes sense to establish an internal company bank. While western MNEs can rely on external providers for inputs and finance, this is not the case in many immature emerging markets. The emerging market companies must integrate activities such as finance, suppliers, and many specialized services into the company's hierarchy. Consequently, companies from emerging markets are often much more vertically integrated and diversified.

The LLL model emphasizes the idea that emerging market companies internationalize *despite* their weak O-advantages and do so precisely to *build* the necessary firm-specific advantages.

---

*Feeling relative comfortable in an uncertain and risky
business environment*

But the model does not explain the aggressive and fast internationalization of emerging market companies. However, the *springboard paradigm* (Luo & Tung, 2007) does. Springboard behavior means these companies try to overcome their latecomer disadvantage with aggressive international acquisitions. Although springboard behavior is related to leapfrog behavior, there is an essential difference. Late entrants "leapfrog" to catch-up with the competitive position of earlier movers, but in many cases, this is a single decision. However, springboard steps are a deliberately designed grand plan to facilitate growth and a long-range strategy to establish competitive positions in the global marketplace more solidly. The springboard model will show a sequence of international takeovers, firmly integrating the foreign activities with those back home.

8.6 Investment Development Path Framework

The above attempted to explain FDI flows from the company's point of view, but we can also analyze FDI flows from a nation's point of view. According to Dunning and Narula (1996), the economic development of a country determines the outward and inward direct investment, the essence of the *Investment Development Path (IDP) model*, visualized in Figure 8.11. The IDP theory differentiates five main stages in a country's development: from poor (phase 1) to high income (phase 5). Each stage corresponds with a specific outward and inward direct investment picture. There is a prominent link to the OLI model. From a country perspective, O-advantages of domestic companies drive outward FDI, and L-advantages such as a large market, low wages, or a stable investment climate determine inward FDI.

The vertical axis indicates the net outward investment position (NOI), defined as the total outward direct investment minus the total inward direct investment of a country. A positive NOI means outward FDI is larger than inward FDI. Conversely, negative NOI means the inward FDI is larger than the outward FDI.

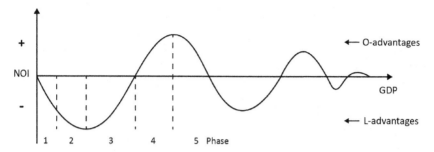

Figure 8.11: Investment development path.

Source: Ebbers (2019) (based on Dunning & Narula, 1996).

The IDP framework assumes the locational advantages of a country change when it develops economically, and, therefore, inward FDIs also change. For example, if the motivation behind a foreign investment is cost reduction, the L-advantage is lower wages. But if the incentive to invest abroad is market entry, the main location advantage will be the purchasing power and market size.

> *We may expect much more FDIs from emerging markets and NEP-9 countries*

The IDP model assumes that as they develop, local companies from emerging markets increase their firm-specific advantages and their ability to compete globally. Consequently, we can expect a positive NOI for several NEP-9 countries in the next decade or so, in line with what we have said regarding the global challenges and the transition from debtor nations to credit nations.

Stage 1

In the first stage, with its low economic and human development, the location-specific advantages of the country are insufficient to attract significant FDI flows. With low per capita income, the local market generates little demand, and immature infrastructure and lack of skilled labor limit the inflow. However, there is some inflow related to natural assets, most of which is resource-seeking FDI. During this phase, the role of the government is vital in attracting FDI. It may give foreign companies substantial preferences, increasing the L-advantage. At the same time, the O-advantages of domestic companies are few and small. They cannot compete in foreign markets and may lack the knowledge to manage international operations; consequently, outward direct investment is minimal, with a negative NOI position as a result.

Stage 2

Due to some economic development, inward investments start to grow. Step by step, the domestic market develops and becomes an important driver behind the increase of the L-advantages of the country. The structure of inward FDI is not changing too much; it still involves natural resources, primary commodities, and low-tech manufacturing. The government's role in attracting FDI is still essential, although it may change slightly from phase one. Now, government policy relates more to creating a stable and transparent business environment and is less focused on giving subsidies and preferences to specific foreign companies. In addition, O-advantages of domestic firms start to emerge as they learn how to cooperate and compete with foreign companies. The government supports the outflow through (export and technology) subsidies. Despite this rise in outward FDI, the inflow of FDI is higher in this phase, and the NOI position falls further. The first two stages in the IDP are associated with the acceleration phase, earlier discussed in this chapter, while the reversing phase relates to the IDP stage 3 and upwards.

Most NEP-9 countries are in the early stages of the IDP framework

---

Stage 3

In stage three, the NOI position increases when the outward flow of direct investment overtakes inward FDI. Production of standardized goods, rising incomes, and growing competitiveness of local firms characterize this development stage. The initial low O-advantages of firms will increase; technology is absorbed, and there are essential learning effects related to management and marketing. L-advantages also change due to the growing local market and its middle class. The (potential) market takes over from low production costs as the main L-advantage. The function of the government at this stage is more indirect than in the previous step: achieving a transparent and stable business climate that stimulates innovative behavior and where foreign companies feel comfortable.

Stage 4

In this stage, the outward FDI equals or exceeds the inward FDI. Local firms are now capable of competing with foreign firms both in their competitive domestic market and overseas. The L-advantages of a country are based on a highly skilled labor force, efficient infrastructure, and a mature consumer market. Higher wages reduce the original L-advantage but are overtaken by skilled labor (still relatively cheap). Inward investments at this stage are mostly market-seeking. Outward direct investment grows significantly as domestic firms further increase their competitiveness and are learning fast from their international experience. The role of the government in this stage is less prominent, concentrating on its regulatory function.

Stage 5

The NOI position of the country hovers around the zero level, although there are temporary surpluses and deficits. The level of inward and outward direct investment continues to increase. A country may emerge as a net outward investor in a specific industry and, at the same time, in other sectors, attract a lot of investments. This may also change over time when companies decide to move operations from one country to the other.

8.6.1 *Some critical notes*

The conclusion is clear: if the NEP-9 countries are following the IDP framework, the West will witness an explosion of investments from emerging market companies. This is in line with the outcome of the BCG report on global challengers, discussed earlier.

As always, a model helps us draw general conclusions, but obviously, using and interpreting the results of such a model are only possible if we know the caveats, therefore, a few critical notes. For example, the IDP framework uses GDP per capita as a proxy for economic development.

However, countries with a relatively high GDP per capita might have lower economic development than countries with a lower GDP per capita. Saudi Arabia or Qatar looks promising for a company in terms of GDP per capita, but the absence of a middle class makes these countries less attractive from a market-motive point of view. Consequently, there is substantially less inflow of FDI in these countries than expected, according to the Dunning–Narula model. The same is true for countries with a low per capita GDP. They may attract much more FDI based on their natural resources than based on the GDP per capita. The consequence is that those specific countries do not fit in the model. Outliers are mainly oil (and other natural resources) producing and exporting countries. The IDP model excludes country-specific factors; it may hold for countries on average but not for every individual country.

There are also some issues regarding the interpretation of data because we cannot see the reason for changes in the NOI position. For example, an increase in the net outward position of FDI is usually interpreted as increased competitiveness of domestic firms as a proxy for the whole economy. But, the rise in NOI position can also be due to a significant decrease of inward FDI stock in response to a deterioration of its investment environment. A final criticism relates to the specific start and end of the phases. There is no clear cut, and we see large differences between the various authors in this field. In our assessment of the IDP model, we link the end of phase 3–early phase 4 to when the country escapes the middle-income trap (Chapter 3). In this period, FDI outflows overtake inflows, and the net outward FDI position eventually becomes positive.

As shown in Figure 8.12, NEP-9 countries are following the general pattern of the IDP model. Except for South Korea and China, all NEP-9 countries are in the early phases of the IDP model. Inward FDI to these countries began to increase significantly during the late 1980s, helped by deregulation and easing of FDI requirements. China has absorbed large amounts of FDI since its opening-up reforms in the 1980s and had a growing negative outward investment position until 2015. Outward FDI was limited between 1980 and 2005 but has expanded fast in the recent decade. In 2015, outward FDI flows surpassed inward flows for the first time, narrowing the NOI deficit position. Because several NEP-9 countries show identical FDI development, only three countries are visible in Figure 8.12: South Korea, China, and Brazil. The latter as a proxy for the other NEP-9 countries.

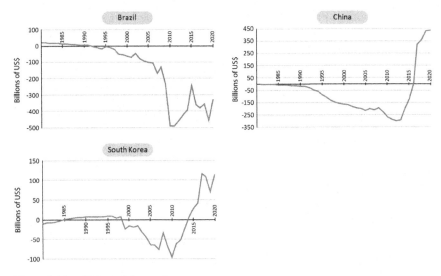

Figure 8.12:   IDP model over the years.

Source: Calculated from UNCTAD database.

Brazil and most of the other NEP-9 countries are situated in the first or second phase of the investment development path in which the inflow of FDI is substantially higher than the outflow of FDI; the L-advantages of these countries attract foreign investors, while the O-advantages of Brazilian, Turkeys, or Indonesian companies are growing but are not yet able to make use of the opportunities given by foreign markets. China is located in Figure 8.12 at the end of the third/early fourth phase of the IDP framework. In line with the BCG overview, Chinese companies are able to compete abroad due to their growing O-advantages and helped by the One Belt One Road initiative. South Korea is moving toward the fifth phase in which inward and outward stocks find their balance.

8.7 NEP-9 and Their Views on FDIs and Foreign MNEs

The views on FDI vary wildly, from the radically negative to the extremely positive. The negative view regards FDI and foreign MNEs as an instrument of imperialist domination, which only benefits the company itself and the home country. Profits are siphoned away, and the MNEs give little value to the host country because most activities are related to low-skilled labor with few domestic linkages. The highly positive view starts with the notion that free markets will result in the best outcome. They see the positive-sum game when countries specialize toward comparative advantages, and international production through MNEs may help in this. FDI increases the overall efficiency of the economy. It generates additional employment and creates competitive pressure, a precondition for innovative behavior.

8.7.1 *Mixed pictures*

As always, most opinions land somewhere in the middle. FDI inflow and MNEs may help the domestic economy but may negatively affect it. Research is not clear on this. The mixed picture also relates to the impact of maquiladoras on the Mexican economy. Maquiladoras are factories in Mexico that import raw materials mostly duty-free and tariff-free. Mexican workers earn income, the Mexican government collects tax revenues, and the Mexican economy gains from technology and knowledge from MNEs through the transfer of technology, competition, and the creation of local linkages and trade. At the same time, you could argue that these maquiladoras are enclaves without relationships to the domestic economy, generating only low-skilled labor, and the MNE makes sure that they hardly pay taxes. The same holds for China. The positive view concludes that economic development after the 1990s is almost entirely due to FDI. Foreign companies have introduced competition, learning effects, and efficiency to a previously command economy. Many Chinese companies learned from competing and cooperating with western firms. Furthermore, the investments created employment, both directly and indirectly, and increased purchasing power of the Chinese people. Others argue that foreign companies hardly affect the Chinese economy and even displace domestic production. Within this view, the inflow of FDI is seen as activities with hardly any domestic linkages and only related to low-skilled and low value-added products, and of little help to the Chinese economy.

FDI policies in NEP-9 countries are driven by pragmatism and achieving positive spill-overs in the domestic economy

---

The NEP-9 countries see FDI inflow and MNEs as helpful under certain circumstances, and we can describe their FDI policy as pragmatic and

Rank	Economy
1	New Zealand
2	Singapore
3	Hong Kong SAR
4	Denmark
5	South Korea
28	Russia
31	China
33	Turkey
60	Mexico
63	India
73	Indonesia
84	South Africa
124	Brazil

Indicator	What is measured
Starting a business	Procedures, time and costs
Dealing with permits	Time and costs related to formalities
Getting electricity	Reliability and costs
Registering property	Procedures and costs
Getting credit	Transparancy and legislation
Investor protection	Shareholders right and corporate governance
Taxation	Regulations and tax pressure
Enforcing contracts	Quality judicial processes
Labor rules	Regulations and flexibility
Government contracts	Public procurement transparancy
Resolving insolvency	Legal framework, time and costs
Trading abroad	Export and import regulations and tariffs

Figure 8.13:   Ease of doing business.

Source: World Bank (2020).

domestically driven. To attract foreign companies, NEP-9 countries are working to improve their business climate. And despite some fluctuations, the general conclusion is that it is gradually improving, as measured by the World Bank report "Ease of Doing Business."

This annual report indicates which countries are attractive to businesses. It shows how easy it is to do business in that country by examining the regulatory environment based on 12 indices. Examples of these indices are the procedures to start a business, dealing with construction permits, the availability of credit, and the rules regarding investor protection, among others. You might expect improvements in ranking to generate greater foreign direct investment inflow because institutional quality must positively impact FDI inflow. But be aware that the World Bank report does not account for some essential business factors. For example, the cultural side of doing business is absent but certainly significantly impacts the decision to invest. In "Ease of Doing Business," it looks like doing business in South Korea is easy (ranked #5), but obviously, cultural differences make it quite complex. Furthermore, the overview may be plausible on a country level, but we know large differences in doing business between cities and regions within countries exist.

Figure 8.13 shows the NEP-9 ranking in 2020. Despite growing international tensions and the perception that operating in China, India, Russia, and Turkey is becoming more complicated, the ranking over the years does not reflect this. For example, China has jumped 15 places from 46 to 31 in the 2020 "Ease of Doing Business." The rankings are benchmarked to May 2019, before the US–China trade war intensified and protests in Hong Kong began, which will have had some impact. Still, the structural trend is toward improving the regulatory environment. The Chinese government explicitly uses the "Ease of Doing Business" report in their policy choices. In 2018, Premier Li Keqiang announced that municipal governments must use the factors of the report as a benchmark when implementing a business reform agenda. South Korea does the same. In the past 10 years, it formed regulatory reform committees that use the *Doing Business* indicators as a key input to adjust and improve the business environment. India is also climbing the ranks, moving up 37 places from 100 (2018) to 63 (2020). This improvement results from measures such as a more transparent and uniform tax system and less government interference.

Too much political pressure and terminating the "Ease of Doing Business" research

---

The "Ease of Doing Business" report used to be an important document and became highly influential as a benchmark for domestic policy measures regarding business climate. However, its success also resulted in more political pressure. On September 16, 2021, the World Bank announced it was discontinuing its *Doing Business Report*. The decision was made after an investigation that found that the research and ranking of countries have been influenced by political pressure. The governments of China, Saudi Arabia, and the United Arab Emirates "asked" the researchers to adjust some of the outcomes. Besides data irregularities, the credibility of the research came also under attack because of its methodology. For example, it appeared that several local experts were not local and not expert. It is to be seen if the "Ease of Doing Business" report will continue after necessary adjustments in the methodology and shielding the organization from political pressure.

Clearly, the 2007–2011 global financial crisis and the COVID-19 pandemic led to more interventionism in national economic policies, some restrictive measures on FDI, and a return of some protectionism. Still, this did not result in a fundamental change in NEP-9 views on FDI and MNEs.

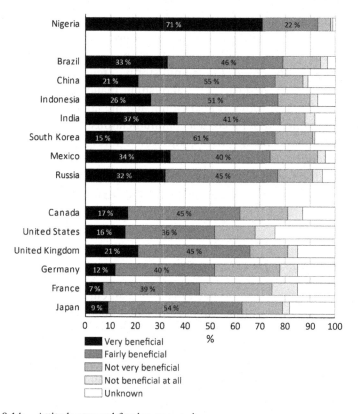

Figure 8.14:   Attitudes toward foreign companies.

Source: Bertelsmann (2020, July)

Figure 8.14 shows the result of the question "What do you think about foreign companies investing in your country?" The NEP-9 countries continue to acknowledge the potential benefits of FDI and have undertaken new measures to promote inward investment in the previous years. For example, in 2020, China passed a Foreign Investment Law that aims to improve the transparency of FDI policies and investment protection. In January 2020, it also published a set of provisional measures to promote foreign investment in the Yangtze River Delta area. Streamlining and a more helpful bureaucracy were also the aims of the Indonesian government under its new foreign investment regime, published in 2019.

India declared in February 2020 that single-brand retailers owned by foreign companies could fulfill their local sourcing requirements by procuring goods produced in outlets based in special economic zones. Furthermore, India eased the administrative regulations for foreign investors in specific industries by abolishing mandatory approval from the Reserve Bank of India. It also eliminated the approval procedure for foreign companies in defence, telecommunications, and private security that wish to open branch offices, and 100% foreign ownership is now allowed in civil aviation. In 2020, Russia and Brazil both simplified the procedures for foreign investors, and in addition, Brazil abolished the different treatment of foreign and domestic investors in the licensing process.

8.7.2 *Changing FDI structure*

Up to the mid-1990s, few countries had investment promotion agencies. Since then, many countries have established such agencies, including the NEP-9. They also have sub-national and even city agencies to attract foreign investments. These agencies combine the general promotion of the country or region with active targeting and searching for foreign investors that fit with the country's development priorities. These investments help the transition to higher value-added production or diversification of the supply side. A related strategy is that NEP-9 countries more and more link FDI inflow to sustainable and inclusive objectives. A decade ago, most NEP-9 countries sought to attract FDI as an important complement to domestic investment in building productive capacity. This focus on the financial aspect of foreign investments is now shifting toward the role MNEs may have in technological transformation. It means that certain direct investments are blocked because they do not fall within industrial upgrading. In principle, the NEP-9 see "good" FDI as a channel for technology diffusion, transfer of tacit knowledge, and know-how. This does depend on the level of FDI spillover to the domestic economy, and that is why NEP-9 governments focus on domestic policies to guarantee these positive spillover effects. Creating positive spillover effects is a key element of how the NEP-9 countries view and assess FDI inflow and MNEs. According to them, the context in which foreign investors must operate can be summarized by the following three elements.

1. Foreign companies must establish links to domestic firms
FDI and joint ventures with a foreign partner, in particular, may generate positive spillover effects through backward and forward linkages. Domestic companies can learn from their western counterparts (demonstration effects), and knowledge is absorbed partly through employee turnover. To ensure that associations arise, governments create policies for local content and the mandatory use of joint venture construction. A joint venture automatically means that the western firm must share its technology and knowledge with its domestic partner. This commonly named "forced technology sharing" issue is at the center of the US–Chinese trade war that exploded in 2018.

The importance of education in absorbing the potential benefits from foreign investors

---

The extent to which FDI can establish domestic links depends on the technological capabilities of domestic firms and the human capital available in the host economy. Highly skilled urban workers are available for a high-tech western MNE in South Korea, and it may be relatively easy to find high-quality suppliers. In this case, spillovers are relatively easy to create. A country such as South Africa finds it difficult to create positive domestic spillover effects because of its educational level and the absence of domestic firms that have the necessary capabilities to supply and cooperate with western MNEs.

2. Foreign companies must not negatively impact the current account
FDI can affect the host country's export and import that form the current account. Although countries may have a current account deficit in certain periods, they generally prefer a current account surplus: export is higher than import. The inflow of FDI can lead to higher imports. FDI is heavily associated with slicing up the value chain, locating various stages of production in different geographical locations. The final assembly of a product in China or Mexico requires importing a substantial part of the components, and in this way, FDI generates imports. On the other hand, FDI inflow may also substitute for imports. Importing heavy equipment from the US by Brazil is no longer needed if US-based company Caterpillar invests in a new Brazilian heavy equipment plant and sells its products domestically. In this case, imports will decline. If Caterpillar's Brazilian subsidiary exports products, this will positively impact Brazil's current account even more. Export in itself is not the primary aim: if the

foreign subsidiary exports, the products should be relatively high value-added products or services. The discussion on escaping the middle-income trap in Chapter 3 clarified that structural changes in the export structure are essential, to move away from low-skilled and low value-added exports toward more sophisticated and higher value-added exports. Foreign companies play a role in this process. For example, the share of foreign companies in China's high-tech exports was around 65% in 2020.

3. Foreign companies must stimulate high-skilled employment
Several developing countries can only connect to the global supply chains through low-skilled labor and assembly activities, a very unfavorable position to be in. These countries need FDI inflow for demonstration and employment effects and compete with other low-wage countries to attract foreign firms. Furthermore, assembly operations of large MNEs are relatively footloose, meaning they can relocate production to other countries if costs of operation increase due to higher minimum wages, environmental regulations, or a stronger social safety net. Therefore, countries concerned about losing employers and tax revenues are not keen to set stricter regulations. These can set off a "race to the bottom," leading countries to essentially compete in setting the lowest possible standards simply to attract businesses.

NEP-9 countries are in a better position today and demand MNEs to create new jobs in the host country. These cannot be just any kind of job but must be relatively high-skilled ones. In addition, MNE must also create both direct and indirect employment through local suppliers or local spending. The NEP-9 countries can implement these measures because of the relatively large market sizes and middle class. Furthermore, many MNEs located in the NEP-9 countries are not truly footloose. Despite increasing production costs, they rely on their high-quality suppliers and the consumer's purchasing power.

8.7.3 *A complex assessment*

In principle, NEP-9 countries stimulate FDI inflow, provided the benefits outweigh the costs. The contribution of FDI inflow to growth depends on the role of institutions (as measured by the "Ease of Doing Business" report) and on the level of educational and technological sophistication (high-quality education and high-quality suppliers). Governments employ several policies to attract the best FDI. The most critical factors are the economic determinants, particularly the size and growth of the market, the quality of the infrastructure, and the availability of skilled labor and science and technology resources. The regulatory framework constitutes another set of FDI determinants and is complemented by specific FDI promotional activities.

The key issue for "good" FDI is the intensity of the connections between the activities of foreign companies and the domestic economy. Foreign investments in manufacturing and even assembly can help transform the host economy by introducing the latest technologies, production processes, and management practices learned by local partners and imitated by domestic rivals. But the big question is if these spillover effects happen on a large scale. Determining (possible) links with the local economy (to determine which inward FDI is "good") and measuring spillover effects is incredibly complex. To complicate matters further, spillover may be low in technology but high for managerial skills. Furthermore, there are significant sectoral differences. For example, technology transfer may be relatively high in specific sectors and regions but non-existent in others. Despite all these uncertainties (and maybe results lagging behind expectations), there is little doubt that FDI has a beneficial impact in the short term (employment, higher income, and consumption) and longer term (increased competition, efficiency, and innovative behavior). The authorities of NEP-9 countries agree and will continue to stimulate future (high-quality) FDI inflow.

8.8 Absence of a Multilateral System on FDI and the Explosion of Bilateral Investment Treaties

A multilateral investment agreement must define the obligations of host governments and MNEs in the host country. Responsibilities of national governments relate to fair and equal treatment of foreign and domestic firms, compensation in case of nationalization, and facilitating fund transfers of foreign firms. Respecting the host country's laws and national sovereignty must be mandatory for the MNEs. Until the 1990s, there was essentially no international framework for governing investments. There were some attempts in the 1920s and 1940s (the commonly named Havana Charter) and the 1990s, but negotiations failed. The latest attempt, within the context of the Organization for Economic Co-operation and Development (OECD), aimed to negotiate the commonly named

Multilateral Agreement on Investments (MAI). Only the advanced nations were involved in the MAI negotiations, and unsurprisingly, the emerging markets, including the NEP-9, rejected the proposal. Their main argument was that it would substantially reduce the autonomy of national governments and give MNEs too much power.

No multilateral agreement to govern and guide foreign investments

---

8.8.1 *Partial agreements*

As stated in Chapter 7, the Uruguay Round of the GATT (1986–1994) included negotiations on foreign investments. Obviously, many services have to be produced where they are sold, and export is not an option. Exporting a McDonald's Big Mac from the US to the Netherlands does not make sense. In this case, investments abroad are the only way to go international. At the same time, export is possible for a substantial part of services, like banking, consultancy, and telecom services. A growing share of international trade concerns services, mostly complemented by foreign investments abroad. A multilateral trade deal that excludes services is not comprehensive. Consequently, members reached some agreement on handling FDI, for example, a ban on the imposition of the Agreement on Trade-Related Investment Measures (TRIMS) inconsistent with the non-discrimination paradigm. Furthermore, the General Agreement on Trade in Services (GATS) also has some provisions that affect investments. But member states were not required to participate in this framework. The WTO reached some agreement on liberalizing trade in telecommunications and financial services in the 1990s. However, there has been little progress toward a universal, multilateral set of rules to liberalize FDI due to protests from several NEP-9 countries like India, Brazil, and Indonesia.

8.8.2 *Bilateral Investment Treaties and Treaties with Investment Provisions*

Absent a multilateral framework on FDI, bilateral investment treaties (BITs) proliferate worldwide and are becoming the dominant mechanism governing FDI flows. BITs are agreements between two countries aimed at promoting bilateral FDI and protecting each other's FDI. Since the signing of the first BIT between Germany and Pakistan in 1959, their number grew to 2,815 in January 2022 (UNCTAD). Growth was particularly explosive during the 1990s, driven by the fall of the Berlin Wall, the consequent opening up of Central and Eastern Europe, and China's acceleration of reforms that opened up domestic sectors for foreign investors. While BITs focus on bilateral investments, countries also use the commonly named Treaties with Investment Provisions (TIPs) to stimulate foreign investments.

The explosion of bilateral investment treaties

These TIPs are mostly trade treaties that have a separate chapter on investments. International investment agreements are inclusive of both BITs and TIPs. Figure 8.15 shows NEP-9 participation in BITs and TIPs. They are quite active compared to advanced countries.

The US had 45 BITs and 69 TIPs signed in January 2022. Japan combined international investment agreements numbered 35 BITs and 22

Country	BITs		TIPs	
	Signed	In force	Signed	In force
Brazil	27	2	19	14
China	128	109	24	20
India	10	7	13	9
Indonesia	42	26	21	17
South Korea	96	89	25	20
Mexico	32	31	16	15
Russia	78	64	6	6
South Africa	38	11	11	8
Turkey	117	81	21	17
United States	45	39	69	51
United Kingdom	102	91	30	5
Germany	122	116	75	58
Japan	35	31	22	20

Figure 8.15:   NEP-9 BITs and TIPs.

Note: Not including the BITs and TIPs that are terminated.
Source: UNCTAD, International Investment Agreements Navigator.

TIPs. These are signed agreements, but there can be a substantial time lag between signing the treaty and the date the treaty takes effect. For example, the 2015 China–Turkey BIT took effect in November 2020, five years after its signing. The South Korean BIT with Myanmar that took effect in 2018 was already signed in 2014. In early 2022, there were 2,815 signed BITs and 2,247 in force. From the total signed TIPs of 421, there were 329 in force.

8.8.3 *Another spaghetti bowl problem*

While the provisions of BITs can differ substantially, most grant protection for MNE contractual rights, financial compensation after nationalization, allow for repatriation of profits and provide a mechanism for disputes and international arbitration. While, on balance, BITs may improve the investment climate, the large number of BITs arguably increases the complexity of rules for foreign investment. It is associated with the spaghetti bowl problem, observed by Bhagwati (Chapter 6). It is interesting to note that many BITs and TIPs with NEP-9 participation have relatively strong investor protection provisions. This contradicts the earlier statement that NEP-9 countries hesitate to give away policy autonomy. However, while governments are reluctant to make such concessions for all countries, governments are willing to do so for a specific country. Whether this proliferation of BITs and TIPs ultimately contributes to or weakens the multilateral agenda is an open question, similar to the explosion of trading blocks being a step forward or backward in multilateral trade.

Growing discomfort about the internationalization of large emerging market companies

---

The EU and China are in the process of replacing the BITs concluded by all EU member states with China with a single uniform legal framework for EU–China investment relations. The aim is to reduce the spaghetti bowl problem and open up more investment opportunities. The new EU–China Comprehensive Agreement on Investment (EU–China CAI) was finalized on December 30, 2020, and involves (binding) market access commitments by China, in particular regarding cars (traditional and new energy vehicles), health equipment, and a broad range of services. Interestingly, the agreement also contains a chapter that prohibits an investment requirement that forces the transfer of technology. However, the agreement is still unratified by the European Parliament and the EU Council (all 27 heads of state) before it can become law. This process was to start in the second half of 2021, but on May 20, 2021, the European Parliament voted to suspend ratification efforts due to growing political tensions regarding the treatment of the Uighurs in Xinjiang. Therefore, at the time of writing this book, China's BITs with all 27 EU countries remain in effect. In principle, BITs and TIPs make it easier to invest abroad. Still, at the same time, we see public and political discomfort about the growing presence of emerging market companies in advanced countries.

8.9 Screening Mechanisms for Assessing FDI Inflow

8.9.1 *Western and advanced countries*

In the West, there are different views on investments from NEP-9 companies. Some see these new foreign investors as stealing technology, and there are fears about the continuity of companies after acquisition by NEP-9 companies. Headquarters abroad may have the power to harm the foreign subsidiary and the country. Another discomfort lies in the takeover of critical national resources by companies from China, Russia, or Turkey, to name a few. This reaction is not new. In 1968, a leading French opinion maker, J.J. Servan-Schreiber, published "The American Challenge." He stated that Europe was an "unprepared victim to the US capitalist predator with its far superior management, technology, and capital." The US would "take over the French economy and society." A far more optimistic view is that the takeover of western companies by NEP-9 investors could rescue a company in crisis. The investment is then a welcome source of foreign capital because the western company can only survive with this capital injection and access to the (new) market through the links with the new owner.

8.9.2 *New neighbors*

In recent years, national policies on FDI from NEP-9 countries have become less welcoming. Partly, this results from the accelerated speed and increased presence of new and high-profile companies from the NEP-9. It is the same discomfort we feel when we have new neighbors from another country. How will they behave? What will be the effect on our daily lives? Should we adjust? We see the same uncertainty when new competitors from different economic systems and with different types of organizational cultures come into the market. This fear grows further when the foreign investor is a sovereign wealth fund or a state-owned enterprise and when the takeovers happen in sensitive industries. Particularly in the US, there is growing hesitation to accept new Chinese owners. This attitude started in the mid-2000s. For example, authorities blocked the bid for US-based Maytag by the Chinese company Haier in 2005. This takeover coincided with the attempted takeover by China's National Offshore Oil Corporation of American oil producer Unocal. This canceled deal created an environment in which the government even blocked the takeover of an American company in a mature and low-tech sector such as appliances. Whirlpool eventually acquired Maytag.

Blocking the takeover by Haier was the result of the US screening mechanism. Several countries have long had screening mechanisms in place, for example, Australia, Canada, and Japan. In May 2018, the Canadian government blocked the proposed acquisition of the Canadian construction company Aecon by CCCI, a Chinese state-owned company and one of the world's largest engineering and construction firms. According to the authorities, the takeover compromised national security: "The Canadian Government is open to international investment that creates jobs and increases prosperity, but not at the expense of national security" (*Reuters*, May 24). UNCTAD identified over 20 cases of large planned foreign takeovers (above $50 million), mostly from NEP-9 companies, that were blocked or withdrawn for national security reasons from 2016 to early 2020. Besides blocking announced takeovers based on national security reasons, foreign investments can also be stopped through competition and regulatory reasons. Some high-profile cases are shown in Figure 8.16.

As a reaction to the rise of foreign investments, EU members recently started to discuss establishing an EU screening mechanism to stop the transfer of sensitive technologies to foreign investors. When they could not reach an agreement, the EU adopted a resolution to launch a system of cooperation and exchange information on FDI in March 2019. But essentially, national governments can decide on the implementation of screening mechanisms. A screening mechanism is complicated because it

National security reasons	China Mengniu Dairy not able to acquire a stake in Lion Dairy & Drinks (Austrailia) Shandong Gold Mining was blocked by the Canadaian government to acquire TMAC resources China based EMST was blocked by German government to acquire radar specialist IMST
Competition reasons	Namibian competition commission blocked the acquisition by West China Cement of Schwenk Namibia America Movil (Mexico) cancelled its plan for a stake in Telefonica Moviles (El Salvador)
Regulatory reasons	Temasek (Singapore) and Hillhouse Capital Management (China) stopped the take over of China-based Kinetic Medical

Figure 8.16: Blocking foreign investments: Several reasons, 2020–2021.

Source: World Investment Report (2021, pages 120–121).

must find the optimal balance between openness and protecting national interests. And obviously, there are different opinions on this.

Finding the delicate balance between openness and protection

8.9.3 *Different scope and design*

Screening mechanisms can be different in scope and design. The scope is the range of sectors covered. Some screening mechanisms cover every sector of the economy, whereas others focus on specific sectors such as critical infrastructure (physical or virtual), energy, health, media, aerospace, and financial services. Some mechanisms assess all types of direct investments, while others look only at M&A, excluding greenfield investments. Another difference is between proactive and reactive screening. The US screening system is proactive: assessing corporate takeovers beforehand to find out if there is a risk involved. It introduced legislation in 2018 to broaden this assertive screening of foreign investment in 27 sectors, including semi-conductors and telecommunications. Proactive screening is not the case in most European countries. However, unease is growing, and some countries are more willing to block foreign takeovers and even foreign companies from operating in their market. The UK blocked Huawei from rolling out the 5G network in the UK, following steps taken by the US government in 2020. Germany is discussing proactive procedures to stop foreign investors in strategic industries. The debate intensified after a Chinese company acquired German-based high-tech company Kuka in 2016. In 2018, the government tightened its screening rules for non-EU foreign companies intending to purchase more than 10% of German companies in industries such as media, critical infrastructure, and defense. Other EU countries are following the same trend. In 2018, the French government published (draft) legislation increasing the number of sectors in which foreign acquisitions must receive prior approval from the Ministry of Economics. This sector-specific screening mechanism (including industries such as artificial intelligence, cybersecurity, and robotics) is also visible in Australia. In 2018 and 2019, it announced further restrictions on investment in electricity infrastructure, telecommunication (5G network), and agricultural land. The Japanese government broadened the scope of sectors subject to screening in 2019, adding sectors such as information processing services and wireless equipment. During the COVID-19 pandemic, screening mechanisms emphasized the need to protect domestic companies in healthcare and biotech.

Unease is growing in western countries, as well in NEP-9 countries

8.9.4 *Screening mechanisms in NEP-9 countries*

Despite the rise reflected in the "Ease of Doing Business" report and the largely favorable view on inward FDI and MNEs, NEP-9 countries are also increasing restrictions on FDIs. For example, South Africa introduced a screening mechanism for foreign investments in 2020. The new law requires the establishment of a special committee responsible for assessing whether a merger involving a foreign acquiring company may harm national security or the economy. Screening mechanisms are important but are only part of restrictions on FDI. The commonly named FDI restrictiveness index measures for types of restrictions on FDI:

- Foreign equity limitations
- Restrictions on the employment of foreigners as key personnel

Country	2003	2020
South Africa	0.103	0.055
Turkey	0.283	0.059
Brazil	0.092	0.081
South Korea	0.148	0.135
Mexico	0.245	0.188
India	0.418	0.207
China	0.577	0.214
Russia	0.338	0.262
Indonesia	0.365	0.347
OECD average	0.098	0.063

Figure 8.17:   FDI restrictiveness, 2003 and 2020.

Source: OECD (2021).

- Operational restrictions such as capital repatriation and land ownership
- Screening or approval mechanisms.

Restrictions are evaluated on a 0 (open) to 1 (closed) scale and are only assessing the regulations on paper, so not the actual enforcement. China, Turkey, and India are among the countries with the greatest decline in restrictiveness between 2003 and 2020 (Figure 8.17). South Korea is an interesting case. Between 1997 and 2010, it was the country with the strongest decline in FDI restrictiveness and transformed from a very closed country with respect to FDI inflow to a very open country toward foreign companies (calculated from OECD database). Important in this process was the switch from using a positive list (FDI are only allowed in those listed sectors) to a negative list system in which FDI is possible in sectors not specified in the list. It does not say that everything is open. The country still has some sectors that are closed to foreigners and in some restricted industries, foreigners need to use a joint venture construction with a local partner. An important learning point of the South Korean case is that substantial domestic reforms and reducing

Country	Main characteristics
Brazil	Only registration of foreign investments is needed No pre-authorization process for most sectors and transactions Blocking FDI based on national security. E.g. heavy restrictions on foreign land ownership
China	Prior security review assessment of foreign investments in specific sectors: defense, critical agriculture, energy, mining and equipment. Several investments in services are constrained (e.g. transportation) Legislation leaves substantial room for interpretation Specific ownership-caps in certain sectors; restricted ownership in media, banks and telecom
India	For most foreign investments, no approval needed Prior government approval is required in sectors such as broadcasting, banking, mining and biotechnology Specific caps on foreign ownership, but in previous years, these caps have been increased. For example, the cap for FDI in insurance companies has been increased from 49% to 74% and cap on foreign ownership in telecommunications has been abolished
Indonesia	In principle, no prior approval or screening, but FDI is prohibited in specific sectors such as gambling, fishing and chemicals; partly based on environmental motives In previous years, new sectors on the prohibitive list; e.g. banking, education and health. Foreign investments are still possible in special economic zones
Mexico	FDI is allowed without prior authorization, except in restricted sectors such as transportation and banking Specific foreign ownership caps. For example, foreign investors cannot acquire more than 10% capital stake in a Mexican cooperative company. And not more than 49% foreign ownership of agricultural land and in sectors such as media and port-administration
Russia	Prior approval needed in so-called "strategic sectors" such as defense, oil and media. The number of sectors increased substantially in the previous years Ownership caps of 25% in companies that are important for the region or country, based on interpretation In general, we see a lowering of control-thresholds; in most sectors from 50% to 25% Obtaining approval is a lengthy process
South Korea	Prior approval for foreign acquisitions of national core technology; in particular when these domestic companies developed this technology with government subsidies and support Mostly, registration is enough, except if it threatens national safety, public hygiene, environment or when the investment is against Korean morals and customs
South Africa	Prior approval for specific sectors (national security), such as defense, infrastructure, technology and healthcare In sectors in which prior approval is not needed, one must wait on the green light given by the South African Reserve Bank
Turkey	Mostly, registration is enough, but in certain sectors FDI is prohibited or restricted or a combination of the two. For example, there is an ownership cap for foreign investors of 50% in a broadcasting company and it is not possible to invest in more than two Turkey's broadcasting companies No FDI allowed in maritime activities and in parts of the real estate sector Foreign ownership cap on land and in commercial airline companies

Figure 8.18:   Characteristics of screening mechanisms, NEP-9 countries.

Source: Based on IISD (2019) and Econpol (2021).

restrictiveness do not generate short-term effects. Companies may come with a substantial time lag and only when a critical mass of reforms are visible.

Today, we see more interventions and restrictions in international capital flows, in particular toward mergers and acquisitions. This is the result of the rise in sensitivity about capital flows in general that started after the financial crisis of 2007, combined with the COVID-19 impact after 2020. As stated before, one aspect of this increase in FDI restrictiveness relates to screening mechanisms. Figure 8.18 summarizes the main characteristics of the screening mechanisms in place in the NEP-9 countries. This reveals substantial differences, ranging from the absence of a formal screening mechanism (Brazil) to the intensive use of screening mechanisms geared at national safety and public security, often motivated by dominant market shares (India). The overview is based on the information that has been obtained at the end of 2021 and several countries were still in the process of restricting foreign ownership further as a result of the COVID-19 impact.

The more restrictive investment screening mechanisms today, compared to the 1990s and early 2000s show that governments are taking a more active role in assessing the costs and benefits of foreign investments on a case-by-case basis, rather than simply assuming that all foreign investments are beneficial. This is in line with what we saw in previous chapters. Full fledge globalization also has a dark side. Free international trade flows may hurt domestic producers and global governance institutions may not generate the best outcome for all members. The same holds for foreign investment: full opening up may not be in the best interest of the host country and a cautious view on this is needed.

Assessing the impact of foreign investments and stimulating
"good" FDI

In Chapters 1–8, we discussed the most important aspects of globalization and the role of the NEP-9 in it. In the final chapter, the Epilogue, we will present how the NEP-9 countries will shape the new global landscape and how the globalization process, in its many facets, looks like in the medium-term future.

Epilogue

I started this book by asking why it was necessary to write (and hopefully read) a book about a group of major emerging markets, a cluster of nine countries dubbed the New Economic Powers: the NEP-9. I trust the subsequent chapters have provided you with the insights and knowledge that inform the answer to that question. In the year 2022, the NEP-9 countries are significant players on the world stage. They are among the largest global exporters and importers and important investors through which unknown companies with unknown brands gain visibility and success in western markets. The NEP-9 middle classes are increasingly spreading their wings. These developments, driven by the catching up process, are fairly recent phenomenons inspiring a certain degree of discomfort in western countries. Policymakers, consumers, and businesses are faced with new neighbors, which tends to lead to some tension and uncertainty. How will I relate to them? Will I have to adapt? And what if we have very different ideas about how to use the front garden?

Discussions within multilateral institutions like the WTO and the IMF reflect the growing importance of the NEP-9. Power dynamics are changing. Formerly dominant (western) countries now have to take these new players into account. Different ideas about the role of government and the market can complicate these new dynamics, especially as these emerging countries are increasingly vocal about the changes they want to see implemented. The NEP-9 no longer see themselves as "takers" of the rules set by the traditional western rich countries (this includes Japan) but see themselves as "shapers and makers" of the new global landscape.

Of course, the NEP-9 are very different in many ways. Russia's economy is built mainly on energy exports, while China and India mostly need to import energy. There are differences in urbanization, aging, levels of democracy, and integration into the global economy. And because they are in different phases of the economic cycle, many argue they should not be viewed and analyzed as a homogeneous bloc. However, these differences arise from aspects that can fluctuate violently in the short term, such as energy prices or trade wars. However, in the long term, where structural features are essential, there are significant similarities.

The shapers and makers of the new global landscape

For example, the NEP-9 think that government intervention is indispensable and structurally necessary in economic transactions. It is vital to note this does not mean they do not trust the market but think the market and government intervention are complementary. They emphasize the market AND government, not the market VERSUS government, as often believed by the West. This difference proved a critical starting point in the book: discussions and analyses that use a (forced) dichotomy are no longer helpful in understanding the current globalization process. Problematic dichotomies such as state versus market, opening up versus protectionism, state capitalism versus private capitalism, and democracy versus authoritarian system create an unnecessarily black and white picture. Often seen hybrid forms make these divisions less relevant. China is simultaneously open and closed in terms of foreign trade and investment. Indonesia participates in 12 trading blocs but focuses strongly on multilateral free trade within the context of the WTO, and India is a democracy but has authoritarian characteristics.

Connecting the Dots

The first three chapters showed the world is changing, and the NEP-9 are claiming an ever-increasing role in it. A multipolar world in which the economic dominance of the West has disappeared in many areas. That does not mean growth in the West will stagnate and increase in NEP-9 and other emerging markets; it implies that growth in NEP-9 is more significant and will remain so for the next two decades, meaning these changes are relative. Of course, the NEP-9 will encounter problems, and we will see cyclical crises here and there, but the consensus is the NEP-9 will show a relatively steep growth path and will be able to implement the necessary reforms. Naturally, this assumes political and geopolitical stability, which is not guaranteed, as evidenced by the Russian invasion of Ukraine and the heavy sanctions from the West against Russia from February 2022 onwards.

The catching up will continue in the medium to longer term

Despite their differences, Chapter 4 showed that the NEP-9 have shared views on the role of government, the pros and cons of globalization, and the modus operandi of multilateral institutions such as the WTO and IMF, whose policies are mainly shaped by a singular focus on market forces. There are also commonalities regarding the rise and attitude of the middle class and the objective to change the economic structure toward more diversification and higher value-added activities.

Chapter 5 recounted that the NEP-9 do not believe in the benefits of a hyper-globalizing world that operates on market forces alone and where global efficiency considerations are leading. They see the advantages of a rule-based globalization process but demand more national autonomy to intervene when necessary. After all, countries are going through all kinds of transformations. Globalization with open borders may create volatility that disrupts these different transformations, leading to all sorts of adverse effects. National policy autonomy can counteract these disruptions. Chapter 7 elaborates further on this premise and focuses on how the NEP-9 view the legitimacy, representativeness, and modus operandi of the WTO and IMF. The conclusion is clear: the NEP-9 expect changes and improvements, supported by other emerging markets and less developed countries. However, their lack of soft power and differences between the NEP-9 countries have so far proved a bottleneck for concrete results.

Fighting disruptions and protecting national policy autonomy

International trade and foreign investments are the two main dimensions of the globalization process. Chapter 6 concluded that the NEP-9 recognize the benefits of free trade, but under certain circumstances, government intervention makes sense. This standpoint is also reflected in the way the NEP-9 view foreign investment. Chapter 8 argued that the benefits of foreign companies to the national economy are recognized, but these benefits do not come automatically. Specific government interventions, such as through regulation that determines foreign companies must use domestic suppliers, are sometimes necessary to ensure that the domestic economy reaps the benefits of foreign investment.

To arrive at an eclectic and consistent picture of past, present, and future NEP-9 influence on the most important facets of the globalization process, the various chapters must be tied together. I will do this from four overarching themes and the key features within these themes. The overarching themes forms the outer ring of the globalization flywheel in Figure 1 and consist of:

1. The catching-up process
2. Role of the government
3. Views on international trade and investments
4. Views on globalization and multilateral institutions

The Catching-up Process

The catching-up process, as we have seen from the 1990s onwards, is unique. Although a few Asian countries transitioned from a poor and agrarian society to a rich and modern one in the 1960s and 1970s, thereby catching up with the western rich countries, these Asian Tigers were the exceptions. Arguably, only from the 1990s onward have emerging markets been catching up on a broad scale, combining high growth rates with solid increases in human indicators. Again, this process of *convergence* is a new phenomenon.

NEP-9 countries started their catch-up at different times. South Korea implemented the necessary transformations as early as the 1960s and 1970s, while China started in the early 1980s while India began in the early 1990s. They also made different choices in their development models. For example, South Korea opened its doors to foreign investment very late, while China encouraged the inflow of foreign companies from the beginning of the reform process.

Strategic autonomy

But despite the differences in timing and other specific choices, essentially, the NEP-9 made the same policy choices during the same period of economic development. We can summarize these choices with the term *strategic autonomy*. In essence, the NEP-9 combine the benefits of the market with necessary government intervention. They believe in the advantages of the market as a source of prosperity, as it has assisted in achieving tremendous growth, decrease in poverty, and increase in human indicators. At the same time, they see the potential dangers of market failures and opening up too early in the catching-up process, when many transitions are happening simultaneously. Many of the necessary transitions and associated reforms (which we summarized with *rebalancing*) were in service of the catching-up process. And according to the NEP-9, many of these structural changes cannot be left to the market. That would take too long and result in extreme volatility during a development process that itself is already unstable, so government must intervene proactively. We have called this state capitalism 3.0. While discussing the *smiling curve* and trade diversification, we also concluded that government, through its policies, can support the transformation to greater prosperity.

The catch-up process occurred at breakneck speed and has changed the global economic landscape. Not only are the NEP-9 important players in exports and imports, but the catching-up process is also happening in the field of innovations, technological advancement, digitalization, the growth of the middle class, and new companies with new competitive strategies. The center of economic gravity has clearly shifted to these emerging economies. Of course, the NEP-9 will experience short economic crises from time to time. Still, the underlying fundamentals (and the continuation of the rebalancing process) are such that the long-term growth path will be higher than in the western, advanced nations. This convergence process is moving quickly and is causing unrest and discomfort in the West.

Role of the Government

In the NEP-9, the government is in the driver's seat. Not only because in 2022, we still face the consequences of COVID-19, but also because within their economic systems, the role of the government is so prominent. Government has always had a relatively significant influence here. Although market forces now complement this influence, there is a significantly different sense of the appropriate role for government, both in the NEP-9 and in the smaller emerging markets. The emerging-market century runs concurrently with the rise of new state capitalism. Increased government intervention is often seen as an alternative economic system that is competing increasingly with western market thinking and the western-dominated liberal world order. From this perspective, sovereign wealth funds and state-owned enterprises exporting this state capitalist model to other parts of the world is often met with suspicion. Hopefully, I have clarified that this one-sided view of state policy in NEP-9 is incorrect. The NEP-9 countries have active governments that *complete* the market: big markets need big governments. The market and government intervention are working together, and government interventions happen within the context of market thinking. We see this, for example, in modern industrial policies aimed at transforming the economy to more domestically added value and moving up the smiling curve. South Korean President Moon Jae-in articulated this idea at the opening of a Special Economic Zone on January 24, 2019: "This new era is a golden opportunity to transform the South Korean economy from a follower-type to a pace-setting one, where government, instead of controlling and administering, renders encouragement and support [to facilitate the private sector]." The addition in parentheses is mine.

Active government that complement, not substitute, the market

---

Because their governments play such prominent roles, it is challenging for the NEP-9 to cede autonomy to multilateral or regional institutions. Government must remain in the driver's seat, and, therefore, *strategic state autonomy* is an essential policy pillar. Again, this is driven by domestic considerations such as the various transformations, possible market failures, and the fact that opening up and market forces sometimes come too early. These must occur in the proper order, which the market cannot facilitate. In that respect, elements of the *Washington Consensus* are hard to understand for the NEP-9. They feel more comfortable rolling out policies that align with the Beijing Consensus where gradualism, stability, and domestic priorities are the starting points.

Views on Trade and Investments

The NEP-9 see themselves as the winners of the globalization model characterized by market forces and opening up. They assume a positive-sum game where there need not be losers in terms of foreign trade and investment, but it is essential to have strategic autonomy. That is why the NEP-9 participate intensively in the WTO, but they also practice government intervention through the *infant industry argument* and the rolling out of various non-tariff barriers. Their view is that there are also market failures in the field of trade where the market does not automatically ensure the optimal outcome. Therefore, governments are strongly proactive, for example, in initiating and promoting a country's latent comparative advantages. This leads to regular conflicts with the WTO. As stated before, the NEP-9 are not against globalization, free markets, and open borders, but they oppose a hyper-globalizing world driven by the tenets of the Washington Consensus where the WTO can set (domestic) rules to which sovereign states must adhere. A rule-based system is good, but this system cannot supersede domestic policies and priorities. The NEP-9 are cautious about the benefits of free trade and opt for *responsible* or *smart* globalization, as I call it. To illustrate, I used the metaphor of the bird (the market) in the cage (the limits set by the government). The NEP-9 are not opening the cage to set the bird free but are making it bigger when possible and reducing it when necessary.

NEP-9 countries: a cautious view on opening up

The NEP-9 are also cautious about foreign investments. In principle, these can contribute to increases in human indicators, but only under specific conditions, conditions that the government must create by, for example, setting terms for incoming enterprises, such as having to buy from local providers, sharing knowledge, and developing domestic linkages.

Views on Globalization and Multilateral Institutions

As indicated above, there are limits to free trade, free investment, and unbridled hyper-globalization. The NEP-9 are keeping the bird (market) in its cage (limits set by the government). In general, globalization is under attack, which also means that the pillars on which the globalization process rests are under pressure. For the NEP-9 governments, the economic paradigm of more market and less government, the IMF conditionalities, and the emphasis on lowering trade restrictions with a focus on global efficiency have lost its appeal. The reality is that the nation state and some degree of policy autonomy are the new pillars the globalization process must build on. Here, we see more elements of the cautious view: globalization can generate benefits, but only if government intervention corrects the market. In this respect, according to NEP-9, the globalization model (based on the market) requires renewal. In this new globalization model, national sovereignty and domestic priorities are central. This means that the rules within which the globalization process takes place need to be in tune with the fact that NEP-9 countries are going through transitions and need time to implement the necessary reforms. The new globalization model should also consider that there is more than one economic system and should not discount these "other" systems.

It is essential to recognize that global governance, or political globalization, is a zero-sum game. After all, when one country gains additional IMF voting rights or power, it is at the expense of another country because the number of voting rights is fixed at 100%. Therefore, discussions about changes in voting rights ratios are even more complicated than those around economic globalization and the benefits of foreign trade and investment. Additionally, perspectives differ wildly. When I talked about this in 2017 with a colleague who also worked at the IMF, he told me that because of the latest voting rights revision (in 2016), countries like Brazil, China, India, and Russia are now among the IMF's largest shareholders and decision makers. He said that the IMF voting power was now more in line with the realities of the global economy. Talking to Chinese colleagues about this voting rights adjustment, they all stressed that China still has much fewer voting rights than it is entitled to, and the adjusted voting rights still do not reflect the economic realities of the 21st century. These are different perspectives, but both are true.

Global governance: the decision power does not reflect today's economic and political reality

---

Despite adjustments, none of the NEP-9 are satisfied with their decision power or with the choices made by these institutions. At the same time, the western, rich countries are dissatisfied with the NEP-9's low adaptability in adhering to multilateral principles and agreements. One consequence is the active participation of the NEP-9 in the proliferation of regional trade blocs. Often these trade blocs go beyond multilateral agreements. For example, many regional trade blocs also have rules on foreign investment protection, and some have lowered non-tariff barriers.

From this perspective, they seem another step toward global free trade. Still, in principle, these regional trade blocs discriminate against non-participating countries and are thus an exception to the multilateral principle of non-discrimination. Again, the NEP-9 do not intend to focus primarily on regional trade blocs and cooperation, but they further complicate discussions within the WTO.

The Inner and Outer Rings of the New Global Landscape

In essence, the four factors of the outer ring, discussed above determine how the NEP-9 countries view the current globalization process and, consequently, they are also the pillars for the new global landscape. Macro and international developments and choices seemingly drive this outer ring primarily, but they also influence the political side of globalization. This is indicated by the inner ring of the globalization flywheel (the inner circle of Figure 1), where we can identify four mutually reinforcing trends resulting from the developments in the NEP-9. The inner ring makes clear that political convergence is not to be expected.

The inner ring of the globalization flywheel

---

1. Due to the economic success and rapid global integration of the NEP-9, we see relative changes in hard and soft powers. The NEP-9 show tremendous growth in many areas, but the development of their soft power is lagging. There is a slight increase, but not enough to shift the moral compass toward the NEP-9. At the same time, we see that many smaller emerging markets have adopted China's macroeconomic growth model, not because they are forced to but because they genuinely believe it is best for their country's future.
2. This will certainly have implications for geopolitical relations, bilaterally and within multilateral institutions. Arguably, for the first time in the history of the GATT–WTO, the outcomes are not solely determined by the US, the EU, Japan, and some other western countries. Alliances among the NEP-9 countries and with other emerging markets and developing countries partly determine the outcomes of talks.
3. Alliance building is also happening on a broader scale. Consider the massive rise of regional and bilateral trading blocs. Global and

regional alliances (formally and informally) where NEP-9 countries find each other in common goals are emerging, both in terms of economic objectives and political goals.

4. Discussions on global rules must consider that differences between cultures, countries, economic structures, and domestic governance models will remain. The inescapable fact is that the world will remain fragmented into nation states. These will always be "different" in culture, institutions, and regulations, which is why hyper-globalization is no longer viable as a starting point for a new global landscape.

In the western discussion of the rise of the NEP-9 and its possible effects, there is a certain amount of *gap thinking*, which aligns with what we said earlier about outdated dichotomies such as open versus closed. This *gap thinking* creates a schism between the NEP-9 and emerging markets on the one hand and the western, rich world on the other. We no longer understand each other and widen the gap between us. In reality, this gap is much smaller than *gap thinking* suggests, especially if we go further back in history. Choices now made in countries like Indonesia and Mexico are the same decisions made by western countries a few generations back. We see the current investment screening mechanisms in both the NEP-9 and western countries. On occasion, the West also sees the impact of the WTO on national legislation as too self-enriching. Some western countries also have industrial policies through which government supports strategic sectors, for example, Global Gateway Strategy, the EU investment fund announced in December 2021. The gap between our views on the role of government and elements of the globalization process is not that big. We just magnify it.

No convergence, but we are overemphasizing the differences: gap thinking

---

Discomfort

History teaches that shifts in economic power often lead to distress, discomfort, and uncertainty, and it is happening all over again. A key question is if we may expect some harmonization or convergence. You might expect the NEP-9 to move toward advanced western nations in terms of policy, which is what we see, for example, in the global middle class. In many ways, a middle-class person in Rio de Janeiro works, thinks, and buys the same way as the middle-class citizen in London. But if we zoom out to the macro or national level, we have to assume that significant differences in per capita income, level of education, and technology will continue in the coming decades. The NEP-9 (except for South Korea) remain substantially poorer, and as a result, domestic priorities and national government policies will not converge across countries, and national autonomy remains essential for the NEP-9. From this perspective, it is not helpful if the West demanded that China privatize its SOEs, that India increases domestic social mobility, and that South Korea dismantle its *chaebols*, the large family-controlled industrial conglomerates. These are structural, country-specific features and are part of its history, economic system, and culture, and so the discomfort about them remains.

The differences are here to stay

Differences in the role of government are decreasing a little, as the goals of NEP-9 and the western advanced nations' government policies are becoming more similar. In recent decades, the role of NEP-9 governments was focused mainly on catching up, and this will continue to play a role. However, many government interventions, such as specific industrial policies, SEZs, and agglomeration effects, are now aimed at joining the fourth industrial revolution. Incidentally, this is also causing discomfort in the West. Fearing the loss of dominance, the US is ringing the alarm regarding rapid technological advancement in China.

The role of government will remain different in the coming decades, creating discomfort in the geopolitical arena as well. Perhaps the Kuwaiti SWF's investments in the London real estate sector and the acquisitions by Chinese SOEs of German high-tech companies are entirely driven by commercial considerations and competitive strategies. Still, there may also be a geopolitical motive behind them. Partly, this is the reason for the emergence of investment screening mechanisms. These mechanisms screen incoming investments before they are made, for the potential negative impact on the national economy, accounting for geopolitical aspects.

Reality and the supporting beans

Increased discomfort in the western countries makes sense from the perspective of the *new neighbor syndrome*. We can also explain the discomfort felt by the NEP-9: why are our wishes not (sufficiently) taken into account in the outcomes of the globalization process? The new global landscape envisioned by the NEP-9 is visualized in the inner and outer rings of influencing factors (Figure 1). This new paradigm is held together by the four supporting pillars. These are the four realities that the West faces in discussions of the new global landscape: the NEP-9 are shaping and making global rules. In doing so, they prioritize their domestic considerations, with governments that structurally intervene in the economic process and which are always looking for the right balance between international strategic partners and competitors.

Changes in global relations and the rise and fall of countries in international trade and investment are of all times. These landscapes are changing continuously. But the current developments associated with the rise of the NEP-9 are different. First, relationships are changing rapidly. Less than 20 years ago, the Chinese economy was smaller than that of the US state of California, and the combined exports of Brazil, India, and Turkey were smaller than that of Italy. The quick change in economic importance also creates discomfort in the West because the speed of the developments puts pressure on adaptability. As change is happening so fast, the population and policymakers in the NEP-9 have experienced different times when wealth creation was uncommon, poverty was typical, and extreme price volatility had dramatic consequences. The memory of how things used to be has increased both the credibility of the market and trust in government.

Factors that makes the assessment even more complex

Some factors of the new global landscape are not shown in Figure 1, but these do further flesh out the picture. For example, the extraordinary role played by China. The rise of China is a defining factor in the shaping of the new global landscape because there is an alternative to the western liberal system of private capitalism. Developments in China will have apparent effects on all aspects of the globalization process, similar to the hegemony of the US in the years following World War II. Consider, for example, the current trade war between the US and China. Of course, it is about trade flows, but underneath the accusations of unfair competition, this trade war is a battle between economic systems.

Other matters, like democracy, corruption, and economic freedom are not in the model either, but arguably, they are related to the circles and

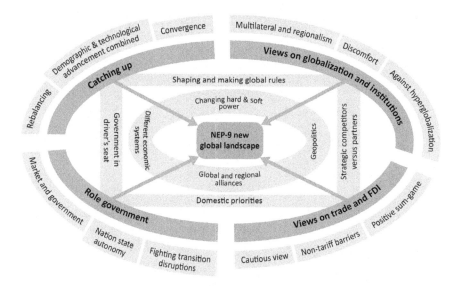

Figure 1:   The new global landscape: the inner circle, outer circle, and supporting beans.

Note: The outer rings relate to what we see today. The inner circle makes clear that no convergence is to be expected with the West in the medium to longer term. The supporting beans relate to the future reality.

supporting pillars. China shows that democracy and eradicating corruption are not necessary conditions for creating prosperity. Of course, democracy can positively affect creativity and innovative behavior. Still, several NEP-9 countries show that economic freedom and the rule of law may be more important than liberal democracy as a driver of prosperity. They prove that autocratic governments can also provide these. In this regard, democracy has been under pressure in recent years as a prerequisite for economic development. The middle classes in China, Turkey, and Russia want democracy and fair elections, but for them, economic freedom, protection of their property, security, and increasing purchasing power are more important today. The discussion of the role of democracy in creating prosperity for all will undoubtedly also affect the discussion on (the future of) globalization.

One thing is certain, in the years to come, the NEP-9 will be the ones defining the new global landscape.

References

Abboushi, S. (2010). Trade protectionism: Reasons and outcomes. *Competitiveness Review: An International Business Journal*, **20**(5), 384–394. https://doi.org/10.1108/10595421011080760.

Acemoglu, D., Naidu, S., Restrepo, P. and Robinson, J. A. (2019). Democracy does cause growth. *Journal of Political Economy*, **127**(1), 47–100. https://doi.org/10.1086/700936.

Acemoglu, D. and Robinson, J. A. (2013). *Why Nations Fail: The Origins of Power, Prosperity, and Poverty* (Reprint edition). Redfern: Currency.

Agénor, P. R. (2016). Caught in the middle? The economics of middle-income traps. *Journal of Economic Surveys*, **31**(3), 771–791. https://doi.org/10.1111/joes.12175.

Aggarwal, S. (2017). *Smile Curve and Its Linkages with Global Value Chains*. MPRA Paper No. 79324. May.

Ahearn, R. J. (2011). *Rising Economic Powers and the Global Economy: Trends and Issues for Congress*. Washington: Congressional Research Service.

Aiyar, S., Duval, R., Puy, D., Wu, Y. and Zhang, L. (2013). *Growth Slowdowns and the Middle-Income Trap*. IMF Working Paper. March.

Akamatsu, K. (1961). A theory of unbalanced growth in the world economy. *Weltwirtschaftliches Archiv*, **86**, 196–217.

Allison, G. (2015). The thucydides trap: Are the U.S. and China headed for war? *The Atlantic*, September 24.

Amann, E. and Virmani, S. (2015). *Is the Evolution of India's Outward FDI Consistent with Dunning's Investment Development Path Sequence?* Lancaster University Economics Working Paper Series.

Angey-Sentuc, G. and Molho, J. (2015). A critical approach to soft power: Grasping contemporary Turkey's influence in the world. *European Journal of Turkish Studies*, **21**. https://doi.org/10.4000/ejts.5287.

Asensio-López, D., Cabeza-García, L. and González-Álvarez, N. (2019). Corporate governance and innovation: A theoretical review. *European Journal of Management and Business Economics*, **28**(3), 266–284. https://doi.org/10.1108/ejmbe-05-2018-0056.

Ashraf, Q. and Galor, O. (2011). Dynamics and stagnation in the Malthusian epoch. *SSRN Electronic Journal*. https://doi.org/10.2139/ssrn.1546257.

Asian Development Bank. (2019). *Asian Economic Integration Report 2018.* Tokyo: ADB Institute.

Babb, S. (2013). The Washington Consensus as transnational policy paradigm: Its origins, trajectory and likely successor. *Review of International Political Economy*, **20**(2), 268–297. https://doi.org/10.1080/09692290.2011.640435.

Babic, M., Fichtner, J. and Heemskerk, E. M. (2017). States versus corporations: Rethinking the power of business in international politics. *The International Spectator*, **52**(4), 20–43. https://doi.org/10.1080/03932729.2017.1389151.

Balassa, B. (1965). Trade liberalisation and "revealed" comparative advantage. *The Manchester School*, **33**(2), 99–123. https://doi.org/10.1111/j.1467-9957.1965.tb00050.x.

Baldwin, R. E. (2008). Managing the noodle bowl: The fragility of East Asian regionalism. *The Singapore Economic Review*, **53**(03), 449–478. https://doi.org/10.1142/s0217590808003063.

Baldwin, R., Ito, T. and Sato, H. (2014). *The Smile Curve: Evolving Sources of Value Added in Manufacturing.* IDE-JETRO Research Series.

Baldwin, R. and Krugman, P. R. (1986). *Market Access and International Competition: A Simulation Study of 16K Random Access Memories.* NBER Working Paper No. w1936.

Banerjee, A. V. and Duflo, E. (2008). What is middle class about the middle classes around the world? *Journal of Economic Perspectives*, **22**(2), 3–28. https://doi.org/10.1257/jep.22.2.3.

Basri, F. and Putra, G. A. (2016). *Escaping the Middle Income Trap in Indonesia.* Jakarta: Friedrich-Ebert Stiftung.

BBVA. (2016). *Emerging and Growth Leading Economies.* Madrid: BBVA Research.

BCG Tech Challengers the Next Generation of Innovation in Emerging Markets 2020. (2020). BCG Research. November.

Bernhofen, D. M., El-Sahli, Z. and Kneller, R. (2013). Estimating the effects of the container revolution on world trade. *SSRN Electronic Journal*. https://doi.org/10.2139/ssrn.2228625.

Bertaut, C., von Beschwitz, B. and Curcuru, S. (2021). *The International Role of the US Dollar.* Washington: FED Notes.

Bertelsmann. (2017). *A Closer Look at Globalization: The Positive Facets and the Dark Faces of a Complex Notion.* Gutersloh: Bertelsmann Stiftung.

Bertelsmann. (2020). *What Do We Need a World Trade Organization for?* Gutersloh: Bertelsmann Stiftung.

Bhagwati, J. (2004). Anti-globalization: Why? *Journal of Policy Modeling*, **26**(4), 439–463. https://doi.org/10.1016/j.jpolmod.2004.04.003.

Bhagwati, J. and Krueger, A. O. (1995). *The Dangerous Drift to Preferential Trade Agreements (AEI Special Studies in Policy Reform)*. Washington: UNKNO.

Bickley, S. J., Chan, H. F., Skali, A., Stadelmann, D. and Torgler, B. (2021). How does globalization affect COVID-19 responses? *Globalization and Health*, **17**(1). https://doi.org/10.1186/s12992-021-00677-5.

Bird, G. and Rowlands, D. (2010). The IMF and the challenges it faces. *World Economics*, **11**(4), 131–156, London.

BIS. (2018). *Globalisation and Deglobalisation*. Basel: Monetary and Economic Department.

Bleiker, R. (2002). Activism after Seattle: Dilemmas of the anti-globalisation movement. *Pacifica Review: Peace, Security & Global Change*, **14**(3), 191–207. https://doi.org/10.1080/1323910022000023138.

Bordo, M. D. (2017). The second era of globalization is not yet over: An historical perspective. *Federal Reserve Bank of Dallas, Globalization and Monetary Policy Institute Working Papers*, **2017**(319). https://doi.org/10.24149/gwp319.

Boston Consulting Group. (2016). *Global Leaders, Challengers, and Champions*. Boston: BGG Research.

Britto, G. (2019). *The Great Divide: Economic Complexity and Development Paths in Brazil and the Republic of Korea*. CEPAL. https://repositorio.cepal.org/handle/11362/44721. August 20.

Calcagno, A., Dullien, S., Marquez-Velasquez, A., Maystre, N. and Priewe, J. (2016). *Rethinking Development Strategies after the Financial Crisis*. United Nations.

Cap Gemini Research. (2021). Capgemini Worldwide. https://www.capgemini.com/research/.

Chesley, D., Everson, M. and Garvey, J. (2016). *Global Power Shift: Winners, Losers, and Strategies in the New World Economic Order*. London: Strategy + Business, June.

Coka, D. A. and Rausch, T. (2020). *Attitudes on Globalization on the Eve of the Corona Crisis; 2020 GED Globalization Survey*. Gutersloh: Bertelsmann Stiftung.

Combarnous, F., Berrou, J. P., Clement, M., Darbon, D. and Rougier, E. (2008). The new Turkish middle class: Identification, behaviors and expectations. *Turkish Economic Review*, **22**(2), 158–184.

Comparing the Real Size of African Economies. (2014). African Development Bank. https://www.afdb.org/sites/default/files/2019/08/27/icp_main_report_2014_-_en-_12_2014.pdf.

Congressional Research Service, Cimino-Isaacs, C. D. and Fefer, R. F. (2021). https://crsreports.congress.gov/product/pdf/R/R45417/12. CRS. October.

Costanza, R., Hart, M., Posner, S. and Talberth, J. (2009). *Beyond GDP: The Need for New Measures of Progress*. Boston: The Pardee Paper Series.

Cowan, G., Cull, N. J. and Nye Jr., J. (2008). *Public Diplomacy in a Changing World (The ANNALS of the American Academy of Political and Social Science Series)* (1st edn.). Thousand Oaks: SAGE Publications, Inc.

Cox, M. (2012). Power shifts, economic change and the decline of the west? *International Relations*, 26(4), 369–388. https://doi.org/10.1177/004711-7812461336.

Crawford, J. A., Fiorentino, R. V. and World Trade Organization. (2005). *The Changing Landscape of Regional Trade Agreements*. Geneva: World Trade Organization.

Davies, K. (2013). *China Investment Policy: An Update*. OECD Working Papers on International Investment, Paris.

Denisia, V. (2010). Foreign direct investment theories: An overview of the main FDI theories. *Academy of Economic Studies*, 2(2), 104–110, Bucharest.

di Matteo, L. (2022). *Measuring Government in the Twenty-First Century*. Vancouver: Fraser Institute.

Dieppe, A. (2021). *Global Productivity; Trends, Drivers and Policies*. Washington: The World Bank.

Djebbouri, M., Laouni, M. and Tahi, A. (2019). An empirical study on the impact of trade war on both the US and Chinese economies, based on the value-at-risk approach. *Applied Science and Innovative Research*, 3(4), 279–296. https://doi.org/10.22158/asir.v3n4p279.

Dollar, D. and Kraay, A. (2001). Trade, growth, and poverty. *SSRN Research Paper*.

Domar, E. D. (1946). Capital expansion, rate of growth and employment. *Econometrica*, 14, 137–147. https://doi.org/10.2307/1905364.

Dreher, A. (2006). Does globalization affect growth? Evidence from a new index of globalization. *Applied Economics*, 38(10), 1091–1110. https://doi.org/10.1080/00036840500392078.

Dreher, A., Gaston, N., Martens, P. and van Boxem, L. (2010). Measuring globalization: Opening the black box. A critical analysis of globalization indices. *Journal of Globalization Studies*, 1(1), 166–185.

Dunning, J. H. (1980). Toward an eclectic theory of international production: Some empirical tests. *Journal of International Business Studies*, 11(1), 9–31. https://doi.org/10.1057/palgrave.jibs.8490593.

Dunning, J. H. (1998). Location and the multinational enterprise: A neglected factor? *Journal of International Business Studies*, 29(1), 45–66. https://doi.org/10.1057/palgrave.jibs.8490024.

Dunning, J. H. and Lundan, S. M. (2008). *Multinational Enterprises and the Global Economy* (2nd edn.). Cheltenham: Edward Elgar Publishing.

Dunning, J. H. and Narula, R. (1996). The investment development path revisited. In *Catalysts for Economic Restructuring, Foreign Direct Investment and Governments* (pp. 1–41), New York.

Ebbers, H. (2019). *Unravelling Modern China*. Singapore: World Scientific Publishing Company.

Ebbers, H. A. (2016). *Internationale bedrijfskunde en globalisering*. Noordhoff.

Eberstadt, N. (2019). *China's Demographic Outlook to 2040 and Its Implications*. American Enterprise Institute. January.

Economist Intelligence Unit. (2020). *The Democracy Index*. EIU.

Edelman Trust Barometer. (2020). Edelman Data & Intelligence. November.

Edwards, H. (2017). What global trade deals are really about (hint: it's not trade). YouTube- TEDxMidAtlantic. https://www.youtube.com/watch?v=-v3uqD1hWGE. May 17.

Eichenauer, V. Z., Dorsch, M. and Wang, F. (2021). *Investment Screening Mechanisms: The Trend to Control Inward Foreign Investment*. Munich: Economic Policy Report.

Engel, J. and Taglioni, D. (2017). *The Middle-Income Trap and Upgrading along Global Value Chains*. Washington: WTO, WTO–WB.

Ferdausy, S., Rahman, S. and Das, A. K. (2008). Impact of globalization on the growth of economies in developing countries. *The Chittagong University Journal of Business Administration*, **23**, 313–330.

Foote, C. and Ezell, S. (2019). *The 2019 Global Mercantilist Index: Ranking Nations' Distortive Trade Policies*. Washington: The Information Technology and Innovation Foundation.

Foxley, A. (2010). *Regional Trade Blocs: The Way to the Future?* Washington: Carnegie Endowment for International Peace.

Foxley, A. and Sossdorf, F. (2011). *Making the Transition from Middle-Income to Advanced Economies*. Carnegie Endowment for International Peace. September, Washington.

Freedom House. (2021). Expanding freedom and democracy. https://freedomhouse.org/.

Friedman, T. L. (2006). *The World is Flat: A Brief History of the Twenty-First Century* (Expanded and Updated edition). New York: Farrar, Straus and Giroux.

Friedman, T. L. (2009). *Hot Flat and Crowded: Why We Need a Green Revolution — and How It Can Renew America* (Rev. ed.). Vancouver: Douglas & Mcintyre.

Friedman, T. L. (2017). *Thank You for Being Late* (Illustrated edition). London: Picador Paper.

Fukuyama, F. (1989). The end of history? *The National Interest*, **16**, 3–18.

Fukuyama, F. (1992). *The End of History and the Last Man*. New York: Free Press.

Gaur, A. and Kumar, V. (2010). Internationalization of emerging market firms: A case for theoretical expansion. *Advances in International Management*, **23**, 603–627. https://doi.org/10.1108/S1571-5027(2010)00000230031.

Glaeser, E. L. (2010). *Agglomeration Economics (National Bureau of Economic Research Conference Report)* (Illustrated edition). Chicago: University of Chicago Press.

Glass, D. V. and Appleman, P. (1976). Thomas Robert Malthus: An essay on the principle of population. *Population Studies*, **30**(2), 369. https://doi.org/10.2307/2173616.

Global Economy, World Economy. (2021). TheGlobalEconomy.Com. https://www.theglobaleconomy.com/.

Goldstone, J. A. (2002). Population and security: How demographic change can lead to violent conflict. *Journal of International Affairs*, **56**(1), 3–21.

Graham, D. (2020). Home. Brand Finance. https://brandfinance.com/. October 14.

Grieger, G. (2017). *Foreign Direct Investment Screening: A Debate in Light of China-EU FDI Flows*. European Parliamentary Research Service. May.

Gygli, S., Haelg, F., Potrafke, N. and Sturm, J. E. (2018). The KOF Globalisation Index — Revisited. *SSRN Electronic Journal*. https://doi.org/10.2139/ssrn.3338784.

Gygli, S., Haelg, F., Potrafke, N. and Sturm, J. E. (2019). The KOF Globalisation Index — Revisited. *The Review of International Organizations*, **14**(3), 543–574. https://doi.org/10.1007/s11558-019-09344-2.

Halper, S., Blumenfeld, R. and Audible Studios. (2010). *The Beijing Consensus: How China's Authoritarian Model Will Dominate the 21st Century*. Audible Studios.

Han, X. (2017). *Re-examining the Middle-Income Trap Hypothesis: What to Reject and What to Revive?* NBER Working Paper. February.

Hanson, G. H. (2012). The rise of middle kingdoms: Emerging economies in global trade. *Journal of Economic Perspectives*, **26**(2), 41–64. https://doi.org/10.1257/jep.26.2.41.

Harrod, R. F. (1939). An essay in dynamic theory. *The Economic Journal*, **49**(193), 14–33. https://doi.org/10.2307/2225181.

Hassi, A. and Storti, G. (2012). Globalization and culture: The three H scenarios. *Globalization — Approaches to Diversity*. https://doi.org/10.5772/45655.

Hayashi, H. (2007). Uniqueness of Russian middle class and its future. *The Journal of Comparative Economic Studies*, **3**, 29–45.

Heldt, E. (2017). Shaping global trade governance rules: New powers' hard and soft strategies of influence at the WTO. *European Foreign Affairs Review*, **22**, 19–36.

Hennart, J. F. (2012). Emerging market multinationals and the theory of the multinational enterprise. *Global Strategy Journal*, **2**(3), 168–187. https://doi.org/10.1111/j.2042-5805.2012.01038.x.

Heritage Foundation. (2021). The Heritage Foundation. https://www.heritage.org/.

Houseman, S. N. (2018). *Understanding the Decline of US Manufacturing Employment*. Upjohn Institute Working Paper. June.

Hu, W. (2019). *China as a WTO Developing Member, is It a Problem*. Brussels: CEPS.

Huang, B., Morgan, P. J. and Yoshino, N. (2019). *Demystifying Rising Inequality in Asia*. Tokyo: Asian Development Bank Institute.

Huang, Y. and Wang, B. (2011). From the Asian miracle to an Asian century? Economic transformation in the 2000s and prospects for the 2010s. *Reserve Bank of Australia Proceedings*. https://www.rba.gov.au/publications/confs/2011/pdf/huang-wang.pdf.

Humphrey, J. (2007). Upgrading in global value chains. *SSRN Electronic Journal*. https://doi.org/10.2139/ssrn.908214.

Huntington, S. P. (1993). The clash of civilizations? *Foreign Policy*, **72**(3), 22–49. https://doi.org/10.2307/20045621.

Huntington, S. P. (1996). *The Clash of Civilizations and the Remaking of World Order*. New York: Simon & Schuster.

Hymer, S. (1976). *The International Operations of Nation Firms: A Study of Foreign Direct Investment*. Cambridge: MIT Press.

IMF Quotas. (2021). IMF. https://www.imf.org/en/About/Factsheets/Sheets/2016/07/14/12/21/IMF-Quotas. July 14.

International Bank for Reconstruction and Development. (2021). *Commodity Markets Outlook 2021*. Washington: World Bank.

Jagersma, P. K. and Ebbers, H. A. (2004). *Internationale bedrijfskunde; van exporteren naar globaliseren*. Amsterdam: Pearson Benelux.

Kanchoochat, V. (2015). *The Middle-Income Trap and East Asian Miracle Lessons*. UNCTAD.

Kappel, R. (2015). *Global Power Shifts and Challenges for the Global Order*. Hamburg: IMVF Policy Paper.

Kasahara, S. (2010). *The Flying Geese Paradigm: A Critical Study of Its Application to East Asian Regional Development*. Geneva: United Nations Conference on Trade and Development.

Kasahara, S. (2013). *The Asian Developmental State and the Flying Geese Paradigm*. Geneva: UNCTAD.

Kennedy, R. F. (1968). Gross domestic product to measure welfare (Speech at the University of Kansas). University of Kansas, Lawrence, Boston, March 18.

Kharas, H. (2010). *The Emerging Middle Class in Developing Countries*. Paris: OECD.

Kharas, H. (2017). *The Unprecedented Expansion of the Global Middle Class: An Update*. Washington: The Brookings Institution.

Kharas, H. and Gill, I. S. (2019). Growth strategies to avoid the middle-income trap. *SSRN Electronic Journal.* https://doi.org/10.2139/ssrn.3526261. Madrid.

Kharas, H. and Kohli, H. (2011). What is the middle income trap, why do countries fall into it, and how can it be avoided? *Global Journal of Emerging Market Economies,* **3**(3), 281–289. https://doi.org/10.1177/0974910111 00300302.

King Jigme Khesar Namgyel Wangchuk. (2009). The Madhavrao Scindia memorial lecture. Lecture, New Delhi, India. December 23.

KOF Globalisation Index. (2021). KOF Globalisation Index — KOF Swiss Economic Institute | ETH Zurich. https://kof.ethz.ch/en/forecasts-and-indicators/indicators/kof-globalisation-index.html.

Kojima, K. (2000). The "flying geese" model of Asian economic development: Origin, theoretical extensions, and regional policy implications. *Journal of Asian Economics,* **11**(4), 375–401. https://doi.org/10.1016/s1049-0078(00)00067-1.

Kotabe, M. and Kothari, T. (2016). Emerging market multinational companies' evolutionary paths to building a competitive advantage from emerging markets to developed countries. *Journal of World Business,* **51**(5), 729–743. https://doi.org/10.1016/j.jwb.2016.07.010.

Kregel, J. A. (2015). Emerging markets and the international financial architecture: A blueprint for reform. *SSRN Electronic Journal.* https://doi.org/10.2139/ssrn.2563721.

Krugman, P. (1986). *Strategic Trade Policy and the New International Economics.* Cambridge: The MIT Press.

Krugman, P. (1994). The myth of Asia's miracle. *Foreign Affairs,* **73**(6), 62–78. https://doi.org/10.2307/20046929.

Krugman, P. (2009). *Citigroup Foundation Special Lecture, Festschrift Paper in Honor of Alan V. Deardorff.* University of Michigan IPC Working Paper 91.

Krugman, P., Cooper, R. N. and Srinivasan, T. N. (1995). Growing world trade: Causes and consequences. *Brookings Papers on Economic Activity,* **1995**(1), 327–377. https://doi.org/10.2307/2534577.

Laffaye, S., Lavopa, F. and PerezLlana, C. (2013). Changes in the global economic power structure: Towards a multipolar world? *CEI, Argentine Journal of International Economics,* **1**, 1–21.

Lagarde, C. (2012). Promises to keep: the policy actions needed to secure global recovery [Presentation]. Peterson Institute for International Economic, Washington, United States. September.

Lawrence, R. Z. and Williams, A. L. (2006). China and the multilateral trading system. *China and Emerging Asia: Reorganizing the Global Economy,* Seoul, South Korea. May.

Lee, A., Hannigan, T. J. and Mudambi, R. (2015). *Escaping the Middle-Income Trap: The Divergent Experiences of the Republic of Korea and Brazil.* Bangkok: Asia-Pacific Research and Training Network on Trade.

Lee, J. W. (2016). The Republic of Korea's economic growth and catch-up: Implications for the People's Republic of China. *SSRN Electronic Journal.* https://doi.org/10.2139/ssrn.2779486.

Levi, M. and Olson, D. (2000). The battles in Seattle. *Politics and Society*, **28**(3), 309–329, Paris. https://doi.org/10.1177/0032329200028003002.

Lewis, W. A. (1954). Economic development with unlimited supplies of labour. *The Manchester School*, **22**(2), 139–191. https://doi.org/10.1111/j.1467-9957.1954.tb00021.x.

Linder, S. B. (1961). *An Essay on Trade and Transformation.* New York: Almqvist & WiksellBoktr.

Lopez-Claros, A. (2020). Global financial architecture and the international monetary fund. In Dahl, A. L. and Groff, M. (Eds.), *Governance of Multiple Global Risks* (p. 205). Cambridge: Cambridge University Press.

Lowy Institute. (2020). *Map - Lowy Institute Asia Power Index.* Lowy Institute 2021. https://power.lowyinstitute.org/.

Luiz, J. M. (2015). The political economy of middle-income traps: Is South Africa in a long-run growth trap? The path to "Bounded Populism." *South African Journal of Economics*, **84**(1), 3–19. https://doi.org/10.1111/saje.12117.

Luo, Y. and Tung, R. L. (2007). International expansion of emerging market enterprises: A springboard perspective. *Journal of International Business Studies*, **38**(4), 481–498. https://doi.org/10.1057/palgrave.jibs.8400275.

Maddison Historical Statistics. (2021). University of Groningen. https://www.rug.nl/ggdc/historicaldevelopment/maddison/?lang=en. December 7.

Mahbubani, K. (2009). *The New Asian Hemisphere: The Irresistible Shift of Global Power to the East* (1st edn.). New York: Public Affairs.

Makoni, P. L. (2015). An extensive exploration of theories of foreign direct investment. *Risk Governance and Control: Financial Markets and Institutions*, **5**(2), 77–83. https://doi.org/10.22495/rgcv5i2c1art1.

Marangos, J. (2009). The evolution of the term 'Washington Consensus.' *Journal of Economic Surveys*, **23**(2), 350–384. https://doi.org/10.1111/j.1467-6419.2008.00565.x.

Mathews, J. A. (2017). Dragon multinationals powered by linkage, leverage and learning: A review and development. *Asia Pacific Journal of Management*, **34**(4), 769–775. https://doi.org/10.1007/s10490-017-9543-y.

McClory, J. (2019). *The Soft Power 30.* Portland.

McKinsey & Company. (2016). *Digital Globalization: The New Ear of Global Flows.* New York: MGI Research.

McKinsey & Company. (2018). *Outperformers: High Growth Emerging Economies and the Companies that Propel Them.* New York: MGI.

Melitz, M. J. (2005). When and how should infant industries be protected? *Journal of International Economics*, **66**(1), 177–196. https://doi.org/10.1016/j.jinteco.2004.07.001.

Morady, F., Kapucu, H. and Yalcinkaya, O. (2017). Development and growth: Economic impacts of globalization. *Global Studies*, **3**, 11–20.

Moyo, D. and Ferguson, N. (2010). *Dead Aid: Why Aid is Not Working and How There is a Better Way for Africa* (Reprint edition). New York: Farrar, Straus and Giroux.

Myrdal, G. K. (1969). The soft states of South Asia: The civil servant problem. *Bulletin of the Atomic Scientists*, **25**(4), 7–10. https://doi.org/10.1080/00963402.1969.11455198.

Narlikar, A. (2022). India's foreign economic policy under Modi: Negotiations and narratives in the WTO and beyond. *International Politics*, **59**, 148–166. https://doi.org/10.1057/s41311-020-00275-z.

Navarro, P. (2008). *The Coming China Wars: Where They Will Be Fought and How They Can Be Won* (Revised and Expanded Edition). Upper Saddle River: FT Press.

Nogueira, S. (2009). The international financial crisis and Brazil in the Doha development round. *BRICS at the Doha Development Round.* Geneva: World Trade Organization Forum, September.

Nye Jr., J. S. (1991). *Bound to Lead: The Changing Nature of American Power* (Revised edition). New York: Basic Books.

Nye Jr., J. S. (2011). *The Future of Power.* New York: Public Affairs.

Nye Jr., J. N. (2008). Public diplomacy and soft power. *The Annals of the American Academy of Political and Social Science, Public Diplomacy in a Changing World Sage*, **616**(1), 94–109. https://doi.org/10.1177/0002716207311699.

OECD. (2007). *Towards Better Measurement of Government.* 's-Hertogenbosch; Van Haren Publishing.

OECD. (2012). *Looking to 2060: Long-Term Global Growth Prospects.* Paris.

OECD. (2017). *Fixing Globalisation: Time to Make It Work for All.* Paris.

OECD. (2019a). *Business Insights on Emerging Markets 2019.* Paris: OECD Emerging Markets Network.

OECD. (2019b). *Under Pressure: The Squeezed Middle Class.* Paris.

O'Neill, J. (2001). *Building Better Global Economic BRICs.* London: Goldman Sachs Global Economics Paper.

Örgün, B. O. (2012). Strategic trade policy versus free trade. *Procedia - Social and Behavioral Sciences*, **58**, 1283–1292. https://doi.org/10.1016/j.sbspro.2012.09.1111.

Osland, J. S. (2003). Broadening the debate. *Journal of Management Inquiry*, **12**(2), 137–154. https://doi.org/10.1177/1056492603012002005.

Oxfam. (2002). *Rigged Rules and Double Standards: Trade, Globalisation, and the Fight Against Poverty*. Oxford: Oxfam International.

Özpek, B. B. and TanriverdiYaşar, N. (2017). Populism and foreign policy in Turkey under the AKP rule. *Turkish Studies*, **19**(2), 198–216. https://doi.org /10.1080/14683849.2017.1400912.

Paape, L. (2020). De langetermijneffecten van Covid-19 op globalisering en het globaliseringsproces. In *Covid-19: een beveel uit het niets* (pp. 182–190). Nyenrode Business University/ Mediawerf, Breukelen.

Pakrashi, D. and Frijters, P. (2017). *Takeoffs, Landing, and Economic Growth*. Tokyo: Asian Development Bank Institute.

Panezi, M. (2016). *The WTO and the Spaghetti Bowl of Free Trade Agreements Four Proposals for Moving Forward*. Waterloo, Canada: Centre for International Governance Innovation.

Paulsson, M. R. P. (2018). Conflict resolution in a changing world order. *Trade, Law and Development*, **10**(1), 1–20.

Paus, E. (2019). *Escaping the Middle-Income Trap: Innovate or Perish*. ADBI Working Paper Series. September.

Perry, E. J. (2019). Making communism work: Sinicizing a Soviet governance practice. *Comparative Studies in Society and History*, **61**(3), 535–562. https://doi.org/10.1017/s0010417519000227.

Piketty, T. and Goldhammer, A. (2017). *Capital in the Twenty-First Century*. Amsterdam: Amsterdam University Press.

Porter, M. E. (1990). *Competitive Advantage of Nations* (Illustrated edition). New York: Free Press.

Portland. (2019). *Soft Power 30*. Soft Power. https://softpower30.com/. October 23.

Prebisch, R. (1950). The economic development of Latin America and its principal problems. *Economic Bulletin*, **7**, 1–22.

Przeworski, A. and Limongi, F. (1993). Political regimes and economic growth. *Journal of Economic Perspectives*, **7**(3), 51–69. https://doi.org/10.1257/ jep.7.3.51.

Puri, H. S. (2017). *India's Trade Policy Dilemma and the Role of Domestic Reform*. Washington: Carnegie India.

PWC. (2017). *The Long View: How Will the Global Economic Order Change by 2050*. London: PWC-LLP.

PWC. (2021). Sovereign investors 2020 a growing force. PWC.com.

Rachman, G. (2017). *Easternisation: War and Peace in the Asian Century* (1st edn.). New York: Vintage.

Ramo, J. C. (2004). *The Beijing Consensus*. The Foreign Policy Centre, London.

Rauch, J. N. and Ying, F. C. (2010). The plight of green GDP in China. *The Journal of Sustainable Development*, **3**(1), 102–116. https://doi.org/10.7916/consilience.v0i3.4498.

Raworth, K. (2018). *Doughnut Economics: Seven Ways to Think like a 21st-Century Economist* (Illustrated edition). Hartford: Chelsea Green Publishing.

Rennie, M. W. (1993). Born global. *McKinsey Quarterly*, **4**, 45–53.

Robinson, S. and Thierfelder, K. (2019). *US–China Trade War: Both Countries Lose, World Markets Adjust, Other Gain*. Washington: Peterson Institute for International Economics.

Rodrik, D. (2002). Feasible globalizations. *SSRN Electronic Journal*. https://doi.org/10.2139/ssrn.349021.

Rodrik, D. (2009). *One Economics, Many Recipes: Globalization, Institutions, and Economic Growth* (Illustrated edition). Princeton: Princeton University Press.

Rodrik, D. (2012). *The Globalization Paradox: Democracy and the Future of the World Economy* (Reprint edition). W. W. Norton & Company.

Rodrik, D. (2017). Populism and the economics of globalization. *SSRN Electronic Journal*. https://doi.org/10.2139/ssrn.2992819.

Rodrik, D. (2018). What do trade agreements really do? *Journal of Economic Perspectives*, **32**(2), 73–90. https://doi.org/10.1257/jep.32.2.73.

Rodrik, D. (2019). Globalization's wrong turn and how it hurt America. *Foreign Affairs*, **98**(4), 26–33.

Rostow, W. W. (1960). The stages of economic growth. *The Economic History Review*, **12**(1), 1–16. https://doi.org/10.1111/j.1468-0289.1959.tb01829.x.

Roth, K. P. and Diamantopoulos, A. (2009). Advancing the country image construct. *Journal of Business Research*, **62**(7), 726–740. https://doi.org/10.1016/j.jbusres.2008.05.014.

Rugman, A. M. and Verbeke, A. (2003). The World Trade Organization, multinational enterprises, and the civil society. In M. Fratianni, P. Savona and J. Kirton (Eds.), *Sustaining Global and Development* (pp. 81–97). Ashgate: Aldershot.

Saad-Filho, A. (2015). Social policy for neoliberalism: The bolsa família programme in Brazil. *Development and Change*, **46**(6), 1227–1252. https://doi.org/10.1111/dech.12199.

Sachs, A., Funke, C., Kreuzer, P. and Weiss, J. (2021). *Who Benefits the Most from Globalization?* Gutersloh: Bertelsmann Stiftung.

Sachs, J. (2006). *The End of Poverty: Economic Possibilities for Our Time* (Annotated edition). London: Penguin Books.

Sara, T. and Hall Jackson, F. (2010). Emerging markets and innovation: A partnership for global progress. *Business and Economic Horizons*, **2**(2), 1–6. https://doi.org/10.15208/beh.2010.11.

Saran, S. (2012). *The Evolving Role of Emerging Economies in Global Governance: An Indian Perspective*. London: FICCI-King's India Institute.

Sen, A. (1999). *Development as Freedom*. Oxford: Oxford University Press.

Sen, A. K. (2002). Globalization, inequality and global protest. *Development*, **45**(2), 11–16. https://doi.org/10.1057/palgrave.development.1110341.

Sen, S. (2010). International trade theory and policy: A review of the literature. *SSRN Electronic Journal*. https://doi.org/10.2139/ssrn.1713843.

Serra, N. and Stiglitz, J. E. (2008). *The Washington Consensus Reconsidered: Towards a New Global Governance (Initiative for Policy Dialogue)* (Illustrated edition). Oxford: Oxford University Press.

Servan-Schreiber, J. J. (1968). The American challenge. *The International Executive*, **10**(4), 1–3. https://doi.org/10.1002/tie.5060100401.

Sharma, R. (2020). *The 10 Rules of Successful Nations*. New York: W. W. Norton Company.

Sheffield, J., Korotayev, A. and Grinin, L. (2013). *Globalization: Yesterday, Today, and Tomorrow*. Marblehead, US: ISCE Publishing.

Shih, S. (1996). *Me-Too is not My Style: Challenge Difficulties, Break through Bottlenecks, Create Values*. Camberwell, AU: The Acer Foundation.

Singer, H. W. (1950). The distribution of gains between investing and borrowing countries. *American Economic Review*, **40**(2), 473–475.

Sovereign Wealth Fund Institute (SWFI). (2021). Sovereign Wealth Fund Institute. https://www.swfinstitute.org/.

Spechler, M. C., Ahrens, J. and Hoen, H. W. (2017). *State Capitalism in Eurasia*. Singapore: World Scientific Publishing Company.

Spence, M., Clarke Annez, P. and Buckley, R. M. (2009). *Urbanization and Growth*. Washington: World Bank.

Statista. (2021). Statista — The statistics portal. https://www.statista.com/.

Stiglitz, J. (2001). Redefining the role of the state. *World Economics*, **2**(3), 45–86.

Stiglitz, J. (2002). *Globalization and Its Discontents*. New York: W.W. Norton.

Stiglitz, J. E. (2003). Globalization and growth in emerging markets and the new economy. *Journal of Policy Modeling*, **25**(5), 505–524. https://doi.org/10.1016/s0161-8938(03)00043-7.

Stiglitz, J. E. (2007). *Making Globalization Work* (Reprint ed.). New York: W. W. Norton & Company.

Subramanian, A. and Kessler, M. (2013). *The Hyper Globalization of Trade and Its Future*. Washington: Global Citizen Foundation.

Taleb, N. N. (2007). *The Black Swan: The Impact of the Highly Improbable*. New York: Penguin Random House.

Trading Economics. Indicators from 196 Countries. (2021). Trading Economics. Com. https://tradingeconomics.com/.

Tran, V. T. (2013). The middle-income trap: Issues for members of the association of Southeast Asian nations. *SSRN Electronic Journal*. https://doi.org/10.2139/ssrn.2266239.

Transparency International. (2021). *Home*. Transparency.org. https://www.transparency.org/en. April 19.

UNCTAD. (2018). *Trade Policy Frameworks for Developing Countries: A Manual of Best Practices*. Geneva: UN.

United Nations. (2018). *Global Value Chains and Industrial Development Lessons from China, South-East and South Asia*. Vienna: UN Industrial Development Organization.

United Nations. (2021). *Technology and Innovation Report 2021: Catching Technological Waves — Innovation with Equity*. Geneva: United Nations.

United Nations Publications. (2019). *Commodities and Development Report 2019: Commodity Dependence, Climate Change and the Paris Agreement*. Geneva: United Nations.

United Nations Publications. (2021a). *World Investment Report 2020*. Geneva: United Nations.

United Nations Publications. (2021b). *World Investment Report 2021: Investing in Sustainable Recovery*. Geneva: United Nations.

United Nations Publications. (2020). *World Population Prospects 2019*. Geneva: UN.

Urata, S. and Doan, H. T. T. (2021). *Globalisation and Its Economic Consequences: Looking at APEC Economies (Routledge-ERIA Studies in Development Economics)* (1st edn.). London: Routledge.

van Grasstek, C. (2013). *The History and Future of the World Trade Organization*. Geneva: World Trade Organization.

Verbeke, A. (2020). Will the COVID-19 pandemic really change the governance of global value chains? *British Journal of Management*, **31**(3), 444–446. https://doi.org/10.1111/1467-8551.12422.

Vernon, R. (1966). International investment and international trade in the product cycle. *The International Executive*, **8**(4), 16. https://doi.org/10.1002/tie.5060080409.

Vujakovic, P. (2010). *How to Measure Globalisation? A New Globalisation Index*. FIW Working Paper.

Wade, R. H. (2016). Industrial policy in response to the middle-income trap and the third wave of the digital revolution. *Global Policy*, 7(4), 469 480. https://doi.org/10.1111/1758-5899.12364.

Wang, L. and Wen, Y. (2018). Escaping the middle-income trap — A cross-country analysis on the patterns of industrial upgrading. *Advances in Economics and Business*, **6**(1), 36–61. https://doi.org/10.13189/aeb.2018.060104.

Wani, H. A. (2011). Impact of globalization on world culture. *Research Journal of Humanities and Social Sciences*, **2**(2), 33–39.

Weisbrot, M. and Johnston, J. (2016). *Voting Share Reform at the IMF: Will It Make a Difference?* Washington: CEPR Center for Economic and Policy Research.

Weiss, J. (2005). *Export Growth and Industrial Policy: Lessons from the East Asian Miracle Experience.* Tokyo: Asian Development Bank Institute.

Wells, L. T. (1969). Test of a product cycle model of international trade: U. S. exports of consumer durables. *The Quarterly Journal of Economics*, **83**(1), 152–162. https://doi.org/10.2307/1883999.

Williams, B. R. (2018). *Bilateral and Regional Trade Agreements: Issues for Congress.* Congressional Research Service. May.

Williamson, J. (1990). *Latin American Adjustment How Much Has Happened?* Peterson Institute for International Economics.

World Bank. (2002). *Globalization, Growth, and Poverty.* World Bank Policy Research.

World Bank. (2010). *Innovation Policy: A Guide for Developing Countries*, World Bank, No. 54893, Washington.

World Bank. (2013). *China 2030: Building a Modern Harmonious, and Creative Society.* World Bank Development Research Center.

World Bank. (2018). *Riding the Wave; An East Asian Miracle for the 21st Century.* World Bank East Asia and Pacific Regional Report.

World Bank. (2020). *Doing Business 2020.* International Bank for Reconstruction and Development/The World Bank.

World Bank Group Publications, World Bank. (2022). *Commodity Markets Outlook, April 2020: World Bank Books Deal with with Deals with Issues Such as Economics Society, Trade, Taxes, Climate and Gender.* World Bank Group.

World Bank. (1993). *The East Asian Miracle: Economic Growth and Public Policy (World Bank Policy Research Report).* Oxford: Oxford University Press.

World Economic Forum. (2020). *The Global Risk Report 2019.* WEF.

World Happiness Report. (2021). WHR. https://worldhappiness.report/. April 20.

World Investment Report | UNCTAD. (2020). UNCTAD. https://unctad.org/topic/investment/world-investment-report.

World Trade Organisation. (2001). WTO | NEWS - WTO successfully concludes negotiations on China's entry - Press 243 (Press release). https://www.wto.org/english/news_e/pres01_e/pr243_e.htm. September 17.

World Trade Organization. (2007). WTO. https://www.wto.org/.

World Trade Organization — Global Trade. (2022). WTO. https://www.wto.org/.

Xu, Y. (2012). *Understanding International Trade in an Era of Globalization: A Value-Added Approach.* Policy Analysis. March, Arlington.

Xuejun, L., Yuan, L., Yefen, X. and Ting, C. (2017). A study on the impact of soft power on international investment. *International Journal of Business and Management Review*, **5**(1), 30–46.

Yalcin, E., Felbermayr, G. and Kinzius, L. (2017). *Hidden Protectionism: Non-tariff Barriers and Implications for International Trade.* Munich: IFO Institute.

Yasheng Huang. (2010). Debating China's economic growth: The Beijing consensus or the Washington consensus. *Academy of Management Perspectives*, **24**(2), 31–47. https://doi.org/10.5465/amp.2010.51827774.

Yeyati, E. L. and Filippini, F. (2021). *Economic Impact of Covid-19.* Washington: Brookings Global.

Yilmaz, G. (2014, September). *Turkish Middle Income Trap and less Skilled Human Capital.* Central Bank Turkey Working Paper Series.

Zhang, C. and Wu, R. (2019). Battlefield of global ranking: How do power rivalries shape soft power index building? *Global Media and China*, **4**(2), 179–202. https://doi.org/10.1177/2059436419855876.

Zinn, H. (1980). *A People's History of the United States.* New York: Harper & Row; HarperCollins.

Index

inted in the United States
Baker & Taylor Publisher Services